History and Obstinacy

Burden of Reason. [Jean de la Fontaine, *Fables choisies
pour les enfants* (Paris, E. Plon-Nourrit & Cie. [n.d.])]

History and Obstinacy

Alexander Kluge
Oskar Negt

Edited with an introduction by Devin Fore

Translated by Richard Langston
with Cyrus Shahan, Martin Brady,
Helen Hughes, and Joel Golb

ZONE BOOKS · NEW YORK

2014

The translation of this work was supported by
a grant from the Goethe-Institut, which is funded
by the German Ministry of Foreign Affairs.

Originally published in German as *Geschichte und Eigensinn*
© 2008 Alexander Kluge and Oskar Negt.

Printed in the United States of America.

Distributed by The MIT Press,
Cambridge, Massachusetts, and London, England.

Library of Congress Cataloging-in-Publication Data

Kluge, Alexander, 1932–
  [Geschichte und Eigensinn. English]
  History and obstinacy / Alexander Kluge, Oskar Negt;
edited with an introduction by Devin Fore; translated
by Richard Langston.
    p. cm.
  ISBN 978-1-935408-46-8 (alk. paper)
  1. Historical materialism. I. Negt, Oskar. II. Title.

D16.9.K5813 2014
335.4'119–dc23
                          2014016770

Contents

Introduction

The Anthropology of Capital

It is hard to comprehend that scarcely a decade separates the first and second collaborations between Oskar Negt and Alexander Kluge, so different are the two works in temperament, focus, and physiognomy. Despite its generally cool analytic demeanor, *Public Sphere and Experience* (1972) still bears distinctive traces of the late 1960s, an era that imagined itself on the brink of rupture with the existing capitalist order. Fueled by the antagonistic spirit of the protest movement, *Public Sphere and Experience* reads like a tactical program for engaging with contemporary social institutions and events still unfolding around it. The heart of the book, for example, is a spirited broadside against the media cartel of the day, whose stupefaction of the populace and gross ideological distortions could be corrected, the authors propose, only by reintegrating systematically obscured aspects of lived existence such as labor and family, production and intimacy, into the public sphere. Similarly, the book's basic distinction between two public spheres, one bourgeois and one proletarian, along with its many references to "capitalist interests," paints the kind of emphatic, high-contrast picture necessary for gathering political energies for historical action. Even the book's more historical elements, such as its critique of Communist Party strategy and the council systems of the 1920s, seek to revisit the earlier organizational failures of the Left in order to get "collective liberation" right this time.[1] To be sure, given its inexorably lucid analysis and the methodical exposition of its arguments, *Public Sphere and Experience* hardly resembles the occasional idiom that one finds in a manifesto, but the program that it presents still calls for political commitment, if not direct implementation. For those readers who still had the events of '68 in recent memory, the book was a line drawn in the sand.

History and Obstinacy, by contrast, is an entirely different proposition. The second book may share the first collaboration's interest in the "microphysics of resistance" (*die Mikrophysik des Widerstands*), specifically, but much has changed in the interim. Gone by 1981 is the prominent role previously granted to the proletarian public sphere and to the proletariat itself as a subject of class resistance.[2] Along with the revolutionary agent of history, the bourgeoisie has also exited, its monopoly on state power giving way in *History and Obstinacy* to more capillary and diffuse mechanisms of control and authority. Tellingly, the second book is less concerned with the "capitalist" than with the generalized "logic of capital." Gone, too, is the hermeneutics of suspicion that fueled the first collaboration between Negt and Kluge, which had argued that "real history is taking place nonpublicly in the domain of production" and that, in the manner of classical *Ideologiekritik*, sought to correct false consciousness by revealing the truth of these obscured and "arcane" realms.[3] Then there is the tone and scope of *History and Obstinacy*, a sprawling congeries of footnotes, excursuses, and illustrations that lacks the polemic élan of its predecessor and reads less like a political program than like an exhaustive reference work.[4] While its analysis remains entirely grounded in the present—even for this 2014 edition, the authors have revised, expanded, and updated the text extensively—*History and Obstinacy* feels, as one commentator has observed, like a "message in a bottle,"[5] a hermetic work addressed not to its contemporaries, but to posterity. Digging deep into the thousand-year rhythms of evolution and geology, as well as into the deep psychic structures of myth and the unconscious, *History and Obstinacy* prospects a temporality much different from that of *Public Sphere and Experience*, which still reflected the protest movement's optimism about the possibility of radical historical change. The slow, churning time of *History and Obstinacy* can be felt in the very scale of the project, which, at its original length of 1283 pages (here edited down to 430 pages in consultation with the authors), is almost four times greater than their first collaboration. A tome of this compass, which cannot be mastered in a single reading, lays claim to an entirely different economy of reception than a punctual manifesto. Its ideas must be acquired over time, through repeated and intermittent forays. If *Public Sphere and Experience* drew a line in the sand, *History and Obstinacy* marks out the plot for a slow and careful archaeological dig into the prehistoric past.

What happened to precipitate such a striking change in the shared vision of Negt and Kluge? First, the 1970s happened. As the exuberance and optimism of the '68 revolts faded in the distance, along with the promise of dramatic social transformation that had motivated them, disappointment set in.[6] Identity-based interest groups pluralized the revolutionary subject, although this diversity came at the cost of expedient political unity: a Marxist analytic that was at once totalizing and focused was now refracted into diffuse *Suchbewegungen*, prismatic movements that were searching for modes of political participation and cultural representation within a generalized "panorama of disorientation."[7] In *Learning Processes with a Deadly Outcome* (1973), Kluge summarized the scene with his characteristic bluntness: "Withdrawal of meaning [*Sinnentzug*]. A social situation in which the collective program of human existence deteriorates at a rate faster than the ability to produce new programs of existence."[8] In response to the likely deferral, if not definitive failure, of the revolutionary project, a melancholic German Left grew increasingly skeptical of the rhetoric of radical rupture, and entrenching itself for the long haul, turned toward distant historical epochs for solace and inspiration. One is reminded of how the *Annales* historian Fernand Braudel came to be interested in the *longues durées* of history: in times of "gloomy captivity," he once explained, when the light of universal history has grown dim, our attention drifts away from the day-to-day events taking place immediately before us and toward deep subterranean pulses of time and vast cycles that exceed the measure of individual endeavor.[9] During such intervals of "decapitated time," as Denis Hollier has called them,[10] people begin to eye the archaic past and the forgotten resources of deceased generations as possible sources of fuel to restart a depleted engine of progress. At these moments, utopia no longer seems to stand before us as a future to be realized, but, reversing its polarity, to lie behind us as a past to be recovered.

German culture of the 1970s is littered with artifacts from distant antiquity. Peter Weiss's monumental novel *The Aesthetics of Resistance* (1975), for example, tells of a German proletarian family that, after the Nazis have come to power, ensconces itself in a room where the windows have all been papered over, and, cut off from the outside world, discusses the ideological contents and political serviceability of the gamut of Western civilization's achievements. Weiss's book uncovers a certain resemblance between the 1930s and the 1970s, two Thermidorian decades that in the wake of failed revolutions and with the accumulating threat of state violence began to scour the deep recesses of historical record and generational memory for surviving fragments of revolutionary experience.[11] Over this interminably long "age of lead" (bleierne Zeit), as the '70s were sometimes called,[12] history became slower and slower until finally stopping altogether in the fall of 1977, when the militarized leftist group The Red Army Faction murdered the industrialist Hanns-Martin Schleyer, killing along with him any lingering utopian sentiment from '68 or confidence in the possibility of purposeful and conscious political transformation.[13] In response, the German government brutally reasserted its exclusive monopoly on violence. One of the most important productions of New German Cinema, the omnibus project *Germany in Autumn* (1978), provides a succinct record of the national imaginary at this historical moment, an imaginary dominated by a crepuscular iconography of funereal scenes and collective acts of mourning.

Although just as in the 1930s, the jarring events of this decade and the reality of state violence forced the German Left into the remote past, one should not be too quick to dismiss this turn to the past as nothing more than a symptom of quietism and political capitulation. For this interval of retrospection also contains a second aspect. As Kluge has recently observed in the DVD project *News from Ideological Antiquity*, it is precisely at moments of social dislocation and disturbance, when the present time is out of joint, that we begin fervently to seek "points of reference that lie outside of current events." Indeed, the more remote and immutable these points are, the more accurately they can help to establish our location within an unfolding present. In the same way that the unalterable and imperturbable stars in the sky assist seafarers to navigate shifting waters, faraway points of cultural reference located in distant epochs and contexts provide a source of tactical orientation at moments when history is no longer making sense.[14]

Meanwhile, as the Left was navigating this "panorama of disorientation in the 1970s," capitalism was itself mutating, not in its fundamental logic, of course, but in its quarry. In response to the victories of the postwar decolonization movements, capitalism was evolving from a phase of overtly violent imperialist expansionism into one in which its energies were focused instead on exploiting the inner resources of the living subject. Using sociological and behaviorist approaches for managing "human capital," neoliberal economics territorialized realms of existence that, although located beyond the formal bounds of the workplace and therefore previously ignored by classical quantitative economists, were now deemed essential for the efficient husbandry of the workforce. This shift in the strategy of capital from exploitation to "imploitation"[15] forced Negt and Kluge to modify a number of the original theses of *Public Sphere and Experience*. For one thing, the book's fundamental claim that the bourgeois public sphere had systematically excluded "the two most important areas of life: the whole of the industrial apparatus and socialization in the family"[16]—the claim that "essential and substantive experiential realms of human existence" such as labor and intimacy "are not organized publicly"[17]—was simply no longer tenable, given the success with which mass-cultural formations were able to integrate public relations, labor processes, and private existence into a single seamless circuit. In turn, the book's corollary proposal to expose occulted spheres of production—a tactic that informed defining works of the late '60s such as Erika Runge's *Bottrop Protocols* (1968) and Günther Wallraff's *13 Unwelcome Reports* (1969) and that can be traced back to Willi Münzenberg's campaign in the 1920s to publish illegal photographs of factory interiors[18]—could no longer be considered a viable solution to the problem of false consciousness. Such previously hidden realms of production were now very much out in the open. In response to the generalized conditions of cultural spectacularization, which reached a tipping point in the 1970s, power interests changed their fundamental strategy from concealment and secrecy to display and exhibition. Negt has recently reflected upon how the political developments of 1970s compelled them to modify their original position:

> The things that had appeared to be excluded from the bourgeois public sphere—production, labor and intimacy, specifically—underwent radical changes. As the result of closely orchestrated cooperation between the surveillance state, which smothered the right to political communication, and the capitalist media industry's partial exploitation

of human needs and interests, the contexts of lived existence in the Federal Republic were expropriated in the 1970s, in particular, through the process of fragmenting and confining that Jürgen Habermas has called the *colonization of the life-world*.[19]

The increasing "colonization of the lifeworld" was not unique to Germany. Across the Rhein, French intellectuals confronted a similar situation. In 1978–79, Michel Foucault delivered his famous lectures on the birth of biopolitics, which examined the genealogy of liberogenic economic strategies and, through this historical reconstruction, presented a bleak assessment of the so-called social state that had emerged to manage populations of human capital.[20] He argued that the founding of the welfare state was motivated not by any altruistic concern for the well-being of the population, but by a need to regulate inherent imbalances in the mechanism of capital (for example, its natural tendency toward violent concentration) and thereby to guarantee the sustainability and longevity of its economic order. Building upon Rosa Luxemburg's theses on accumulation, Foucault explained that the same expansionist impulses that once defined capitalism in the imperialist era were now being applied to investments made "at the level of man himself."[21] Negt and Kluge describe the transition from exploitation to implotation in similar terms: "In the same way that the Western mindset of the early nineteenth century thought that 'empty' continents inhabited by indigenous peoples were all that was left on earth to colonize, today, the enormous continents within the subjective landscape of the human appear uncultivated and unpopulated."[22] Approaching the limits of spatial extension and recognizing the finite number of global markets, capitalism began taking up residence in the inner space of man, establishing new sites of concentration in his body and psyche.[23]

It is no accident that the theoretical vanguard that, in Foucault's account, first mapped out the biopolitical turn — the Freiburg School of ordoliberal economics, with its conception of a "socialist market economy" — was based in Germany, of all places. As a largely landlocked nation whose imperial ambitions had always been limited (and historically belated) compared with those of its neighbors to the west, Germany was of necessity one of the first to redirect the expansionist energies inward, toward the populace. This "blockaded nation" was forced to become a social laboratory of introjected imperialism long before other European nation-states.[24] Indeed, as the analysis of German fairy tales in *History and Obstinacy* shows, biopolitical violence has haunted the collective imaginary of this Central European territory for centuries: from the tale about "smithing human beings so that they are able to work" (see "The Rejuvenated Little Old Man," in Chapter 5) to the fabrication of the homunculus in Goethe's *Faust*, which anticipates current prospects of genetic engineering with uncanny accuracy,[25] the German psyche has long been preoccupied with the theoretical and ethical questions raised by human capital. In contrast to the mythological traditions of Mediterranean countries, which depict lines of movement and feats of cunning, the German cultural imaginary, forged under geographical conditions of immobility, has focused instead on the problem of distinguishing the boundary between inside and outside. Whereas the itinerate, seafaring heroes of Greek myth have thus supplied the archetypes for bourgeois subjectivity during capitalism's heroic, imperialist stage — consider, for example, the brilliant analysis of Odysseus's adventures in Horkheimer and Adorno's *The Dialectic of Enlightenment* — the characters in German folktales and literature constitute the archetypes for subjectivity in capital's new, postimperialist phase. Given recent transformations in the logic of capital, it could be argued that the collective noetic resources contained in the fairy tales of Germany have in fact superseded the Oedipuses and Odysseuses of ancient myth in currency, becoming indispensible assets for human existence today, when we are faced with countless incursions into and disturbances of the ecology of the human subject. In their analysis of "The Wolf and the Seven Little Kids," for example, Negt and Kluge emphasize the importance the story places on the ability to differentiate between an intimate who can be trusted and an intruder who must be kept out. The questions raised by this tale are ultimately of an epistemological nature: On what basis can we recognize a threat from without? What belongs properly to the self, and what is foreign? Further: Where is the line that divides subject from object?[26] For Negt and Kluge, the complex and artful epistemology of German fairy tales exercises our *Unterscheidungsvermögen*, the faculty of critical distinction, cultivating a sophisticated cognitive framework on a par with today's highly mediatized world in which the distinction between self and other, like that between human and thing, has dissolved into sprawling and diffuse actor networks. At the historical transition when capital has shifted its locus to targets within the human subject, our capacity to distinguish between inside and outside has become increasingly important, if not vital to our very survival. These tales are the "instruments of thought" for our age.[27]

Out of the biopolitical laboratory of Central Europe emerges *History and Obstinacy*, a book that its authors describe as an investigation into "the capitalism within us." Despite receiving little public attention at the time of its appearance, not to speak of substantive critical engagement, it is a book that is increasingly acknowledged to be the nucleus of Negt and Kluge's three decades of collaboration. It has been justifiably heralded as the missing half of *Capital*, a project that Marx left unfinished at the time of his death.[28] Whereas Marx's opus supplied the foundational analysis of the forces of production in all of their objectivated, material formats, ranging from factory machinery to communication technologies, but left the organic dimension of capitalism largely unexamined, *History and Obstinacy* at last examines the other, human side of political economy: the living forces of production, the anthropology of labor power, the soft tissue of capitalism. It takes seriously Raymond Williams's insight that "the most important thing a worker ever produces is himself."[29] What happens, Negt and Kluge likewise propose, when we apply the tools of Marx's analysis not to dead labor, but to its living and breathing counterpart, to the subject? "Can capital say 'I'?" they ask in Chapter 3, the book's nerve center. The answer is a breathtaking archaeology of the attributes of Western man as they have developed over the last two thousand years. Like *Public Sphere and Experience*, this book is designed to "open the analytic concepts of political economy downward, toward the real experience of human beings,"[30] but *History and Obstinacy* now extends this analysis all the way down to the lowest strata of unconscious thought and cellular life. To do this, it dives below the surface of discrete historical events and the life spans of individuals, descending into the deep temporalities of collective memory and the slow pulses of evolutionary cycles.

History and Obstinacy supplements classic political economy with elements from disciplines not typically admitted into the orthodox Marxist hermeneutic, fields ranging from phenomenology and mythology to evolutionary science and systems theory. In its nonlinear construction, historical breadth, and catholic methodology,

History and Obstinacy is comparable only to the philosophical nomadism of Deleuze and Guattari's *A Thousand Plateaus*, which had appeared one year before, although without direct impact on Negt and Kluge's work.[31] Both books renounce the Left's infatuation with heroic dramas of historical rupture, turning instead toward the subversive energies and potentials located in the multidimensional processes of geology, chemistry, and biology. (Both, it could be added, come precariously close to the territory proposed in Friedrich Engels's *Dialectics of Nature*, even if the recourse to scientific positivism in *History and Obstinacy* never decenters the humanist subject or naturalizes the movement of the dialectic quite as radically as Engels did.)[32] Foremost among the theoretical instruments used by Negt and Kluge to explore the political economy of labor power is the apparatus of psychoanalysis, which complements Marx's sophisticated analysis of machine capital with a correspondingly nuanced account of the subjective dimensions of capital and its complex intervention into the human psyche. "Like the whole of preceding history in general, the outside world of industry governs our inner world and establishes powerful forces (of motivation, of the capacity for distinction, of feeling), a kind of parallel regime that merges with our classical psychic equipment," notes Kluge.[33]

Unlike fixed capital, whose historical development follows a tempo that is mechanical and predictable, human capital for Negt and Kluge is an unstable assemblage of dissimilar and often ill-fitting components, some flexible and some obstinate, some acquired (for example, education and socialization) and some endogenous (for example, genetic disposition and anatomy). Together, all of these elements form a delicate, dynamic, and highly reactive subjective economy. While machine capital does not observe any inherent limits or proportions — it accumulates exponentially, in the manner of a logical algorithm — living labor, by contrast, always follows principles of measure. It possesses a sense of harmonious balance that capital lacks. This is in fact what makes *History and Obstinacy*'s proposed analysis of the political economy of human capital such a Gordian task, for unlike the simple linear development of fixed capital, living labor power occupies multiple dimensions (sensory, intellectual, psychic, physiological), many of which are incompatible with one another,[34] but all of which are together subordinated to a basic law of self-regulation. Within the metastable system of the organic subject, each force always summons an equivalent counterforce and is offset by what Negt and Kluge call "balance labor." The laborer meets every abstract operation with a corresponding feat of concretion, every act of violent coercion with one of intransigent willfulness. In this way, *Homo compensator*, as Kluge sometimes calls this subject,[35] establishes the equilibrium that is necessary for survival. Faced with the complexity of this subjective ecology, Negt and Kluge respond by extending the parameters of what constitutes labor far beyond the limited forms of valorized work normally recognized by classical economics: for them, political economy must address not only the mechanisms of production and their quantifiable output of material commodities, but also the qualitative counterstrategies that the working organism is forced to develop as a result of its need for self-regulation and stability. Chapter 3 provides a concise *Denkbild*, or thought image, for this process, a female welder who pauses intermittently at work to sweep her arms back in the "winglike fashion" of a bird: here, the system of mechanized labor provokes a corresponding act of balance labor in the working subject, a Deleuzian becoming bird that counteracts the becoming machine of the Taylorized workplace.[36] "In this respect, the balance economy is in fact an economy, albeit under specific conditions."[37]

In order to provide a properly dialectical account of the labor process, then, *History and Obstinacy* attends to the compensatory activities that are necessary for the reproduction and maintenance of human capital, taking into consideration not just the physical labor of the assembly-line worker, but also, for example, the cognitive labor of the intelligentsia, the affective labor of the circus clown, and the reproductive labor of the parent. For Negt and Kluge, labor processes extend far beyond the walls of the workplace, reaching into distant realms seemingly unconnected to what we normally recognize as work: in their discussion of warfare, for example, they note a morphological resemblance between the movements that an army uses to "process" an enemy and those that are found in factory production; likewise, their analysis of rituals of erotic intimacy suggests that these tender *Feingriffe*, or "precision grips," share the same ontogenetic origins as the sensitive labor gestures used by the machine operator. (More on this below.)

An Inversion Machine

The anthropological foundations for this natural history of capital is man's status as a "deficient," or "auxotrophic," mutant (*Mangelmutant*), a being that "depends on specific associations with others because it is not metabolically autonomous."[38] Here, Negt and Kluge draw from two currents of thought, philosophical anthropology and psychoanalysis, which have both argued that humans, unlike other animals, are born into the world ill equipped and featureless, lacking the concrete material resources necessary to survive out in the world. For this reason, Arnold Gehlen, perhaps the most significant philosophical anthropologist of the twentieth century, defined man as a "deficient" or "defective being" (*Mängelwesen*).[39] At once a source of profound disorientation and existential freedom, both a liability and an opportunity, man's fundamental deficiency engenders a cultural imperative in this "vulnerable, needy, exposed being" who makes up for its ontological poverty by devising artificial constructions in language and technology, symbols, and instrumentation.[40] In this way, human defects are compensated through acts of labor, Gehlen explained.[41] In *Civilization and Its Discontents*, Freud similarly described how the creaturely infant enters into the world as a "helpless suckling," although this lamentable "inch of nature" eventually constructs technological organs as substitutes for the evolutionary equipment that it lacked at birth. Thus, suggested Freud, man is thrown into the world prematurely, without having gestated fully,[42] but he will build for himself a "house as a substitute for the mother's womb," for example.[43] Through such supplementations, the "deficient being" (Gehlen) transforms himself into a "prosthetic god" (Freud).[44] With reference to Gehlen, Kluge describes this dialectic as follows: "On the one hand, we are deficient beings [*Mangelwesen*]. We are naked, poor, and lacking. Our faults are sometimes also our virtues.... On the other hand, we are prepared: we have been armed with constructions that required 4.2 billion years of existence on this blue planet—the planet *on* which we have emerged and *with* which we have emerged, together, in a most improbable way."[45]

If evolutionary development can be described as a process of increasing specialization and differentiation that allows an organism to thrive within its particular environment, then the negative anthropology of the "deficient being" presents us with a certain paradox, namely, that humans, unlike other animals, have stopped evolving. Based on morphological analysis of our anatomy, for example, Gehlen argued that we resemble nothing so much as fetal monkeys whose growth was stunted at an early developmental phase: our organs undifferentiated, our bodies hairless and exposed, our neural mass lamentably uncoordinated, but for that reason also extremely plastic and adaptable, we are unfinished and open to the world. Gehlen would in fact go so far as to argue, against Freud, that man is born lacking even the hard-wired impulses—the psychic drives—necessary to orient him in the world and for this reason requires fixed social institutions and rituals to give meaning to his life.[46] Like the physical technologies that endow this open and shifting being with a prosthetic anatomy, culture and tradition must therefore furnish man with life instincts, vital programming that nature had denied him.

Gehlen thus argues that the development of our species reached a conclusion some time in the past, at which point the site of human evolution began to migrate outward, beyond the perimeter of our bodies. Walter Benjamin summarized the paradox well, pointing out that the individual human organism stopped evolving anatomically long ago, but that mankind qua "species being" (*Gattungswesen*) has only recently started to evolve collectively: "Man [*Mensch*] as a species completed its development thousands of years ago; but mankind [*Menschheit*] as a species is just beginning his. In technology, a *physis* is being organized through which mankind's contact with the cosmos takes a new and different form from that which it had in nations and families."[47] Evolution no longer takes place within our bodies, but between them, as it were. Our species evolution thus follows a curiously centrifugal course: the more the human perfects itself, the more its being is objectivated in the artifacts of technology and culture. The philosopher Bernard Stiegler recently designated this movement of exteriorization as "epiphylogenesis," the development of the biological species through external, inorganic means.[48] In the work of Negt and Kluge, this development recapitulates the familiar circuit of the Hegelian diremption, an ontology of alienation in which the anthropological machine that we call "man" individuates and achieves subjectivity through a two-part process, first by splitting and projecting itself and then by reappropriating those objectivated fragments of self from the world around it.

Since this process is ongoing and constant throughout the life of the individual, extending even into advanced adulthood, Negt and Kluge emphasize the importance of "learning processes" (*Lernprozesse*) as an anthropotechnical injunction: for humans, who lack the innate programming of other animals, sociality and shared existence must be practiced and performed, again and again.[49] Human life, Giorgio Agamben similarly writes, is "what cannot be defined, yet precisely for this reason, must be ceaselessly articulated and divided."[50] We are works in progress forever engaged with our own self-fashioning.

This understanding of the human as a deficient and therefore ontologically groundless creature belongs to a tradition of thought that long precedes Freud and Gehlen. Before the twentieth century, it appeared in Nietzsche's description of man as the "not yet determined animal" (*das noch nicht festgestellte Tier*) and in Johann Gottfried Herder's essay *On the Origin of Language* (1772), which defined the human negatively vis-à-vis the determinate abilities and fixed contours of other animals. Indeed, as Negt observes, existential apprehensiveness about the unfathomability and pluripotentiality of man is as old as philosophy itself, discernible already in the words of *Antigone*'s chorus: "Many are the wonders [δεινὰ, strange and mysterious, but also terrible and powerful], none / is more wonderful than what is man."[51] This negative anthropology of the "deficient being" has motivated thought across the political spectrum. Take the case of Gehlen, a social conservative who joined the National Socialist party in 1933: for him, man's ontological lack generates a need for control, constraint, formalized convention, and authority to provide relief (*Entlastung*) from the existential pressures of indeterminacy. Whereas Freud argued that man's premature birth and his protracted extrauterine gestation, by contrast, form the basis for "the need to be loved which will accompany the child through the rest of its life": in this way, the helplessness experienced by the "auxotrophic" human infant constitutes the biological foundation of intimacy and intersubjectivity.[52] Thus, despite very different political agendas, both Gehlen and Freud recognize that it is man's basic condition of lack and dependency that perforce makes him a preeminently social animal.

Negt traces this notion of the social animal back to Aristotle's definition of man as *zoon politikon*, a form of life that requires the polis for its self-realization.[53] It is a notion that constitutes the cornerstone of Marx's anthropology, as well: "The human being is in the most literal sense a *zoon politikon*," Marx writes, "not merely a gregarious animal, but an animal which can individuate itself [*sich vereinzeln*] only in the midst of society."[54] This political ontology is evident even in our physical architecture, literally in our bones. "Humans were not designed for balance," Negt and Kluge write. Our upright gait suggests a process of constantly tumbling forward, of walking and falling at the same time. Even a "soldier at attention does not so much maintain his balance as rotate around an imaginary point of equilibrium," and is therefore unstable and prone to stumble.[55] What is more, as they note in the book's final image on page 441, certain parts of our anatomy such as the hip's weak femoral neck, are designed to fracture with this inevitable fall. But this inescapable fracture is not an evolutionary flaw in our construction. Here, the defect of the isolated person (*Mensch*) turns out to be an asset of the species (*Menschheit*), an opportunity for the *Mängelwesen* to realize its potential within the collective body: since a person immobilized by a broken hip must be cared for lest he or she die, the weak femoral neck of this deficient being serves as a natural mechanism to guarantee interdependency with others, forcing autonomous individuals out of their self-sufficiency and insuring that each remains a "being that presupposes society," as Negt and Kluge put it.[56] This is the "violence of relationality."

In addition to augmenting the anatomy of man, who acquires a new prosthetic *physis* in the collective, the evolutionary mechanism of exteriorization also transforms the fabric of human consciousness. Like the body, thought, too, leaves its center, migrating out into the world of cultural artifacts that range from alphabetic writing to industrial factories (the "open book of human psychology," Marx called them). According to Gehlen, this displacement of man's cognitive faculties outward generates a "hiatus," or opening, between willed action and its effect. This interval, which takes the form of a dissociation between the needs of the present and the contexts for their gratification, makes the human into "an anticipatory creature," he wrote: "Like Prometheus, man is oriented toward what is removed, what is not present in time and space; in contrast to the animal, he lives for the future and not in the present."[57] As direct manual engagement with the world is diverted through various artifacts, a gap opens between the subject and its environment, a delay that engenders the experience of time itself and that marks us, in Heidegger's words, as fundamentally "historial" beings. Through cognitive acts of protention and retention, the human perforates the immediate sensation of the present with past and future events, giving rise to a complex temporality full of deferred actions, nonsynchronicities, anticipations, and recollections. Kluge likewise writes of the "uncanniness of time" (*die Unheimlichkeit der Zeit*),[58] since the temporality of being is always experienced as something that is simultaneously both familiar and strange, both ours and alien, both intrinsic and yet also disquietingly inauthentic and external. Commenting on Heidegger's idea of historial being, Stiegler has noted that the "temporality of the human, which marks it off among other living beings, presupposes exteriorization and prostheticity: there is time only because memory is 'artificial,' becoming constituted as already-there *since* its 'having been placed outside of the species.'"[59]

By fashioning a "second nature" in which to live, humans distance themselves from the "first nature" of their organic body, acquiring in the process a bank of memories that are collective, but for this very reason also uncannily foreign. Many different times are coursing within this historial animal, some punctual and primary, others repetitive and cyclical. "Short and long times coexist within the same body and mind," Kluge writes.[60] This insight is reflected in the formal construction of *History and Obstinacy*, whose montage composition, which interleaves dense theoretical passages and pithy narrative sketches together with diagrams, photographs, and other images, is designed to link up and bring into dialogue the disparate temporalities that otherwise remain disjoined within the subject. Negt and Kluge's method of splicing together fragments of experience and language that are circulating at different cognitive speeds induces a learning process in the reader: "Nothing is more instructive than intermixing different scales of time," Kluge observes.[61]

Kluge has noted in an essay on the ecology of consciousness that "the distance between feeling and action"—Gehlen's hiatus—has gradually increased over the course of the development of our species. One illustration from this essay depicts an evolutionary ancestor of ours and suggests that the bridge of nerves connecting this creature's brain to the extremities of its limbs grew longer with evolution toward *Homo sapiens* and that furthermore, our reaction time as a species slowed down with this development. With the expansion of this interval between brain and hands, between thinking and doing, our involvement in and connection to the world grew more attenuated. We became more absent than present. Here Kluge adduces Herder, the founder of philosophical anthropology, who proposed that "we differ from animals not in the fact that we develop, but in the fact that we do so cautiously and slowly."[62] Thus, as our species evolves outward through epiphylogenesis and our collective forms of symbolic mediation grow more intricate and tangled, the delay between consciousness and action grows ever longer. To give one memorable example from *History and Obstinacy*: the American response to the events of 9/11, which was to dispatch an aircraft carrier to New York in defense of the city, would have been an appropriate reaction to Pearl Harbor, but was entirely out of place within the new historical scenario of asymmetrical partisan warfare. In other words, the military reacted to the terrorist attack of 2001 with a strategy from 1941. History is slowly dilating. This collective process of gradual deceleration is evident at the level of individual experience, as well, on the ontogenetic register: unlike other creatures, the human infant, again, is not "subordinated to a program" that has been preestablished by nature (instinct), but learns gradually and cautiously, its emerging consciousness taking root, Kluge proposes, in "the gaps of its sluggishness."[63] In acquiring language, for example, the developing child takes leave of the world in its sensory immediacy and learns to engage instead with signs that stand in for absent people and objects. Time becomes complex, involuted, uncanny.

We are, in sum, beings out of synch with the world around us. Despite our status as auxotrophic mutants that, in Negt and Kluge's words, "presuppose society," humans are fundamentally alone, cut off from their conspecifics.[64] Even the libido, the drive that promises to connect us to the primary realm of embodied pleasure and the supposed basis of human relationality, is essentially blind,[65] easily duped by substitute objects or tricked into circuitous schemes of sublimatory gratification. Despite efforts to connect with the world, the brain, the seat of human consciousness, remains a windowless monad that floats suspended within a hard skull that blocks all direct access to the world outside. In order to penetrate the walls of this ossiferous prison, external sensory data must undergo a complex process of translation and synthesis.[66] With reference to Freud, Negt and Kluge consequently define the human as "an inversion machine," a life-form that engineers time through strategies of condensation and displacement, enciphering experience and then rearranging the resulting code. All experience, they write, takes shape through a "series of necessary distortions."[67] Like the media historian Bernhard Siegert, who has argued that subjectivity is little more than an effect of relays and lags in transmission,[68] Negt and Kluge suggest that the "distance between feeling and action" defines us as a species. Indeed, such detours, delays, and retardations, Kluge writes, are "precisely the core of the human and of the living."[69] Thus, for all of the emacipatory power that the collaborations of Negt and Kluge have vested in the category of "experience" (*Erfahrung*) as the root of material particularity and as a source of resistance to capitalism's principle of abstraction, empirical experience, for them, is neither primary nor pure. It is not given, but hard-won, assembled through acts of labor. (It is revealing that in German, experiences are actively *made*—"man *macht* Erfahrungen"—while in English, a language that has nursed so many positivist philosophies, experiences are instead passively *had*.) Already, by the second illustration of *History and Obstinacy*, for example, Negt and Kluge have pointed out that "the eye works" (p. 75), that this organ of perception is not an indifferent photographic plate, but a biased and highly specialized muscle that searches the visual array in a procedure more akin to scanning than to contemplating. The eye doesn't simply "take in," but synthesizes. Against the epiphanic epistemology that, since Lessing's *Laokoon*, has granted phenomenological immediacy to the image, Negt and Kluge show here that vision is never in fact punctual. Every sensation takes time. And indeed, the ornamental tracery of the ocular movements in this illustration resembles nothing so much as a complex graffito, an elaborate text that is gradually inscribed over time. Vision, like writing, is sedimented with traces and delays. It is *éspacée*, to use Derrida's phrase.

Here, Negt and Kluge follow the precedent of their Frankfurt School mentor, Adorno, whose aesthetic preference for time- and language-based arts such as music and literature over the visual arts was underwritten by a deep-seated skepticism about the image's claim to sensory plenitude. Kluge observes that "Adorno's relationship to film was based on the principle: 'I enjoy going to the movies;

the only thing that bothers me is the picture on the screen.'"[70] In his own practice as a filmmaker — which, by his own admission, has always remained secondary to his textual production[71] — Kluge has consequently emphasized the interval between the shots over the shots themselves. He likes to remind us that "on average, half of the time spent in a movie theater is darkness."[72] Not the image, but its negation, not presence, but absence, is the basic unit out of which his films are assembled. *Ecce homo clausus*: a blind monad sitting in the dark.

Be that as it may, man's existential absence is not an entirely bad thing. For Negt and Kluge, it is also key to many of the distinctive successes and accomplishments of our species. The gap between mind and sensation is a source of alienation, but our absentmindedness is also the wellspring of the imagination and its salvatory promise. Writing on the imagination, Sartre explained that it is by distancing itself from the empirical exigencies of the present, from Heideggerian *in-der-Welt-sein*, that the mind is able to shatter a monolithic and indifferent world "as totality" and reconfigure it anew according to models that are more hospitable, more human.[73] Such an anthropology of the imagination was anticipated already in Marx's *Grundrisse*, which famously observed that "what distinguishes the worst architect from the best of bees is that the architect builds the cell in his mind before he constructs it in wax."[74] For Kluge, in turn, the powers of the artistic imagination are predicated on an ability to remove oneself from the world, to close one's eyes and withdraw into the solipsism of dreams. On the subject of writing, for example, he urges that "you have to leave gaps in prose,"[75] intervals of absence; he likewise describes film as a medium that "comes into being" not on the screen before our eyes, but "in the spectator's head."[76] He consequently situates the seat of human intelligence in the blockades in and diversions from our traffic with the real. "Why is human thought slow?" Kluge asks one of his regular interlocutors, Dirk Baecker. The latter replies, "thought is slow because that's its only chance. Thought means stopping short, hesitating, not reacting immediately, inhibiting reflexes, meeting instinct with mistrust, and only then doing something."[77] These delays and hesitations reflect what Kluge identifies as the fundamentally "anti-realistic attitude" of human thought and fantasy, a defiant attitude that raises "protest against an unbearable reality," against *in-der-Welt-sein*.[78] Negt and

Kluge's recurring emblem for human intelligence, borrowed from their teachers Adorno and Horkheimer, is the land snail, a sensitive animal that retracts into its shell when overstimulated or confronted with danger. Isolation and stupidity, not action and intervention, are the properly human response to what Horkheimer called *Wahrheitssadismus*, the sadism of reality.[79] Following Benjamin, who once remarked to Adorno that philosophical concretion can be achieved only by taking leave of the sensuous world and setting out "through the frozen desert of abstraction" (*durch die Eiswüste der Abstraktion*),[80] Kluge speculates that the human capacities for distinction and higher symbolic reasoning first emerged in the Pleistocene era, when the globe was covered with ice, and the experiences of warmth and of being at home in the world were but a distant genetic memory.[81] As reality turned sadistic and inhospitable, man recoiled and began to think.

Refusing the brutal exigencies of the present, thought shrinks away from the Now and seeks refuge in the intervals established with this delay. Cognition is always behind the times, especially at moments of rapid political upheaval, when history leaps erratically and unpredictably ahead of consciousness: "Thoughts cannot follow revolutionary action," Negt and Kluge write: "They are slow. Gradually they begin to arrive five days after the action."[82] For this reason, theory—which for them remains necessarily *critical* theory—should never be translated directly into practice, whatever the militants may think. Instead of trying to keep pace with the breakneck speed of reality, we need to slow it down, to arrest and capture it so as to make it comprehensible. For Negt and Kluge, this inhibiting function is one of the defining virtues of poetic constructions, especially in the contemporary age of turbocapitalism.[83] "Faced with unendurable experiences, [poetry] creates vessels, labyrinths, spirals that slow down the horror so that we can experience it through the senses without being injured by it, so that the feelers of the snail—our sensitivity—can remain outstretched, even though it goes against human nature to experience horror at all."[84] In both his prose and his films, Kluge's oeuvre teems with examples of events that have been manipulated temporally in order to render their underlying structure fathomable. Through these manipulations, he aims to produce what he calls *Zeitorte*, sites where, as in the cinema of Andrei Tarkovsky,[85] time condenses and regains an auratic dimension of permanence and duration (*Dauer*)[86] so that these moments "give back more time than they cost."[87]

Obstinate Traits

It is a popular misconception that the last ice age ended ten thousand years ago. The Enclosure Acts of the late eighteenth century, which fulfilled the several-centuries-long campaign to separate the peasants from the shared resources of the commons, inaugurated a new glacial period, the inhospitable "stream of cold" (*Kältestrom*) in which we live today. Thus began the era of high capitalism, an epoch characterized by division, distance, calculation, and icy abstraction in social relations.[88] Negt and Kluge describe the fundamental mechanism of capital's expansion as a process of *Trennung*, or "separation," that takes place simultaneously in two different registers, one economic and the other phenomenological.[89] On the one hand, there is the division of the laboring subject from the means of production, brought about historically through the forcible separation of the peasant from the land and the physical migration of those subjects into urban areas. If, as Ernst Bloch once wrote, the premodern peasant "still held the means of production in its hands," in being separated from the land, the laboring subject now loses its hold on these means.[90] Previously "embedded in a working and living community that occurred naturally,"[91] the laborer now becomes "free and rightless" (*vogelfrei*, in Marx's language). In other words, the laborer becomes proletarianized. According to Negt and Kluge this foundational act of expropriation (*Enteignung*), which Marx called the moment of "primitive accumulation," is not just a historical event that can be traced back to the enclosure initiatives and their transformation of the commons into private property. It is an ongoing process by which the logic of capital is interiorized and reproduced, over and over, within the individual subject. (Marx himself suggested as much when he described primitive accumulation as an "encounter" [*ein Gegenübertreten*] or a set of relations [*das Kapitalverhältnis*] that "reproduces itself on a constantly extending scale.")[92] Today, the properties that capitalism targets for appropriation are not spatial territories found out there in the world, but the personal assets located within us, properties such as "the capacity for learning, discipline, the capacity for abstraction, punctuality." In this way, "the violence migrates inward," notes Negt.[93] For Negt and Kluge, primitive accumulation is less a discrete historical event in the past than a permanent and continuous campaign to expropriate subjective capacities,[94] or, as others have written, an "endlessly iterated event"[95] that results in a "basic ontology of alienation."[96]

This process of dividing and requisitioning the capacities of the laborer can only ever be a partial and limited operation. "'Expropriation,' or 'the permanence of primitive accumulation,' which is the same thing, [is a process] that relates to separate or several human characteristics, but never to entire people," explains Negt.[97] The total subordination of multidimensional life to the linear, mechanical logic of capital is simply unsustainable, since, as experience has shown, such forms of outright depredation quickly result in the death of the worker.[98] So instead of commandeering the body of the worker in toto, capital pursues a more discerning "microphysics of power."[99] "Since Marx, we have known that capital would optimally renounce living labor entirely, if it could still make profit that way,"[100] but since it can't in fact forego its organic half, capital instead chooses to underwrite and develop certain human abilities "like a hothouse" (*treibhausmäßig*), while allowing other capacities to stagnate and go to seed (*verwildern*). This strategy may allow for the basic reproduction and maintenance of living labor, but in the course of overcultivating a limited set of very specific capacities, capital still deforms the natural ecology of the human body and psyche, making the biological self-regulation of the subject increasingly difficult. Capital's one-sided investments in living labor power, to repeat, lack any sense of proportion and balance.[101] Characteristics that can be readily monetized are singled out and quickly overbuilt, while those with no immediate value are left fallow and drift into the netherworld of the collective unconscious. For every trait that is capitalized, another is shunted aside. As a result, alongside a primary economy of labor traits established through the historical mode of production there emerges within the human subject a secondary, black-market economy, where, isolated from the authority of the ego and capital's logic of valorization, repressed and derealized traits take on a intransigent life of their own. "Whenever something is repressed, it becomes autonomous and intractable," Negt and Kluge observe.[102] Capital's violent expropriation is countered by the subject with obstinacy, *Ent-eignung* with *Eigen-sinn*. Like Marx's old mole, a favorite image of Negt and Kluge,[103] marginalized traits vanish from sight, but, exiled to the hinterlands of the psyche, they do not die. Instead, they mutate and enter into unexpected alliances with other capacities. Once taken out of circulation, these obstinate traits—"more durable than concrete"[104]—seethe below the threshold of consciousness, where they grow even stronger and more resistant to subsumption by capital. To use a term central to the thought of Negt and Kluge, these subdominant traits are *unterschätzt*, in two senses: "undervalued" by capital, they have little worth and are held in low regard, but precisely for this reason, they are also "underestimated" as potential sources of revolutionary force.

The word *Eigensinn*—rendered variously into English as "autonomy,"[105] "willfulness,"[106] "self-will,"[107] and, here, "obstinacy"—implies a degree of stubborn obtuseness, an imperviousness to directives from above. Hegel, for example, famously defined *Eigensinn* as "a freedom" that is "enmeshed in servitude."[108] Kluge, in turn, describes *Eigensinn* as "the guerrilla warfare [*Partisanentum*] of the mind."[109] Obstinacy is the underside of history: for each entry in the valorized record of human culture—a record that, as Benjamin wrote, is always a documentation of barbarism[110]—a countervailing act of obstinacy pushes back against the thrust of so-called progress; for each luminous vista cleared by instrumental reason, a dense scotoma of stupidity emerges to blight the view; for every human trait that is singled out and capitalized, a resistent trait gathers force underground. "It is not…some primal 'self' that has *Eigensinn*, but rather a whole range of historically acquired and developed skills, drives, capacities, each of which makes its own 'stubborn' demands and has its own distinct 'meaning,'" writes Fredric Jameson about Negt and Kluge: "Such forces, however, can be residual or emergent; they often fail to be used to capacity; and their unemployment generates specific pathologies, as does their repression, alienation, or diversion."[111] Here, the differential method of Negt and Kluge is more dialectical than psychoanalysis is, with its foundational ontology of the drives. For them, emancipating repressed traits in the way in which radical Freudians such as Wilhelm Reich and Otto Gross proposed to liberate the drives will not bring about sustainable social transformation, since, according to Negt and Kluge, the valorizion of these declassed traits will cause only further imbalances within the economy of the subject. For them, the solution lies not in the spontaneist "infantile disorders of the Left" (to recall

Lenin's memorable formulation), but in the careful recalibration of the political economy of labor so that these marginalized characteristics and feelings can enter into an enduring configuration with other traits. What is needed, then, is a new psychological subject. Without the stable framework that such a subject provides, these volatile energies will continue their twilight existence, erupting only fleetingly in the gaps of consciousness and at moments of felicitous stupidity.

Since these unruly traits do not answer to any ego, they lead a life independent of the humanist subject, transecting and joining individual biographies according to their own patterns, cycles, and historical periodicities. And since they are not the property of any one "self," such traits do not simply disappear with the death of the individual. Rather, like the "obstinate child" who, in the eponymous Grimms' fairy tale discussed on pages 291–94, refuses to be put to rest and continues stubbornly to thrust forth its arm from the grave where it has been buried, these uncontrollable traits continue their insurgency from the afterlife, defying the authority and will of the society that seeks to repress them. These traits inhabit the temporality of the deep historical cycles that Braudel, in his theorization of the *longue durée*, designated as the time of the "conjuncture"—the time of enduring *habitus* and collective institutions, which is located somewhere between the slow geological pulse of structural history, on the one hand, and the "microhistory" of individual biographies and political events, on the other.[112] "So you take it as given that the individual faculties of labor have their own history?" one interviewer asked Negt and Kluge after the publication of *History and Obstinacy*. "Yes, certain faculties of labor have been taken out of circulation," Kluge responded: "The division between private and public traverses all of history, not just that of capitalism, where this division of course is particularly exacerbated. Because they work in the manner of a mole, faculties of labor that have been taken out of circulation can once again be reactivated even after two or three hundred years." To this Negt added:

> But this mole is also there in plain view. It is of no interest to us whether a trait that can be emancipated exists within an integral system or has been taken out of circulation. Just because a working trait came into existence and was cultivated within a capitalist context or within the laboratories of the Third Reich such as the *Organisation Todt*

37

doesn't make it more stable than any other. Just like any other, it can also be reconstellated.[113]

The real agents of history, then, are not the Napoleons, the Goethes, or any of the other celebrated figures whose names we associate with revolution and innovation. Nor do Negt and Kluge bestow this distinction on any particular social estate or class identity. For them, the actual subjects of history are instead the enduring capacities themselves, the cache of properties out of which the auxotrophic mutant assembles its identity. Each such trait is a "splendid natural force in its own right," as Jameson puts it.[114] The class known as the bourgeoisie, for example, is not some kind of elementary social substance, but merely a label that identifies one specific arrangement, one particular economy, of more fundamental and enduring traits that began to coalesce historically at a moment toward the end of the Middle Ages. It is a stabilized configuration of aptitudes for things such as work discipline and compound accumulation, combined with a psychological disposition toward deferred gratification and value abstraction. But no steadfast boundary divides the bourgeoisie categorically from the proletariat. Indeed, disenfranchised proletarian traits occasionally erupt within the bourgeois subject, perturbing its regular psychic economy.

For Negt and Kluge, one of the chief differences between the bourgeoisie and the proletariat is that the former possesses a stable historical configuration and psychological identity, while the latter does not. Here they touch upon a persistent asymmetry within Marxist theory: whereas the capitalist, a position defined by the economic mode of production, has a political and psychological counterpart in the bourgeois class, the proletariat, also an economic category, has no such equivalent representative in the realm of political ideology.[115] Negt and Kluge consequently write not of an integral proletarian subject, but of proletarian traits, in the plural. In this regard, they move beyond an essentialist conception of the proletariat, a social category that traditional Marxist criticism mistakenly tailored to the contours of the humanist individual. They use the word "proletarian" not as a "concept for a substance,"[116] but as a placeholder for the sum of the repressed characteristics of man. For there is no proletarian subject, properly speaking. At least not yet. Underwritten by cultural technologies ranging from the *Bildungs-*

roman to single-point perspective, the bourgeois self learned several centuries back to stand at the center of its universe and say "I," *ego*. But the vital question, posed by Negt and Kluge at the beginning of Chapter 3, is whether *capital* is itself similarly capable of doing so.[117] In other words: Can the proletariat become a stable and self-identical subject? Can it lay claim to an ego?

Marx provided no answer this question. He presented a road map for revolutionary transformation, but he did not provide a psychological profile of its agent. "As a singular substantive which implies the representation of a personality responsible for a historical mission," the word "proletariat" "almost never appears in *Capital*," notes Étienne Balibar.[118] In his own study of *Capital*, Brecht, too, observed that proletarian subjectivity remained for Marx necessarily multiple: "Marx addresses the workers with a new name: as *proletarians* (not as proletariat)."[119] Brecht consequently described the revolutionary masses as a protean liquid that is diffuse, undifferentiated, and shapeless. One of his filmscripts from 1931, entitled "The Bruise," characterized them as follows: gathered "in a mute march, transparent and faceless," the masses "are coming together, they are marching, their ranks are closed, as wide as the streets, they fill everything, like water, they seep through everything, like water, they have no substance."[120] This line, which is composed, indicatively, in a single flowing cascade of words, reveals two important features of proletarian traits. On the one hand, these traits are highly mobile and difficult to contain or capture. They move along those vectors that Deleuze and Guattari famously called *lignes de fuite* (a phrase that "covers not only the act of fleeing or eluding but also flowing, leaking, and disappearing into the distance").[121] For this very reason, their appearances are also, on the other hand, impermanent and fleeting. Whereas the bourgeois ego has erected a grand psychic architecture for its particular assemblage of valorized traits, proletarian traits remain orphaned and homeless. Under capitalist rule, they have, at best, improvised encampments within the individual. "Mute" and "faceless," as Brecht wrote, their self-will (*Eigensinn*) most often finds only a negative expression, by interrupting the status quo, by deranging the dominant discourse, by triggering parapraxes and other productive failures.[122] These sudden outbursts provide only a partial glimpse of the vast network of emancipatory traits coursing through the underground of history. Thus, it is not yet possible to speak of the proletariat's class consciousness as such, since consciousness, that integral mental image of human identity and self-awareness, is a privilege that has been denied to these revolutionary traits. These liquid forces still lack a psychological "vessel" (*Gefäß*) in which to gather and accumulate, as Kluge puts it:

> I don't know of a single example of socialist behavior that was sustained for a long period of time. Evidently no vessel has been found for it yet. If the bourgeois subject is not a new characteristic, but the sum of all preceding characteristics placed in a new vessel, then the worker that is expressed in acts of mutually coordinated labor—the spontaneous worker—is himself a character utterly distinct from the bourgeois. The worker lacks the aspect of accumulation: he is more powerfully at home in the moment and in the felicitous venture, which is to say, he is a character type that is thoroughly and powerfully rooted in the economy of pleasure [*Lusthaushalt*]. This is what is new about him.[123]

Until a durable anthropomorphic container can be found for this new subject, the components of its personality will remain, as Norbert Bolz observed, "strewn about as messianic fragments in the world of commodities."[124]

Following Marx, Negt and Kluge designate this noncohesive and thus strictly "hypothetical" subject[125] the "collective worker" (*Gesamtarbeiter*), which they define as the "embodiment of all of the productive activities within a society that aim at forming a collective existence."[126] Despite the fact that the specific actions of this collective worker look plural, disjointed, and even contradictory from the vantage of individual ego psychology, considered from a more global, transsubjective perspective, the actions of this "collective ego"[127] appear highly systematic and patterned, indeed, "structurally integrated" (*gefügeartig*). Take one episode from *History and Obstinacy* that describes a manifestation of the collective worker at the Battle of Verdun, when the French and German armies, each bent on destroying the other, burrowed toward one another from opposite sides of a hill in 1916: Negt and Kluge observe that the movements of these armies, although motivated in the minds of the individual soldiers by a desire to annihilate the enemy, actually exhibited the features of a well-organized cooperation. With minimal modification, a mere change in political valence, this coordinated burrowing could have instead resulted in a tunnel connecting the two peoples to one another. In a second appearance of the collective worker, this time on the Eastern Front during the Second World War, a captured Russian tank driver sitting among German soldiers unintentionally allows his gaze to linger too long on a technical defect in one of the tanks in front of him—a screw that is loose and that would damage the tank if not repaired: following the Russian's sight line, a German tank driver notices the problem, discerns his enemy's concern, and has the screw fixed. "This understanding, which runs either below or above the structure of enmity and which is grounded in the experience of production: this would be a proletarian element."[128]

In both of these episodes, the appearance of the collective worker suspends the distinction between friend and adversary, making possible unexpected and even politically undesirable alliances across enemy lines. For Negt and Kluge, the proletarian element always seeks cooperation. It is, they write, the "subterranean association of all labor capacities."[129] The result is an unconscious choreography of solidarity that supersedes the will and interests of the ego, which remains confined within domains of individual identity such as nation-state citizenship, family genealogy, class affiliation, and social standing.

Emotional Life

If the distinction between friend and enemy, per Carl Schmitt, is foundational for the concept of the political as such, then the previous examples show that the collective worker is not a political being.[130] It doesn't know party slogans or recognize ideological divisions. For this reason, the search for proletarian traits today is more likely to discover bonds of solidarity and social cohesion in the realm of the human emotions than in that of politics, which ceased to be a practice of collective being (Gemeinwesen) back in the eighteenth century.[131] According to Negt and Kluge, proletarian traits in fact share the same ontogenetic origin as feelings: both are grounded in the primary sensation of touch and contact as originally encountered by the young animal clinging to its mother. "This haptic sensorium, the proximity of the mother—this is the first thing that motivates the development of the hand and, with it, of labor. All further characteristics will then be developed out of this motivation."[132] The infant's foundational experience of skin contact and of its qualitative aspects—pliancy, firmness, timing ("seizing"), and so on—will subsequently be diverted and refined, one portion of this sensation allocated in the body of the adult to the realm of erotic sensitivity and another portion allocated to the repertoire of gestures found in labor. One of Kluge's favorite examples of a work gesture that requires a degree of sensitivity on par with erotic tenderness is the gesture of fastening a screw, which, when correctly fitted, should be neither too tight nor too loose.[133] (One could surmise too, that, as our machines for production become outfitted with more touch screens and keyboards [in German: *Tastaturen*, or "touch boards"], the future promises an even greater convergence between the delicate haptics of labor and those of the erotic encounter.) In the words of Isabelle from Godard's *Passion*, "work has the same gestures as love."[134] But this shared origin has been obscured. Cultural practices such as Western opera, an institution that Kluge has dubbed a "power plant of feelings" (*Kraftwerk der Gefühle*),[135] specialize in taking the elemental units of human emotion such as the experience of contact and assembling those microfeelings into elaborate and bombastic ideological commodities of such complexity that we are no longer able to recognize the commonalities between the feelings expressed on the stage of the opera house and the activities taking place in the factory.[136] As a result, "an emotional approach is really no longer possible in a power plant," Kluge notes. "I can't suddenly operate the tools of a cockpit or a power plant in a playful or libidinous or erotic way."[137]

Because the arts of the West, along with their latter-day descendants in the culture industry, have captured and assembled feelings into ready-made ideological clichés, misprision abounds in the realm of human sentiment. These "highly synthetic compounds" of emotion "must be examined for their elemental components," urges Kluge.[138] Much of his narrative prose and film analyzes these complexes, revealing these emotional artifacts to be composed of elements and impulses that are entirely different from than the ones that we would normally expect to find in them. What purports to be an opera about love, for example, turns out to have been one about war (Verdi's *Aida*, as seen through *The Power of Feelings*). Or a case of kleptomania is revealed to be motivated by a utopian longing for a world without property ("Anita G.," from *Case Histories*). For Negt and Kluge, feelings cannot be observed in their pure state, since, like highly reactive chemical elements, they enter spontaneously into "coalitions with other feelings,"[139] giving rise to highly complex emotional assemblages with new valences and receptors. The proposal of the authors to analyze the "high-rise constructions"[140] of emotion that have been erected by Western culture and to dismantle them into their constituent blocks therefore encounters the same methodological obstacle that Freud faced in his attempt to distinguish between the libido and the death drive: these "two kinds of instinct seldom — perhaps never — appear in isolation from each other, but are alloyed with each other in varying and very different proportions and so become unrecognizable to our judgment," Freud remarked.[141] When bound up in complex, alloyed forms, emotions begin to function in illogical ways, becoming "unrecognizable to our judgment." In their elemental state, however, they are exceedingly precise and anything but irrational. Being based in the haptic surface of the skin that is our source of direct contact with the world, feeling, or *Gefühl*, is wholly inclined to reality. As Negt and Kluge note, feelings are in fact the origin of the cognitive faculty of distinction (*Unterscheidungsvermögen*) and are essential to making critical judgments about the world, to analyzing the things and people around us, and to establishing foundational contrasts such as attraction-repulsion, association-dissociation, inside-outside. In these individual judgments, "feelings never err," Kluge notes.[142]

But when these microfeelings are fused together in more complex sentiments such as patriotism or nostalgia, they lose their essential accuracy and begin to misfire. It would seem that Machiavelli's observation that "men are apt to deceive themselves in general matters, yet they rarely do so in particulars" pertains to emotions as well.[143] Above all, it is the timing of feelings — their punctuality — that becomes impaired when they are trapped within elaborate compounds. Assimilated to recurring clichés, feelings acquire an aura of destiny and fatefulness and are no longer able to respond realistically to the exigencies of the present. Either they are triggered too far in advance, or they react too belatedly. An episode from Kluge's famous story collection, "The Air Raid on Halberstadt" (1977), tells of Gerda, a German mother who tries in vain to protect her children from the bombs that rain down from Allied planes in 1944. As the narrator observes, in order to save her children from the bombs, Gerda would had to have agitated against the threat of fascism six years earlier. She didn't recognize the very real danger before, but now, when it is too late, she does: "the question of organization is located in 1928, and the requisite consciousness is located in 1944."[144] Likewise, with reference to the Holocaust, Kluge points out that that the appropriate German reaction to the atrocities—one of outrage and protest—did not occur until 1979, long after any such outcry could save the victims: "we in our country are always shocked at the wrong moments and are not shocked at the right ones," he comments.[145] So much historical misery, so many catastrophic events, have resulted from a failure to exercise the faculty of distinction—to feel—at the appropriate time.

By breaking down emotional complexes into their elemental microfeelings, Negt and Kluge provide an account of psychic experience that is far more nuanced and internally differentiated than the model of subjectivity proposed by traditional ego psychology. Crack open the psyche, and you find a multiplicity of vying voices and impulses, an elaborate dialectical configuration of forces and counterforces arranged with a sense for equilibrium. The internal dynamism of *Homo compensator* is, again, what distinguishes flexible human capital from the monologic of its fixed, mechanical counterpart. Despite the efforts of the rational ego, the psychic authority of capital, these feelings will not be tamed through an act of conscious will. In looking past the ego, past the authority that occupies the pronoun "I," and attending to the more fundamental emotional states and traits out of which subjective identity is constructed, Negt and Kluge call into session what they call a "general assembly of feelings." This "grassroots democracy" of affect suspends the vertical system of representation established by the "narcissistic 'ego,'" which seeks to install itself at the top as the sole deputy of all feelings.[146] Unlike this parliamentarian hierarchy, the "general assembly" found in books such as *Chronicle of Feelings* (2000) allows elementary emotions to confront, provoke, challenge and liaise with one another without the mediation of consciousness.

For Negt and Kluge, it is on this deeper stratum of existence that human history is actually written, not on the surface composed of proper names and personal identities. "Real historical developments do not move on the side of the 'complete person' and 'whole proletarian,' but on the side of their individual qualities."[147] These qualities are the actual quanta of history; we personages are merely their vehicles. The resulting blow to the notion of individual agency renders traditional subject-centered tactics of political transformation problematic, of course, but at the same time it also establishes new axes of political solidarity that are not hedged by fixed identitarian coordinates. Like the proletarian trait that crosses enemy lines, feelings pierce the claustral walls of individual biography, transecting and linking these monads together in often unexpected ways. In response to the explosion in the 1970s of kaleidescopic *Suchbewegungen* whose identity-based activism derailed attempts to organize politically under a single banner or agenda, Negt and Kluge thus recover a platform for coalition within the experience of multiplicity and diversity itself.[148] For them, the self is always plural, or, as Brecht put it, the individual is always "dividual." Following Freud's analysis of human development as a "beginning twice over" (*ein zweizeitiger Ansatz*), which suggests that we are in fact born two times—first as infants, and then again, after an unusually long latency period, at the age of puberty—Negt and Kluge explain that the individual is actually a doublet, if not an entire multitude (see the section "The Second, Third, Fourth, Etc. Social Birth" in Chapter 2). All of the distinctive stages that the growing child passes through, along with all of its particular temporalities and experiential acquisitions,[149] are retained permanently within the psyche, layered incongruously one on top of the other in the manner of Freud's Eternal City. "It is a luxurious condition that we were created—that we were made by evolution—to lead two lives," notes Kluge.[150] As a result of this extravagance in our biological design, the individual mind turns out to be far more complex and far richer in assets and resources than the blinkered ego will ever know.

As an art form that over centuries has developed an exceedingly precise and refined language for the analysis of emotion, literature is a cultural technique particularly well equipped to identify and map these feelings in their historical migrations across people.[151] Following the models of Kleist's *Berliner Abendblätter* anecdotes and Brecht's calendar stories, Kluge states that the goal of his own fiction is to write "stories in which the alchemy of feelings can be displayed as if in a vial."[152] Because most of these primary feelings, in existing reality, already are bound up in elaborate emotional compounds such as melancholy or aesthetic pleasure, the only way to ascertain their fundamental composition is to increase the sample size, as it were, and deduce their elemental properties based on their interactions

with other feelings under the pressures exerted by distinct historical conditions. Kluge's increasingly massive collections of fiction,
some of which contain hundreds of stories, most fewer than five
pages in length, provide a breathtaking panorama of these feelings
as they cut across individual case histories and are passed down from
one generation to the next. Viewed at a cosmic scale as if through a
reversed telescope, the individual characters in his stories look more
like miniaturized specimens or lab models than like traditional narrative protagonists. Above all, they lack the latter's subjective depth.
This distant, clinical coldness and rigorously analytic approach to
human psychology has won Kluge little acclaim among fans of the
literature of sentiment.[153] "He is and he remains a heartless writer,
and this would be the main reason that people cannot bear him,"
Hans Magnus Enzensberger once noted.[154]

But Kluge's disregard for the psychological depth of his protagonists is a calculated strategy to redirect attention toward the real
heroes of these stories, the feelings themselves. "Feelings are the
true inhabitants of the lives that people lead," he observes in the
introduction to one of his most recent collections.[155] Looking past
anthropomorphic units such as "character" and "personality," he
instead looks at the subjacent feelings that, at a fundamental level,
are what determine the lives of individuals, their subjective experiences and complex motives. In the same way that Brecht's drama
depicted a scientific *Gestentafel*, or grand periodic table of human
gestures, Kluge works with a diagram of emotions such as they exist
outside of the diegetic pressures of the plot system.[156] But reverse
engineering the emotional elements from the empirical episodes of
lived existence, again, requires an operation of some scale. Here,
too, Kluge is like Brecht, whose first attempt at a *Gestentafel*, the
play *Fear and Misery of the Third Reich*, took the form of a massive
cycle of scenes far too long to be performed in a single evening. Only
when individual incidents are arrayed alongside one another in enormous collections such as the recent *Chronicle of Feelings*, over two
thousand pages in compass, do they shed the external appearance
of accident and display their obstinate core. Out of a jumble of random parapraxes, personal tragedies, and felicitous events emerges
a pattern of regular elements that traverses and unites different life
stories, revealing commonalities between unconnected individuals and unanticipated networks of solidarity across political lines.

The reader should not be distracted by the dazzling and distinctive appearance of these individual historical episodes, for below this chaotic surface, there is a "subcutaneous" structure linking them all together: "My books are never single stories, but 12, 14, 16 facets that together make a single story; they *are* the same story."[157]

Endowed with an insuppressible "capacity for metamorphosis,"[158] feelings mutate and transform as they traverse peoples' lives, assuming disparate forms as they enter into coalitions with other feelings and are subjected to new psychic economies. Little wonder that the poet Ovid holds a prominent position in Kluge's pantheon, alongside the likes of Marx and Brecht.[159] For Kluge, metamorphosis offers a conceptual model for thinking about time and change outside of the unidirectional teleology of history. This grammar of transformation is akin to the natural laws that govern the phase transitions between two states of matter: just as water can be transformed from a liquid to a solid state and from there into a gas, and then back to a liquid, emotions, too, can assume different states, some more stable and others more volatile (echoes of Engels's *Dialectics of Nature* again). Like labor faculties, feelings can be frozen and taken out of circulation for centuries and then reactivated, or liquefied, at a much later historical moment.[160] If Kluge's periodic table establishes the basic inventory of individual human feelings and traits, it is the logic of metamorphosis that defines the combinatory laws according to which these elements interact and fuse outside of history's causal series of events. The mechanism of this metamorphosis can be described as a process of "transcoding," Jameson suggests.[161] There is no punctual beginning or end to the lives of these obstinate feelings and traits, just an ongoing and virtually endless series of "forms changed into new bodies" (Ovid).[162]

History and Obstinacy updates Ovid's notion of metamorphosis with theoretical instruments taken from cybernetic and systems theory—in particular, the concepts of self-regulation and autopoeisis. The latter ideas provide a method for tracking recurrent patterns across these elaborate chains of transformation, revealing the continuities within their rolling play of variation. And like that of metamorphosis, the concepts of self-regulation and autopoeisis used by Negt and Kluge "are essentially a matter of correcting German idealism's mistaken belief that there is only one kind of subject."[163] Indeed, there are almost too many subjects in their work. The chain of metamorphosis does not conclude within the realm conventionally arrogated to the human, or even to organic life, for that matter. A recent formula of Kluge reads: "All things are enchanted people."[164] Like Ovid, who sang of the transformations between rocks, people, vegetation, animals, and celestial constellations, Negt and Kluge draw diverse phenomena ranging from newborn infants to industrial enterprises into a supervening chain of becoming. This red thread is far longer, far more encompassing, than the life span of the individual. For example, Germany's industrial heart, the Ruhr district, appears from this view as a gigantic "biotope" composed of five human generations,[165] while the construction of a naval fleet entails a historical accumulation at least seven generations in measure.[166] In turn, Germany itself is revealed to be a two-thousand-year-old "life-form" (Lebewesen) made of eighty-seven generations.[167]

Negt and Kluge's account of metamorphosis is based on Marx's own understanding of the object world as a great storehouse of dead labor. Capital had described work as a process through which dynamic, living forces are captured and given a stable, objective format: "During the labor process, the worker's labor constantly undergoes a transformation, from the form of unrest [Unruhe] into that of being [Sein], from the form of motion [Bewegung] into that of objectivity [Gegenständlichkeit]."[168] Industrial enterprises function like gigantic transformers for converting human life, in all its dimensions, into inorganic matter. "Dead labor is no mere arsenal of things," comment Negt and Kluge. "Rather, it is a social relationship, subjectivity that has assumed an objective form, human connections."[169] Here Negt and Kluge blur the distinction between biology and mechanics (a distinction that, according to Stiegler, is foundational for Western philosophy)[170] and insist instead that machines and humans are ultimately consanguineous, their fates intertwined. If machine capital is indeed composed, as Negt and Kluge suggest, of "entire associations of generations" (Chapter 3, note 12, p. 485), every act of labor, every operation performed with a machine, is in turn an act of communicating and collaborating with the dead. Industrial societies such as ours cannot escape the fact that despite our attempts to remove them from our everyday existence, past generations are still with us. Even after their departure, they will not stop desiring, as Bloch once wrote: "transformed...the dead return, their acts want to be realized once again with us."[171] We moderns are in fact far deeper in the thrall of dead generations than the so-called primitive cultures that we deride for their spiritism and animism. This is so because of two cultural features central to industrial modernity. First, our mode of production is increasingly based on the compound accumulation of machine capital bequeathed to us by previous generations: following the economist Jean Fourastié, Negt and Kluge observe that "more and more dead labor is utilized in the place of living labor."[172] And second, through the elaborate administrative frameworks and institutional superorganisms that function independently of their individual human operators, modern bureaucracies ensure that plans and strategies established at a point in the past will be realized in the future, even long after the plan's original authors have passed away, thereby securing the will of the dead over that of the living.[173] Considering the stockpiling of dead labor in industrial enterprises and the creation of decentered bureaucratic structures that guarantee the fulfillment of past (that is, dead) directives, our presentist fantasy of autonomy and self-determination looks less and less convincing. On the contrary, at this point the industrial West looks more like a giant necropolis. But unlike Marx, who summarized this predicament in the famous observation that the "tradition of the dead generations weighs like a nightmare on the minds of the living,"[174] Negt and Kluge do not regard the influence of the dead to be purely negative, as a paralyzing burden. Instead, they emphasize the dialectical potential of past generations, which they see as an encumbrance that immobilizes the present, but also, in a Benjaminian mode, as a resource whose reanimation under transformed conditions could also contribute to the liberation of the living.

The work of Negt and Kluge is rife with instances of the dead returning to life. Perhaps the most memorable example is the talking knee of a certain Lance Corporal Wieland killed at Stalingrad, which comes back in *The Patriot* in order to set the record straight: "I have to clear up a fundamental misunderstanding, namely, that we dead were somehow dead. We are full of protest and energy," the knee insists, after which it proceeds to recite an obscure text in Latin.[175] The vast crypts of accumulated dead labor that surround the living are in fact full of untold "treasures,"[176] Kluge notes, if only these encrypted resources could, like the mysterious Latin text, be deciphered and comprehended. "Again and again we have to exhume the dead, for our future can only come out of them," explained the playwright Heiner Müller, a close interlocutor of Kluge. "Necrophilia is a love for the future. We have to accept the presence of the dead as partners or obstacles in dialogue. The future can come into being only through dialogue with the dead."[177]

The Lazarus feat of resurrecting the subjects imprisoned in the world of inorganic things requires a profound understanding of history and its diverse temporal currents, which range from deep cycles of biological evolution to the more turbulent time of technical invention. "Resurrecting the dead presupposes a profound knowledge of history."[178] This history does not proceed in a straight line. In a series of knight moves, obstinate characteristics and traits instead leap unpredictably across peoples and generations, back and forth between living and objectivated forms of labor, significantly complicating our attempts to track the course of their movements. The difficulty is compounded by the fact that as a result of constant metamorphosis and recombination, these traits seldom assume the same outward appearance with each instantiation. Take the episode from *The Patriot* again, which leaves the audience to ponder what exactly it is that links a German lance corporal killed at Stalingrad in 1943 to a knee babbling in Latin in 1979. The connection in this case certainly cannot be based on any manifest external likeness — a relationship of resemblance — since the knee does not look like Wieland any more than Ariadne, in Ovid's account, looks like the constellation of stars that she becomes.[179] Nor can the connection between the two be that of part to whole — a relationship of synecdoche — since, as the knee explains, every last piece of Wieland's anatomy, including adjacent parts such as the calf and the thigh, was obliterated at Stalingrad. Indeed, the knee claims to have survived only because it did not in fact belong to the material body of the corporal, but was just connective tissue — not a substance, but a "mere in-between" (*ein bloßes Dazwischen*).[180]

How exactly are we supposed to track — and what do we even call — this "subjectivity that mysteriously continues to have an effect"?[181] Identifying the elusive constant of these metamorphoses is no mean feat. Freud faced the same theoretical problem in his phasal account of the developing libido as did Marx in his description of the historical evolution of the forces of production. As Balibar has observed, these two projects each encountered an identical pair of questions: "What form does the development take and what is its subject, what is it that develops?"[182] For Freud, the development of human sexuality takes the form of a continuous process in which the libido—the "subject" of sexuality, as it were—moves about the infant's body restlessly, establishing erotogenic zones in specific sites and achieving gratification in activities that from the perspective of the valorized genital pleasures of the adult body "are *least obviously* of a 'sexual' character" (thumb sucking, for example).[183] Likewise, for Marx, the development of the forces of production necessarily entails activating certain labor capacities that are least obviously of a properly industrial character (artisanal practices, for example): industrial manufacture "is not only a continuation of handicrafts from the point of view of the nature of its productive forces, it also presupposes the persistence of handicrafts in certain branches of production and even causes handicrafts to develop alongside itself."[184] Thus, rather than concluding with the triumphal emergence of the mature and fully vested subject (of sexual pleasure or production), these examples suggest a nonteleological process of constant metamorphosis and reconfiguration, an open-ended development that recalls the structure of creative evolution once described by Henri Bergson.[185]

So what is the invariant across this string of transformations? As Balibar suggests, the ongoing process of metamorphosis calls into question the very integrity of the subject, which cannot be anchored either at the beginning or the end of the evolution: "In Freudian (and Marxist) pseudo-development, we do not even find the minimum [foundation of history]—we are dealing with the radical absence of any pre-existing unity, i.e. any germ or origin." Just as the development of the libido does not conclude with the genitalization of the adult body,[186] the development of the mode of production does not conclude with the victory of industrial mechanization over premodern handicraft. The factually consecutive evolution of the subject is offset by the permanent retention of all developmental phases through which the subject has passed: modes of artisanal labor flourish within—indeed, are produced by—industrial manufacture, just as the adult body continues to experience sexual pleasure in libidinal zones established during pregenital phases of development.

So, too, Negt and Kluge argue that even the earliest developmental acquisitions are never fully displaced by the ones that succeed them. These primitive experiences are not eliminated, but are instead frozen, suspended in a state of latent potentiality from which they can be reactivated under the right circumstances. Negt and Kluge discern these potentialities everywhere: consider the striking return of "the peasant in me" and forms of archaic work in their analysis of the most advanced forms of intellectual labor; or the prominence they give to "extremely valuable materials from the evolutionary archive"[187] such as the lost tree shrew (the *arche* of all mammalian life (Chapter 7, pp. 369–73); or the oldest form of nonmalignant HIV, which holds the key to disarming the disease today;[188] or the recrudescence, in Kluge's "stone-age television," of eclectic nickelodeon gimmicks taken from the early era of silent cinema.[189] From peasant craft to industrial machine, from thumb sucking to genitality, from Lance Corporal to Latin-speaking knee: each of these displacements represents not a linear historical development of successive forms, but a manifestation of one particular capacity of the respective system in response to the concrete pressures of lived history.

The Underground of History

Like Bloch, who envisaged world history as "a house which has more staircases than rooms,"[190] Negt and Kluge see time as a dynamic process that is full of transitions and passages, but that offers few sites of rest or stasis, not to speak even of discrete and clearly demarcated phases. Their understanding of history not as a linear course of supersession, but as an ongoing and even occasionally reversible process of metamorphosis has important consequences for the concept and practice of revolution. With reference to Thomas More's *Utopia*, Negt has pointed out that the word NO WHERE (from the Greek, *ou-topos*) can be made to spell NOW HERE through a simple displacement of the word's letters.[191] Much like these letters, all of the component elements of socialist society are already at hand, although they would need to be reconfigured to awaken them from their state of latency. Even in 1946, in the immediate shadow of Auschwitz, at a historical moment far darker than our own, Bloch could still claim that utopia was not a distant and chimerical fantasy, but entirely concrete and, indeed, even immanent in current conditions of existence: "Since Marx, we have overcome the abstract character of utopias. Improvement of the world takes place as labor in and with the material dialectic of a developing history that is consciously produced."[192]

But because we have not learned to socialize the forces released through new discoveries in the sciences, history continues to be produced only unconsciously. Shunted aside, many of the most progressive resources of the human psyche have likewise been rendered incomprehensible and dismissed as irrational. But they haven't disappeared. It just requires a feat of imagination to realize their productive capacities. For this reason, Kluge writes of a "utopia which, contrary to the Greek meaning of *ou-topos* = no place, is in existence everywhere and especially in the unsophisticated imagination."[193] As an example of a human trait with both baleful and utopian potentials, take reliability, a psychological characteristic cultivated in modern bureaucratic regimes: this particular combination of dependability, technical precision, blind credulity, and submission to authority is a trait that made the industrial genocide of Auschwitz possible, but as Negt and Kluge point out in an anecdote from Chapter 5, it is also the characteristic that at a very different moment in time, in a different historical conjuncture, thwarts the American bombing of Cambodia when a "reliable" pilot reports to Congress a technical irregularity in his flight path and assigned bombing pattern.

As another example of a trait with a similarly dual aspect, we could cite the elitism found in aristocratic society in the early twentieth century: on the one hand, this outdated form of social distinction was antagonistic to the democratic, mass-cultural developments of the era; on the other, the same elitism also established within the aristocracy nests of unyielding resistance to the demagoguery of National Socialism and its pseudopopulist ideology.[194] Like reliability, then, elitism is a deeply ambiguous quality. But even the most nefarious human trait, when felicitously reconstellated under the right historical conditions, can reveal a latent utopian potential. Evil is nothing other than "good that has been transposed in time," observes Kluge.[195] "Through an improbable turn, the same facts could also be organized differently; if it were possible to translate individual wishes back into a context (into the collective body of wishes), they could be arranged into a successful life, not into catastrophe."[196]

With reference to Foucault, Kluge chooses to call the emancipatory reorganization of traits as a heterotopian project, rather than a utopian one. The latter term, Foucault observed, refers to sites "with no real place…that have a general relation of direct or inverted analogy with the real space of Society," while the former has a concrete "location in reality": heterotopias are "real places—places that do exist and that are formed in the very founding of society—which are something like countersites, a kind of effectively enacted utopia in which the real sites, all the other real sites that can be found within the culture, are simultaneously represented, contested, and inverted."[197] Which is to say that heterotopias are not phantasmatic in the manner of utopias. They are "available, but not tangible."[198] What is so perplexing is that these countersites aren't even necessarily obscured from view, but are, on the contrary, quite out in the open: "this kind of counterpublic sphere would take place in the midst of the public sphere," Kluge notes.[199] These progressive elements are not hidden, then, but are instead unidentifiable or unintelligible, falling either below or beyond the hegemonic horizon of meaning. "We are dealing today with forms of counterpublic sphere that are so embedded in the official public sphere that they are often no longer even recognizable."[200] Because they are out of phase with the socially dominant reality, these sites are mostly encountered elliptically, as effects without explicable causes. The conscious mind experiences them as an incoherent heap of particularities, not as systematic knowledge and certainly not as an organized context for living. This analysis, again, represents a strategic development beyond the claims of *Public Sphere and Experience*, the previous collaboration that still associated ideology with secrecy and tactics of deception, and that consequently called for the integration of obscured realms of everyday existence such as family and work into the collective purview of the public sphere. In contrast, *History and Obstinacy* calls not for revelation, but for reconfiguration, for a shift in perspective that would demonstrate the motivated connections between seemingly unrelated particularities and incidents. "We are seeking an economy of combined trivials" (*eine Ökonomie der kombinierten Nebensachen*), writes Kluge.[201] Although little effort would be required to induce this simple shift in perspective and realize a utopian state that is in fact already here, this shift turns out to be virtually impossible, precisely because of its very obviousness. Confronted with the increasing spectacularization of postwar consumer society, Adorno and his colleagues at the Frankfurt School likewise observed, all too presciently, that ideology is no longer a veil, but the menacing face of the world. It is transitioning into terror, not just by force of being interlaced with propaganda, but in accordance with its own appearance. However, because ideology and reality have moved so close to one another—because, for lack of any other convincing ideology, reality has become its own ideology—only a minimal effort would be necessary for the mind to cast off an illusion that is at once omnipotent and insignificant. But that effort seems to be what is the most difficult of all.[202]

When deception has given way to terror and the shrouding of power to its adulatory display, politics takes on a very different meaning than the one it had in the classical bourgeois public sphere. Accordingly, the later work of Negt and Kluge no longer identifies the political with arcane power nexuses or Bismarckian *Realpolitik*, but instead describes it as an art of configuration, balance, and proportion. For them, the goal of leftist politics today, in turn, is not to invent new revolutionary traits within the subject or fashion utopia from whole cloth, but to organize already existing, if still neglected and underestimated human capacities in a way that activates their dormant emancipatory potentials.

Their third and final major collaboration, *Politics as a Relation of Measure*, develops this principle into full-blown ecological paradigm of the political. This book's point of departure is Hegel's thesis that the true essence (*Wesen*) of any phenomenon is revealed only when it enters into a felicitous historical configuration or proportional "relation of measure" with other phenomena:[203] "Only when conditions are such that phenomena assume a certain constellation—when they discard their previous mode of existence to encounter other existences—only then do the relations that they carry within them begin to condense and transform into a unique structure that constitutes an *essential context*. This inner structure is identical with measure. Phenomena arrive at their essence only through relations of measure."[204] Responding in part to the dissolution of the high-contrast ideological binarisms of the Cold War, the third collaboration between Negt and Kluge, published in 1992, proposes here a far more nuanced and sensitive framework for the analysis of geopolitical configurations, one that does not divide the world into axes of good and evil or categorical oppositions between capitalist and socialist. Indeed, the identical human trait can be found in both revolutionary and reactionary constellations.

This is an approach that has been justifiably characterized as "a kind of secular political alchemy."[205] Just as water (H_2O) and carbon dioxide (CO_2) reveal different potentials of the oxygen molecule that they share, individuals come to exhibit certain of "man's essential powers" (*die menschlichen Wesenskräfte*) within particular social configurations. Only when the right configuration has been found will these latent capacities of the individual be released. Until then, they remain in a dormant state. For this reason, Negt and Kluge explain that objective reality is located not at the level of immediately evident empirical properties, but at the level of the relations connecting these isolated phenomena: "the issue is not how to describe so-called 'reality' accurately, in the way that we directly perceive it; instead what matters is that the proportions be correct."[206] Like Lance Corporal Wieland's knee, the "mere in-between" that outlived the calf and thigh on either side, or like Ariadne, who lives on as a celestial pattern created by the relationship between individual stars, the connections and constellations themselves are more essential, philosophically speaking, than the physical substance in which they manifest themselves historically, and they endure far longer than the transient and incidental facts out of which they are composed.

More recently, this dialectical understanding of essence as an expression of relations, rather than of substances, has shifted the thought of Negt and Kluge toward territory identified today with the philosophy of emergent properties.[207] Although to be sure, this was in fact a feature of their thought all along, evident, for example, in their appropriation of Marx's analysis of the collective worker. Indeed, an application of Hegel's law of "relations of measure" to sociopolitical phenomena can be found throughout Marx's work. Take the important chapter titled "Co-operation" in *Capital*, which described the appearance of a novel social macroentity that is irreducible to its individual members (the basic definition of an emergent social phenomenon): "a dozen persons working together will, in their collective working-day of 144 hours, produce far more than twelve isolated men each working 12 hours, or than one man who works twelve days in succession." "Not only do we have here an increase in the productive power of the individual, by means of co-operation, but the creation of a new productive power, which is an intrinsically collective one." Marx used an English phrase to

designate the mysterious surplus that arises within a society of combined *zoa politika*: "animal spirits."[208] According to Negt and Kluge,
when elements, whether material or psychological, are emplaced
within a "condition of condensation," they reach a "new degree of
intensity," giving rise to a complex system that possesses objective
qualities and energies not manifest in any of its individual components.[209] Like the social process of cooperation, the physical process
of condensation involves a slow and gradual accumulation, or "transition" (*Übergang*), that eventually leads to a tipping point (*Umsturz*),
in which one system is transmuted, quasi-alchemically, into a different one.[210] At each distinct level of synthesis, the system exhibits different structural principles that correspond not only to its particular
organizational state (for example, liquid versus gas, artisanal versus
industrial production), but also to its relative magnitude: thus, just
as smaller physical bodies are subject to the intermolecular force
of van der Waals adhesion, while larger physical bodies instead
observe the law of gravity, the forms of ideation that are contained
within the individual mind and that are expressed in conscious
thought differ fundamentally from those that are found in collective
activity and that are instead expressed unconsciously, in statistical
curves. Kluge calls this latter social condensation a "fusional group"
(*fusionierende Gruppe*):

> The "fusional group" is an element of every revolution. People join
> together. Even without their knowledge, they are forming a novel con-
> dition that is distinct from their lives thus far, a condition in which their
> characteristics merge together without their intending to do so—below
> the threshold of the force of will, as an effect of the unrest that has
> seized the city, on account of the ability to intuit and of the force of
> action. Human reinforcements from the countryside. They integrate
> themselves. The "new revolutionary man" (at first an unstable element)
> does not consist of individuals, of the previous people themselves,
> but arises between them, out of the gaps that divide people from one
> another in everyday life.[211]

Needless to say, personal motives play little to no role in this
understanding of the political. Nor do ethical criteria of behavior,
for that matter. In one episode from a recent story collection, for
example, Kluge writes of one particular fusional group that formed
at a demonstration in Kiev one day in 1905 and that contained indi-

viduals from diverse social backgrounds, including a lawyer and, notably, a pickpocket. All of these characters were subsumed into the contagious mass of bodies that day, the narrator reports. We are also told that the pickpocket, despite the potential profits to be gained in the fervent and distracted crowd, forgot his trade, stole nothing, and was left to hunger by the time evening came. "On that day, he possessed nothing but his enthusiasm."[212] For the duration of the fusional group's existence, the pickpocket was transformed, despite his own interests, from a selfish thief into a passionate revolutionary element. A previously dormant characteristic—a capacity for cooperation and mutualism—had been released, if only fleetingly. This episode suggests that politics, as the science of collective existence (*Gemeinwesen*), is beyond psychological or ethical criteria and is instead a matter of assembly and proportion. Ultimately, the right fusional configuration will decide whether human history produces acts of mass violence, the hell of Social Darwinism, and the tragedy of the commons[213] or whether this group of egotistical monads can instead be joined together to create an integrated collective existence. Quoting Kant's "Perpetual Peace" essay, Negt, like Kluge, sounds an optimistic note: "The problem of setting up a state can be solved even by a nation of devils, as long as they have reason."[214]

Given their emergentist understanding of history, it is not surprising that Negt and Kluge never romanticize political revolution as a punctual break with the past. Years such as 1789 or 1917 may possess great symbolic power, but, for them, there is little to be learned from singling these dates out from all the others. For no revolution can be consummated in a year. Politics is instead "a slow and powerful drilling through hard boards," to cite a phrase of Max Weber's that has returned in Kluge's recent work.[215] As a tactical response to the harsh lessons of the 1970s, when, in the wake of the failed insurrection of 1968, German activists turned to "strategies of hibernation" (*Überwinterungsstrategien*), *History and Obstinacy* privileges measured political tenacity over manic demands for revolutionary convulsion.

The ethos of "slow and powerful drilling" is conjured in an episode central to the book: Rosa Luxemburg's haunting ventriloquism of the revolution on the eve of her own death in 1919, when she wrote the words "I was, I am, I will be."[216] As she conjugates the copular verb "to be" through its different tenses, Luxemburg evokes the multiple temporalities of the revolution and its capacity to suture together distinctive historical materials, underscoring with this grammatical recitation the fact that the revolution is not a singular event, but a process that is repeated across time, in each instance taking on a different form with historically variable features.[217] However, this temporal conjugation of the revolution is ultimately a distortion of its essential qualities. For "revolution does not function like a language," Negt and Kluge note:[218] whereas the grammar of spoken language is based on sequential concatenation, the revolution's "dialectical relations are nonlinear" and thus fundamentally "ungrammatical."[219] The pressure chamber of lived history causes the fine filigree of logical relations to buckle and collapse (*zerbeulen*), rendering these dialectical relations and emancipatory constellations of traits unrecognizable.[220] The logical structure of the revolution is refracted into past, present, and future—"was," "is," and "will be." Only at those extremely rare conjunctures when the competing gravitational forces of human history cancel one another out—the moment of suspension that Negt and Kluge identify in Chapter 7 as the "abaric point"—is the "pulverizing effect" (*Zermalmungseffekt*) of time interrupted long enough for this abstract dialectic to become temporarily legible.[221] One such moment, Negt and Kluge propose, was the period in Germany immediately after the end of the Second World War, the so-called Stunde Null, in which the reality principle of history was held in abeyance, if only for a short time. During brief intervals of freedom such as this, when the syntagmatic rules of lived experience are temporarily neutralized, it becomes possible to glimpse revolutionary relations in their pure, paradigmatic state, outside of time. Within this zone of historical indifference, lived experience becomes a logical object of philosophy, and the subterranean connection between all of the outwardly dissimilar historical iterations of the revolution becomes visible, if only for a moment. Like water at a temperature of 212° Fahrenheit, history hovers at this point on the threshold between states as a reversible, isometric field that can be read either forward or backward. "At the interface between gravitational fields, at the abaric point (which is always only theoretical), gravitational forces have no effect, only 'freedom.' For a moment, the attributes of the sphere and the funnel are identical. Above and below reverse their polarity."[222]

Luxemburg's words "I was, I am, I will be" thus suggest, on the one hand, that the revolution is inevitable, since revolutionary capacities cannot be eradicated by force. Proletarian traits will never fail to "return [*wiederkehren*] if they are violently repressed."[223] But on the other hand, her words simultaneously suggest that revolution*izing*, as a practice, is an interminable process that will never culminate in a singular event or dramatic peripeteia. It will instead be played through again and again, each time with different results. *Wiederkehren*, after all, means both "to return" and "to repeat," as in Nietzsche's doctrine of eternal recurrence (*die ewige Wiederkehr*). In Commentary 4, Kluge refers to Aleksandr Bogdanov and Aron Zalkind, two Proletkult theorists who calculated that socializing the objectivated forces of production (that is, machinery and technology) would require only seven years, whereas socializing the human subject—forging a stable psychological vessel for the marginalized proletarian traits—would take at least ten times as long.[224] Even this estimate is far too optimistic, according to Kluge: "It took eight hundred years to develop capitalism to the French Revolution; and it will take quite a lot of years to prepare experience and organize a period that could make a more socialist society. It will probably take more time, more activity, and more interest than was needed to invent this capitalist society."[225] Regime change and technical revolutions are relatively swift affairs, but human revolutions have an exceptional *Zeitbedarf*, he writes: they "need time."[226] And without the psychosocial reconfiguration of the subject and its essential powers, no political revolution can succeed in the long run. Marx himself had mocked as "political superstition" the conceit of overthrowing the government in a grand coup, as if seizing the state's command centers, symbolic assets, and means of production would be the culminating stroke of the revolution:[227] to be sure, it would be a start, he argues, but the concrete mores and habits of the population, not the state apparatus, are what actually holds a society together.[228] For similar reasons, Negt observes, "it is not just a matter of overthrowing [*Umsturz*] the state, but of something like a transformation and of self-transformation as a feature of living people."[229] Bastilles and Winter Palaces can be stormed in a day, but redesigning the affections and pleasures of a population, their intractable habits and everyday comportment, demands an intervention that is nothing less than evolutionary in scope.[230] There is no

Umsturz without *Übergang,* no tipping point without transition, no revolution without emergence.

This reminder that revolution cannot take the form of a radical historical caesura is especially timely in our post–Cold War moment, when the Left, tempted by the rhetoric of eventhood and the neo-Stalinist promise of a Great Break, is increasingly captivated by forms of political messianism as the only remaining hope of deliverance from a global capitalist system that now expands unchecked. But a total break with the past will not provide the necessary solution. As Negt and Kluge caution, radical thought's implicit opposition between two structures of time, one of "rest" and "duration" and the other of "a dramatic, abrupt, sensational, and fleeting movement" is itself a theoretical legacy of the classical bourgeois age.[231] More than anything else, the go-for-broke strategy of political messianism is a symptom of a generalized loss of "trust in a historical process that can be directly shaped by the consciousness of people."[232] Rather than exacerbate the differences between the "time of waiting" (*Wartezeit*) and that of the "quantum leap" (*Quantensprung*),[233] conscious political transformation would therefore dictate that these two temporalities instead be integrated. The past, in other words, must be reorganized, rather than renounced. "We are separated from yesterday not by an abyss, but by a changed situation" reads the epigraph for Kluge's film *Yesterday's Girl*. Unlike the romantic generation of '68, Negt and Kluge, as obstinate '58ers, maintain that in times of revolutionary transition, the elements of existence and experience are exactly the same as those found in nonrevolutionary times, only they have now been arranged in a way that causes them to coruscate and demonstrate new qualities. Even the precarious abaric points of history, such as the years in Germany immediately after 1945, are not necessarily more susceptible to human intervention and influence than any other moment in time. For Negt and Kluge, these intervals of crisis (from the Greek word meaning "discrimination" or "judgment") are in fact more valuable as thought objects, as opportunities for cognition, than they are as narrative peripeteia in the revolutionary drama of human history.[234]

Kluge compares the historical record of man's essential powers to a typewritten sheet of paper that has been overwritten four thousand times by a continuous text with neither spacing, punctuation, nor vowels.[235] *History and Obstinacy* exfoliates this dense laminate that has been passed down to us, layer by layer, in the hopes of locating emancipatory characteristics that can be actualized in our own time. For contrary to their appearance of technical novelty, the problems faced by the present generation are seldom, if ever, genuinely new. In order to explore these paradigmatic connections, Negt and Kluge bring together disparate historical expressions of human traits, aligning them in a way that reveals the resemblances between these seemingly incommensurable moments in time. So, for example, the political powder keg in Serbia of 1914 returns in the Kosovo conflict of 1991;[236] the experience of huddling in shelters during the Allied carpet bombings of 1945 recalls that of being buried alive in ancient Egypt, as depicted in Verdi's *Aida*;[237] and the cemeteries' refusal to accept the bodies of the Red Army Faction terrorists in 1977 echoes Creon's denial of Antigone's claim to bury her rebel brother.[238]

As random as such juxtapositions may seem, Negt and Kluge insist that these likenesses are not merely pseudomorphic. For them, the fact that these episodes have been repeated again and again in our history is a symptom of a collective failure to learn from them the first time around. Instead of brushing distant episodes aside with the gesture of historicism, we must instead revisit them if progress is to be made and the endless cycle of repetition broken. Only by "working through the problems of the past that were left behind" can the tautological loop of myth be transformed into conscious human history.[239] "The phantom existence of the past, which crisscrosses the present's plans for the future, can be suspended only through socially conscious, collective labor that will put an end to the deadly repetition compulsion and stem the return of the repressed. Transforming the cultural legacy into contemporary social forms, however, requires a process of engaging with history publicly, a process that cultivates learning impulses only under specific conditions."[240]

Recently, for example, Negt and Kluge have each returned to the distant era of the Thirty Years' War as an important "provocation to learn" (*Lernprovokation*) for us today. In their account, the diffuse, total European war that preceded the emergence of the modern nation-state four centuries ago anticipates the current geopolitical crisis in which the territorial sovereignty of the nation, together with its exclusive monopoly on violence, are being undermined by supranational organizations and corporations that do not observe the political or economic borders of individual states. What lessons about justice and the right to violence were confronted in the decentralized conflicts of the seventeenth century, but still remain to be worked through today?[241] Do the theologically tinged knowledge structures of the seventeenth century, so many assets of which were disavowed under the Enlightenment's project of secular modernization, in fact provide us with solutions to some of the problems that we are facing now?[242] With the proliferation of forms of asymmetrical, postnational warfare and with the uptick of politically motivated religious fundamentalisms worldwide, we may need the resources, intelligence, and ingenuity of pre-Enlightenment thought more than ever before. Like Bloch, who sought to recover the protosocialist elements within the chiliastic dreams of medieval theology,[243] or Agamben, who has recently investigated prefigurations of modern political economy and strategies of governmentality in early Christian doctrine,[244] Negt and Kluge hope to learn from the strategies of revolutionary consciousness (and unconsciousness) that existed long before the philosophical formalization of the Marxist dialectic in the nineteenth century, and that might ultimately prove indispensible for progressive politics today.

The remote past may hold the answers to many of the questions now facing us, but these solutions are not readily available. Accessing them requires what Kluge calls "counterhistory" (*Gegengeschichte*) or, in the famous phrase of Benjamin's seventh thesis on the philosophy of history, brushing history against the grain. In his writings on the *longue durée*, Braudel likewise enjoined historians to "react against the advantages of their professions, and study not only progress, the prevailing movement, but also its opposite, that harvest of contrary experiences which fought hard before they went down."[245] *History and Obstinacy* is the yield of that harvest. On the one hand, the inventory of experiences and capacities that this book provides seems utterly factual and objective, delivered in the rationalist idiom of a reference work, but at the same time, this counterhistory also appears fundamentally unrealistic, if not outright bizarre and fantastical. Kluge explains that these scenarios appear so utterly improbable because they have been systematically marginalized by the dominant ideological narrative of our culture, a hegemonic fiction that he dubs the "novel of reality."[246] Even such a hardened realist as V. I. Lenin defended the merits of revolutionary imagination and counterhistory when he insisted, against the crushing force of fate, that "there is always a way out."[247] And finding this way out requires thinking unrealistically, imagining that "the same story can take a different direction." Running against the entrenched patterns of "realistic" thought, the heterotopist wins positions from which the irregularities and unmotivated incidents of history begin to appear as necessary and interconnected.[248] The heterotopist establishes an "economy of combined trivials" that challenges the dominant economy of reality. Although purely hypothetical, these positions are in fact of inestimable tactical value, as the shrewd military theorist Carl von Clausewitz proposed when he observed that the battles that never actually took place are just as important as the ones that did.[249] "What you notice as realism... is not necessarily or certainly real," Kluge in turn explains. "The potential and the historical roots and the detours of possibilities also belong to it. The realistic result, the actual result, is only an abstraction that has murdered all the possibilities for the moment. But these possibilities will recur."[250] The imaginary will inevitably one day return as reality.[251]

Recovering these murdered possibilities requires a bent for counterfactual thinking. It is a talent that Kluge has in abundance. Over decades of writing and filmmaking, his rehabilitation of the lost futures that were smothered by a hegemonic reality principle has yielded a body of work that is difficult to situate generically, poised as it is on the boundary between documentary and fiction. "One never knows whether what Kluge reports as fact is indeed fact," Jürgen Habermas notes. "But the way he reports events makes it clear that it could have happened like that."[252] Subjunctive and indicative are on par in Kluge's work. Just as his thought experiments in prose regularly place historical figures in invented scenarios to consider how they would have responded (and what we can learn from this response), many of Kluge's films, conversely, place invented characters in real-life, documentary situations in which the fictional protagonist interviews well-known political figures or joins in actual historical events such as street protests and public performances. By undermining the boundary between reality and fiction in this way, Kluge demonstrates that the hegemonic conception of reality is neither objective nor unassailable. Our blind faith in facts and the immutability of reality is just a secular equivalent of the religious fetish, Negt and Kluge explain. Against currents of modern positivism that seek to conceal the manufacture of reality, they therefore emphasize its madeness and its susceptibility to revision.[253]

Negt and Kluge's counterhistory of Europe coalesces around those moments when the dominant frameworks for human experience became brittle and collapsed, rendering a shared reality momentarily vulnerable to imaginative reconceptualization. Take, as a dramatic example, the precipitous ideological deflation of the Berlin Wall over one night in November 1989: during the time of the Cold War, this structure had appeared permanent and eternal, but with the sudden annulment of its political foundations, the Wall was transformed within hours from a seemingly timeless pseudo-objectivity into what Hegel called a *realitätsloses Gebilde*, a construct with no symbolic authority or even basis in reality.[254] Even the most concrete of realities can be liquefied, revoked in an instant. The work of Negt and Kluge is rife with such instances of rapid ideological decommissioning that reveal the fragility of our conception of reality and of the sociopolitical institutions that sustain it. These episodes of collective derealization are both traumatic and liberating, experiences of loss, crisis, and potentiality all at once: thus, the firebombing of Kluge's birth town Halberstadt in 1945 caused an entire community to disappear from one day to the next, but in so doing, also exposed the permanence of the thousand-year Reich as pure fantasy. Likewise, the activities of the Red Army Faction in the 1970s shattered the utopian ideals of the German Left, but the desperate state violence that the terrorists provoked also revealed the fundamental insecurity of the Federal Republic and the tenuousness of its claim to democratic legitimacy. At moments such as 1945, 1977, and 1989, the monolithic account of reality becomes permeable to counterhistories. And by imagining alternative courses at these critical historical junctures, it becomes possible "to disarm the fifth act," as Kluge puts it, and dispel the aura of destiny and fatefulness that enshrouds our conception of reality.[255]

In our present era of uneven development, when the pluralization of history globally has scumbled the contrast between progress and regress, the untimeliness of Negt and Kluge appears timelier than ever. Revolutionary activity today entails as its corollary the kind of radical historiography practiced by Negt and Kluge, which draws connections between distant and noncontiguous episodes in time.

As Joseph Vogl notes in conversation with Kluge, the figure of the revolutionary can be recognized by his unique ability to "dissolve and stitch together different times. He assembles history. He is a vessel for temporal states."[256] And so where, at the current post-Cold War moment in which the "possibility of a European revolution seems to have disappeared,"[257] can these orphaned emancipatory traits, these nests of obstinacy, still be found today? Given history's incessant thimblerigging of human traits from one site to another, these revolutionary resources are never located where we think we'll find them. For Negt and Kluge, they crop up in the unlikeliest of places and at the least probable historical moments: in Detroit techno, in the labor habits of the premodern peasantry, and in the crude thinking (*plumpes Denken*) of Leibniz's unrealistic proposal for a network of windmills in the Harz region.[258]

Take, as a concluding example, the migration of the European Enlightenment's revolutionary project to the Caribbean, where, under new social conditions, the bourgeois ideal of freedom and promise of equality acquired a second life in the political revolt of black slaves. Like Heiner Müller's play *The Mission*,[259] which was written in 1979 while Negt and Kluge were at work on *History and Obstinacy*, Kluge's recent story "Revolutionary Experiment on the Margins of France" follows the itinerary of these radical impulses after their emancipatory contents had been evacuated in France, first by Thermidor and then by Napoleon's coup. As the stories of Müller and Kluge both suggest, these ideals lived on long after they were abandoned by their original European authors, igniting anti-imperialist struggles for self-determination in faraway parts of the world. After a period of agitating unsuccessfully in the colony of Louisiana, during which time the French Revolution was degenerating into terror and dictatorship, Kluge's revolutionaries finally arrive in Haiti, where at last "the citizens of humanity saw before them exactly the raw material that they needed."[260] It was in fact the revolutionaries in Haiti, not those in France, who alone were able to "surpass the confines of the present constellations of power in perceiving the concrete meaning of freedom."[261] As history would have it, the most enlightened and progressive ideals of the European bourgeoisie—a class that was itself ultimately incapable of realizing these abstract concepts in practice—found their radical actualization on a distant island thousands of miles away, reborn as a slave revolt.

Delays and displacements such as these remind us that history, according to Negt and Kluge, is "not a criterion of substance, but rather a search criterion."[262] Since time subjects all phenomena to a sea change that renders them unrecognizable, we are forced constantly to revise the rubrics under which we organize historical knowledge. If we want to learn about the most progressive ideals of European culture, for example, perhaps we should open the file cabinet of history to *H*, for "Haiti," rather than *F*, for "France." The Enlightenment's promise of radical freedom never disappeared. Like other proletarian traits, it was simply mislabeled and archived under a different heading. And one day, if we get the search criterion right, the global margins may return to us the European revolutionary ideals that were betrayed upon its own soil and that have been waiting patiently abroad for their repatriation.

Devin Fore
Princeton and New York, 2014

Notes on the Translation

History and Obstinacy is a significantly revised edition of the German publication of *Geschichte und Eigensinn* that originally appeared in 1981. *Geschichte und Eigensinn*, completed over the course of roughly three tumultuous years of West German history, was originally a twelve-chapter, three-part book spread over 1,283 pages. The revised English-language edition is roughly a third this size. The authors, Negt and Kluge, wrote the massive tome sentence for sentence together, often with three assistants on call. In the brief afterword to the book, the authors explained: "This book drained us. It remains a fragment. In light of our estimation of the subject we are dealing with, we wanted this book to be nothing more than this. Readers will have to look for gaps."[1] A collaborative process that itself has lasted years, the translation of *Geschichte und Eigensinn* has entailed several substantial revisions of the original text, made by the original authors in consultation with both the editor and translators. While no chapter from the original has gone unchanged, some are largely edited down in size (for example, chapters 2, 3, and 7 in *History and Obstinacy*). Others contain a considerable amount of new material interwoven into abbreviated versions of the original (for example, chapters 1, 4, and 6 in *History and Obstinacy*). Chapter 5 stands out as a condensation of the most important portions of whole chapters from of the German original not preserved in this translation (chapters 7, 8, and 9 in *Geschichte und Eigensinn*). Deemed inessential by the authors for a book intended for an English-language audience in a new century, chapters 5 (on German identity) and 12 (on orientation) from *Geschichte und Eigensinn* appear nowhere in *History and Obstinacy*, and yet their traces nonetheless lie scattered throughout all of the following pages. The Appendix, a glossary of terms, is entirely new and gleans essential concepts from the entirety of the German original. Although previously published in German, the stories interspersed therein, as well as those that conclude chapters 4, 6, and 7—forty-four in all—are also entirely new to *History and Obstinacy*. While both authors were involved in the revisions, Kluge undertook the bulk of the work, and thus readers have before them a book authored by Kluge and Negt and not Negt and Kluge, as the duo had long been known in both the German-speaking and English-speaking worlds. To be sure, the transformation of *Geschichte und Eigensinn* into *History and Obstinacy*—a metamorphosis, in part, of writing history (*Geschichtserzählung*) into telling stories (*Geschichten erzählen*)—is itself a story of the Old Mole resurfacing in the twenty-first century, a tale in itself worthy of careful study.

Readers will quickly recognize in *History and Obstinacy* a remarkable synthesis of theoretical concepts and ideas taken from throughout ancient and modern Continental philosophy, Western literature, and film history. The translators have made every effort to identify the origins of these ideas and to incorporate consistently the most widely adopted, up-to-date, and viable scholarly English translations that still remain true to the contexts of the original. (The original occasionally cited different editions of the same title.) In the case of entire bodies of work by single authors such as Karl Marx, of which Kluge and Negt make extensive use, the translators have instead consulted comprehensive standard editions such as the Marx/Engels *Collected Works* (*MECW*) in order to ensure consistency and accuracy within the cited sources. In those few instances where existing English translations either did not exist or did not correspond to the quoted German in Kluge and Negt's text, the translators either provided their own translation or modified existing translations. As is the case with the German-language original, many of these sources are named by the authors either in the body of the text or in its critical apparatus. In addition to these references, the translators have intermittently inserted essential footnotes and commentaries into the English-language edition in an effort to illuminate the provenance of quotations and concepts never recognized in the original; some notes provide definitions of translated concepts that go beyond the reach of those provided in the glossary, while others explain the rationale for chosen translations of thorny concepts that would otherwise go unnoticed by English-language readers. These addenda are identified thus, [in square brackets], throughout the translation. Similarly, the translators have inserted German-language concepts at those junctures in the text where the best English-language equivalent still fails to capture all the valances of the original. Those few quotations lacking sources are either Kluge and Negt speaking or have remained unidentifiable. In his seminal article on *Geschichte und Eigensinn* from 1988, Fredric Jameson writes of a "typographic revolution" in which "everything has already begun to flee into the footnotes and appendices."[2] With *History and Obstinacy*, the original's typographic revolution is muted and the disruptive role the original's many footnotes plays on the reader's eye is relegated to the endnotes in the name of readability. In spite of all of these precautions and extra measures undertaken for this translation, readers nonetheless would be wise to keep the German original at hand, because *History and Obstinacy* rests like the tip of an iceberg atop a massive critical apparatus preserved here, but yet not entirely transferred over from *Geschichte und Eigensinn*.

Negt and Kluge once explained that speed and efficiency was of utmost importance in the writing of *Geschichte und Eigensinn*: after five minutes of debate, unresolved formulations were recorded as-is by their amanuenses.[3] In other instances, some sentences were initiated by one author and completed by the other. In wrestling with the formal traces of their idiosyncratic labor processes, the translators have strived for maximum readability in English while preserving the meanings and voices as well as the unique punctuation and abbreviations of the original as much as possible. At the level of sentence and paragraph construction, this has sometimes entailed deciding between solving or retaining semantic ambiguities. In other cases, it has entailed making difficult decisions for how to render into English excessively protracted syntax and concatenated dependent clauses, not to mention ambiguous relative pronouns, peculiar adjectival nouns, and unique compound nouns. In so doing, the process of translation has very likely smoothed over the shifts and breaks between Negt's and Kluge's individual voices in some passages of *Geschichte und Eigensinn*. Careful attention, too, has been paid to preserving the rhetorical distinctions between Negt and Kluge's theoretical voices and Kluge's poetics of storytelling. Given both the aforementioned addenda as well as the inevitable transformations that result from any translation, it is arguable that *History and Obstinacy* has mitigated ever so slightly the radical provocation intended by the original's polyvocal character and its renegade art of citation. A trade-off made in the name of accessibility for a foreign-language audience, this polishing, we hope, has not made the work any less fragmentary or challenging.

Like the German original, this English translation was a long and exhaustive process; it has involved a handful of researchers and translators working in three different countries with very different intellectual relationships to Negt's and Kluge's heterogeneous bodies of work. Nonetheless, every precaution has been taken to ensure a consistency from cover to cover. To these ends, Rory Bradley and Richard Lambert painstakingly located most of the extant English translations of source material quoted in Chapters 1, 2, 3, 4, and 6. Samantha Riley mined sources for Chapter 7. Joel Golb completed drafts of Chapters 1 and 2. Cyrus Shahan cotranslated Chapters 3 and 4, as well as the Appendix. Martin Brady and Helen Hughes translated Chapter 6 and the stories in Chapter 4. Richard Langston translated the Preface, as well as Chapters 5 and 7. He also cotranslated Chapters 3, 4, 6, and the Appendix. In addition to completing Chapters 1 and 2, he also oversaw the preliminary research for the translation and together with the brilliant assistance of copyeditor Bud Bynack oversaw the preservation of the translation's overall consistency and readability. He also determined the provenance of most of the images with the invaluable help of Julie Fry and Meighan Gale, who also secured permissions. Devin Fore masterminded the English-language edition, set the project in motion, and ensured that it saw the light of day. Beate Wiggen provided administrative assistance. Thomas Combrink prepared numerous German editions of the manuscript. And Alexander Kluge and Oskar Negt actively presided over and authorized the entire translation process. Underwriting for this translation was provided, in part, by the Alexander von Humboldt Foundation, the Goethe Institut and Inter Nationes, and the offices of Alexander Kluge.

Richard Langston et al.
Berlin, 2012

Preface

The following book is about the human ability to change matter purposefully. We call this ability "labor."[1] It not only consists of commodity production, but also engenders social relations and develops community. It possesses OBSTINACY. Its product is HISTORY.

We are interested in what confounded perception in the twentieth century, derailed by Auschwitz, and what continues to do so now in our twenty-first century, eclipsed by asymmetrical warfare and pervaded by debt crisis. Whereas on the one hand, the debt crisis has led to a widespread loss of trust in politics, it has also proven conducive, on the other, to embark in new directions and constituting counterpolitics. This is precisely what is contained in HISTORICAL LABOR CAPACITIES [ARBEITSVERMÖGEN]. In abbreviated outline form, this book is about the POLITICAL ECONOMY OF LABOR POWER [ARBEITSKRAFT]: Of what do those human characteristics capable of bringing about material change consist? How do the "essential powers" of humans come into being, so that we are able to work, control our own lives, and become autonomous? The economy of this labor capacity is the capital's polar opposite. It constitutes COUNTERCAPITAL.

Hundreds of years passed before the certainty and fear of God's existence in modern societies metamorphosed into thriftiness, fiscal exactitude, credit, and productivity. The precise feeling with which a person in China, Europe, or the United States tightens a screw ("it fits," "like a glove," "it wiggles," "has clearance") is a characteristic that all workers mutually recognize, but that evolved over the course of a long chain of relays. Thousands of years would pass before resistance against incompetent and unjust overlords transformed into wit, the spirit of invention, and political self-consciousness.

A photograph. [Alexander Kluge Archive]

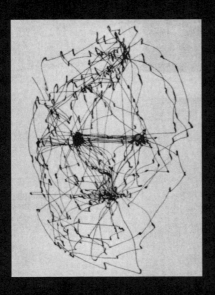

Eyes contemplated the adjacent photograph for several minutes. A two-dimensional rendering of eye movements according to Alfred L. Yarbus, *Eye Movements and Vision*, trans. Basil Haigh (New York: Plenum Press, 1967). Eye movements are spontaneous. **The eye works.** But it does not do this in a linear fashion. The motion of work has its own prehistory.[2] *Note:* "The sleep of reason" does not mean reason that has passed away or that has temporarily fallen asleep. Rather, it means sleep in the form of reason. Logos (as the dead labor of all egocentric standpoints in history) is especially alert and "produces monsters." Such reason protects its sleep from awakening with violent dreams.

The Critical Theory of the Frankfurt School once observed that humans first built the Tower of Babel only to see it then crumble. Centuries later, this building constituted itself anew inside humans. This was modernity. Silicon Valley is full of people carrying around Towers of Babel inside them. And now Marxists have risen up to build Shanghai into a megacity.

Empirical processes of this kind have been of great interest on both sides of the Atlantic. Both "drawing maps of experience" and "rendering history accessible" are what are at stake for us in the ensuing pages before you. For this reason, the kind of analysis is necessary the likes of which Walter Benjamin, Max Horkheimer, Theodor W. Adorno, Jürgen Habermas, Bertolt Brecht, Richard Sennett, Niklas Luhmann, and Michel Foucault always demanded. We need a new encyclopedia, and it is essential that it be accessible to the public.

We apply the term "political economy of labor power"—in other words, the battle between OBSTINACY and HISTORY—to domains not traditionally associated with industry: the politics of love, war, and the "capitalism within us." We have matter-of-fact reasons for adopting this cross-mapping approach. For one thing, it disrupts our habitual ways of seeing. Labor capacities rule daily life, just as they react virulently when societies create monsters such as fascism, for example. It is essential that we recognize our labor in all its aggregate states, and not solely in those belonging to midlevel functionality.

For this English-language edition of our text, which was originally published in 1981, we have excised several chapters and drastically revised others. We did this, on the one hand, out of deference to experiences anchored in the national histories of our new English-language readers in the United States, which are markedly different from those of Central Europe's. We undertook these changes, on the other hand, because of the radically altered perspectives that already have emerged at the end of the first decade of the twenty-first century.

Alexander Kluge
Munich, 2011

Oskar Negt
Hanover, 2011

An elephant posing underneath a mastodon. A comparative study in size. [Alexander Kluge Archive]

PART ONE

The Historical Organization
of Labor Capacities

CHAPTER ONE

The Origins of Labor Capacities

in Separation (The Permanence of

Primitive Accumulation)

Humans, by their very nature, are hunters of their own fortune. In the course of six thousand years of agricultural revolution—from their beginnings in Mesopotamia and the birth of cities to our present day—people learned to work. On account of a historical caesura, modern labor capacities— working according to one's own incentive, without the interference of outside taskmasters—emerged only late in the game. These capacities are a precondition for both nineteenth-century factory work and the founding of Silicon Valley companies (that is, labor in the twenty-first-century sense). As a universal, material-altering activity, labor is one of the world's unsolved riddles.

Work is not a natural product. Even classical economists such as Adam Smith and Karl Marx emphasize this point. Instead, work emerged as a human counterreaction to a dreary process these economists call PRIMITIVE ACCUMULATION. This ORIGINAL EXPROPRIATION demolished forms of property and then, in the wake of this violence, annihilated labor capacities, as well. There is evidence that this primitive accumulation not only stands at the beginning of modern human development, but also permanently renews itself in every present moment. It is the impetus for both capitalism's extraordinary structural potential as well as of its crises and general lack of measure. But what is truly amazing is its ability to furnish the STRUCTURE OF ALL LABOR CAPACITIES with a fixed code.

Different Forms of Property
For classical economists, the original or "primitive" assets that humans once possessed were seen as elemental: their life spans and their individual characteristics.[1] These are two instances of *original property in the narrow sense of the word.* Another form of property

derived from this is autonomy, the special case whereby individuals live off either their own production or the cooperatives that they founded themselves. In prehistoric societies, such instances were rare, at best. It may have simply been an idea developed by descendents. Regardless, the image of such a GOLDEN AGE is as significant as it is attractive. As a claim staked out by humans vis-à-vis their present moment, the notion of a golden age seems irrepressible. In this respect, it makes no difference whether what is at stake here is myth or bygone reality. According to Immanuel Kant, humans will never allow themselves be dissuaded from the expectation that this *original property in the broader sense of the word* will return (at every stage of the emancipatory process).

The image of such original property — an image of the ground on which humans stand, their means of production, and their capacity for cooperation — lives on in the ideas of modern society's middle class and free entrepreneurship. It also lives on in Adam Smith's observation that a million egotists *involuntarily* further a nation's prosperity.

In contrast, Marx indicates that nothing belongs to capital except the consolidation of "the masses of hands and the instruments which are already there."[2] This is a highly abstract network. The ground, tools, people and machines, morality, and discipline, indeed, the society itself, merely serve as a pretense in order to achieve an essentially more abstract form of "property" based on the PROCESS OF CAPITAL. Using the very same epic narrative form that Homer used to recount the siege of Troy, Bertolt Brecht retold Marx and Engels's *Communist Manifesto* (1848) in HEXAMETER.[3] He underscored the fact that 70 percent of Marx's revolutionary text is an encomium for the machinery characteristic of capital that ended the torpor of the Middle Ages. Only the remaining 30 percent of Marx's text is dedicated to arguing that this machinery could not run economically and for this reason should be abolished by one of its very own products, namely, the proletariat.

It is essential for our analysis to keep in mind both capital's generative and combinatory potency, on the one hand, and its interconnected exploitative potency, on the other. These two sides of capital are inseparable from one another. Without demonstrating detailed proofs, classical economists have presumed that the periodic crises in the capitalist process resulting from a loss of equilibrium actually arise out of a separation of humans from their original mode of production. The trouble seems to lie in what Marx called the human's "essential powers," which tacitly remain anchored in early modes of production and only superficially comply with more recently established economic formations.[4]

Both the question regarding the demands that humans make on their societies and the question regarding labor and the maneuvering capacities of human societies are fundamental.[5] In this respect, in 1914, widespread ignorance derailed the twentieth century. The inability to keep the peace and the uncontrollability of chaotic productive forces resulted in what amounted to a Thirty-One Years' War (1914–1945). At the derailment's core was Auschwitz. This is, to be sure, not the only twentieth-century example of a "loss of history." What is frightening is the fact that there is no guarantee that the twenty-first century will not incur a similar derailment.

What is beyond question, however, is the fact that the capitalist process, which in difficult times even accommodated itself to fascism, knows of no anchors or ways out that would allow for a historical production process about which humans could be at all certain. Humans need to find ways out of the historical structures of labor capacities, which is to say that HUMANS MUST FIND ANCHORS WITHIN THEMSELVES. The evolutionary and historical reserves residing in humankind's essential powers have been insufficiently studied.

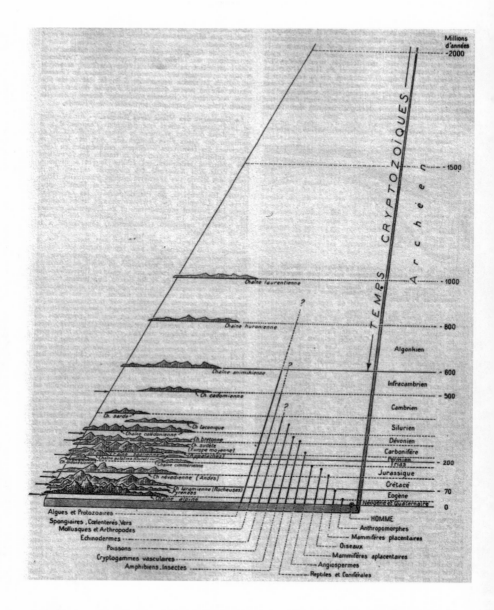

A *historical narrative* [*eine Geschichtserzählung*] taken from a French manual on the passing of time (Earth's first interval): "L'édification de l'écorce terrestre, la fuite des tempes." Lower right corner: Man ("Homme"). [*Encyclopédie française*, vol. 3: *Le ciel et la terre* (Paris: Société des gestion de l'Encyclopédie française, 1935–66)]

"The Secret of Primitive Accumulation"

There exists a capitalist economy fueled by automatism that both presupposes and contains within itself primitive accumulation.[6] In addition, there constantly exists a crude grasp [*Rohgriff*] of what, on account of separation energies, is supposed to accumulate anew within the context of capital. This crude grasp, however, is devoid of any economic measure or principle, because it lacks any and all necessary regulation.[7] Its particular grasp annihilates what is actually supposed to be accumulated. It also *explodes* the economy, insofar as its annihilatory impact never completely succeeds in the final analysis. In the context of capital, we find therefore two distinct economies: one that resembles a legislative machine and a second, cruder one that is unavoidably bound to the first. Unlike the former, the latter fails to adhere to the rules.

We focus our attention here on the following: (1) the depth and severity of primitive accumulation (not only with respect to England); (2) the permanence of this process; (3) the dialectic of the two different modes and their gravitational fields (the expanded process of accumulation and the continually renewed recourse to primitive accumulation); (4) the specific encipherment of individual labor and life capacities by violent separation processes that expand and renew themselves, processes that section off both the means of production and productive characteristics that always exhibit processes of appropriation in the event of any and all instances of expropriation (estrangement); (5) antiproduction; and (6) the antagonistic reality principle.[8]

If processes of separation are the organizing moment of history, and if reality has its motor and substance rooted in these processes, then every single real context separates itself into a representative and an antagonistic form. The point where classical theory turns serious is where it tacitly circulates around the following proposition: IF REASON IS REAL, THEN REALITY IS RATIONAL. But what, then, is real? We can also read this sentence in the optative mood: Because reason is the formal designation of association and the objective possibility of universal consensus expressed in terms of real cooperation—because, in short, it is a sum of radical needs—it **should be real**. Furthermore, it can be real only when it brings forth the requisite forces from real relations. But reason may not consider the prevailing synthesis of relations fused together from the separations of the real as something actually real. What presents itself as reality is fictitious. It is constructed out of the separation of essential portions of history. But history is hidden within it. We therefore need to disassemble it. History is absorbed neither by its economies nor by the reality principle.[9]

This brings us back once again to the concept of "primitive property." It embodies a human behavior (whether real or imagined) toward the natural conditions of production — the ground upon which humans toil and the community of which they are a member — as something belonging to them, something "which constitutes, as it were, only an extension of his body."[10]

In accordance with Adam Smith, Marx repeatedly designates this relation of original property as a "natural workshop" of human characteristics.[11] More precisely, this relation is the notion of something of one's own (such as identity or subjectivity), one's language, an association with a community, or one's labor and life capacities. Ultimately, it is the subjective precondition for successful separation. With primitive accumulation, a second, "historical" laboratory emerges, its "vessels and alchemical apparatus" producing the shape of labor's future discipline: its **capacity for precision maneuverability**. This is separation energy assuming the form of human character. Marx describes this process as it relates to particular relations in England. He indicates in dramatic terms how primitive accumulation transpired. Over a 150-year period, England's original peasantry was practically destroyed when it was divided into two classes: wage workers and outlaws. A series of twelve engravings glossed in German by Georg Christoph Lichtenberg, William Hogarth's *Industry and Idleness* (1747), characterizes this result aesthetically in the form of two careers. One person, the "Idle 'Prentice," does not fit in and is eventually executed as a criminal. His companion, the "Industrious 'Prentice," adapts, becomes a craftsman, marries his master's daughter, and dies peacefully. If we look for the attributes of primitive accumulation in countries other than England, we cannot expect to find such schematic repetitions.

On the European continent, the peasantry underwent processes of gradual depletion that were interrupted by revolts and peasants' wars. These peasants saw the products of their labor taken from them; they became serfs, but the means of production remained in their hands. Their depletion exhibited the characteristic of a loss of meaning. Well into the nineteenth century, male children low in a family's birth order (third sons on downward) were prompted to move away from their fathers' farms and settle first in urban centers and then later in the New World.

In cities, handwork was not directly expropriated, but rather its specific products, of which a handworker and his guild were especially proud, were overtaken by the dumping of industrialized, mass-produced articles onto the market. A maelstrom emerged in early capitalist urban areas from which the surrounding regions could not escape. The result was industrial production much like a hothouse, both forward driven in its temperament and bound to the underdevelopment characteristic of protocapitalist and nonindustrial regions. At present, the process is still unfinished in the European Union. Over centuries, such devolutionary processes have led to terrible congestive effects: (1) alongside the industriousness of handwork, so-called agents (remotely similar to today's investors) formed a network of opportunities in the countryside where many still longed for work (Gerhard Hauptmann documented these historical processes in his play *The Weavers*).[12] These early entrepreneurs brought the early industrial **production in cottage industries** under their command before they, too, were overtaken by processes emanating from the sphere of circulation, so that they, like the artisans, continually started something only to abandon it shortly thereafter; (2) industrial zones with a strong immigrant labor force abruptly emerged in the Ruhr Valley, Saxony, and elsewhere; (3) flight to the cities took hold of country life; and (4) the process culminated in an exodus overseas.

In the nineteenth century, the immigration of laborers to the United States from Ireland, Poland, Germany, Scotland, Galicia, Italy, and other parts of Europe brought individuals to that country who developed new communities and, to a certain degree, new labor capacities. THE LAND OF UNLIMITED OPPORTUNITIES is also the land that expanded the potential for devotion, skill, and self-consciousness. The regions where these people originated knew nothing of the American state of mind and its affirmation of the "pursuit of happiness." The immigrants brought their inner experiences of bitter want and oppression with them. This was the basis for the astonishingly rapid development on the North American continent. (This was the case with Australia, as well.) It transpired in a mere four hundred years and has seemed to know nothing of its own primitive accumulation. But it simply has been unrecognizable because it was imported from elsewhere and operates subterraneously.

Man's Essential Powers

The subject of our book, the political economy of labor capacities, is not a matter for specialists. This has long been the case because human self-consciousness in modern societies, in other words, the reflection of one person in another, manifests itself at its core in a person's labor. Conversely, nonlabor produces losses of both identity and social contact. This also applies to portions of society that appear to be postindustrial. In this respect, the concept of labor capacity also applies to communication societies, along with lingering forms of participation typical of previous modes of production, such as, for instance, systems of exchange in the **World Wide Web**, in which we no longer see the factory chimneys, the sweat of our forefathers, or the careers this structure brings forth. We will never understand the potentials and capacities of the human side of the equation, which now, as before, generates the essential achievements in the process of capital, if we avoid looking directly at what classical economists call "humankind's essential powers." These powers "work" in every society on this planet as subjective and unconscious partisans, as conscience, as amour propre, as skill, as intelligence, or as a derivative of these characteristics.

Hammer, Tongs, Lever: Violence as a Labor Characteristic

The basic form of most mechanical labor characteristics that humans perform and that, when transferred to tools and machines, stands between them and the objects of their labor relies on the use of direct violence. This violence is more or less ambivalent when two people embrace. It is nonviolent when it preserves the autonomy of each person embraced. It is violent (as is the case when pushing, prying, wedging, reaping, or hammering) when it engages in misappropriation, initiates a wrestling match, or traffics in political tactics that allow for the counterposition to perish in the political embrace.

88

Above all, the difference lies in the direct or indirect application of any such violence or whether and to what degree any such violence (that is, the constituent of entrapment or guile) incorporates the other's counterreaction. Starting with this distinction, we can then say there exists violence that enters into an object's characteristics and violence that does not. The Otto engine, for example, is based on the principle of permanent explosion. All individual components of this invention are destructive. As an aggregate, they propel motor vehicles forward. Incomplete production processes (for example, an unsound assembly of labor characteristics or their naive application in realms where they were never tested) regularly end up being damaged.

We consider all applications of the principle of "trial and error" (in the context of both phylogenetic and individual histories) as a *single* labor characteristic. A vast arsenal of tools stands at its disposal. They are all highly robust. However, their problem lies in their proportion, for the labor characteristics of violence provide no criteria for their precise control.

Cautiousness, Self-Exertion, Power Grips, and Precision Grips
Of all the characteristics responsible for **unifying** the muscles and nerves, the brain, as well as the skin **associatively** with one another—in other words, for the human body's feedback systems, its so-called rear view [*Rücksicht*]—the ability to distinguish between when to use power grips and precision grips is the most significant evolutionary achievement. It is the foundation of our ability to maneuver ourselves, an ability that is most easily disrupted by external forces. These forces are also capable of disturbing our self-regulation. Self-regulation is the outcome of a dialectic between power grips and precision grips.[13]

When measured against an external violence, internal cunning appears, by its very nature, to be something lacking in violence. When I act in a cunning manner, I refuse to attack things frontally and instead try to bring the inner power relations of objects into motion for myself. In actuality, cunning behavior is tied to the powers of the opponent, so that it leads to a reversal of their direction until a point in time when they revert into their opposite. These powers are steered toward a place they inherently do not wish to inhabit. This reversal is violent, as well.

Gripping

Most physical work begins by gripping tools, levers, or other devices and then putting them into motion. The way the human hand grips a tool and the movements to which it gives rise are mutually dependent. A purposeful grip facilitates a string of movements. A pointless grip only obstructs potential motion. Releasing or setting aside an object is similarly dependent upon previous kinds of movement. The same goes for when a movement involves zooming in on an object or, say, operating a control panel.

In such manual activities, the hand's task is not only to hold something. It must also function simultaneously as an organ of perception. The pressure required for operating knobs, buttons, and switches on a control panel must be dispensed in *just* the right a way, so that corresponding sensitivity in the hand is still possible. The dependence of a grip on factors such as necessary grip pressure, the possibility for perception, the kind of object to be grasped, and the movement to be performed produces such a variety of possible types of grips that a classification capable of doing justice to all the many variations is hardly possible. According to Sauerbruch, three basic types can be discerned (Figure A, taken from von Baeyer). The wide grip allows for the greatest holding power; however, it permits movement only in the wrist, elbow, and shoulder. All of the more refined grips result from the especially versatile and variable pinch grip, which also allows for the finest play of movement.

Figure A From left to right: wide grip, pinch grip, thumb grip. Taken from Hans von Baeyer, *Der lebendige Arm* (Jena: Fischer, 1930), plates 7 and 8.

Referring to an array of graspable objects, Giese arrives at twelve types of grips that he represents pictorially (Figure B). Of these, nos. 3, 6, and 11 are clearly wide grips. Nos. 9 and 12 are variations of the same grip involving specific features. Nos. 2, 4, 5, 7, and 10 are pinch grips, and no. 8 is a thumb grip. No. 1 could be considered an additional wide grip, but probably represents a special type that could be designated as a holding grip.

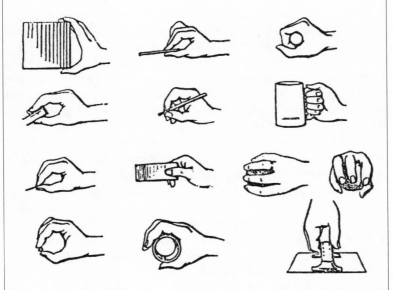

Figure B Types of grips. Taken from Fritz Giese, *Psychologie der Arbeitshand* (Berlin: Urban und Schwarzenberg, 1928), p. 32.

The Internalization of Labor Characteristics

All external forms of labor, as well as the tools they involve, replicate themselves on the subjective side of humans. In the interiority of humans, they almost always assume a new form, as either echoes or transformations. Similar to an internalized Tower of Babel, in terms of their subjective processes, hammers, tongs, levers, and nets are something other than what they were as external tools. This is not meant to suggest that a fisherman's net has anything to do with the InterNET. However, it is unequivocal that the invention of the WORLD WIDE WEB is based on labor characteristics with a rich archaeological record rooted in their networks of social relationships and presumably even in the brain's evolution. (It is important to note nonetheless that the Internet and the brain's synapses function in markedly different ways.) We thus refer to the subjective return of external tools in the form of maneuvering, motives, and feeling. Of particular interest to us is the composition of two capacities: differentiation and balance. The public image of classical industry, for example, may have vanished from reality, but it still perpetuates itself in highly animated fashion within humans. In fact, it is observable that characteristics reemerge in the subjective realm after the passing of three generations or their equivalent (a century) when a prevailing social practice has fallen into decline. In every one of us urban dwellers, we thus find "an inner farmer."

On the subjective side, violence, precision grips, self-exertion (especially when the latter characteristic develops from an individual virtue into a collective custom) — in other words, all the manifestations of material transformation — undergo permanent change. At the same time, the elements remain anchored and thus the same.

As is the case in the following pages, we can consider these HISTORICAL LABOR CAPACITIES using the categories of classical economics (Marx, Adam Smith, Ricardo, or Keynes). Or we can utilize the empirical instruments of various French philosophers (Foucault, Derrida, Deleuze, Guattari, or Michel Serres). We can also observe them using either the instruments of Critical Theory of the Frankfurt School or the occasionally opposing views of SYSTEMS THEORY (Parsons, Luhmann, or Dirk Baecker). Or we can assume the especially unprejudiced vantage point of someone such as Richard Sennett, who is indebted to no theoretical school. What consistently emerges, regardless of perspective, are the same themes and key points, namely, the OBSTINACY we argue for in these pages and the historical roots that the special form of humankind's essential powers have taken, as well as the general appearance they have assumed throughout modernity. We do not believe that any of these methods of investigation, even when applied with unparalleled thoroughness, alters the historical labor capacities or their relationality we seek to illuminate.[14] The principle of CROSS-MAPPING—the application of mutually contradictory maps, methods, or theories—is a robust and useful practice.

At stake here is not a linear narrative, but rather a CONSTELLATION. When comparing social relations to gravitational processes—the movement, attractions, and gravitational fields of planets and stars—Walter Benjamin pointed out a drawing by J. J. Grandville:[15]

If revolving bodies such as real moons and planets were actually connected together by an iron construction, as they are rendered in this drawing, each end of the imposing bridge linking the earth with other celestial bodies would be torn apart at any moment. It is plausible that such moving bodies can be described only multidimensionally, with special consideration of the long-distance effects they exert on each other (which are not directly visible), and hence as a *social context*. Often based upon labor performed long ago, twenty-first-century social formations and their underlying forces thus resemble the stars, which obey neither a central command nor an engineer, but rather follow solely the self-regulation of their inertial and gravitational masses. [J. J. Grandville, *Un autre monde : transformations, visions, incarnations... et autres choses* (Paris: H. Fournier..., 1844)]

Upright Gait, Balance, the Ability to Separate Oneself, Coming Home

According to some anthropological texts, the development of language, along with the decisive organ of auxotrophic mutants [*Mangelmutant*], namely, the brain, (not to mention the contrivance of the precision grip and the eye's characteristic ability to perceive horizons at roughly five feet and ten inches above ground) are what make us specifically human. In fact, it is a reasonable hypothesis that our upright gait freed our ancestors' hands for work and sign language, thus making the mouth available for language. It should suffice to note that an upright gait does not correspond to the skeleton's original structure. Humans were not designed for balance.

If not for the subtle countermovements made possible by their musculature, humans would fall on their noses when walking forward. A soldier at attention does not so much maintain his balance as rotate around an imaginary point of equilibrium. These countermovements go entirely unnoticed by his superiors.

According to the way fairy tales describe subjectivity, the ability to separate oneself from the home of one's parents and the possibility of later returning home form a constellation that determines whether people remain stuck in a state of regression—like dwarves, frog princes, or distorted images of themselves—or are rescued [*erlöst*].

Our focus, however, is not on fairy tales, but rather on individual human labor capacities. Engels once argued for the "*the transition from ape to man* ... through the medium of labor," in other words, the purposive function that forces transformations of nature.[16] Yet Darwin's analysis is so abbreviated that it prompts misunderstandings. It would be far more productive to start by observing how at every moment, learning and working beings derive their approach to time (on both phylogenetic and individual historical levels) with the help of their environs. Time frames such as "one's own time," "the time of childhood," "long pregnancies," "the time of day," "patience," "long-windedness," "temporal reserves," "repetition," "idleness," and "the mnemonic faculty" are all formal determinations initially linked to human reproduction. In evolutionary theory, an auxotroph is a living being that depends on specific associations with others because it is not metabolically autonomous.

It was presumably not labor that spurred hands, the brain, and "the optical capacity for maneuvering" to develop. Rather, those early living beings that eventually became human initially clawed their way into their parents' fur when faced with danger. Their parents would then carry them on their backs to safety. The mark of this tender grasp is present in the distinguishing prints they bear on our fingertips.

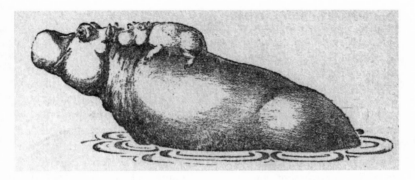

"Hippopotamus carrying its young." A drawing by R. B. Brook-Greaves, in P. Chalmers Mitchell, *The Childhood of Animals* (New York: Frederick A. Stokes Company Publishers, 1912), p. 172.[17]

Robo sapiens, *the Internet, A Relapse back into* *"Simple Lived Time"*

The need for accelerated communication among scientists working on the CERN particle accelerator led to the invention of the Internet. This network, once a research aid for a small circle of specialists, became a motor for a new kind of public sphere that evolved like an explosion. The architecture of this network can be compared to the construction methods used in factories that propelled the Industrial Revolution forward in the eighteenth and nineteenth centuries. Within their life spans, working humans do not so much exchange commodities in this new context as actual portions of their lives. THE CONCEPT OF LABOR HAS CHANGED.

But just as evolutionary processes are misperceived when they are understood as "working upward toward higher levels" (instead of being thought of as a product of nature's *tinkering*), so, too, is it misleading to think that human labor loses its elemental character on account of both its transformations and modernity's economic systems. *Following its ascents, labor always reverts back to simple labor.* We observe this in every crisis. The real element remains the investment of lived time by actual humans. The fact that this is not taken into account only at the moment of insolvency, but rather at every moment that precedes it, is a decisive contribution to PRECISION MANEUVERING and represents an antidote to the VIOLENCE OF PROCESSES.

Maieutics: The Midwife's Art

Sometimes a fetus lies twisted in the so-called breech presentation in the mother's womb. If the midwife does not turn it in time, the child will be strangled at birth. She does this "by applying violence [*Gewalt*]." Using a power grip is not an option she would ever consider. Instead, she uses a precision grip in the middle of the procedure, one that corresponds to the delicate limbs and agility of "the object." It is entirely impossible for the midwife to use her hands in a violent fashion and move the infant's arms so that they lie crossed atop its chest. In order to allow it to pass through the birth canal, her grip must provoke the child's own movement. Such violence as applied by the midwife is distinct from the violence of hammers, sickles, hoes, or saws.

Translated by Joel Golb and Richard Langston

"Reading. Storytelling [*Erzählen*]." [George Romney, *Serena Reading*, 1780–85 (Harris Museum and Art Gallery, Preston, Lancashire, UK / The Bridgeman Art Library)]

CHAPTER TWO

Self-Regulation as a
Natural Characteristic

The fact that humans voluntarily give away the entirety of their best possessions, their labor capacities and their matter-of-fact devotion when they cooperate with one another is a testament to their ability to oppose oppression and coercion. They otherwise retain a reserve.

Every act of fettering, plundering, and exploitation inflicted on a human characteristic entails, on the one hand, a loss. Every adversity elicits, on the other hand, resistance, invention, a possible way out.

This is the phenomenon of FREEDOM as discussed by champions of the Enlightenment on both sides of the Atlantic. They include Immanuel Kant, Adam Smith, Friedrich Schiller, Ralph Waldo Emerson, Thomas Jefferson, and Richard Rorty, among many others. Self-regulation is a natural characteristic (and the locus of obstinacy). Vis-à-vis obstinacy, coercion is only as powerful as its ability to contain such supplemental labor [Zuarbeit]. As a species, we humans have retained, against all odds, our place in the evolutionary process because we internalized this principle of self-regulation.

The Social Senses

We refer to humans in terms of a second nature, the nature of society. At the same time, we are interested in the nature of cells, the skin, bodies, the brain, the five senses, and the social organs constructed on top of them: love, knowledge, mourning, memory, the sense of family, the hunger for meaning, the eyes of society, the forms of collective attention. Some of these things really do exist. Others exist merely as a capacity never exercised, as protest or as utopia.

Marx anticipates the following: "the senses and enjoyment of other men have become my *own* appropriation. Besides these direct organs, therefore *social* organs develop in the form of society; thus, for instance, activity in direct association with others, etc., has become an organ for *expressing* my own *life*, and a mode of appropriating *human* life," And "for this reason the senses of the social man *differ* from those of the non-social man."[1]

"For not only the five senses but also the so-called mental senses, the practical senses (will, love, etc.), in a word, the **human** sense, the human nature of the senses, comes to be by virtue of *its* object, by virtue of **humanized** nature. The *forming* of the five senses is a labour of the entire history of the world down to the present."[2] A metaphor Marx uses elsewhere is related to this: "And windows are to a house what the five senses are to the head."[3]

When referring to natural characteristics, what is meant — especially in the case of those essential characteristics possessed by individuals — are both those from **first nature** as well as their productive extensions engendered under the conditions of **second nature**. This is done in such a way that both natures always exert equal influence on both the foundation [*Basis*] and the superstructure [*Aufbau*], both on human beings' originary nature and their social organs.

It is obvious that the origins of the human's social organs (loving, knowing, and so on) are relatively recent. In contrast, their originary organs reach back into the cells; they are products of the entire history of both the earth and the species. When measured against the high degree of suggestibility common among the social organs and their characteristics, they show very little variation, even under the drastic circumstances of advanced societies. It thus remains to be seen whether the latest advances in the epoch of capitalism have altered the brain and the cells, as is the case, for example, with the skin, the stomach, and the eyes, the last of which now follow a "sense of having."[4] We need only compare the extraordinary imprint of social circumstances on the social organs with at least the relative resistance exerted by a body's material construction (for example, the brain and cells) **against** variation. **What** constitutes cells, how their environment poisons them, **what** the brain works out—these questions are subject to the influences of social nature. **How** they really function according to their own specific nature and the manner of their material construction, the answers to these questions have scarcely changed for millennia.

These oldest of senses within human nature nevertheless project themselves into a society's most advanced crises; their natural characteristics take part in these crises and impede their advance. It is precisely their invariability—the fact that they form both the foundation and the pyramid at once—that provides for the development of their material force at the tip of the pyramid. If they were more variable, they could make compromises. This innate hardness characteristic of contradictoriness repeats itself in the relation between the sensuous social organs and the sensuous originary organs. Neither knowledge nor want can oppose the brain's nature absolutely.[5]

"And windows are to a house what the five senses are to the head." Here: eyes without eyelids. [Alexander Kluge Archive]

"This is an important moment. For this reason the eyes are shut." [Alexander Kluge Archive]

The extreme, the realization of which is made at the expense of willpower, is when cells work under the illustrated conditions. They work here according to the same principle present under all other conditions until the point in time shortly before their destruction. [Alexander Kluge Archive]

A laboring assemblage is obliged to take into account the elemental nature from which it is derived, through which it can finally express itself, and that is its proviso. Let us scrutinize the following sentence: **"A revolutionary situation emerges when those below are no longer willing and those above no longer can."**[6] Consider, for example, the hierarchy of mental constructions (within a cultural-social organ). When conflicts can no longer be solved through redistribution, they enter into the bones or cells. The dissociation is then decided in favor of the cells, meaning psychosomatic illnesses, circulatory disorders, or even collapse occurs. In other words, the cells unfurl their original independent activity, but not with respect to the socially assembled human being. **There are no victories possible here that start from high above and permeate downward.**

An Interpretation of the Sentence: "When those below are no longer willing, and those above no longer can."
This formula defines the revolutionary situation. **Revolution takes place when those below are no longer willing and those above no longer can. Furthermore, this is not measured according to intentions or commands, but rather in the self-regulation of forces. This does not solely involve the forces of production, whose regulations grow and at a certain point burst the shackles of the relations of production. The various self-regulating levels must be examined simultaneously.**

It should be evident by now that if cells and cellular clusters—the corporeal organs from below—are no longer willing and, by contrast, both the individual's higher assembled capacities and the objective coercive relations from above can no longer assert themselves, what transpires does not correspond to the image of revolution, but rather to decomposition.

Concerning another position from "below," that of the libidinous structure, which is much more aggregated than cells, Freud says: "The strangest characteristic of unconscious (repressed) processes, to which no investigator can become accustomed without the exercise of great self-discipline, is due to their entire disregard of reality-testing; they equate reality of thought with external actuality, and wishes with their fulfillment—with the event—just as happens automatically under the dominance of the ancient pleasure principle."[7]

In this case, self-regulation is principled indifference, a conservatism of elemental forces that are no longer willing from below and that put the ego to flight when the ego no longer lords over them. Once again, the result does not so much evoke the image of revolution as appear like a defensive barrier, an exclusion carried out by the ego in flight. In the activities of the ego collective, this exclusion assumes a different guise, namely, that of a powerful authority [Gewalt] hidden within culture, morality, and the reality principle. In this instance, it resembles neither decomposition nor the image of political revolution, but rather the cement holding a social system together.

Self-regulation's next higher stage of composition produces motives. In bourgeois revolutions, they initially explode the political relations of production by first deposing the king's and the nobility's sense of self and then their actual persons, as well. **This is political revolution.** It behaves toward its motivational foundation like something from "above." As soon as the motives no longer are willing and those above (that is, the political and economic relations) no longer can, they burst open the chains of revolution, and a return to that state transpires where only economic relations change. In such an instance, a political revolution reverts to an economic one. On account of the self-regulating structures from *below*, the revolutionary process appears different at every level. The self-realization of human production can take place as a revolutionary process only when **everything** below is no longer willing and the

various positions above no longer can. Without taking this into account, the revolutionary process has no continuity and is thus not emancipatory.

The Cantankerous Brain
The most complicated organ in human nature is the brain. It is striking that human brains do not at all operate according to the forms of so-called rationality. According to either their nature or their constitution, they work neither logically nor teleologically (they are not goal-oriented). They are neither theological (myth-forming), nor do they really generate the huge pauses that seem to emanate from them when they function in a disciplined fashion or follow operating instructions. Rather, human brains achieve their highest operational level more often than not precisely when they are "doing nothing," according to the criteria of entrepreneurial enterprise. Conversely, they become paralyzed when long-term coercion imposes inactivity on them. When someone "thinks nothing at all," encephalograms show "white noise," extreme activity. According to its developmental history, the brain is obviously thoroughly prepared for complexity, movement, and a natural relation to those human and objective worlds composed of a wealth of connections and diversity. It can adequately handle the most confusing overabundance of impressions, because its **basic form** is grounded in a specific type of self-regulation, one that is distinct, we should add, from all other types of self-regulation found both in nature and in other human organs.

Ice Age
There is no self-regulation in and for itself. We could say, for example, that the fundamental difference between the coldness of an ice age (it regulates itself *for* itself according to nonhuman, physical laws), the self-regulation involved in the homeostasis of the human body and the specific self-regulation of the brain, which perceives both the outside world and feels the human insides, constitutes **unrest.** On account of this unrest, humans began to work (inter alia). The difference between the nonhuman outside (nature) and the inside of humans (nature) is the brain's world of codes, a mediator that organizes a hermetically self-contained and engaged mode of regulation while at the same time functioning as an imaging organ [*Abbildungsorgan*]. Consequently, the brain is by no means just

a window. Reality does not penetrate the brain and then migrate downward into any of the deeper organs. **What** the brain **does** and **how it does its work** are fundamentally different. With respect to "how" it works, the brain is autonomous **for itself**; its essence consists of staying both alive and active according to its specific laws, which initially are neither concerned nor congruent with either the outside world or anything else in the human being. Only when this autonomous activity is carried out by billions of synapses does it become clear that it was capable of fulfilling its functions at the same time. From the start, the brain's own formal determination and its contents are nonidentical. It behaves like a monad **and** a window.[8]

Cells

Among the human's many natural characteristics, the simplest element is the cell. However, the cell is not something simple. Both the autonomous way a single cell works and the basic autonomous behavior of all cells have been described thus: **"As much inside as possible, as little outside as necessary."** (There is, in fact, no organ that establishes a direct and perceptible contact between the brain and the cells, via the nerves, for example; there exists no notable contact to individual cells, only to cellular clusters.) Cells repeatedly seal off their autonomous activity as individual entities from the whole human being and the outside world. At the same time, they preserve within their internal programming the complete memory of the entire prehistory of the species, as well as every one of its characteristics. In this respect, it is not merely the cellular genome, but the entirety of all cells that inwardly possess this experiential potential.

Disobedience

Were capital or a person in command to try to order a cell around, it would not obey. The **individual,** a **single** cell's master, certainly cannot put a cell into motion. I can command my muscles or even an entire person to march, but I cannot break cells and cellular clusters away from their own regulation and then expect them to march. Self-regulation is therefore something specific that acquires character in every organic whole, that is, character that maintains hermetic contact—which is to say that it is distinctly untranslatable and accessible only through mediation and the exchange of codes—with every other organic whole of a higher nature. Observe, for example, the temporal difference at work in phylogenesis when we compare the individual cells of the human body (essentially no different in their basic working cycle from those of animals or the single-celled creatures that once populated prehistoric oceans) with the working cycle of brain cells, the approaches to self-determination among children, or examples of self-regulation that play a role in social labor.

Fraternité

All forms of self-regulation have a spatial, rhythmic (or temporal), and specifically encoded world of their own. They would never be anything universal [*Allgemeines*], like the bourgeois concept of freedom, something to be practiced only in various constitutions and by various individuals. In the first article of the French Declaration of the Rights of Man and of the Citizen from 1789, the concept of equality immediately follows that of freedom and thus criticizes in a sense a program of freedom merely "from something." But a specific process of self-regulation was designated only in the associational interests captured by the third word of the Revolution's short-lived tripartite slogan, "fraternity." For a circle of revolutionaries (that is, for the revolution's associated producers), this concept contained, at the very least, a call for the self-regulation of their conflicts.[9]

Self-Regulation as Order

"There is no self-regulation in and for itself." As living labor, self-regulation develops from friction with an object. The concept of order to emerge from this differs from a concept generated by a violent command (for example, a **supply network**) insofar as its self-regulating order is more multifarious. In a school that allows for self-regulated learning, two children are engrossed in deciphering letters. Three children are climbing a pole. One group of children is making a ruckus, while another has placed tables together to form a house and squats beneath it. Other children focus intently on solving a puzzle, and yet others are making artistic cardboard figures. The teacher moves between the different groups. No one group disturbs any other, although there is repeated traffic and contact between them. The highly animated children, as well as those working quietly by themselves, remain fixed on their respective activities. Evidently, invisible forms of order are present in the room, forms of

106

order that preclude disturbances. This order could not be produced by, say, a traffic policeman, because he would know nothing of the rules of right-of-way and waiting that are in play.

The Specific Capacity for Disruption

A self-regulating order is just as capable of being disrupted as one controlled by supply networks. In this snapshot of an elementary-school pilot project, it is not self-regulation in itself, but the **form** in which it has been authorized that brings about order. The children previously experienced that form as "private workers of their own primitive property"; they gain recognition and mutually transfer this recognition to various activities reciprocally. At any given moment following a sudden shift in interest, the children intently concentrating on their labor can start to hop around, and those who had been climbing the jungle gym can move to more focused work that suits their shifting interests. The form of their order rests on both their own knowledge and their concomitant recognition of what the others are doing. For all intents and purposes, it is a stroke of good fortune. Within the experience of children, the subsumption of such flukes creates community.

If a stranger unfamiliar with the order of play intrudes and wishes to disrupt the ongoing activities, the self-confident children — depending on how experienced they are in matters of their self-regulating order — will ignore him for a while. However, if the disruption persists, it will have an impact that potentially destroys the self-regulating order altogether. But whereas a new order resulting from a command collapses into near chaos akin to a traffic jam, the order of self-regulation, when mastered by all its participants, possesses a certain degree of idleness. It is not difficult for the children to devise a new form of order after the old one was disrupted. For instance, they show solidarity with one another against the disruptive party.

In a shared apartment committed to self-regulation, two members are working on a manuscript. In the adjacent kitchen, a couple is quarreling. Probably agitated because of the fight, their children stage a disturbance by running wildly between the kitchen and the study. Self-regulating forces are at work here to a degree, as well. The fight regulates itself over the course of the afternoon and evening **in its own way**; the children later abreact their anxiety caused by the incomprehensible quarreling and the impenetrable work on the manuscript. With every disturbance, pertinent ideas in the minds of the two authors are reduced in a self-regulating manner. In this example, only the possibility of mutual recognition has been removed. Without it, **self-regulation** is essentially **disruption**.

Self-Regulation against Consignment to the Junk Heap

The autonomously protected reserves of labor power [*Arbeitskraft*] evince an entirely different form of self-regulation. Without the consciousness ever in the know, living bodies hold some of their capacities in reserve.

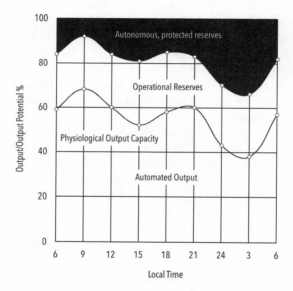

Distributed over twenty-four hours, the curves show so-called productive capacities. Humans take care of automatic activities (e.g. resting, expressions of life, the handling the daily life tasks) without ever having to exert special amounts of will. This is especially the case when it is not the middle of the night. Physiological motivation already demands effort, and with the exertion of forces, energy reserves can be updated. But beyond this, humans have additional reserves that they cannot retrieve by simple exertion of the will. They would first need to out-smart their bodies. Only a **condition** involving the entire person allows for a breach of the self-regulation protecting this reserve; no **intention** can accomplish this. Forces mustered by the human will could never generate the necessary excess.[10] [Alexander Kluge Archive]

Fingertip Feeling, Selectivity

The skin's sensory function reacts to six different sensations: pressure, touch, warmth, coldness, vibration, and pain.[11] If I exert pressure on the back of my hand using a caliper composed of two sliding ivory tips used for measuring pressure points, **a single** punctiform stimulus results from the pressure. This is different for my fingertips: there, I would feel two such stimuli. The pressure points in the fingertips' tactile corpuscles are far more numerous.

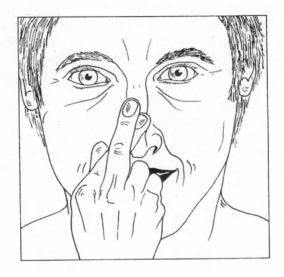

When you cross your index and middle fingers and pass their interstice over the tip of your nose, your nose appears doubled: this is the so-called Aristotelian illusion. Through the fingers' dislocation, the natural cooperation between the processing brain and the tactile feeling at your fingertips is outsmarted. Correcting this sensory illusion cannot transpire through self-regulation, but via the labor of experience. [Alexander Kluge Archive]

The particularly fine sensory selectivity of the fingertips is presumably an evolutionary trait. Conscious processing in the central nervous system takes place through a separate self-regulation process. The two forms of regulation are cooperatively flexible; if cooperation is disrupted, each form remains rigidly fixed to the standpoint of its own regulation.[12]

What the eyes perceive is not subject to commands or orders. The system involved in producing retinal images corresponds to a radically different mode of regulation. The retina consists of rod cells that developed from flagellate cells; specialization stunted them in such a way that only information transmitted transversally leads to the execution of stimulatory potential. The periphery of the retinal image sends particularly weak impulses. Precisely because the stimulatory lines at the edges of the retinal image make less sensory noise, the brain's nerve bundles responsible for optical perception are capable of interpreting the border zones of an image. In other words, they are able to lay impressions **side by side** and account for meanings. The result is a form of perception that, when juxtaposed to the retinal image, is far more certain *at the edges*. The contours of the comprehensive image are subsequently worked out by the brain more sharply than if they were to have actually reached the eye's retina.

In this case, several different kinds of autonomous activities cooperate within a single sensuous relationality. For their part, the interfaces are subject to their own self-regulatory laws. (For example, a zone containing particularly weak impulses emerges at the interface between stronger and weaker bundles of energy; its weakness constitutes the strength of its interpretations).

These forms of self-regulation are markedly different from those in nature, from the autonomous will of tools or furniture, and from the autonomous reserves. They are, after all, components of conscious sensory activity. Self-regulation is grounded in **cooperation** between autonomous activities working according to their own very different laws of motion.[13]

Self-Regulation of Syntheses

A person's two eyes see something different from what is seen by the collectively unified eyes of a group of people. The collective production of goods develops images of exchange value that cannot be tested by two pairs of eyes. Political images and images of the world unfold their own laws of motion that cannot be refuted by individuals opposing them using their own visual scrutiny. When the sense of having takes hold of the eyes, they actually see value, instead of concrete objects.

Two modes of perception can be distinguished at this point. The one is horizontal and the other vertical. They never appear in pure form, but rather are always mixed. This corresponds to the observation that workers involved in dangerous production processes successively orient themselves according to each and every one of its steps, one after the other. They do not initially form a concept. They do not consider the big picture or elaborate an interpretation. Rather, they track each individual dangerous moment, and only when they do so do they manage to avoid damaging, say, their fingers. What is at stake here is **experience**. In a public political discussion, the procedure is different. First, concrete impressions are registered and placed side by side, as is the case with the horizontal form of perception. Then and there, an impression considered significant is extricated from the horizontal relationality and placed atop an interpretive pyramid. A concept or general impression is developed on whose abstract level a vertical search is then undertaken in order to classify other meanings and concepts. At stake is the formation of an opinion. A linkage formed this way can be reduced to the dimension of the eyes only through an overpowering counterconcretion. This is how those who work *sit* on their eyes.

Something constructed lives off of its piece of nature. From this, it draws forth its own nature, a collective self-regulation. And this autonomous life made of syntheses detaches itself from the autonomous activities of underlying concretions. For the most part, it forms less relationality than concretion and can be overthrown on this basis. However, there are syntheses (for example, those composed of wishes) that form such a rich mass of self-regulation vis-à-vis perceptible reality that they are immune to the merely real perceptions of the senses.

Self-Regulation as History
Shortly after the destruction of a city, beaten tracks extend out over the ruins. In a certain way, they restore the old relations of pathways that existed before the destruction, while at the same time, they mark out manifestly new shortcuts and detours. If one were at work like an archaeologist, these tracks could be interpreted as a picture of the city's prehistory.

In the interior of humans, the pathways along which inner and outer impressions are processed practically never lead directly from point *A* to point *B*. Rather, they follow variable tracks of associational streams, much like the emergence of trodden paths.

111

Milkman, "The Emergence of Beaten Paths." [Fred Morley / Getty Images]

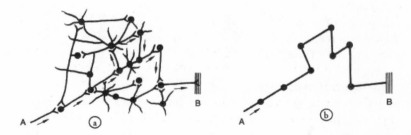

Figure ⓐ shows a piece of the nervous system's network. A gap is located before each of the receptor's points; each synapse represents an effector. The entire system resembles a bad stretch of road pitted with potholes, so that all routes—both the main roads and the detours—offer travelers the same chance of reaching their goal. An association can thus assume the route represented by figure ⓑ, but can also take countless other routes. This constitutes the rich range of neural connections. The history of all previous neural facilitations informs the variants of each and every present facilitation. They are never identical with their prehistory and can never remove themselves from it absolutely. [Alexander Kluge Archive]

The particular laws governing such neural pathways and the emergence of beaten tracks free of police regulation in heavily bombed cities are related to one another according to their obstinacy. They are forms of self-regulation of the relations between actuality and history.

The Double Meaning of Self-Regulation: (1) A General Category of Relationality; (2) A Category of Living Relationality

Death is in vain. In other words, it is self-regulating. Self-regulation has various meanings. First and foremost, it is a **category of relationality** by virtue of the fact that it characterizes every individual activity as emanating from relationality. In the more narrow sense, it is the category of the **relationality of living labor** by virtue of the fact that it draws attention to the subjective obstinacy contained within it.

Finally, as a **category of social relationality**, self-regulation focuses on the autonomous forces that continually constitute the gravitation between dead and living labor when the relationality of living labor comes into its own and tips the balance. In this particular constellation, the primary universality of natural materials and the subjective vitality of humankind's natural substance are mixed; an extra dose of subjectivity joins the subjective and subjective-objective components that work in a self-regulative manner. Our attention focuses on this third and still-rare case of self-regulation: it manages to incorporate the overabundance of primary regulations, which elude human will in itself and remain alien to it, into the relationality of living labor without resorting to any exclusionary mechanisms. When this succeeds to a sufficient degree, it gives rise to an autonomous force field that occurs *naturally* neither in nature nor in history as an enduring condition. This is the meaning behind the phrase the "naturalism of man and the ... humanism of nature."[14]

Birth

We encounter self-regulation on yet another new level with the birth of a human. What occurs during birth and in the first weeks thereafter — when the first impressions are formed between the infant and the world — can be followed from very different perspectives. For example, it can be viewed from standpoint of the reduction, which sets in from the start, of what the child expresses as its body and its general movement (the two are identically encoded, something not necessarily understandable to adults). All told, the "program" announcing itself in infancy seems to be richer than what emerges later with the onset of growing and learning. Compared with other creatures, humans are born especially naked and helpless, but they have yet to encounter the reality principle. It would be incorrect, however, to describe human birth as the birth of a "creaturely" human; there is no place for such creatures in society, especially because the infant enters immediately into the adult environment of divided spaces, social organizations, and the organized units of time.

The Second, Third, Forth, Etc. Social Birth

Biological birth can thus be understood only in connection with a sort of second social birth in which the young child encodes its inherent goals and processes its earliest experiences (that is, the original language of its self-regulation), only then to abandon this in order to learn the code of its social environment. This second birth encompasses, at the very least, the time of basic disruption (that is, the time until it acquires language and a minimum of body control) and, at most, the formation of the mental authorities, a process Freud argues is completed at age six. In this period, the child can develop into a social human being who is either "fully born" or "not yet fully born."[15]

In all processes of first and second births, as well as in all subsequent developments constructed atop them, concrete reality (third, fourth, fifth births, the so-called upbringing of a child), the natural law of available energy (that of the libidinal economy) and its human or social transformations are always determined by underlying forms of self-regulation. In actuality, child-rearing methods composed of harsh, aggressive interventions—the most successful result of self-mastery—cannot be understood without considering how it came to be that the self-regulating energy of the drives could be constructed and organized thus with the involvement of their will. Mechanical in nature, the external pressure typical of child rearing—as it appears, for instance, in the apparatuses of Dr. Moritz Schreber or in different sorts of mechanical exercises—are effective only through a gain in self-regulation in spite of the counterproductive methods used for intervening.

Kant emphasizes that character does not change piecemeal, neither through child rearing nor through empirical declarations of will:

> The human being who is conscious of having character in his way of thinking does not have it by nature; he must always have *acquired* it. One may also assume that the grounding of character is like a kind of rebirth, a certain solemnity of making a vow to oneself; which makes the resolution and the moment when this transformation took place unforgettable to him, like the beginning of a new epoch. — Education, examples, and teaching generally cannot bring about this firmness and persistence in principles **gradually**, but only, as it were, by an explosion which happens one time as a result of weariness at the unstable condition of instinct. Perhaps there are only a few who have attempted this revolution before the age of thirty, and fewer still who have firmly established it before they are forty. — Wanting to become a better human being in a fragmentary way is a futile endeavor, since one impression dies out while one works on another; the grounding of character, however, is absolute unity of the inner principle **of** conduct as such.
> — Immanuel Kant, *Anthropology from a Pragmatic Point of View*, trans. and ed. Robert B. Louden (Cambridge: Cambridge University Press, 2006), p. 194.)[16]

Kant does not use the terms "explosion" and "revolution" to describe social relations anywhere else. The observation that what is at work in character formation is a restoration of unity according to the measure of one's own fundamental powers is found today in Piaget's writings, as well (for instance in his *Psychology of Intelligence* [London: Routledge and Paul, 1950]). For an overview, see Mary Anne Spencer Pulasky, *Understanding Piaget: An Introduction to Children's Cognitive Development* (New York: Harper and Row, 1971). Piaget describes learning, in particular, in the form of a **crystalline lattice**. In math instruction, for example, students learn next to nothing from mere exercises or the quantity of regular instruction. Then, all of the sudden, whole units of math are learned and retained as a whole when contact and autonomous organization rooted in the realm of self-regulatory forces transpire. A step-by-step learning process facilitated by instruction and lesson plans divided into in small segments does not really take place.

115

The Politics of the Body

Using examples from the earliest stages of physical education, Michel Foucault describes the institutionalization of rule in terms of a microphysics of the body.[17] He speaks of the politics of the body, as well as its political economy. The child's body desires general activity involving all of its skin, muscles, limbs, cerebral impulses, and everything its eyes and hands can grasp. But even well-meaning adults will not respond to this general interest. *For the child's benefit*, adults are interested that it learns to sit, stand, and walk. Sometimes children do not bathe completely, but rather wash only where they see pollution. A selection process develops. At the same time, this process entails a constriction and manages to omit certain movements and areas of skin from the child's attention. At this point, we cannot yet speak of "punishments," relations of violence, or barriers that trigger, for example, the incest taboo or the fact that children are not only meant eventually to walk upright, but also to become willing working adults. Each of these steps involved in the confrontation between the self-will of the child and the barriers through which it learns and suffers—through which it finds its own form, only then to curtail it—is a struggle between self-regulation and its opposing concretion. (With respect to self-regulation, even teachers shaped by reality behave like objects). In this struggle, child rearing wins only insofar as it incorporates autonomous energy into its distinctive forms according to its own nature. It is a crude illusion to say that child rearing makes something. Children achieve this using their own powers.[18]

The collective labor process involved in giving birth, in the development of new societies, and in revolutions is determined by specific elements that rest on self-determination, elements that develop into a productive force that runs into barriers and searches for new forms of determination through which it can objectify itself. The entire way of thinking about the capitalism that entered the pores of feudal rule was thus incomprehensible to feudal lords. The historical chain of mistaken actions and judgments that mounted on the side of France's royal government and the nobility of the French Revolution was not incompetence or stupidity. At the same time, the same circles produced or at least tolerated elements of the Enlightenment. The code at work in self-regulation—what the Third Estate desired—was unclear to them. What they saw as a question of power or tax law was in fact the development of a form of production. Similarly, the Girondists could not later factor the force of the *sans-culottes* in the Quartier St. Antoine into their normally highly flexible calculations. (They were, after all, merchants and accountants). This led to their downfall.

Many have focused on the power of the new ideas that pushed the French Revolution forward. It is said that Paris constituted the center of a gravitational field that led to the revolution. The court considered whether separating the capital from the rest of France would extirpate both this center and thus the revolution, as well. We encounter once again the fallacy concerning what labor actually accomplishes according to its own laws, from the text of the Terror on up to its faulty revolutionary design. If the particular nature of revolutionary energies can no longer express itself as labor, Thermidor will follow.

Thermidor

In his *Social Origins of Dictatorship and Democracy* (Boston: Beacon Press, 1966), Barrington Moore Jr. offers new insights that clarify the actual dynamic at work both in the period of the French Revolution and in its pre-history. Abbé Sièyes, one of the Revolution's chief theorists, once asserted: "What was the Third Estate? Nothing. What will it be? Everything." This was, in fact, not the case at the time around 1789. The Third Estate, in other words, evolving bourgeois society, did not form the main mass of people in France. This role was actually filled by both peasants and the petty nobility, whereby the latter group engaged itself in a manner resembling bourgeois economic activity, in the wine trade, maintained small country estates, performed military service, and so forth. Nevertheless, it was indeed bourgeois forces—those centered in the trading cities—that, on account of the obstinacy typical of their form of production, recognized the most characteristic phenomenon in France, the exhibitionism of central royal authority, as something worth acquiring for themselves.

At an early point in his work, Marx insisted that the object of capitalist predation was not only exploiting labor power and appropriating the resources of the soil and objects, but also theft from the state. Using the example of peasants from the Mosel region, he shows that capitalist landholders not only appropriated the peasants' longstanding rights, for instance, the right to gather wood, but also the (unpaid) labor power of foresters and policemen protecting this robbery. Whoever steals a piece of the state gets unpaid labor.

For this reason, the seizure of power in 1789 by the elite of France's Third Estate can be described not only in the stirring form of the breakthrough of new ideas and the debate over the constitution, but also as the brazen robbery of all of France by a single class of property owners. They now had the state, which had so strikingly offered itself in Versailles as an object for acquisition through centralization and self-display. They had what they wanted, and could now settle down with the same obstinacy with which they had previously seized it. It was this self-interested withdrawal, and not the fierce Convention debates, that sealed the Girondists' defeat. The *sans-culottes*, which is to say those dwelling in Paris's suburbs (with the mass of people consisting mainly of handworkers and store owners), had an entirely different way of regulating their interests. Represented in the daily politics of the Montagnards (in the clubs and Convention), they were incapable of expressing themselves through representatives. Their language was deter-mined by a contradiction: on the one hand, they had to feign being all of France, a state; on the other hand, they had to represent concrete competi-tion and production interests characterized by the immediate senses and handwork. Representatives would have done their best to level the contradic-tion, which was unrealistic, or to oscillate between its extremes, which was equally unrealistic. Consequently, as soon as the principle of representation of a bourgeois public sphere was seen through by the Convention and Com-mittee of Public Safety—the Jacobin constitution of 1793 had just been readied for a vote—they lost the possibility of continuing to express the self-regulation of their revolutionary interests in their own particular form. Whereas the *sans-coulottes* still saw in themselves their opposite—some-thing less than whole men—their interests withdrew from the Revolution; the result was Thermidor.

Translated by Joel Golb and Richard Langston

Gérard David, deputy from Rennes, Jacobin, painter, 1793. A family portrait. Reflecting revolutionary predilections of the day, Gérard wears peasant clothing. The children's generation does not follow his lead. They adorn themselves fashionably. [Bulloz, Musée de Tesse, La Mans, France © RMN-Grand Palais / Art Resource, NY]

CHAPTER THREE

Elements of a Political Economy

of Labor Power

The subtitle of Karl Marx's central work, Capital, *reads:* CRITIQUE OF
POLITICAL ECONOMY. *Based on the observations of the Anglo-Saxon
economists Adam Smith and David Ricardo, this work poses the following
of many possible questions: If capital could speak, how would it explain
itself? Can capital say "I"?*

*The political economy of capital stands in opposition to humans who
live in societies structured by capital, but who — along with large portions
of their subjectivities, their ancestors, and elements of their labor capacities and essential powers — at the same time also belong to social relations
not structured by capital. For a more complete economy, we must pose the
question: "Who is the subject of history?"*

*Six thousand years of Chinese social history, for example, could serve
as an object for such an analysis, or the three thousand years of European
history and economic praxis that were later forced in the hothouse of the
Industrial Revolution and accompanied by the rise of very young nations
such as the United States, Australia, and Canada. In what follows, elements of a political economy of labor power are sketched out. At stake are
the questions: What is real? Are humans spectators of their own lives, their
realities, and the histories they produce? Could they even perhaps be the
producers of their own lives?*

The Two Economies
We begin with a simple observation: We clearly possess an elaborate
theory of the political economy of capital: Marx's *Capital*. The polar
opposite of this would be a **political economy of labor power,** for
which no theoretical groundwork has ever been laid. Marx never
recorded any such political economy of labor power, even though his
thought system immanently presupposes it as the opposite of capital.

We assume that **this** is the reason why he never wrote on **politics**. Politics necessarily presupposes a theory of the proletarian public sphere, and this in turn requires a theory of the developmental history of each and every labor capacity.

What Does the Political Economy of Labor Power Mean?

The expression **economy** transfers the laws of physics in second nature onto production and exchange in society. The attribute **political** designates a contradiction: a conscious and collaborative form of interaction capable of forming associations with the quasi-physical intercourse of an economy. According to Marx, the word *critique* in the "critique of political economy" refers to previously developed theories of political economy (for example, Adam Smith, Ricardo). Critique is not a way to deal with things themselves. Above all, critique defends the authenticity of facts. Critique is directed against the metaphysics of the political economy. In contrast, political-economic praxis can be addressed critically only by using *counterproduction*.

Marx uses different expressions in this context. He speaks of the **political economy of the working class** when it pertains to the confrontation with a single capitalist class (for example, the middle class as the most important producing class of capitalists, or it can refer to the fact that capitalist rule enters into certain alliances with feudal upper classes, state authorities, the army, the church, the Tory upper class and so on, and then stands as an agglomerate in opposition to the political economy of the working class).[1] In contrast, when referring to the confined spaces of factories where labor power is transformed into labor, Marx speaks of the political economy of labor in exactly the same way that the affected class would express itself in a concrete battle. The counterpart to this designation is **property**, that is, concretized capital.[2] When referring to the potential, the constitutional history, and the emancipatory possibility of historical labor, Marx speaks conversely of *"real essential powers of man and nature"* or *"real essential powers and faculties [Vermögen]."*[3] He thus avoids using a metaphoric concept [*Oberbegriff*].

Incidentally, it is to be expected that what constitutes the political economy of labor power does not itself tolerate a metaphoric concept in the classical sense. What we are investigating becomes incomprehensible when we cannot name it. The use value of the category "political economy of labor power" lies exclusively in the power of differentiation contained within this designation vis-à-vis all the other reflections of human labor, as well as in its developmental history. This is therefore not about a metaphoric concept that eventually constitutes itself as a **concept** on account of the ever-more concrete variations produced by close examination. Rather, it pertains to a moving form of critique that contrasts the history of the individual characteristics of labor power with the heteropolar history of associational needs. That is to say: there can be no labor power **in itself**, and what labor power is **for itself** has to be queried.

Whoever cannot think of something intelligible when we invoke the expression "political economy" needs only ask what an **unpolitical economy** or an **uneconomic politics** would be. Whole branches of social sciences concern themselves with the analysis of labor capacities and empirical labor: industrial and organizational psychology, business economics, industrial sociology, social psychology, drive economics, education economics. They tend, however, not to develop the integrated theoretical relationalities of a political economy of labor power.

As an "immense accumulation" of prehistories of characteristics, labor power draws its specific energy for change from the fact that it could not become a historically existent energy "for itself."[4] But it is empty with respect to the conception of its own concept. This is not because it is something, but because it can become something only if it has the capacity to assume all the many different appointed forms. Under the given historical conditions, on the contrary, it has the form of **nonidentity**. This is its stinger [*Stachel*]. Were we to imagine that a kind of identity accompanied it, it would already have the "capacity above and beyond itself" and would be equally empty on account of its prehistory. IT THUS HAS A SPECIFIC CAPACITY TO EXPLODE METAPHORIC CONCEPTS OVER AND OVER AGAIN, BUT NOT TO INSTALL ITSELF WITHIN THE SHELL OF A METAPHORIC CONCEPT.

We arrive now at a differentiation: the political economy of labor power is itself a laboring concept, and this is the reason why there is no metaphoric concept for it. However, we strive to avoid definitional circumlocution at the beginning of our work on this concept for entirely different reasons. In other words, we first need to seek the locus of the contradiction originally responsible for generating the object on which we work.

The Two Economies in Relation to Wage Labor and Capital

The **owner of money** confronts the laborer in such a way that he appears as the **owner of the commodity labor power** itself. Possession by the owner of labor power, however, is a fiction, since he acts as if he's the vendor of this commodity, but by no means has it at his disposal at the time of sale. He may have in his head the requisite willingness, even when all his senses, his organs, and the perfidy of his education constitute such willingness, but he must first still do the work. For example, if his consciousness does not obey him, his movements evince self-will [*Eigenwillen*]. He then makes mistakes, and fantasies of escape ensue. **As the owner of the commodity labor power, he constantly has to acquire the labor power anew that he is expected to deliver.**

In this labor process transpiring within labor power itself, both the natural characteristics and the labor that is already mastered by the **disposition to work [*Arbeitsdisposition*]** and derived from the economy of these very same natural characteristics either do battle or enter into an exchange. Owing to the rearing of labor power, originary self-regulated forces rooted in the libidinal economy shrink to a kind of solidified dead labor, a character machine. To a certain extent, they form the prior *objectification* of labor power *within* labor power.

This is the *one* side of labor capacity. Only on account of the friction with these ontogenetically and phylogenetically acquired influences — with the one side of labor capacity — can the natural characteristics bind themselves to labor power anew. A certain quantity of this natural force that appears anew in concrete labor processes is necessary so that the supply of acquired labor capacities effects the change in condition that we then call "labor."

There are *two* products where the capitalist or national economist only sees *one*. One product arises in the relation of exchange between capitalist production and wage labor; the other consists of the exchange of the inner relation of labor power with itself, which is to say, **in the production relations of labor power as commodity with respect to itself as created.** From the perspective of the political economy of labor power—contrary to the vantage point of the logic of capital—the result of labor is the by-product, whereas the process within the laboring individual—a piece of real life—is the primary product. The other side of labor power as commodity is thus not the character of its use value. What arises, rather, is an entire chain of differentiations of which only the last link contains the core contradiction: the application of natural forces/abstract labor/labor power as commodity/use-value character for capitalist production of meaning/use-value character for the obstinacy of labor capacity/internal production relations of self-alienation. The final link is the core of the political-economic contradiction of labor power. This contradiction permanently explodes the concept of the political economy. In other words, a real economy does not obey the aforementioned potential for contradiction; the analyzed field of experience breaks the rules of the economy. At the same time, the attribute *political* breaks down, because the political draws its substance from the power of this contradiction; this is obviously a very traditional notion of the political. Essentially, this pertains to the invalidity of all economic and political conditions at the moment when they strive to hold down and generate historical labor capacities under the contradictory conditions typical of production relations. And this break becomes clear as soon as the change in perspective focuses on the **unity of the individual and phylogenetic history,** instead of imagining the **unity of capital and labor.**

We have just observed the following: when an exchange is finished for the owner of money, a twofold form of work begins for the owner of labor power. **He works for capital, and he performs work on himself in order to engender within himself the aptitude for his labor.**

The First Contradiction in the Political Economy of Labor Power

Self-exploitation; the instrumental, the calculating ways in which the brain functions; obedience; or the way organs and cells refrain from drawing attention to themselves (to the point of a psychosomatic sickness or death)—all these factors belong to the **external law.** In comparison, the **inner law** reads in the reverse: without the supplemental labor of what works alone—the self-regulative economy of drives—none of these processes would take place. This contradiction between appearance [*Schein*] and essence [*Wesen*] of the real process expresses itself in the fact that the history of self-regulation in our culture has to be written as the history of disruptions. This is one of the reasons why the powerful labor of self-regulation so seldom leaps into consciousness. Were we to investigate at this point the aforementioned question regarding the separation of labor power from the means of production, it would revolve around the **separation of motive from labor power**. If the tasks that are assigned to natural force (that is, to the self-regulative forces that encipher their own value system, namely, the idea of what they *can* do) are so inadequate that this force cannot express itself, then the **object of labor** becomes separated from **the capacity for labor** within labor power. Conversely: if the produced motivation is focused on something impossible, then the same torturous separation of labor capacity from the object of labor arises *within* labor power. The worst that can happen to labor power is the total separation of *ability* from the *field of activity*.

The question regarding the separation of producers from their labor resources or the objects of production does not pertain only to the manufacturing of goods in factories. This image prevails because this appears historically to be the primary application of labor power. However, we are interested above all in labor power inadequately reflected in traditional consciousness: labor both inside and outside the factory. This includes, for example, protest labor and the power of resistance. If the rebellion of the cells, the senses, the brain, or the feelings of protest pent up in a labor situation lacks an adequate means of production and an object for friction, a tension arises. A proletarian situation emerges capable of directing itself explosively outward or inward against the agent of labor power. The same goes for when a protest or the power of resistance is assembled into aggregates that do not correspond to individual laws, to the self-regulative, natural development of these forces; in this case, alienation arises full of similar tensions. If such protests are politicized incorrectly, they, too, direct themselves either outward in an uncontrolled fashion or inward against the agent of these forces. For the self-regulative natural force active in every social labor, the other person is a need; the power [*Macht*] of labor power [*Arbeitskraft*] that goes into relationships must not be underestimated. Here, too, the question revolves around "the separation of the means of production from the objects of labor."[5]

What this cast of characters as relatively "thin abstractions" suggests is, in reality, hidden in the surplus of the objective, an immense abundance of experience. In this real form, nothing is abstract. Rather, everything is so substantial that the acrimony tied to it is one of the reasons why consciousness finds it so difficult to deal with the processes of labor power according to its own proportions. How much easier it is to occupy oneself with things or with fields of knowledge such as physics, the biology of animals, or meteorology that lend themselves to be organized objectively according to their material! As if there existed something more objective than the historical stamp of labor power! The production of this labor power entails **raw materials** (self-regulation, forces organized **from below**), **labor resources** (education, the influence of all previous instances of objectified labor power, learning through the reality of labor), their modes of production (it is as heterogeneous as the labor of a composer, that of an assembly-line worker, and like the labor in a love relationship or that of the producers of a revolution), and finally their **relations of production** (as the relation of exchange between self-exploitation of the subject, that is, already constituted labor power, and the obstinacy of the natural force acquired from it over and over again). All of this is an **organic whole**. In the introduction to "Outlines of the Critique of Political Economy" (*Grundrisse*), Marx comprehended the process of production, distribution, and consumption exactly this way: as an organic whole whose parts all react with one another so that the respectively acquired relations of production morph again into raw materials, out of which the process of the production of labor power later asserts itself in stages down the line. This transpires, in fact, in two directions: (1) the destruction of historical labor power, and (2) in the form of a larger abundance of collective labor capacities. As a **social abundance**, however, this is paid for by the **individual impoverishment** of productive forces. At this point, it is not a matter of counting these movements in their entirety, but rather of pointing out the fundamental application of all criteria postulated by Marx to the commodity production of labor power.[6]

The separation from both the means of production and the subjective object is the stinger, a sensation of difference that enters like a motor into self-regulation. For this reason, it is **unrest,** and not **calm,** that again and again creates a backwardly projected sense of hope in the form of an image of an originally happy human being. Or it occupies some fleck of futurity as compensation for all that unrest in the fantasy, a sign of historical labor capacity.[7]

But then the reverse is also conjecturable regarding what determines the need for **association:** the core of radical needs. History produces a division of labor, competition, parceling, Robinsonades, absenteeism, protests generally directed against labor, the devaluation of consciousness, **and** the labor of resistance precisely because they have brought about nothing in so many numerous examples throughout highly industrialized societies. A loss of reality thus results, a loss that the radical needs must endure. A daring hypothesis emerges that partially flies in the face of the bulk of historical empiricism: **all this points to the core of labor power's self-will.** The need for the confederation and association of producers (as a subjective labor capacity and labor power) **does not objectify itself because of the obstinacy of these needs.**

Two elements are always present in a useful concept: **authentic interest** (as well as its anticipation) and a **horizon** (or its anticipation). Order derived not from reduction, but from autonomy. This is the **motor** driving the concept as it works toward the completeness of relationality. In Brecht's "Conversations in Exile," Ziffel says to Kalle: "Concepts . . . are grips with which things can be moved."[8] That concepts are to a certain extent like hands is the very reason why we should take on the "exertion of the concept" at all. Concepts "work."

As we have already indicated, the political economy of labor power therefore neither allows a concept to stand **for itself** nor permits itself to be gauged according to length, width, prehistory, or futurity. So that a production process within the concept arises, a confrontation with the root of its interest is far more necessary: this is the **associational need of human producers who require the horizon of a political economy for what constitutes their strength, namely, labor power**. It appears as if this associational need is a second concept that could be investigated on its own. However, it is only the first concept by means of which the other operates to any extent. In this respect, only the conflict between both, a working **organic whole**, constitutes a **single** useful concept. The one (the political economy of labor power) is the material, the other (the confederation or association, the need for society or for the unification of forces) is the motor, the measure, and the order of workmanship [*Verarbeitung*]. But then it reverses itself, for the measure necessary for associational needs lies in the previous history of labor power and this, in turn, is the workmanship necessary for associational needs. This now forms the horizon for the horizon and then reverses itself once again. The one without the other would be without object and interest and would lead nowhere. It is with this nonpragmatic sense in mind that we must understand the Marxian phrase: ideas have always embarrassed themselves when they are not associated with an interest.

When it presents itself purely in the mind or in the form of written letters, the labor process possesses something playful.[9] This is different in reality, where real concepts work effectively with one another or go to battle. The conceptual fragment "I want to survive" among occupants in a basement during an air raid and the conceptual fragment "obliterate the city, do the job right" in the armada of bombers, together with their highly unequal instruments of power, form a single situation, a single experience.

However, this situation is at the same time a publicly legible code that in everyday life or in times of so-called peace discloses a hidden relation of an entire society to humanity. This is a *single* concept. Concepts, or at least real concepts that refrain from isolating out factors such as the critical mind, should therefore be imaged as deriving from not only a **single** laboring pair of opposites, but also as an organic diversity of numerous parts working both with and against one another. It makes no sense to apply such working concepts to categories such as *right* or *wrong* or *truth* or *meaning*. Seen from the perspective of human use value, that would entail incommensurable units of measure. Rather, what is initially involved are proportions, a relation, questions regarding the completeness or incompleteness of the relationality.

The Contradiction between Living and "Dead Labor"

My name is Milchsack Number 4
I guzzle grease, you guzzle beer
I devour coal, you devour bread
You haven't lived yet, I am still dead.
I do my daily rounds
I was here in the Ruhr before you.

When you're no more, I'll still have long to go
I know you by the way you walk.
—Bertolt Brecht, "Song of the Crane Milchsack IV"[10]

Living labor is reflected in production and disappears therein. Marx calls this solidified form of labor "dead labor."[11] Such dead labor is, for example, machines, trodden paths (relationships), the social relations of production, the product of history, money, the state. *Living* labor stands in opposition to the entirety of its prehistory: *dead* labor.

The second contradiction in the political economy of labor power reads as follows: The bulk of dead labor turns out to be superior to living labor.

The relation of living labor to labor already rendered into a product is experienced in *life spans*. Seen from the perspective of the history of already materialized production, these are extremely short periods of time. Dead labor organizes itself in far longer time frames: the lived time of machines and their heirs,[12] in the period of entire social formations, in the time scale of the course of history, and finally in phylogenetic durations entirely unimaginable in the rhythms and modes of sensuousness typical of individual time spans.[13]

This is initially a contradiction in the mode of experience; the interrelation between living and dead labor cannot be perceived individually on account of its vastly diverse times of production. In addition, the bulk of dead labor in a modern society is superior to living labor.

According to *basic principles*, superiority rules by both oppression and dead labor, an alliance against living labor. Conversely, no class can feel itself in the undisputed possession of dead labor **practically**. Rather, trench warfare over both points of contact and portions of dead labor takes place in a similar fashion, as in the permanent war over the limits on working hours, the distribution shares of the social product, or at the interface with the life-context [*Lebenszusammenhang*].[14]

A strike, for example, is the temporary conscious separation of living labor from the resources of dead labor; it is supposed to win portions of dead labor for the realization of living labor. A general strike presents the functional incapacity of dead labor as entirely sensuous and manifest.[15]

In revolutions, the relation of living labor to dead labor is determined anew from the side of living labor. The productive forces of people in society rebel against the relations of production by revolutionizing them; an alliance of living and dead labor is always contained in these revolting productive forces. Within dead labor, the already-acquired abilities revolt as a mute coercion of progress seized, enunciated, and set into motion against the relations of production by living forces. The goal of this motion is to bring living labor to power.

In praxis, battles over dead labor en masse run their course in more confined scenarios. It is a matter of punctuality. Strikes, revolutions, and general strikes seldom occur, compared with real battles. The theoretician Carl von Clausewitz provides us with a differentiation between possible and real combat. Possible combat has the same real consequences as real combat. This empirical rule refers as well to the battles between classes in the confrontation between dead and living labor. In this confrontation, possible strikes, revolutions, or a general strike are real determinations of social relations at any moment, even when they are not currently taking place.

We hold fast to the view that the contradiction between living and dead labor encompasses the entire basic understanding of a society.

A single machine thrusts the worker into a position, be it corporeal or temporal, best suited for it. The entirety of machinery and acquired social relationships exercise — like history — a force on the producers of living labor, regardless of their actual will. This overpowering process does not reflect itself exhaustively, not even in the experience of producers. In order to deal with this aforementioned political relation, we first need a public sphere, a public sphere in whose production processes the historical movement of dead and living labor allows itself to be converted into experience.

The Contradiction between Individual Labor and the Total Labor of Society

Marx says in *Capital* that the creation of social wealth, the wealth of an entire society, is tied to the impoverishment of the individual laborer. This means that the worker, who divests himself and disposes of his essential powers, does not really take part in this wealth he produces. What he gets in return is always just the minimum of self-preservation that he needs in order to reproduce his individual living conditions at a respective cultural and material level. This concept of impoverishment is not a physical determination, like hunger, but describes a specific relation between the wealth of relations, relationships, and products objectively available in the whole of society, as well as the individual possibility of using these relations, relationships, and products for the expansion of the individual's life context.

Yet pauperization reaches over into the realm of production. The rich composition of a society full of productive forces goes hand in hand with the individual impoverishment of labor qualifications. Increasing one-sidedness and the abstraction of individual labor correspond to the general expansive activity of the whole of society.

Both sides of the contradiction also lend themselves to be described as the relation of social production to private appropriation. Individual labor power is locked into its life span; it looks on the prehistory and the present totality of society from this individual, distorted angle. **Individual labor is thus determined not individually, but rather socially.** Appropriation occurs individually by owners of private property.

Labor Power as Result and Process
A process is never completely absorbed in its result. The result is itself an immobilized excerpt of the process. The prevailing process of labor is assembled from two very different dimensions of the divestiture of labor power. One dimension consists of the multitude of more or less coordinated activities that are always available, but that never enter into consciousness during this process. It appears as if they operate only on the side, when in fact, they form very diverse forms of supplemental labor not at all aimed directly or selectively at the product. However, this labor forms the production basis for the **second** dimension of labor, which is much more intentionally concentrated on producing a certain product and organizing the means. This dimension's activities, which are equally necessary in prevailing labor processes, can lead, under certain social conditions, to an immense summation of labor resources, with the result that individual stages of this labor activity and the actual expended energy are no longer recognizable at all. Attempting to reconstruct this process retroactively from its result is not possible for several reasons. One reason for this resides in the fact that in its entire diversity, the labor process is not in any way objectified in the product, but rather only in selective portions. Another reason pertains to

131

fact that considerable portions of these activities expire, as it were, **below the threshold of consciousness** and then become, through their partial objectification in the result, neither more visible nor more conscious. Just as it is correct to say, on the one hand, that the process is never completely absorbed in the result, so, too, it is correct to say, on the other, that the result is not absorbed by the process, which is to say that the result is itself reflected in the process. A fundamental **incongruence** between process and result arises at this stage, one that is grounded in the structure of labor capacity. Marx names an additional reason for this limit of recognizability when he cites the example of the broken fork. He says: whereas all recollection of the labor process is consumed by the **successful** product, only the **broken** fork brings people to contemplate and recollect whether something in the production process itself went awry. The **successfully** functioning product erases the memory of production in such a way that we can also say that the successful reconstruction of a society uses up both memories of suffering and the efforts that are connected with it.

"The Broken Fork." Richmond after the Civil War. The capital of Scarlett O'Hara's Confederate States of America. [Library of Congress]

Within the **multifaceted product** of the labor process, which stands vis-à-vis its result, there lies the inner rationale for Marx's observation that one hundred workers achieve more per hour than one worker in one hundred hours. Marx calls this phenomenon *animal spirits*.[16] However, it has nothing to do with the enthusiasm that might arise "if animals were gathered together." The labor process transpires on account of the comprehensive activity of various labor capacities. Out of this variable flow of actions—be they reactive in nature, full of detours, riddled with potential errors, or even containing a minimum of freely and newly invented variations—the intervention of labor leading to the result selects what is suitable under the concrete circumstances. **Possible** actions are initially as real as real ones. With the collaboration of numerous modalities of labor power, free or learned variants or even the interventions of labor unite with one another and bar erroneous actions, so that in between jobs (that is, below the surface of conscious labor), inter-subjective alliances of labor capacities occur that are capable of enriching the result or expediting the labor process.

The relation of ends and means reverses itself frequently in the process, but not in the result. Basically, two kinds of production usually transpire: labor powers turn out a **product** and simultaneously manufacture among themselves a sense of understanding, a solidarity through mutual error correction—in other words, teaching processes—that enable pieces of reciprocal vitality to branch off. For the process of value creation, this is merely the underside of life. For real life contained in the labor process, it is the main portion of this vitality.[17]

In a meritocracy, all attention is directed at results. Results appear as the real. Conversely, the processes from which the real emanates appear as extenuated reality, as a private matter, so to speak. But for the political economy of labor power, it is precisely the processes, and not the results, that fulfill the conditions necessary for an analysis of how **labor and real life** are **identical**. They are not to be found as such in the result. It turns out that abstract labor consists of the privation and the partial refund of concrete, lived time. The time during which a female punch operator stands at her machine is virtually struck from her lived time; it is not she—a living person—who stands there before the machine, but rather her abstraction. If she makes extraneous movements that rationalization

133

experts advise her to avoid, she infringes — as something real — upon the unreality of labor's time frame. An important question for the political economy of labor power lies in the way this punch operator is able to prepare herself for this abstraction by using her own powers. She does not have to exert herself in order to operate the machine; it is strenuous and consumes her powers, but the machine dictates her will. She must exert herself in order to **endure this abstraction**. Job performance therefore lies in the product she produces with herself. Without a doubt, this clearly does not enter into the results of her labor. Whether an unwilling or satisfied female worker produced the result cannot be observed in it, as long as the workplace created by a third party bars her will and restricts her capacities from making mistakes.[18]

> The social scientist Marianne Herzog describes a female pipe welder who sweeps her arms backward in a winglike fashion after welding approximately thirty spots in order to proceed with her functional labor that entails welding yet another thirty pieces of pipe or so. The sweeping movement is real for her person (that is, her lived time). The rest of her movements are unreal. For the process of value creation oriented toward the result, the opposite is the case.
>
> This winglike movement, scratching one's head, catching the glance of a fellow female worker, exchanging a few words, a short breakfast break, these things, when taken together, do not constitute life. The results of partial products unreal for employees, which incidentally appear as equally unreal single products, unite into one sellable relationality.[19]

The Reversal in the Relation of Flow and the Disruption in the Political Economy of Labor Power

According to the punch clock, the intervention of labor is a flow, whereas the pauses that a worker makes constitute interruptions. For the lived time of labor power, the exact opposite is the case: labor is the interruption. Only an entirely different form of labor, a nonalienated kind, is "a necessary condition, independent of all forms of society, for the existence of the human race; it is an eternal nature-imposed necessity, without which there can be no material exchanges between man and Nature, and therefore no life."[20] The need for such labor, labor that "breathes natural forces in and out," so to speak, acts like a stream with respect to alienated free time and alienated labor. The flow of protest, for example, must sedate the extant protest within itself via self-alienation so that someone can endure both work and their free time.

The reversal refers to all basic materials from which labor capacities are produced. These basic materials reside in no way merely in a period of rest or empty movement. Rather, they are presupposed by every objectification of labor itself. They are there because they are uncompensated, separately not noticeable, and inconspicuous in their flow. Memory consists of such a permanent flow; the circulation or set of spirals active in the mnemonic faculty are interrupted when memory enters into consciousness. The **conscious** circulation then sedates its unconscious counterpart for a certain period of time, during which memory again weakens and ostensibly vanishes. Thereafter, the unconscious flow begins anew. In school, a child's permanent interior flow of oblivious ideas is **interrupted** when the child attends to something, gives answers, or is called upon by its teacher. In this respect, children's activities in school are full of interruptions.

The flow of the community within the body consists of the rest energy of nerve cells, which is later interrupted by stimulation in order to revert it back into its independent flow. By nature, muscles have the ability to tighten and relax permanently. This is their potential, their flow. A complicated system of inhibitions avoids this storm of movement and facilitates **concerted action** via interruption. The compiled labor capacities themselves flow as a **potential**. A surplus is always operative when a single act of labor approaches; from this surplus, the capacity for interruption selects those essentials necessary for the concrete labor process and fortifies itself by immobilizing the remaining flow. This is generally the reason why conscious, purposeful activity evolves out of the trial-and-error method. This procedure would not be possible if the result did not materialize out of a rich flow of unrealized potential.

The Balance Economy of Labor Capacities
A result of the principle of double labor, those labor capacities belonging to streams invisible in labor's result and seldom seen in the labor process must exert labor power on account of the First Contradiction in the political economy of labor power. This

flow of labor power, which is constantly spent so as to endure the demands of alienated work, objectifies itself in the form of a **balance economy**. It expresses itself, for example, in culture's production of detours, the activities of fantasy, the labor of protest and interpretation, mourning [*Trauerarbeit*], and in the plethora of consolations of the self and other. As a reservoir, it is a component of practically every labor process and at the same time a compensatory form of praxis based on counterproduction. In today's society, its size corresponds roughly to the two largest visible fields in which labor capacities are applied, namely, in the workplace and in the realm of socialization. It exhibits the tendency of drawing on more and more human energy and subsuming it into its praxis because the endurance of every additional instance of alienation also demands additional countermaneuvers. However, it may extract labor power to a more limited degree vis-à-vis the powerful agents of reality presiding over factory work. This is why the balance economy culls forces from less-guarded life-contexts. If the extraction of power for balancing results in the further dilution of the life-context, this requires, in turn, an additional effort on the part of the balance economy in order to withstand this drain. For this reason, power preferably is drained from general interests and labor capacities but particularly from political ones, as well. Since interests and labor capacities expended in this universal direction constitute self-consciousness, ulterior kinds of balancing are also required. The balance economy thus drains what would render it unnecessary. It goes without saying that it is not a balance economy per se—and thus an arsenal of labor capacities exhibiting this balancing character—but rather involves *different* kinds of balancing necessary for every class, every mode of production, children, women, and the elderly, depending on their position in society.[21]

Navigational Labor
The balance economy is a special case of a maneuvering of the self [*Selbststeuerung*].[22] Every expenditure of labor power contains a portion of this navigational labor. What appears in Marx as the difference between carpenters, builders, and bees is this portion of specific labor capacities for maneuvering and navigating. They must not be sought after in those realms of consciousness so easily

remembered, but rather can be found scattered in routines and particular skills. They catch the eye, above all, in the form a **loss of control** [*Steuerungsverlust*] that results from breakdowns in the balance economy. The same result can ensue on account of balance imperialism, that is, from the logic of extracting navigational energies necessary for balancing.

A special case of losing control is to be found in aggressive tendencies in society. They are almost always based on a collapse of the balance economy; in other words, they are ingrained dissatisfactions not processed in public. These aggressions do not gather only in the form of an "imperialism directed outward," that is to say, in the form of aggression toward other peoples. They also exist as an "imperialism directed inward." This latter form has the aggressive tendency of importing "as much world as possible" into the intimacy of the family, for example, and thus exporting problems far off into the distance. This retreat into the family is fed by a loss of control and aggression and is in no way a peaceful process.[23]

Labor Capacities Aimed at the Unification of Forces

Let us return now to the countermovement that responds to both a loss of control and the balance economy's tendency to drain power. We saw that a system of labor capacities that emerges historically, but not as a relationality, always develops labor capacity as something cobbled together. Something cobbled together (that is, an amalgamation) is itself also a flow of labor capacities. Without a specific **economy of association**, the appearance of cooperation and **solidarity** that evolves underneath industrial processes is unthinkable. These capacities could not emerge by force. From the viewpoint of non-emancipation, that is, from that of industrial processes, this question boils down to how these powers function; evolved out of the processes of separation and contradictions, they do not exhibit the tendency to unify with one another above and beyond their already existent collectivity. From the viewpoint of emancipation, we must pose the question: In which context would these powers exhibit an autonomous tendency to abandon their inability to amalgamate and come together? The accent lies on the word: **autonomous**. The perspective of our investigation must therefore direct it toward the autonomous moment of these labor capacities—not the point where they **ought** to unify, but the point where they **actually** do so.

What is astonishing is the fact that the concentration of empirically ascertainable abilities to unify does not reside in labor or life processes. These predominant and compulsory amalgamations contain just as many dispersal capacities as associative capacities. In fact, they exist opposite [*quer*] from the context of labor and life. Accordingly, a self-evident and spontaneous form of cross-referencing [*Querbeziehung*] rooted in respective disciplines arises between all specialized labor capacities—for example, all linguists, physicists, engineers, but also philatelists, bloggers, artists, and other laborers possessing specific skills—around the world.[24]

On account of hierarchy and competition, the accommodation of these same qualifications within the workplace is inhibited. Neither cross-referencing within a concrete labor process nor the relationships within a collective political organization possesses the strength to secure specialized disciplinary cross-links for independently producing, by virtue of tacit recognition, an ability to work as soon as said abilities effectively drop out of the immediate forced relations of their production. As with factory labor and the cooperation within the generally constituted nonspecialized public sphere, this also applies to the forms of labor within relationships in the realms of socialization and life.

As impossible reaching an agreement on erotic matters may appear to be within a single relation of relationships, for example, it does nonetheless happen spontaneously in the ostensibly anonymous realm of cross-links, insofar as an exchange of experience therein is feasible. In love stories, solutions fall into place that could not otherwise be found in a nonerotic relationship between two people. The public sphere comports itself not only toward experience, but also more specifically toward intimacy as the kind of realization of experience whereby I test myself—in fact, secretly—as to whether something is in agreement with my own experience. Such intimacy is the opposite pole of the public sphere. It is a fact that a public sphere useful for humans ought to possess this intimacy as a testing mechanism. Cross-referencing intimacy is a way to aim labor capacities toward amalgamation within the labor of relationships that is otherwise neither possessed by the representative (that is, general) public sphere nor controlled by its exclusionary mechanisms.

Trust as the Basis of Labor Capacities Aimed at Realism

In an antagonistic reality, a realistic attitude is characterized by the fact that it recognizes the antirealism of feelings—their protest against unbearable relations—as the motor for realism. This poses demands, since the antirealism within the senses (feelings of the self cobbled together from both sensuousness and the labor capacities that are, in turn, cobbled from them) violates the obviously powerful reality principle, namely, **self-confidence**. Self-confidence can subsist only on collective confirmation. The central point of realism—and the labor capacities operating within it—is the production of epistemological procedures based on solidarity. This is not something individually producible.[25]

No human is objective by nature. The antirealistic labor of motives is autonomous, as are both the labor that changes matter and unrest. Construction is necessary if an objective attitude is to arise from this. One of the realistic attitude's most important constructive activities consists of accommodating within itself the foreign and the adversarial and transforming them into something of its own. If such constructive labor fails, the foreign and the adversarial must be banished and fended off; this **appears** as objectivity, but is actually the highest form of **impertinence**. In contrast, it would be impossible either to exclude or to appropriate by recognition the foreign and the adversarial, since this would suspend the autonomous activity of living labor. Part of such a misdirected attempt is contained in the exclusionary labor of defensive barriers. That this does not exclude the return of the repressed and the disruption of the order based upon repression shows that the autonomous activity of living labor cannot be stopped. A person can act as if he were dead, but he does not die because of it.

The trust necessary for the labor involved in constructing the realistic attitude, the attitude from which the recognition of the other produces itself, has adversaries in the factions that constitute the inner community: (1) natural mistrust, a fear of strangers; (2) ambivalence, the unpredictability typical of strangers and what is not mine, a lack of **credibility**; (3) the lack of trust that others will endure my contradictions and dissonances: concealment.

Recognizing **a** stranger presupposes that I am allowed to maintain my contradictions, my ownness [*Eigenes*]. Seen from the other, more positive flip side, this pertains to: (1) a certain amount of basic trust, a subsidy from an earlier developmental period; I must have had a bit of good fortune to treat reality so fairly; this is the principally unfair and disproportionate thing about the problem of realism;[26] (2) self-confidence; (3) trust toward others so that they can endure me (my dissonances when I introduce something real of myself) and not continually exact revenge on me. In the same way that self-confidence always returns to the sparks of basic trust, so, too, must I consider myself to be trustworthy if I am to assume that others will tolerate me. Mistrust leaves its mark when I doubt myself. I trace the image of the other's abilities, an image in which I recognize my own contradictions from within myself.[27]

> Objectivity is seen best when understood as the scarring of experience. It fluctuates between the **good will** to submit to the friction of objects (their pressure) and the **feeling of omnipotence** (a specific obstinacy and the exuberance of knowledge). The roots of trust, as well as those of **selectivity** and those of **relationality**, develop in a twofold manner from both (1) omnipotence and (2) the point of contact. As long as the cognitive faculty remains a **potential**, it persists in this double form; in all **objectifications**, an injury arises due to the dual nature of the root. Later it becomes a scar. Herein, the realistic attitude is always at the same time both dead and living labor.

The Differentiation of Strong and Weak Social Forces and of Hermetic and Associative Forces

If we render concrete the political economy of labor capacity from an emancipatory perspective, praxis reveals a distinct differentiation: the way repulsion and attraction operate in spheres of socialization, in particular within the family, clearly differentiates them—by virtue of the degree of their emotional intensity—from those motives that enter into either public affairs or the basic materials in industrial labor processes. In fact, the latter determine social relations in fundamental ways, but in individual humans, they are weak motives. The strongest of fantasies do not revolve around work and efficiency. Instead, strong ideas and motives concentrate on reaction formations that trigger dissociation. Jealousy, ego strength in the form of character armor, the sense of having, unflinching love, stinginess, self-aggression (flight from reality, flight into death), and panic—all of these formations bind and divest the strongest of forces. They act hermetically, but the capacities laboring therein are not capable of forming associations. When they do accumulate, they are often more likely to explode, rather to bind themselves to a related accumulation of forces. Twenty-two Medeas, forty-six Othellos, five Shylocks, multiple Michael Kohlhaases, twelve Hamlets, four Beethovens, and fourteen Lady Macbeths can gather together a tremendous concentration of forces, but they do **not** form **a society.**[28]

Without the dramatic moment—that is, the one-sided concentration of forces, which is also the principle of the bourgeois mourning play [*Trauerspiel*]—the hermetic structure of labor capacities proves itself to be the essence of those methods of production that have the particular [*das Besondere*] as their object. What makes me particular—for example, **my** dignity, **my** acre of land, **my** wife, **my** animals—is **what I would not sell for any price**; it is what constitutes my steadfast customs and the transmission of generations. These particulars are what stand opposite to exchange, as well as to the unification of forces (association). As a category of primitive property, the particular is finally something powerful and universal [*Allgemeines*]; it also produces a community that emerges out of multiple particularities, my own community, which prevents me from **really** forming a collective community with others.

It is imaginable that interest in universals such as money and logic can be aroused in an agrarian society untouched by the process of capital. This interest can be developed in an individual born into a consanguineous or tribal society only in the form of a weak force. What I would never sell for any price will keep stronger force fields inside me occupied; no attendant weak notion could ever provide me with an abstract universal capable of uniting the world. A complex process transpires under the influence of capital and its many abilities that is responsible, on the one hand, for unifying strong foreign factors within its circulation and, on the other, for transforming a weak need—such as characterizing and exchanging something from the particulars I can do without as something universal—into a strong characteristic. This is possible only because the reaction to the suggestions of capitalism weakly present in each individual [*Einzelnen*] behaves **associatively** toward the same weak force in other humans. (Similarly, capital makes suggestions only formally, following a violent separation from the primitive means of production and the violent implementation of the commodity as the category of reality.)

When viewed externally, the cumulative effect of this assumption—namely, that there exist universal signs such as money and logic—leads to neither explosions nor dissociations. As soon as it becomes collective experience, this assumption lays the groundwork necessary for capital's suggestions. If one day individual weak forces are generalized—that is, if, through a common exchange of experience, a collective general inventory of conduct arises—money and, to a limited extent, logic prove themselves to be **dominating powers** that retroactively allow weak forces in individual humans to appear as strong motives. In reality, weak forces do not become strong, like individual characteristics, but rather associate themselves with the whole of society. Instead of speaking of a society, one could speak of **each and every association**—for example, that of **money**, that of general welfare, that of collective defense of the community as **fatherland**, that of **civility** and helpfulness (in other words all **weak forces** in the individual)—as belonging to a society, a concrete association of characteristics.

When collectively translated as social characteristics, strong characteristics, like weak ones, can act immediately as **inductive forces**; when **compliant** or constituting a **countermovement**, they act as a motive for displacement [*Übersprungsmotiv*], substitution [*Ersatzhandlung*], or transference [*Übertragung*], and so on. For example, a relationship to the father can encompass attraction and repulsion. Due to the strength of the area of contact and crystallization—in other words, because of the injuries caused by paternal authority and the attraction to this authority—both can become **strong forces**. They induce a chain of imitations and avoidances, each of which enters into either the ego's strength or its armor plating. They can refer to the state or its leader in the form of a transference or a misunderstanding. Because of the irrepressible libidinal loss in transference, these transferred forces are thus weaker vis-à-vis the concrete father, but through the rejection of the father again are freed from inhibitions and therefore appear strong.

The high degrees of intensity of motives that yield strong labor capacities are rooted in what is relevant to me. The danger of loss affects me; I defend these forces, and they belong to my primitive property. Their entry into cooperation—their collectivization—

presupposes trust that as a rule is not produced anywhere. It is a function of their strength that they tend more often to explode during their assembly than to integrate with one another. The same does not hold true for the weak forces that unite as labor capacities, whose defense and demarcation do not appear so necessary to me. In this sense, even terror can produce only weak characteristics.

> In physics, we differentiate four relations of forces: Coulomb forces, strong and weak interactions, and gravity. Electrical attraction and repulsion — that is, Coulomb forces — differentiate themselves in their strength at the order of magnitude of 103^6 of gravity. The negative load of electrons and the positive load of the nucleus exclusively structure the relationships inside the atom; we are omitting here some additional factors. At this level, gravity is so weak that no physicist takes it into account. The strong Coulomb forces do not coalesce above a certain mass; an association above and beyond this mass makes the aggregate explode. The weak effects of gravity act completely differently in an individual atom. Bound together into entire suns — our sun contains 10^{56} atoms — this association of forces determines the paths of planets.

The Fulcra of Labor Capacities

Labor is the category of social transformation. This becomes comprehensible via its opposite pole: naturally occurring (in the social sense of the word) indeterminate transformations. Voltaire protested against the earthquake in Lisbon. The earthquake brought about a transformation, but it was not labor.

Another example: a city was built. An industrial zone arises. This particular landscape is now transformed in a specific way: the numerous inanimate objects, the construction materials, and the relationships moved and transformed by humans. A social relation emerges in which human interests and needs are built into inanimate objects: **this is labor.**

One dimension of this transformation is measured as capital value; everything that remains untransformed is not measured. The unit of measurement called the erg used in physics measures something of this transformation. It is not identical with value in the capitalistic sense; nevertheless, what is measured is only a result (force times distance). Significant portions of social transformation are left out.

A More Specific Designation of the Category of Labor

Crops of grain sown in the fields grow. This process is not **labor**. It is a necessary constituent in the relationality of production processes called "cultivation." The conceptual difference between growth and productive intervention by humans is inconsequential for the production process. Regarding the question as to what in a production process must be paid for as labor power and what unpaid labor accomplishes — that is, what is subject to the subjective will and what remains unaffected by it — this differentiation is, conversely, **essential**. The acuteness of the analytical interest applied to this differentiation results first from an interest in exploitation and second from an interest in comporting oneself realistically toward the production process — that is, determining what a laborer is actually capable of doing. Analytic answers will result in varied demarcations, depending on which of the many interests I follow.

The summation of instrumental egoisms that generate the historical product expresses itself negatively. An individual interest in exploitation is vehemently interested in a greater allowance of unpaid labor; "natural labor" therefore refers only to that labor whose interventions are absolutely necessary. The lifelong labor of the beating heart is remunerated just as little as the double labor of labor power that must be expended in order just to get by. In contrast, utilization interests are especially interested in how the leftover **remainder** of instrumental labor still functions after its subtraction from a human being's essence.

The summation of all exploitation interests proceeds differently. This is culture's view of labor. It has no interest whatsoever in bringing up the contradiction between paid and unpaid labor, and as we will see later, it completely masks the contexts of labor and life as processes; it is unconcerned with differentiations.

Yet the interest of labor power is again itself different. The question as to what still counts as labor and where so-called privateness begins is a battlefield of class disputes.[29] The unification of all labor powers is not capable of developing an independent concept for the category of labor vis-à-vis bourgeois culture because precisely here, agreement cannot be achieved; no public discussion takes place.

We have no reason to search for a firm border between labor and its opposite pole, as if any such boundary could assume the form of a fence in the first place. Up to this point — and in general — it is labor: above all, nature, growth, a "sheer activity." Instead, we attempt to determine its force field from the fulcrum of the individual, historically developed labor capacities. These laws of motion, poles, or fulcra lie at the center of characteristics, in their **motives**. They act rather indifferently toward the exact determination of borders.

The Antagonistic Reality of Labor

From every class-specific interest that necessarily contradicts another interest there arises yet another question about the concept of labor. The interest in differentiating translates into answers. The results are heterogeneous demarcations. Seen from the interest of **vitality**, broad sections of abstract labor are unreal; conversely, for utilization interests, they are a particularly hardened form of reality. The instrumental concept of labor, as it correlates with the logic of capital, contradicts the emancipatory concept aimed at the general development of labor characteristics. But the one differentiation is not incorrect if the other one is correct; they coexist next to one another, signifying different perspectives, much like the way contradictions in labor processes are at odds with one another.

As indifferent as a general dividing line may be, each social observer in motion and in contradiction with every other observer is still interested in the fulcra and nodes where conflicts provoke specific experiences and labor capacities. Particularly important is the heterogeneity of aspects when their differences bind with further differentiations. Labor capacities differentiate themselves externally depending on whether they are investigated functionally, historically, or analytically according to the contradictory composition of their basic characteristics. The basic elements that are concealed in empirical labor by synthesis all possess **obstinacy** individually. IN AN ANTAGONISTIC REALITY, REALITY CHARACTERISTICS FLUCTUATE BETWEEN UNREAL, ANTIREAL, AND REAL.

Seen from the standpoint of the subtraction of contradictions (that is, from an unrealistic perspective), this pertains to simultaneous characteristics or processes. From the realistic standpoint of real interests, this clarity does not exist. If the fact is recognized that human producers conduct themselves like spectators, but not as adjudicators with respect to the historical products they produce, the total capacity is the historical synthesis of empirical labor power, that is, something **real**. IN THIS DETERMINATION, THE ANTIREALISM OF PROTEST IS JUST AS MUCH CAST OFF AS THE CATEGORY OF EMANCIPATION. Following a reality principle excised of its antirealistic traits, this is something unreal, something utopian.

The party of emancipation interests — scattered, yet effective as they are in material relations — represents the exact opposite standpoint: a social relation whose constitutive feature consists of the fact that producers are ruled by their own products; this is an **unrealistic** relation.

In a context of crises [*Krisenzusammenhang*] — the kind that leads to modern war — all individual elements are labor processes that, in their isolation, can be seen as being functional. The collective process that is assembled out of these elements is **unreal**. The individual elements consist of concrete stages in the labor process. However, the direction of movement of the entire relationality [*Gesamtzusammenhang*] is **lacking** the most important determination of reality: concreteness. Conversely, individual processes of abstract labor that confine themselves to partial delivery lack specific concreteness. They prove themselves to be derealized. Only after the fact does the abstract [*ungegenständlich*] partial product become a commodity, that is, an object [*Gegenstand*]. In the total relationality, a high level of industrial production is generated, something real.[30] Seen from the life-context of those affected, the derealized basic situation, however, was real life. At the same time, the antirealisms based in the emotions of those same affected persons say: **It cannot have been real life**.

The polymorphy of the reality concept contains order, and not confusion. It is confusing, though, to apply a general concept to something heterogeneous.

Our main investigatory interest focuses on the category of labor — among so many others — that investigates the ability of **labor capacities** to **control the historical product, and not to be ruled by it**. One might initially think that for such an emancipatory intention, the material aggregation of capacities and forces [*Kräfte*] must be much larger than is the case for labor capacities established in alienation. In fact, the materiality of the object (of historical production) and the materiality of labor capacities compete with one another. But this comparison does not pertain just to quantities. In certain circumstances, the materiality of labor capacities that ensconce themselves in the existing conditions is even quantitatively higher than the labor capacities necessary for a breach. This is because high volumes of labor power must be expended in order to endure those conditions. The material difference — and therewith the central point of the comparison — lies in the different shape and in the quality of alliances that labor capacities enter into among themselves. This depends not on any quantity, but rather on a phenomenal degree of cooperation.

We seek to expand the concept of what constitutes labor, just as we previously did with the concept of production in *Public Sphere and Experience*. On the other hand, we seek to center it by starting from the stinger and the fulcrum of contradictions active within it. We must do this for all **individual** labor capacities as they emerge historically from different histories.

COMMENTARY 1: THE PRINCIPLE OF SKIN-TO-SKIN CLOSENESS

In *The Principle of Hope*, Bloch turns vehemently against a series of Freud's supposed misinterpretations. Because of his aversion to the theory that the libido is the most reliable basic drive, Bloch introduces the idea of self-preservation and insists in lieu of the sex drive, as he calls it, on the historical transformation of **hunger**.[31]

By reducing everything to an unambiguous materialistic point — it is something that can be grasped — Bloch is misled into making a violent proposition: that hunger is central. What repulses him in Freud's manifold interpretations (he is even stronger in his engagement with C. G. Jung) is that the origins of libidinal binding — for Freud, they are chained to the development of linguistic expression, and for C. G. Jung, they dissolve into imaginary historical images — do not appear graspable enough in order to bind the intensified sublimation that the labor of hope presents. It is the tendency to grasp and cling that motivates Bloch to take corporeal privation, and not any *unnecessary eroticism* (from the Protestant standpoint), as the foundation for the edifice of his thought.

Surface and Depth

Bloch knows that the ego is an entity that could initially be empty. According to Freud, the ego regulates the relationships between inner representations and the outside. It mediates this regulation through the pleasure principle and the reality principle. In this regard, it deals with forces foreign to it and does not itself add anything new. This assumption also eliminates Bloch's desired facilitation principle, which ideally arrives at the new from the id. Bloch: "*there is nothing new in the Freudian unconscious.*"[32] Freud is so earnest about grasping things that all hope vanishes on account of his grip. Bloch grows his materialistic protest from this.

Clinging to the skin of another creature — the skin's senses — is located at an idiosyncratic border between materialism and idealism, between inside and outside, between safety and danger, between conscious and unconscious, between **perceiving** something and **belonging to it**. As something that goes back to radical roots, this **surface principle** resists both the strong sublimating and weak desublimating grips of thought. It resists thought's desubliminating grip especially at the juncture where it should consolidate a sublimation that forcibly transcends the reality principle (Bloch). This

148

surface principle likewise resists the sublimating grip responsible for representing the image of the living and hiding away the invisible figure of God in one of the primary drives (Freud). **At its core,** the surface principle **does not arbitrarily root self-regulation down deep or pin it up high. Rather, it affixes it to what presupposes the first thing in any environment: the skin.**[33]

The Nature of Love

In his essay "The Nature of Love," Harry F. Harlow deals with the "question of the primary drives."[34] According to the prevailing doctrine, he says, the basic motives are, above all, hunger, thirst, loneliness, pain, and sex. The relations between mother and child are interpreted as gratifying the primary drives, and the mother-child relationship materializes through secondary strengthening mechanisms. What is correct about these observations is the fact that no other binding influences the subsequent fate of the drives and their generalization as intensively as the mother-child relationship. It is nevertheless striking that all secondary strengtheners that are bound to the gratification of the aforementioned drives or needs disappeared in experiments after a certain period of time. In contradistinction to this, the human contributions invested in the mother-child relation never completely disappeared; instead, they exhibited much more of a tendency toward broad generalization.[35]

 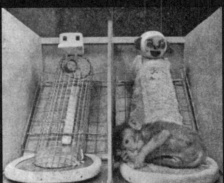

Cloth mother.   Wire mother, left.

Harlow proceeded experimentally. In the process, his experiments encountered difficulties insofar as they ran up against the inadequate development of motor skills in newborn humans. Initially, the human child does not have an adequate means of expression. This, Harlow says, is different with newborn macaque monkeys. Immediately after birth, their motor skills are more mature and develop faster. In comparison, their basic responses related to love ("affection, including nursing, contact, clinging, and even visual and auditory exploration") do not exhibit any fundamental differences from those of human children. For this reason, Harlow initially studied monkey children in a three-year experiment in which he offered two ersatz mothers — a cloth mother and a wire mother — to two groups of equally strong babies.[36] **The experiment was carried out in such a way that milk was administered first by the wire mother and then by the cloth mother.** In every case, the babies concentrated exclusively on the skin-covered mother, even when the cloth mother could no longer still the baby's hunger.[37]

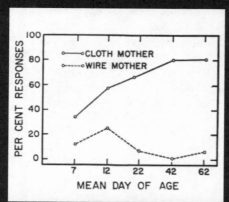

Flight to the skin-covered mother.

A bear playing a drum and moving (a typical fear stimulant).

The researcher generalized his observations thus: as long as the surface of the child's skin remains unsatisfied, neither hunger nor despair could draw it to a wire mother, or to a wire woman, for that matter.

"The socioeconomic demands of the present and the threatened socio-economic demands of the future have led the American woman to displace, or threaten to displace, the American man in science and industry. If this process continues, the problem of proper child-rearing practices faces us with startling clarity. It is cheering in view of this trend to realize that the American male is physically endowed with all the really essential equipment to compete with the American female on equal terms in one essential activity: the rearing of infants. We now know that women in the working classes are not needed in the home because of their primary mammalian capabilities; and it is possible that in the foreseeable future neonatal nursing will not be regarded as a necessity, but as a luxury—to use Veblen's term—a form of conspicuous consumption limited perhaps to the upper classes. But whatever course history may take, it is comforting to know that we are now in contact with the nature of love."[38]

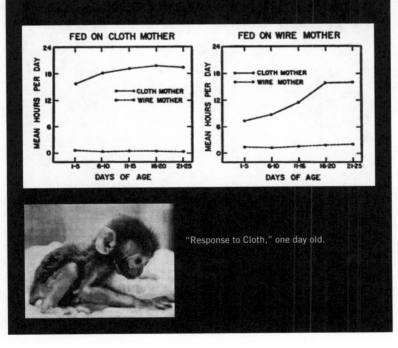

"Response to Cloth," one day old.

Absence of the skin-covered mother.

Flight from danger to the skin mother.

The rigorous experimental researcher, who presumed that the foundations of protection, security, and contact that are communicated through the surface of the skin build the core of needs, unexpectedly quotes — in the middle of his behavioral reports — verse that the translator failed to render into German.

The Snake
To baby vipers, scaly skin
Engenders love 'twixt kith and kin.
Each animal by God is blessed
With kind of skin it loves the best.

The Hippopotamus
This is the skin some babies feel
Replete with hippo love appeal.
Each contact, cuddle, push, and shove
Elicits tons of baby love.

The Crocodile
Here is the skin they love to touch.
It isn't soft and there isn't much,
But its contact comfort will beguile
Love from the infant crocodile.

The Rhinoceros
The rhino's skin is thick and tough,
And yet this skin is soft enough
That baby rhinos always sense,
A love enormous and intense.

The Elephant
Though mother may be short on arms,
Her skin is full of warmth and charms.
And mother's touch on baby's skin
Endears the heart that beats within.[39]

COMMENTARY 2: THE CONTEMPORANEITY OF MENTAL HISTORY

Dilapidated Rome in the Late Middle Ages. [Hieronymus Cock, "Rvinarvm palatii maioris prospectvs," *Praecipva aliqvod romanae antiqvitatis rvinarvm monimenta...* (Antuerpia: per Hiro. Coc, 1551)]

"Now let us, by a flight of imagination, suppose that Rome is not a human habitation, but a psychical entity with a similarly long and copious past — an entity, that is to say, in which nothing that has once come into existence will have passed away and all the earlier phases of development continue to exist alongside the latest one. This would mean that in Rome the palaces of the Caesars and the Septizonium of Septimius Severus would still be rising to their old height on the Palatine and that the castle of S. Angelo would still be carrying on its battlements the beautiful statues which graced it until the siege by the Goths, and so on. But more than this. In the place occupied by the Palazzo Caffarelli would once more stand — without the Palazzo having to be removed — the Temple of Jupiter Capitolinus; and this not only in its latest shape, as the Romans of the Empire saw it, but also in its earliest one, when it still showed Etruscan forms and was ornamented with terracotta antefixes. Where the Coliseum now stands, we could at the same time admire Nero's vanished Golden House. On the Piazza of the Pantheon we should find not only the Pantheon of today, as it was bequeathed to us by Hadrian, but, on the same site, the original edifice erected by Agrippa; indeed, the same piece of ground would be supporting the church of Santa Maria sopra Minerva and the ancient temple over which it was built. And the observer would perhaps only have to change the direction of his glance or his position in order to call up the one view or the other. . . . Our attempt seems to be an idle game. It has only one justification. **It shows us how far we are from mastering the characteristics of mental life by representing them in pictorial terms.**"[40]

Self-regulation **in** the mental apparatus and the brain is another indication that their prehistory remains permanently present in their working capacities; in other words, it shows that self-regulation is a matter of living labor. At every moment, self-regulation constitutes a historical essence and, as such, **its** relationality; it would be a mistake to regard the utility of this arsenal for instrumental processes as belonging to it own life [*Eigenleben*].

Mental events have their history in the present. As we will see, nothing physiological **transforms** into psychology, nothing individual into society or history. A transformation does not exist; there are different encryptions and different methods of observation, but there are not different objects. The sublation of historical time—the contemporaneity of history—is related to all events of evolution, history, the genesis of labor capacities and the future. **When seen solely from this perspective, self-regulation is the real relation.** We do not see it, because this perspective is obscured by the arbitrary details of historical order. However, its own life has consciousness—the internal history of living labor and human property—in this real relation; in other words, it is rooted in something different from what masquerades itself as reality.[41]

COMMENTARY 3: ON THE CONCEPT OF THE REAL

In the course of history, a mass of subjective characteristics goes into products and remains dispersed within them. **Rotating around the gravitational center of this dead labor are social relations and humans**. In order to assemble a human-centered world out of this arrangement, one would have to turn to the actual movement (that is, dispersion) by recognizing and collecting subjective splinters.

For experience, this entails a Copernican turn. The curiosity of the senses is capable of this on its own; their intentions are as of yet unable to do so. The Copernican turn (Galilei, Kepler, Copernicus, Newton) — the Einsteinian turn is propped up upon it — is external and is recognized by us as a foreign method; internally, a Ptolemaic image world dominates. The reason for this lies in a coercive dialectic. In the worldview of antiquity, humans gazed full of emotion at stars that were themselves cold; as a closed way of seeing, **this** filled their hearts with warmth. The image fulfilled a collective wish. It was daring individuals who shook this worldly edifice that sheltered humans around the earth. The new knowledge did not warm their hearts. If everything moves with a precision either too cold or too hot, there is no way that we can hope to constitute a center. There is no cozy home to be found here. **The colder social relations become, the less I desire to look at them with the gaze of cold knowledge**. The gaze that mimics both familial and collective closeness and that resides in the root of my self-consciousness (= ego) does not allow itself be exchanged for the promise of effort, distraction, and coldness. Different from the curious senses, motives need the warmth of a nest.

Our earth has the sun as its neighbor. The Milky Way, composed of several hundred billion suns, in which our sun moves at the periphery of one of its spiral arms, has neighboring Milky Ways. For natural relations, this is closeness. Faraway galactic clouds and pulsars act, comparatively speaking, from a distance.

Below the dimensions of humans, elementary particles exhibit similar distances. Accordingly, the mass and speeds of both history and evolution move completely askew. Collective experience and practical labor capacities do not deal with all of these real relations. In fact, doing so is unrealistic. In order to deal with them, the recognition would suffice that using our senses, we can know nothing of this. This would be certain and result in veneration.

"Labor and language are older than man and society."[42] Elemental characteristics that enter into labor capacities have as their foundation the temporal dimension of evolution. They therefore have their reality simultaneously in this temporal distance and in the closeness of today. If the one is subtracted from the other, either closeness or distance becomes abstract.

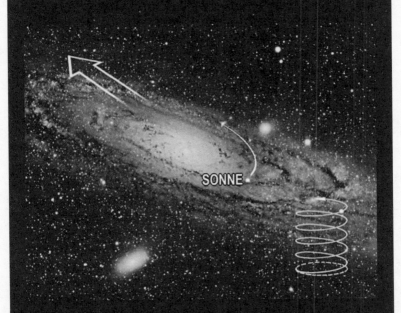

The Milky Way is a flat stellar mass arranged in a spiral shape. Here, a view of its center. The Earth moves around the sun. The sun moves at 750,000 kilometers per hour around the center. One orbit takes 250 million years. Planet Earth is roughly four billion years old. [From Alexander Kluge's *Labyrinth der zärtlichen Kraft* (Frankfurt am Main: Suhrkamp, 2009)]

> Intercourse with four billion years of evolution, two thousand years of historical time, the cumulative landscapes of industry, and the emotions of the entire body is both objective and definite. Cells know everything under the stars. Either the head has never experienced anything of this sort, or it has forgotten it altogether.

Determinacy, Indeterminacy; Concreteness, Abstraction

We saw that reality — as a mere accumulation of things in antagonistic social relations — can prove to be real or unreal. People things [*Menschendinge*] are real in a social relation only according to the categories of determinacy and concreteness. They are **determinate** with respect to the antagonism intrinsic to interests in reality; they are **concretely** real with respect to immediate interfaces and the completeness of relationality. Labor that yields changes in real relations follows the dialectic of reality relations in a society in terms of its determinacy and concreteness. The delineation of **nonlabor** can thus not be reliably determined according to anything external, neither by imagined purposes nor through the realm of activity. The **concreteness** of a determinate transformative production process distinguishes itself much more from indeterminate or abstract activities.

Determinacy and concreteness have labor capacities (1) far below the level of the ego (that is, in their prehistory, in their corporeal **community**, in their partly unconscious **whole** movements) and (2) far beyond the ego in the landscape of industry, including the relations of commodities that radiate outward from these landscapes (that is, in their history, in the thinglike and partly unconscious noncommunity). Their movements in this collective laboratory are exhaustive.

Ptolemaic subjectivity acts like a maverick with respect to such movements. Three instances of confinement constitute this realm: the insularity of the body, the enclosure between birth and death (a life span), and the brain, surrounded like a coffin by bones, which arrives at interpretations from corporeal impressions and insights acquired throughout life that normally block out the real movement between social macrostructures and historical microstructures. This is not about individual decisions **exchanging** this mode of perception for another one more suitable for reality. The distorted mode of experience is anchored in the center of primitive property, in the massive needs for security that humans must have for themselves.

The internal community is another expression for the laboring physiology of the human being. In this respect, human producers carry the phylogenesis of their species around with them for the duration of their entire lives. All subjective-objective relations designated in this way together form a contemporary social and historically **real** totality. Their relationships run through individuals and all collective representations of society. It should now become clear that throughout history, humans have attempted to position themselves individually, collectively, or, using the ruling forms of production and intercourse, **between** these real movements and that these attempts, which incorporate ever-increasing portions of the self into the web of appropriations by expanding fictional concreteness dynamically, act like a barricade with respect to both real relations and its praxis. This barrier conceals concreteness.

Translated by Richard Langston and Cyrus Shahan

A group of egos around 2,600 B.C. [Detail from *The Standard of Ur*, *"Peace,"* 2600 B.C.
© The Trustees of the British Museum/Art Resource, NY]

"Ego." [Stone statue of Kurlil, 2500 B.C. © The Trustees of the British Museum / Art Resource, NY]

PART TWO

The Public Sphere of Production

CHAPTER FOUR

The Labor of Intelligence

We usually do not speak of INTELLIGENCE WORKERS. Instead, we refer to designers, philosophers, teachers, journalists, and clergymen. Or we call attention to "heavenly liars," such as Odysseus, doctors, lawyers, economists, and so on. It is nevertheless worth going to the trouble of investigating the operative elements flowing underneath the activities associated with intelligence, for they are thoroughly robust and typical of all forms of intelligence. In so doing, we seek to undermine the stereotypical usage of the word "intelligence." In short, if labor is tilling a field, then the labor of intelligence is tending a garden.

Along with countless other functions, intelligence includes the natural navigational organ in humans. Men and women orient themselves intelligently. At the same time, some deviations and losses of control can be observed when exercising intelligence. Intelligence also is ambivalent. The god Hermes, whom we associate with intelligence and to whom the French philosopher Michel Serres dedicated a five-volume work, is also the god of communication, merchants, and thieves.[1] Shakespeare's Iago, Richard III, Napoleon's minister of police Fouché, Machiavelli, and Dr. Goebbels are all obvious laborers of intelligence. The opposite type of thinker (such as Socrates, Rosa Luxemburg, or Einstein) has remained in the minority for the longest of times. Using the word INTELLIGENCE in the affirmative sense is not simple.

What "toils away" in humans and their many different organs when they act intelligently possesses—every element in its own right—its own rhizome. (We mean here not only the intelligence of the head, but also that of the skin, the hands, the diaphragm, social intelligence, the materialist instinct, in short the intelligence of feeling.) "The heart has its reasons which reason itself does not know."[2] Knowledge of this foundation—it is, in fact, not a structure, but rather a system of branching

165

rivers—is of current relevance. In the face of the evolution of artificial intelligence and the astonishing new public spheres of the Internet in the twenty-first century, the strain on traditional acitivities of intelligence (for example, the capacity for memory) has been relieved. New capacities for intellence are emerging, becoming dominant, and establishing a need for more heightened forms of orientation. "The migration of thought out of the brain" corresponds to an innovative occupation of newly freed-up interal terrain, in part by older, forgotten, and often repressed forms of intelligence.

That Someone Is an Intelligence Worker Says Nothing about the Intelligence of the Product That Person Produces, but Rather that Someone Has Gone about Its Production in a Professional Manner

Military intelligence. Staff officers out on maneuvers. Front row, left: the future chancellor von Papen. [Oscar Tellgmann / Bundesarchiv]

Political intelligence workers. "Intelligence without foresight." The signing of the Treaty of Versailles, 1919. Shown is the Hall of Mirrors. The German Empire was founded here in 1871. In the foreground are Hermann Müller and Johannes Bell signing the treaty. At the other side of the table: Henry White, Robert Lansing (advisor to the president), Woodrow Wilson, Henri Clemenceau, Lloyd George, Bonar Law, and Lord Balfour. [Imperial War Museum]

Adolescent intelligence at the book burning of 1933. [Keystone / Getty Images]

Hyman Rickover, an admiral and intellectual who developed the first American atomic submarine. Here, he is climbing up a ladder in the tube of an atomic power plant. A short focal length.
[Yale Joel / Time Life Pictures / Getty Images]

"Knowledge is food." A dining room in the ruins of 1945. [Alexander Kluge Archive]

That Portion of Intelligence Involved in the Process of Self-Alienation

Domination's point of penetration in antiquity and in the Middle Ages — and later the point of penetration for the economic exploitation principle of capital — was the side of the personal will in humans that previously cultivated itself through the labor of precision grips and cunning. This portion of the will made it possible to respond to those instances of economic or extraeconomic violence where they indirectly express themselves via precision grips. However, this is the substantive point for both kinds of exploitation: feudalism is not possible as long as it functions only where soldiers are currently present. There can also be no capitalist circulation if a society's members repeatedly forget the principle of exchange after every individual transaction. Without intelligence, there is no will that can seek its salvation in exploitation. If I am sufficiently unintelligent — not even intelligent enough to understand the basis of power's claim on me — I cannot be subjugated.[3]

Its Decisive Role in the Political Economy of Labor Power

The labor that subjective labor capacities expend, as well as its circulation among the imperatives of external object relations (which in turn forces them into this labor) takes place essentially in the internal relations of labor power. The necessary linkages can be imagined only as the labor of intelligence. Whereas labor capacity develops out of separation, labor power does not directly deal with the separation. Rather, it manages the cognitive representations that mediate its separation, wherein a new family, species, subspecies, or even a whole variety of labor capacities is assembled. Once again, linkages transpire in the internal community of the subject via representations that are simultaneously those of intelligence labor. **It is immediately apparent that the labor expended by the tools of reason or by thought in general cannot be solely understood using intelligence. Practically all the capacities of consciousness act on this subjective labor that consciousness carries out within labor capacities. That labor pertains to the production of the production of labor capacities.** At this point, it is therefore necessary to take a closer look at the concept of intelligence labor.

Feeling, thinking, perceiving, sensing, acting, remembering, imagining something, laughing, crying, and so on are all labor processes of consciousness. Thinking is one characteristic among many. It thus is a mental form of labor. Intelligence designates whether thought is carried out well or poorly. **Intelligence** evaluates a result. It is an interpretative concept, not a processual one like, for example, thinking.

All real activities left over from mental processes — laughing intelligently, keeping silent intelligently, remembering intelligently, acting intelligently ("faster than I thought") — are also intelligent insofar as they can be differentiated according to whether they are good or bad. There are additional designations that merely vary the perspectives under which a process of consciousness is seen: as **Spirit** [*Geist*], as "sensations" [*Empfindung*] (as a stronger designation for the emotional cathexis of a single perception), or as a synonym for perception (as the empiricists maintain).

The word "consciousness" itself has a heterogeneous meaning in the vernacular that is not anchored in its own labor process. (1) Conscious = the opposite of unconscious; "I am the proprietor of an inner world." (2) Conscious = I concentrate my attention on a thing. I see it consciously when I strengthen perception through precise intention. (3) I am conscious of a thing. = I explicitly recognize it. (4) "It is a matter of my consciousness" = I come to a partisan differentiation, for example, politically; this also designates the difference between "correct" and "false" consciousness. (5) Conscious = deliberate; as opposed to random, unintentional. (6) Conscious = to be penetrated by something, to come to terms with one's identity, that is, consciousness deploys not only a part of its character, but rather its entirety; I reside in my limbs and experience something, in this respect, **consciously**. Each of these relationships entails different results arising from the labor capacities.

As is the case with the designation "intelligence," interpretational concepts are: motivation, attention, personality, and disruption. In contradiction to processual concepts, they do not betray the elements out of which they are assembled; they view a result according to the measure of its success ("strong motivation, weak motivation"), and that, in turn, underlies social agreements and valuations considered to be successful. Thus, for example, a strong motivation is constituted out of forces and counterforces. How these forces come into existence — whether their production processes merely disrupt one another or respond to one another in an organized fashion — develops from the result only insofar as traces of the preceding battles among various motivations appear within it.

Personality and identity are similarly constituents that have as their object a valuation and the description of an appearance. In terms of personality, we cannot even say whether the concept describes a real result or the point of view from which we investigate it: the Latin word *persona* = a mask, something behind and through which an actor speaks. It is something that, as the bearer of individual life spans, *establishes borders*, and as a social living being, it is something *permeable*. A person is *sociated* [*vergesellschaftet*] through his or her personality.[4]

Other designations for the mental labor process include the differentiations of the ego, subconscious, and superego. These mental authorities are the interpretation of a social relation that describes the main classification of mental processes. What are described are processes, conflicts, and internal class relations that simultaneously interact with the mental representations of the external world. The laws of motion and translations transpiring within the highly organized systems of the internal community within a human being are described by this classification. Libido theory offers an elemental theory of these processes. There are phylogenetically underpinned drives whose modes of labor psychoanalysis follows throughout the individual life history of linguistically gifted social beings. Because these concepts describe production processes, it becomes apparent that consciousness proves itself to be only a narrower portion within a much richer portion of mental experience. The libidinal energies that Freud broke down into their elements were not, however, not broken down as social products. In our context, we must therefore first see them as elements within an already composite system, so that the question regarding the process of the consciousness's mental foundation is not exhausted by its ascertainment.[5]

Within this variety constituting the foundation and process of consciousness, thought is only one characteristic. Rationality constitutes a narrower portion of thought. **Theory labor**, on the other hand, is a collective application of a highly organized system in an even broader system of self-will [*Eigenwilligkeit*].[6] To this end, the intelligent labor of entire societies conducts itself, in turn, as praxis. We thus proceed conceptually with a richness of layers that were previously cloaked by the keyword "intelligence labor."

Knowledge Is Not Primary, but Thievery Is

We do not assert here that there are primary cognitive drives. On the contrary, it appears that work and knowledge—along with the phylogenetic development of the cerebrum's organization—develop as partial concepts of labor, as an inhibition of urges in primary predatory behavior. This specific drive inhibitor first enables the beginnings of collective conduct, of society, upon whose foundation human labor, as a cooperative confrontation with nature, becomes possible.

All of these labor processes form a high degree of independence among the individual characteristics that the labor concept, subtending the entire social process, comprises. Specialization and instrumentalization, to which the sensibility of theoretical and scientific brain workers is subjected, creates an arsenal of tools that—when seen from the point of view of foundational characteristics of human labor—are completely unnatural. They demand an extreme output of effort and the activation of individual abilities while other human characteristics and interests stand idly by, as it were. The high instrumentalization of individual characteristics is possible only with a simultaneously forced and crimped linkage with the libidinal substructure that both guides knowledge and navigates perception.

> The tools used by the rationalistic disciplines negate the mimetic foundation that is necessary for them to operate.[7]

This risky production method is repeatedly brought to its extreme through competition and commodity relations in science. When a scientist performs research, he must exclude from the results of his labor the fantastical reasons that motivated him; he must weaken and domesticate the reasons why he is scientifically active. If he mobilizes the foundations of his activity, he must, in turn, rein back in these rational exclusionary mechanisms and attenuate the rigidity of the grasp of his thought. Only a labile connection develops between the substructure of the drives and labor. Brain work that develops in a greenhouselike manner therefore possesses a particular production structure whose individual parts and connections are extremely weak and sensitive. This organizational structure thus seeks out collaboration with the robust organizational mechanisms within the relations of competition and commodities on account of their strong potential to forge linkages.

The material foundation of cognition in science and theory—relieved from the production process through the division of labor—lies, above all, in the libidinal-economic fact that the satisfaction of sexual interest—the motor of curiosity and the cognitive drive—is already inhibited in the earliest stages of socialization and that through a series of further developmental and socialization processes at higher levels of schooling and scientific training, that interest is continually exhorted to engage in additional sublimation efforts. In this respect, scientific and theoretical activity is the form of human labor most closely based on the **pleasure principle**. In the course of working through the scientific reality principle, which is more strongly structured than the reality principle of daily life and than that of healthy human understanding, it continuously changes its form. Its material foundation nevertheless remains the pleasure principle.

Desire is a goat. On guarding a house with goats, as well as an interpretation of goats as the *devil's creature*, see page 285. [Alexander Kluge Archive]

On Building a House

If I regard the sum total of all cognition of pure and speculative reason **as an edifice** for which we have in ourselves at least the idea, then I can say that in the Transcendental Doctrine of Elements we have made an estimate of the building materials and determined for what sort of edifice, with what height and strength, they would suffice. It turned out, of course, that although we had in mind a tower that would reach the heavens, the supply of materials sufficed only for a **dwelling** that was just roomy enough for our business on the plane of experience and high enough to survey it; however, that bold undertaking had to fail from lack of material, not to mention the confusion of languages that unavoidably divided the workers over the plan and dispersed them throughout the world, leaving each to build on his own according to his own design. Now we are concerned not so much with the materials as with the plan, and, having been warned . . . yet not being able to abstain from the erection of a sturdy dwelling, we have to aim at an edifice in relation to the supplies given to us that is at the same time suited to our needs.

By the transcendental doctrine of method, therefore, I understand the determination of the formal conditions of a complete system of pure reason. With this aim, we shall have to concern ourselves with a **discipline**, a **canon**, an **architectonic** . . . of pure reason.[8]

Alexander Kluge, pipes underneath the city, "intestines." [Alexander Kluge Archive]

175

The Relationality of Life and Labor; The Unity of Sensory Relationships

Albert Einstein was a professor of physics at the University of Prague when he was preoccupied with the interaction of mass and energy (light). The rooms of his institute had high windows from which he could look out at a park of sorts. Looking down from the window, Einstein often wondered about the groups of people he saw at specific times walking about in unusual configurations.

At one particular moment, his inner eye was occupied with something completely different: were I to move at the speed of light — so his thought experiment went — and were I to lie prone upon a wave of light that constantly moves at the speed of light, then I would lie either on the lower or higher inflection of the amplitude, but never on both. In this state, there would be no light. However, I am able to exclude this condition as nonphysical, he said, without ever having seen it with the eye.

Later, Einstein discovered that the groups walking in the park were inmates of the Prague asylum. He was flummoxed by this news, seeing that his visual impression appeared to confirm something remarkable. He had not been able to explain what was so remarkable about it. Conclusions are of no use.

A farmer thrown in jail in the twelfth century. [Alexander Kluge Archive]

Einstein and Oppenheimer in Princeton. [Alfred Eisenstaedt / Time Life Pictures / Getty Images]

André Gide. [Apic / Getty Images]

Nineteen-year-old Thomas Mann. [Keystone / Thomas-Mann-Archiv / STR]

Bismarck at twenty-one. [Philipp Petri, "Otto von Bismarck als Student," 1833. Otto-von-Bismarck Stiftung]

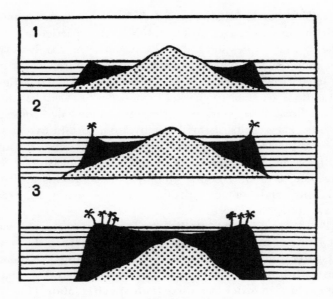

The growth of a coral reef. [Alexander Kluge Archive]

Usefulness

Intelligence labor is useful to the extent that it can be appropriated in all parts of society. The character of its use value is measured by its ability to produce a public sphere. The production of intelligence is the production of a public sphere.

Some of the traditions that operate within the intelligence class *according to the division of labor* in the realms of science, the arts, the production of news, or technical intelligence are inconsistent with their claims. For example, *technical intelligence* and *the kind of scientific intelligence directed at the domination of nature* both have at their command a density of communication and high levels of generalization in this *subject-specific exchange*. They are *particularly narrow* according to the selection of their objects, as well as their knowledge-constitutive interests and with regard to the communicability of their methods. In their specific results, however, they are virtually unprotected from being appropriated. The *intelligence that produces news* (including narrated news) works directly on its product, the public sphere. As the sole form of intelligence labor with an interest in general mediation, it is particularly interested in forms of mediation and exchange. However, this labor in particular is bound to the forms of expression and the exclusionary mechanisms typical of the representative public sphere; it is, in turn, mired in circuitousness and narrow-mindedness. What remains is **critical intelligence.** Its traditions avoid narrowness. Critique [*das Kritische*] has the tendency to break through the constrictions of knowledge-constitutive interests. The results of this labor live to a certain extent in the particular [*Besonderen*], from which it strives to combine the universal [*Allgemeine*] **realistically.** Therein lies the emphasis of critique: on account of the intercourse common to commodity exchange it barely withstands contact with all members of society. **Inadvertent narrow-mindedness arises.**[9]

All of these forms of intelligence labor have selective usefulness. None of them possess practical usefulness in the sense of foodstuffs that are useful to every human being. What each of these traditions lacks in order to become a foodstuff is what they must exclude in order to realize their specific labor. They publicize only representative excerpts of real relations.

The adjective "representative" denotes the principle of exclusionary mechanisms. These mechanisms never produce complete products of truth. Instead, they must strive to acquire the appearance (that is, a representation) of completeness at the price of their domination, on account of the fact that they live off loyalty taxes [*Loyalitätsabgaben*] paid by the dominated productive class.[10] For the benefit of this appearance, they must exclude their inherent incompleteness. This involves an additional exclusion, the consequence of which is again another set of exclusions. This process behaves similarly to the dialectic of the bourgeois public sphere as developed in our *Public Sphere and Experience* (pp. xlv–xlix and 54–95). The exclusion comports itself as idealism; it actually is situated in goodwill, in the idea that one takes great pains indefinitely. This is why the exclusion of incompleteness injures the method's core. Compared with the *material* of intelligence labor, the exclusion is performed unwillingly: the exclusionary mechanism prefers to **succeed at the costs of the nonprofessional participants in this public sphere. This embodies the tendency of all professional intellectual public spheres to exclude the majority of social producers.**

Of concern here is a knowledge-constitutive drive different from the one that social position and the proletarian life-context objectively exert in members of the proletariat. Compared with the objective necessity felt by the proletarian, the knowledge-constitutive drive of a scientist to use knowledge in order to break through the obstructions in his life-context appears downright artificial. He is, after all, also culturally produced by a deferral of real satisfaction made possible by multifaceted fictions. In a word, the proletarian needs the organization of his experience in order to *change* his living conditions. The scientist organizes his scientific experience in order to maintain his standard of living.[11]

The Weakness of Intelligence Lies in Its Motive

In contradiction to the proletarian process, which consists in the separation of the means of production and expression, professional intelligence amasses tools and methods. It appropriates a public capacity for expression.[12]

However, its knowledge-constitutive interests are insufficiently rooted in motives. It draws its knowledge-constitutive interests from the traditions of dead labor and therefore borrows from the ruling annex, that unproductive class always already provided for by the loyalty taxes paid by a society's laboring producers—rather than producing knowledge-constitutive interests anew from one's own needs or living, subjective reasons. This motivational weakness corresponds to a strength: the ability to mediate between differing social situations and class characteristics, neither of which can really sustain the intelligence professional. This happens by leaping over borders in a way possible only in thought. But this would not practically be possible if a lifetime's feelings, actions, and objective moorings were also to be transported.

While this functions for primary, nonprofessional intelligence (the kind that each social producer has according to the law that reads, "necessity is the mother of invention"), for professional intelligence labor, it is nothing less than the immobilization of the immediate impressions of necessity that is the precondition for labor.

A concentrated ability to think can hardly develop if it does not originally arise from separation processes and suffering—for example, during childhood—as a highly aggregated **unnatural productive force** for daily life and normal vitality. The initial motive arose from a profound rationale to change something oppressive. In the phase of intelligence's self-exploitation, on the other hand, this stinger increasingly recedes; the labor capacities for saving it—for preserving the motive until death—are rare and specialized. As a rule, professional intelligence labor, particularly the institutionalized kind, defends its acquired authority representing commercial interests **against further changes**. Its original motive runs out after overcoming a moment of listlessness.[13]

The Weakness that Results from the Intangibility of Intelligence Labor

Aside from natural scientists busy experimenting in laboratories and inventors, behavior in the stage of its mental rehearsal [*Probehandeln im Geist*] is a form of praxis in which the nature of a situation enclosed in objects does not contain a sufficient critique of the experiments in question.[14] Hegel's sentence—"But first of all, the one thing I shall venture to ask of you is this: that you bring with you a trust in *science, faith* in *reason....* [The] closed essence of the universe *contains no force* which could withstand the courage of cognition..." has the flip side that only with serious difficulty can the artificiality of highly composite intelligence labor establish whether it is working on something real or merely concocting something.[15] First and foremost, professional intelligence labor has relationships and relations, not individual objects. This is also the case for art. Art must therefore develop specialized and **artificial** labor capacities in order to bring into use once again materiality, simplicity, robustness, and natural relations, all of which it had previously marginalized in order to go about its labor. The extent to which it succeeds is dependent upon the use value of their products, alongside the general interchangeability of their products.

The Core Symptom of Malfunction

Propped up on such a foundation, the professional labor of knowledge lacks a **materialistic instinct**, the **unity of life, and labor contexts**. Such knowledge-constitutive activity is terrified by the proximity of **personalization**, but equally so by the distant effects of **fantasy**. It constructs **linguistic barriers**, produces a specific **exclusionary industrial public sphere**, and comes to a halt before each **obstruction** of public experience that it has not wrought itself.[16]

Cunning and Its Trade

Hegel and Engels conjoin cunning with the irony of history. For example, there is irony in the fact that the Proudhonists and Blanquists in the Paris Commune were practically forced to do exactly the opposite of what they had planned to do. Engels was endlessly delighted by this. This joy expresses something that, thanks to its cunning behavior in these relations, performs a supplemental labor in objective relations necessary for its own prediction. In other words, both factions of the Paris Commune categorically turn against Marxism, yet insofar as they are forced to act practically, they realize a part of Marxist theory. The same cunning relations, however, effected the downfall of the commune. It would have been much better had Engels been sad.

This irony has to do with the objective cunning of relations within compulsory laws. But it behaves using subjective cunning as soon as it has been stripped of its rural character and has learned nothing other than the rules of trade. The inversion of identity inflicted on the enemy recoils backward onto itself, insofar as it would not know how to perpetuate this inversion without disavowing itself and its identity. Odysseus therefore says: My name is nobody. He proceeds from the inversion, but at what a price. The archaic form of entrapment underlies cunning. In this trap, cunning entraps itself, along with the victim.

A Comparison of Intelligence Labor and Trade

According to Max Horkheimer, the destruction of the sphere of circulation also destroys the autonomy of intelligence. For him, one rationale for the formation of National Socialism and the sublation of the critical distance from reality is that a compulsory exchange society can do without a market. Cunning and maneuverability, which constitute a substantial part of intelligence labor, developed alongside trade. Thinking, feeling, and praxis were indivisible in Medea's society along the Black Sea, which subsisted on cultivating the land. *They* could not jump, play, modulate, transpose. They were bound to the particular [*Besonderen*], so they neither needed any of the intelligent forms of labor, nor could they put them to use. In the case of the Colchians, the whole human being was always linked to a piece of earth, so one could indeed be intelligent, but could not libidinally occupy any **forms of behavior in a state of mental rehearsal**. It was always real action, not trade. The Phoenicians, Odysseus, and Jason were completely different in this respect.

The principle of mental rehearsal, which jumps between situations and uses them as thought without really working them through, excludes the moment of objective production. Letters of the alphabet, speeches, discourses, and relationships are its products, which are in effect ways of safekeeping the living labor of thought and not actual products. In this respect, intelligence toils without producing a product. Viewed vis-à-vis its results, it administers an exchange. Only as such (that is, within a public sphere) is it a product. Intelligence laborers as laborers of the public sphere are thus not pure merchants. Rather, the sole similarity that their labor has with production, distribution, and consumption lies in the domain of trade. The comparison with the publisher—that midwife of the Industrial Revolution who had no intention whatsoever to trigger a revolution—is thus not absurd.

Henry Kissinger describes how the relation of intelligence labor and power develops. In principle, intelligence labor cannot be linked to bureaucracy and power at all. Its product consists of a supplemental labor, in the rendering of options, that is to say, in sorted processes in the relations of reality. Its task is said to be neither decision nor the exercise of power, and it also refrains from disrupting the process of labor.[17] However, Kissinger must (1) supply the president with options and categorize news items, and (2) educate the president in the use of intelligence labor. Because the framer of politics does not know the advantages of reflection that distinguish the intellectual, Kissinger says of his president, "his problem is that he does not know the nature of help he requires."[18]

If Kissinger wants to make the usefulness of his intellectual supplemental labor conspicuous to the president, he can do so only by taking over the bureaucracy, power, and finally (for the sake of simplicity) decision making. He says he assumed this office only for the purpose of producing the right kind of decisions, but that there was a hitch: the Pentagon comprises approximately five thousand people, the State Department approximately two thousand, a staff "that all want to do what I'm doing." He must initially immobilize this labor power by directing a plethora of queries to officials so that "they spin their wheels."[19] Only in this way can he create the **calm** that is the precondition for **his own** labor. In other words, all this laboriousness runs up against the job, something that he must subsequently eliminate in order to be able to work at all. It is nevertheless urgently necessary, because without the production of the right instructions, the tasks that intelligence labor accomplishes could not occur. These operating instructions remain incomprehensible to politicians if they do not express themselves by taking over an office, by assuming a position of power.

The Origin of Intelligence's Mode of Labor in Handwork
Intelligence does not correspond to a distinct method of production, just as intelligence laborers hardly constitute a distinct class. Rather, all previous stages of production revert to the "behavior in mental rehearsal" that demarks the labor of intelligence. Intelligence pertains to an aggregated method of production, and the laborers of intelligence (who externally appear like yet another class unto themselves) are assembled out of all the many disparate class characteristics.

Particularly apparent is the principle that intelligence labor allows itself to be only **formally subsumed** or positioned alongside the ruling social production process. In the instance of **real subsumption,** it is destroyed as a specific form of labor and reverts to simple labor. The predefined self-determination and freer relationship to material typical of simple labor was a feature of manual methods of production. But whereas the handworker always objectified his labor power into a thing, the principle of intelligence labor allowed for the experimental practice of mental activity reclaimed by the human interior to operate more extensively with the tools of **proximity and distance.** Objects, in particular, are not only things, but above all **relationships**, as well. They appear to be more abstract because we do not see them, just as I do not see the laws of nature in the behavior of things that obey them. Actually, the relations of relationships are as concrete as pieces of iron, gold, or the table that a handworker once produced. Cautiousness, a sense of materiality, and skill all return in augmented form as virtues in handling things meticulously and naturally.

We saw how in preindustrial societies, the manual method of production—with the exception of those who cooperate with the primary sector in directly cultivating the soil—toiled away on demand for the nonproductive annex, also known as the ruling class. This tradition of dependence carries over to modern intelligence, except for those who provide unsolicited labor in the gaps of primary production processes. Intelligence feeds on taxes, works on demand by the ruling class, lives off allocations, and draws particularly on an immaterial stream of revenue drawn from decentralized annexes:[20] **The idea among social producers that critique, the search for truth, news, loyalty, as opposed to mental effort and science, belong to the inventory of reality produces the foundation for the limited independence of intelligence labor.** Thus, as intelligence positions itself vis-à-vis authority, it sets in motion the social recognition of its activity previously produced by others, that is, as a power relation against other power relations. It remains trapped in an economically dependent circulation of domination.[21]

For handwork, this dependence on limited revenue streams means it must be productive in three different ways; it must produce: (1) the needed product; (2) the idea within the ruling class that precisely such a skillfully produced product is needed; that is, the **production of commissions** that would otherwise not occur in the mind of the purchaser; and (3) the **measure of exchange**; the incompetent purchaser who knows nothing of the production process (the values and costs intrinsic to materials) would indeed always order too much or too little. Thus, both checks and balances and incentives (that is, a measure of relations [*Maßverhältnisse*], a commensurability) must be supplied by handwork. A labor that orients itself only to the usefulness of the product is insufficient. A level of appropriation, which incorporates within itself the encipherment of each of the two additional processes, must remain in the product. At that point, the product is **not** primarily about **usefulness**, but rather about the **principle of additional laboriousness.** The presentation of skill, a particular kind of craftsmanship, originality, the inability of others to produce it—that is to say, its irreplaceability—arise, as well, a wealth of **markers** identifying handicraft production, and are all bound to **professional honor**, as well as to the checks and balances typical of guilds.[22]

For the same reasons, professional intelligence labor cannot occur merely in the form of a simple labor of the head. If so, it would be considered trivial. Its discrete value, which in the last instance undermines the characteristic of use value (as opposed to an ordinary commodity that simply carries inside itself use and exchange as differentiated values), consumes a real portion of effort. And this

marking labor really [*reell*] does subsume intelligence labor, as if it were itself a capitalist, something that a capitalist fails at entirely. This defines occupational intelligence labor principally as a composite form of labor and excludes it from simple labor. Although every form of intelligence labor, even that multiplied by a particular originality or genius, has its life in simple intelligence labor. This would be noticeable by analyzing the individual stages in the labor process.

Exclusionary mechanisms make **one** step, in which usefulness among all social producers becomes separate from usefulness within the circle of intelligence laborers. Another step is summed up in the **social relation** of intelligence labor based on the division of labor. If one searches for intelligence labor outside the circle of intelligence occupations, it can be found again in **every** producer as a simple **and** composite form of labor. Additionally, it is located in all aggregations of dead labor as the intelligent head in which each commodity, each machine, each tool, money, buildings, houses, or walls store their value. Value is the objective representation of relationships among intelligent humans. Stored value = stored intelligence. This intelligence labor contained in all raw materials of society is the practical, perceptible critique of specialized labor.

"Everyone's intelligence is the practical critique of professional intelligence." [Lewis Wickes Hine, Library of Congress]

Intelligence Labor and Industrialization

The industrialization of society and intelligence labor, which both retain the status of handwork and nowhere attempt to rise to the level that is occupied by large machinery and cooperation, *coexist* with great tanacity.

The incapacity of intelligence labor to industrialize itself is an impression that arises if one misconcieves the process of industrialization anachronistically, as if industry developed directly out of handwork, as progress. In this manner, handwork would not have integrated itself into modernity, nor would intelligence labor have industralized itself along such a direct path. Rather, it would just have been annihilated. The historical process ran parallel to manual production. We wish to investigate here how, through mimicry of this process — under real relations there are putatively third ways — a resolution of the mere juxtaposition of intelligence labor and industry could be imaginable. Indeed, their mere juxtaposition accounts, at its core, for the dependence of intelligence, its inability to unify itself in a useful manner with the intelligence of all producers into an intelligent public sphere.

> The word "intelligence" denotes the **position of "those with insight."** But those with knowledge — collectors, sorters, messengers, experimenters, inventors, bibliophiles, entertainers, architects, designers — engage in a wealth of activities that the word "intelligence" does not convey. The difference in the **use value for all** expresses itself in the form of aphasia, as is generally the case with labor.

"The beginning of industrialization" is a different way to designate the incursion of early capital into the **primary production sector**. In Central Europe, this sector was composed of farms. On these farms, land was cultivated, but shoes and clothing were also manufactured. Individual merchants — the system of so-called cottage industries [*Verlagswesen*] — began aquiring the weaving and production of cloth that previously occured as a form of self-substitence in the primary production sector. It then proved to be easier to subsume the parceled-out activity under a unifying command. At its core, however, this was centralized collection for the purpose

of trading. Take, for example, the Brothers Grimm. They collected
fairy tales in a similar manner. It is a simple form of labor to interview people (that is, to gather the self-sustaining praxis of intelligence and experience from around the world). And it is imaginable
that encyclopedias of extrodinary relevance could be to constructed
from this. Collectively, websites such as Wikipedia, Wikileaks, the
Stanford Encyclopedia of Philosophy, and the Internet in general
have shown how this happens in praxis. Here, the labor of the so-
called cottage industry repeats itself, but according to a completely
different mode of action. Long ago, handwork and guilds were
overtaken by mass production, up to the point where early entre-
preneuers of the cottage industry were themselves overtaken by
factories. Likewise, the EXPANDED PARTICIPATION produced by
the Internet takes place today independently from the instutional
knowledge of universities, schools, opera houses, and museums.
But at the same time, it takes up their labor and uses it as a point of
orientation. The new public spheres of the Internet are not part of
a process of industurialization, but rather part of a process of innovative participation, that is to say, a postindustrial process whose
progression is unknown to industry.

It seems prudent to search for the exploitation of intelligence
labor in the classical process of industrialization. We will see that
such an exploitation cannot not really succeed. By taking intelligence labor under its command, industry does a number of things:
(1) human producers manufacture more with intelligence than they
previously needed for their own self-sufficiency; (2) a new market
develops that did not previously exist, a market in the primary sector of experience that is not bound to the professional sector; (3)
intellectual labor capacities are separated from their original self-
sufficiency. This seperation contains a provocation; no knowledge
can suffice, not even the earlier condition of self-suficiency. In other
words, the golden age of intelligence is reproduced on an expanded
level. And (4) a **public private property** develops, a particular form
of anticapital that generates a surplus value that cannot be appropriated by the purchaser. The intelligent product does not become dead
labor, but rather liquifies into living labor.

Since a wage is directly identical with pleasure—I enjoy the intelligence of others as my own, and they delight in the products of our
collective mind—a **social relation**, which exchanges not products,

but relations of relationships, develops instead of wage labor. This is similar to love relationships.

> In such an industrialized state — the Latin word *industria* literally means "understood as the proliferation of industriousness, of **effort**" — something programmatic appears to have become praxis. In this instance, the following slogan is within earshot: "The *head* of this emancipation is *philosophy*, its *heart* is the *proletariat*. Philosophy cannot be made a reality without the abolition [*Aufhebung*] of the proletariat, the proletariat cannot be abolished without philosophy being made reality."[23]

The Brain as a Social Organ

Sorting perceptions, deciding whether to attack or flee, and searching for sustenance hardly explain the striking enlargement of the human brain vis-à-vis those of our most closely related primate relatives. In fact, evolutionary biologists agree that the formation of the human brain and its intelligence result from the complex necessities of living in close groups, that is, in societies. Intelligence is above of all a function of stress reduction. That a human becomes a mirror for another requires powers of observation to the fourth degree, the consideration of visible and invisible relationships that are able to make out the difference between homicide and cooperation.

Evolutionary biologists have observed that a clan of chimpanzees — ever ready for self-defense and specialized for collective hunting — lessens the stress triggered by the closeness of being together through reciprocal personal hygiene: the ritualized cultivation of both corporeal contact and sufficient distance. This caring for another in order to preempt strife is commensurate with what Stockholm zoologist Olof Leimar claims humans did in premodern times, when they produced commonality through collective narration or the consumption of drugs (alcohol, mushrooms).[24] Today, *entertainment in the form of the media industry* obviously fulfills this function. According to the Berlin biologist Peter Hammerstein, the development of social communication has made the growth of the brain and networked intelligence into a social-evolutionary advantage: the anticipation of the other.[25] This characterizes the path of

192

human beings as a species, a path composed of a never-ending chain of echoes leading up to the formation of general laws.

The Fish in Us
In this context, researchers attribute the complex phenomena of our present to robust elemental rules that possess an astoundingly long prehistory. This is why swarm intelligence—an obviously old evolutionary achievement evident in flocks of birds, in schools of fish, in the flight of herds, but also in congregations of human beings—can be reconstructed in computer games using three simple rules:

(1) move forward;
(2) keep a necessary distance from your neighbor, so-called elbowroom; and
(3) remain within society.

Such ancient formations (50 or 500 million years old) clearly become part of the potential of intelligence, which has at its disposal a reservoir of characteristics still unused well into our present.

The Pharaohs' Storehouses of Intelligence:
The Transformation of Knowledge and Education
We humans easily overlook the fact that writing and schools are recent social inventions. A long period dominated primarily by oral communication preceded them. It was accompanied by the invention of religions and magic. Protection was needed against the dangerous "excesses of speech." With the traditions of writing and education, momentum toward modernity emerged. This development progressed in fits and spurts and experienced long desertlike stretches, too. With the fall of the Roman Empire, the ancient form of handing down knowledge was momentarily forsaken in parts of Europe and was resumed again only with the reception of antiquity during the Renaissance. In the Byzantine Empire, in which abrupt interruptions did not occur, a variant of intelligence production developed. It coexisted with an intelligence that was likewise handed down, but not by books or schools. The intelligence produced in Europe's illiterate zones formed an effective undercurrent to the academicism still in effect today. It governs the rules of wit and trustworthy speech. If, in fact, today's forms of participation and methods of dissemination—and not only just those shaped by

the Internet—are indeed transforming themselves, one must turn an eye to the ways in which these different labors of intelligence are hoarded and transcribed. How do societies obtain provisions of intelligence in good years that can endure for future bad years? Are the balance sheets of this intelligence a concern of pharaohs, or do the autonomous attractors of knowledge prevail in the way Adam Smith described the "wealth of nations," not as a hierarchical process of concentration, but rather as a flexible process of dispersed interests?

The Balance Economy versus the Excess of Information

A group listening to a Homeric singer such as Odysseus makes use of other senses (the oral tradition) than the ones used by monks skilled in writing at the court of Charles the Great. The curious young men in Tuscany to whom the carriers of knowledge from antiquity (that is, the Byzantine scholars) fled and who were driven from their city by the Turks in 1453, developed a new style of intelligence. Young scholars after the catastrophe of 1918 and contemporary bloggers are again completely different from one another.

With Gutenberg, the inventor of the printing press, the mass production of printed matter and the era of writing were superimposed on oral transmission. Alongside the emergence of printing, a tradition of memorizing—a mnemonic culture of quotations—persisted.

More striking today is the radical superimposition of learning and mnemonic cultures fueled by the Internet. The carrier of intelligence splits itself into a traditional individual and a joint partner involved in the "communities" of the Web, a communication network consisting of a virtually countless number of humans.

Following Niklas Luhmann, Michel Serres and Dirk Baecker have laid out in greater detail some of the processes that arise with such shifts in emphasis in the communication of knowledge. When the front paws of our ancestors were no longer needed for hunting due to the evolutionary move to upright walking, according to Serres, hands became free for tender touch and for labor.[26] When the snout was no longer necessary for sniffing, snapping, and hunting, it stood poised for speaking. Extending the metaphor further, he adds that the digital and virtual world of today has unburdened individuals as personal carriers of knowledge and has therefore facilitated their becoming navigators of their own knowledge, much like the helmsmen among Portuguese and Spanish mariners, the so-called pilots who invented nautical charts. Frank Schirrmacher has described this thoroughly ambivalent process as the "migration of thought out of the brain."[27] According to Serres, rarely would one human organ that lost its previous function persist without gaining a new one. The question then arises as to what occupies these newly freed areas today. Another question would be: Are there elements of handed-down thought that remain indispensible in every instance of orientation? The stratification of intelligence activities must be imagined according to the depths of time in much the same way that Freud described it as discussed in Commentary 2 in Chapter 3.

An observable partial aspect in the mutation of the concept of intelligence comes from the **resistance** against the excess of sub-stance that a new medium imposes on it. A *Homo sapiens* is always also a *Homo compensator* (equilibrator).

In this respect, the invention of magic, which mitigated the power of speech and allowed for a counterpower to emerge beyond the field of vision and everyday discourse, reacted to the shock that the achievements of speech triggered. (Our excursus here is based on the ideas of Dirk Baecker).[28] A reserve in the parallel world guar-antees balance: I do not need to hear and understand everything in order to be able to preserve my trust.

Writing functions just as radically. From now on, whatever once was merely said can be recorded and (impersonally) proven for pos-terity's sake. The reaction to this is the explosive development of fiction in theater and novels. Even though a primary reality codifies all fundamental things, it is in the realm of a second reality where freedom is reclaimed. It preserves what is approximate and variable at a moment's notice: in the "story" [*Erzählung*]. Ever since juridi-cal processes entailed parallel public events and ended in a verdict, an extremely rich arsenal of questions and emotions have remained unsettled: art.

Even more elementary is the reaction of humans to the tsu-nami of printed texts that Gutenberg's invention unleashed onto the world. We forget today that the lion's share of printed material contains calls for religious or civil war. And how much fictional and informative junk was printed! The defensive reaction to this was embodied in the emergence of *critique*. It distinguishes what I need not know from that what I should know. It is like the drainage

system in swampland, the new construction of a house with a surrounding fence, the constitution of a particular intelligence against
the collective stream of printed materials, the assertion that *one owns
an understanding of the world*. Those are the elements of the indivisible individual. They later formed the indivisible French Republic, out of which the Revolution emerged. And prior to that, the
resistance against the excess of printed material was documented
in the work of Immanuel Kant. His three great *Critiques* can also
be understood as providing their readers the chance to deselect
what we humans need not know. We describe the context insufficiently when we consider only the positive and negative instances of
printed media. **Counterproduction** that evolves from humans must
also be considered.

No one foresaw the powerful implementation of the Internet,
even though it conforms fairly accurately to the radio theories developed by Hans Magnus Enzensberger and Bertolt Brecht.[29] Both
authors describe conceptions of an apparatus held to be utopian in
their respective times. The core for both lies in the fact that every
receiver can become a sender. The effect of today's worldwide network transcends radio's reciprocating relationship, which has always
remained dualistic. In our context, we concentrate on the individual
aspect of the defensive reflex that participants obviously develop
spontaneously and collectively. Their need for balance contains a
positive aspect. Initially, it pertains to the need to deselect information from the existing surplus, to abate what Jürgen Habermas calls
the NEW OBSCURITY.[30]

At first, classical media such as newspapers, as well as radio
and television programs, were weakened by the new digital networks. Simultaneously, the need for a stronger means of selectivity
emerged. The question "What actually interests me in general?"
cut paths through the information overload. This was not "channel
surfing," as is the case with TV programming (that is, the search for
something better), but an activation of a sense of orientation: I want
to see less in favor of something more trustworthy. All offerings on
Facebook (a social network), Twitter, the principle of "communities"
themselves, gardens of knowledge such as Stanford's Encyclopedia
of Philosophy, and collection sites such as Wikipedia all have as
their common denominator the need to perform a supplemental
labor focused on **reduction**. A television channel corresponds to a

window, and the Internet, in contrast, more readily corresponds to a table or a serviceable machine. The difference lies in the position of the user; I lean back for TV, whereas I lean forward for the computer. For the present question regarding the restructuring of intelligence activity and the concomitant emergent need for balance, the concern is not to explicate the Internet's mode of operation, but rather to differentiate the transmissions of knowledge.

We speak metaphorically of Henry the Navigator,[31] Columbus, and their pilots as intelligence laborers. Using GPS, I can measure every position on the globe to the exact meter. The traveling land surveyor therefore has been rendered expendable. Measuring stars and beacons—the traditional means of orientation—has become superfluous for piloting ships. We transcribe this metaphor onto orientation as it applies to the practical experience of life, onto navigating the ship of life. In this case, new questions prevail: *In which direction should I head? Which goal do I seek?* In these instances, GPS trackers cannot furnish any useful information. On the subjective side of humans, it all comes down to the transmitted means of orientation.

And at this point, the old monuments of the public sphere—the *New York Times*, the *Washington Post*, *Der Spiegel*, the *Guardian*, *Der Freitag*, the *Frankfurter Allgemeine Zeitung*, *Süddeutsche Zeitung*, *Neue Zürcher Zeitung*, *Le Monde*—come back into view. They bind trust to thoroughness, making it possible at the same time to deselect from great masses of exess information. Our view widens even further when we examine academia, for example, instead of journalism: the Ivy League universities on the East Coast of the United States, the Grandes Écoles in France, the London School of Economics, the British Royal Society, the Institutes of the Max Planck Society, the Wissenshaftskolleg in Berlin, Germany. In these cases, the markers of the classic public sphere work their way into the much broader and junglelike public sphere of the Internet. They are not carried by impulses or intentions of the Internet. Instead, they owe their new authority to the resistance unleashed by it.

Intelligence that Seeks the Universal in the Fullness of Particularities

The classicists sought out the universal [*Allgemeine*]. That was the case in the political sciences, the natural sciences, mathematics, and economics. They searched for universal laws and rules. Out of respect for phenomena, a minority operated according to the counterprinciple. This was the case in medicine, law, the individualizing historical sciences, as well as philology. The theoretical work of southern German neo-Kantianism (Emil Lask, Heinrich Rickert, Wilhelm Windelband) and Max Weber's *modus operandi* positioned them against the search for laws and concepts as Kant and Hegel had once carried it out. (With Hegel, we see his regard for the particular [*das Besondere*], but it never grasps the whole; against this, Adorno laid down the maxim "The whole is the false.")[32] The Frankfurt School's preference for the particular, a similarly oriented tendency, had different roots: Critical Theory imagines the universal as an elementry undercurrent *beneath* the particular (similar to the labor of partisans) or *immanently* in the midst of the particular. Accordingly, a concept would always be accompanied by a plentitude of particularities that are neither encompassed by it nor capable of transcending it. This is especially commensurate with Walter Benjamin's mode of observation.

Intelligence must proceed according to a division of labor. Otherwise, it does not satisfy its claim to recount complex relations. On the other hand, the roles that navigation and strategy play in the doling out of intelligence labor are necessary: What matters to us? What should a trustworthy science investigate? Neither managers of science nor specialists, not to mention philosophers, can carry out this role under contemporary conditions. In this respect, Heraclitus, Socrates, Heidegger, or Kant would appear like oddballs at a convention of particle physicists. Equally absurd would be interventions on the part of chiefs of secret service agencies or lobbyists from think tanks who claim to have the wellbeing of the entire nation in mind.

Intelligence labor in the present has a distinct need for balance, which Immanuel Kant defined in the following metric:

> Thoughts without content are empty,
> intuitions without concepts are blind.[33]

The governance of the masses of aggregated perceptions that accompany modern societies can be constrained by concepts only to a practical degree. But as is the case with thinking in general, for this navigational function, concepts require the apperception of the other and, above all, of what is excluded. They do not confront the other authoritatively, but rather with the humility of reality. The situation is similar to the lowering of the ego barrier, itself a precondition for successful communication. Only in this way can concepts command the necessary authority. The reason why intelligence labor cannot be understood instrumentally—why, as the labor of navigation and orientation, it is indispensible for the life of socities—becomes clear if one considers Theodor W. Adorno's proposal for a modification of Kant's categorical imperative. For Kant, this imperative reads: "*act only in accordance with that maxim through which you can at the same time will that it become a **universal law**.*"[34] As a representative of Critical Theory whose thinking was confronted by fascism, Adorno commanded: "arrange [your] thoughts and actions so that Auschwitz will not repeat itself."[35] This demand is the motive behind our entire book.

The Principle of "Cowardice in Thought"

Kant describes the faculty of reason as a force of nature. Nature wishes to put to use, what it developed, Kant says. What appears for Kant as the labor of intellectual powers returns in Marx as the thought process of real relations. In reality, it is labor that thinks. Jürgen Habermas addresses this in *Knowledge and Human Interests* in the context of Nietzsche's vehemently critical countermovement.[36]

It is clear that the differences between taxonomies do not actually allow for any such contextualization. Marx does not mention Kant—he reads him (and we know little of his readings) according to the treatment that Hegel's system gives him. It is also questionable to impute a reception of both Hegel and Marx to Nietzsche. Taking this into consideration, relationships nevertheless arise out of all the many differences.

According to its form, Nietzsche's polemic is entirely antidialectical and "sets out to expose all the mystifications that find a final refuge in the dialectic." According to him, three leading ideas determine the dialectic: (1) the power of the negative "as a *theoretical principle*"; (2) the value of "suffering and sadness," "the valorisation of the 'sad passions,' *as a practical principle* manifested in splitting and tearing apart"; and (3) "the idea of positivity *as a theoretical and practical product of negation*." "It is no exaggeration to say that the whole of Nietzsche's philosophy, in its polemic sense, is the attack on these three ideas."[37]

It would be an exaggeration to say that we do not adhere to the dialectical principle. In this principle, it is the bondsman, for example, who produces an image of his lord according to the image of his own misery. In other words, the lord, who previously produced the bondsman, is no lord. He only speculated "à la baisse." This dialectic is too exclusive for us. On account of practical principles, the inflection of every perception by the "sad passions," and the recognition of the reality principle, which guarantees misery when rebellion fixes its attention on it, the perception of real misery can account only for the rigid, hopeless gaze. Critical praxis establishes itself in misery and does it justice; this is not the task of critique: *critique behaves inequitably toward misery.*

If positivity—as a theoretical and practical product—is the extended organ of primitive expropriation (that is, negation), then a nudge—via a third party—can lead the way out of the original negation. (This is never on account of the inertia of relationality itself.) It is never the negation of the negation, but rather an entirely different position that can suddenly change into emancipatory positivity. To this end, we call on an idea from Nietzsche that concerns fortune: that of throwing dice. For more on this, see, for example, Deleuze.[38] Laboriousness—the **need on the part of particular achievements** that adhere to thought to mark themselves—sees no laboring capacity in what is variously called in English "chance," "good luck," or "fortune" [*Glück*]. Chance is a straightforward matter of finding. No one is ever paid for good luck. Fortune is not identified in history enough because it is considered unreliable. It does not bear the sign of an unrelenting effort. Only a diligent person can attain it. From an evolutionary standpoint, what has brought about changes in characteristics, yielding transformations, anticipation, and continuity are the probabilities of real life, and not the appearance of any work ethic. As for the subject, a reserve long since prepared for in the mental faculty of his or her attention stands ready to respond to chance and the nudge of fortune. The category of fortune and that of courage do not allow themselves to be separated from one another. The core of this assertion is to be found where a person **dares** to make separations. Human beings have in what they separate what they can ideally reassemble.

Nietzsche's polemic does not undercut the dialectical principle, even when it acts absolutely antidialectically in its form. Instead, it provides a helping hand, much as the substructure of the central nervous system responds to plus-minus relations by fabricating alliances at the breaks between the tiny power plant within one cell and another residing within an opposing cell. But this also transpires with third cells until associations with thousands of other cells are created.

Realism, a central product in the ideal of intelligence labor, begins not with the production of knowledge, but with the production of relations of trust. They are what produce the relationality that constitutes the sole objective and effective corrective within the labor of knowledge. However, self-confidence — the foundation for relations of trust — is produced from a third set of characteristics. It can arise only from the power of the negative, the "sad passions," and from the positivity that results from it (on account of the ruling reality principle) in the form of ideology. Contrary to assumptions, the object of the theory labor is therefore initially relations of trust, and not the immediate production of knowledge itself.

"Sense perception is the basis of all science"
This sentence from Karl Marx's *Economic and Philosophical Manuscripts of 1844* ("The Paris Manuscripts") orients itself polemically against the spiritual heavens of Romanticism, but also against the reign of classical philosophy since 1800.[39] Vis-à-vis a philosopher such as David Hume, polemics would be unnecessary.

There are the five senses that Marx designates as the product of world history. Additional social senses exist, upon which twenty-four or more forms of sensuousness have established themselves.

The eyes, for example, have a specific intelligence: the perception of dangers out of the corner of one's eye or the differentiation of nothingness. It is possible to shut one's eyes. They say that Homer's blindness might have imbued him with a special poetic sense. Iconoclasts (image wreckers) claim that images are disruptive to the understanding of the world. An entire rhizome of human intelligence is joined together by the eyes. We can differentiate up to sixteen images in a second; thereafter, we transmit "film."

The ear is capable of perceiving up to 360 different tones per second. It passes judgment on trustworthy pitches. It is remarkable that the organ for hearing is simultaneously the organ for balance. The ear cannot close itself off. In medieval illustrations, the Holy Spirit communicates through a dove into the ear of a monk, who then writes down the message. Obviously, an intelligence different from that of the eyes assembles itself when listening is the matter at hand.

These different roots of intelligence can be observed when we characterize their polar opposite: **the sensuousness of having**. It is a social sense that is of great importance for the production of identity, self-consciousness, and status. The sensuousness of having that prevailed in ancient times in the form of King Croesus's arrogance appeared as a characteristic presented by the "new human being," the bourgeois character after 1600. In the twentieth century, Max Weber analyzed the transformation of medieval faith declared through external rituals into the internalized knowledge typical of the Protestant world. Predictability, credit ratings, a sense for annual balance sheets, motivation in all seasons, the concept of duty as a form of motivation independent from concrete situations, and with them an abundance of echoes and derivatives of natural intelligence were created. All of this belongs to the fundamentals out of which the sensuousness of having first developed. The senses that the CEO of Lehman Brothers made use of in the last ten minutes on that catastrophic Sunday before the stock market in Tokyo opened were at that moment the very same ones operating in any other human being's organs in our present time. This goes especially for those senses of *having* and *suddenly not having*.

More concrete than the sensuousness of having is the **intelligence of the diaphragm**. The muscle called the diaphragm, dividing the body through its midriff into an underworld (the sexual organs, the intestines) and the higher bodily regions (the heart, breathing, thinking) has its prehistory in upright walking. This established the bisecting of the body and thus the diaphragm as the seat of (uncontrollable) laughter. Together with the sole of the foot (the seat of reactions against unexpected stimulation), this sensuousness is active much like a partisan is. If the diaphragm is upset—this was already the case with Olympic gods—neither prohibition nor authority can help. Intelligence based upon it is disseminated by the stories of Rabelais, Till Eulenspiegel, and Mother Goose and in the British pun, in the world of Chaplin, and in comics.

We limit our presentation to these few examples. They evince the autonomy of the substructure of the human labor capacities focused on intelligence. That they form hierarchies and catacombs independent of one another makes them complex and is the reason for their undomesticability.

It is often asked whether the Internet in a future phase of its evolution could develop consciousness. A related question is whether evolution, whose laws allow for scant modifications in the complexity of human beings, could operate to the benefit of artificial intelligence. If one compares the substructures and potentialities of natural intelligence with those of artificial intelligence, including its further development, the rationale for self-consciousness lies, if anything, on the side of natural intelligence. We carry around with us a formidable mass of "computational times" in our cells.

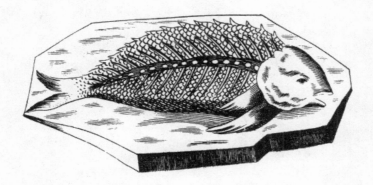

"The Fish of Fortune in Us." [Alexander Kluge Archive]

COMMENTARY 4: FIVE STORIES ABOUT INTELLIGENCE[40]

An Unintentional Stroke of Good Fortune: A Story of Displacement

While flying his plane over Far Eastern territories, a young fighter pilot of the United States Air Force had an object in his sights that he believed to be a bunker. Those who sent him here suspected that a terrorist gang had set up its base in the vicinity when, in fact, it was merely a farm where, at that very moment, a wedding reception was taking place. Once the fighter plane locked onto the target, the intelligent weapons it had at its disposal could have destroyed the area in a matter of seconds. According to the report subsequently compiled by the auditor and university lecturer E. S. Davidson-Miller, who investigated the incident from his home base in North Dakota, the pilot experienced a convulsive evacuation of his bowels at the very moment he was to fire his weapons. This irritated the young man ("he was filled with shame") and led him to yank at the controls of his fighter. The missiles landed in muddy fields where no one was injured.

What, the auditor was asked, was the point of conveying such a repugnant story in a seminar at Stanford University, where he held the chair for CAUSAL ECONOMICS.

— What is it that you want to say with this story, Professor, given that it relates to an incident demonstrating a relative absence of successful communication?
— You will have observed that the story contains all the ingredients pertaining, in one way or another, to a person living in modern society.
— What do you mean by "in one way or another"?
— The pilot was "filled with shame," that is, he had a conscience. He was qualified to aim a tool of war at a target, and to that extent he was "rational." Indeed, one could say that he was in competition with the intelligence and energy of the intelligent weapons built into his aircraft. He possessed both a strength of will and obedience, and thus the ability to commit himself.
— With everything rather jumbled up?
— Thanks to the intestinal colic.
— Inside his hermetically sealed flight suit?
— Yes, that was embarrassing for him. He was in control of everything else. Something had come undone.

— And that was enough to avoid a huge disaster?

— Yes, it would have been a disaster if he had aimed at the original target.

— It would have been an incident with international repercussions?

— If it had come to light that he had liquidated a wedding reception, that would certainly have aroused considerable international attention.

— It was to be expected that it would come to light. Troops reached the spot the following day.

— He could count himself fortunate.

— A bodily malfunction. Do we know what caused it?

— You mean whether he had eaten something not quite right the night before?

— Or whether he was stressed? Was he afraid?

— No one has a clue.

— Why did he report the embarrassing incident in the first place?

— He had to. There's no way you can clean the flight suit yourself.

— Was the pilot punished for his mistake?

— Not directly. He was deemed not fit for flying jets and transferred to different duties.

— Why "unfit"? The wedding reception had been spared, after all.

— The weapons had been misused. An uncontrollable bowel movement is one of the many factors deemed egregious enough to declare a pilot unfit for further military action.

In the seminar, Davidson-Miller wanted to provide an example of "an unintentional stroke of good fortune." It provides a chance when all fortune has run out.

Unintentional Revolution

Scholar of French literature and author of the *Proust–ABC*, Dr. Ulrike Sprenger believes it strange that although the revolutionary Paris Commune of 1871 left no works to posterity—only the wall against which the Communards were executed by the counterrevolution survives as proof of its impact—it still produced offspring that changed the world. This was very different from the way the Communards intended it. These months of the revolution saw, for example, the birth of Marcel Proust, who revolutionized the EXPRESSIVENESS OF BOOKS:

— That wasn't one of the aims of the revolutionaries?

— Certainly not.

— Proust himself wasn't interested in revolution?

— Neither the political nor the social kind.

— Could one describe him as the opposite of a revolutionary?

— Certainly. He was interested in the erotic side of social distinctions. He would have never considered tearing down the social distinctions that separate people.

— But he does that all the time in his descriptions.

— Yes, he does exactly that.

— And he is, as you put it in *Proust–ABC*, the one who predicted the great processes of the twentieth century.

— Of course.

— Then he is a child of fortune. A revolutionary achievement?

— And without the intentions of the revolutionaries.

In Praise of Crudeness

On the instructions of his rulers, Johann Friedrich and Duke Ernst August, the well-known intelligence worker G. W. Leibniz was commissioned for a fee of 1,200 thalers to propose inventions for improving the profitability of the mining industry in the Upper Harz. The details were left up to his own discretion.

Having actually traveled to the workplace, there were complicated pumps and conveyors operated by horses and water power to be inspected; these pumped the water out of the mine shafts and active seams onto a hill in the Harz, while at the same time a hydraulic mechanism brought the mined ore to the surface. In summer and during hard winters, the mines suffered from drought. The silver mines stood idle. The miners had no jobs, and their families were starving.

The experimenter climbed down from his carriage and examined the arrangement of reservoirs. Chief Mining Officer von Hahn mistrusted the learned gentleman, who suggested trying windmills, namely, post mills from Holland. However, the winds from the Harz mountains are not consistent, like the westerlies from the North Sea. They would smash into the proposed windmills and instead of propelling them would merely lead to their destruction. The chief mining officer remained skeptical. He thought the learned gentleman was something of a busybody and sightseer.

The important thing, Leibniz said, is to channel the water back up to the reservoirs once it has done its work driving the conveyors and wheels. He compared the local terrain, which clearly consisted of mountain ridges and a valley, with the circulation within the human body, which pushes its liquids upward to just below the skull and then lets them flow down again like a cascade. The mining officer did not need a description of the terrain, but the learned gentleman kept talking about the chest, shoulders, and neck of the water flow. What kind of energy do you have at your disposal, he asked? Nothing other than the wind and some equipment for making fire, the chief mining officer retorted. For that, you would have to develop a method of circulation to transport the coal to the top of the hill. That would consume as much energy as it would produce. Although wood is readily available up there, it would burn too quickly, Leibniz replied. The wind is all we've got. He imagined huge windmill sails on every mountain ridge. By this time he was hungry, and departed.

The chief mining officer's suspicions were fed by those of the miners themselves, with whom he was well acquainted. They sabotaged the learned gentlemen's experiments when these subsequently arrived in written form from the provincial capital. It is difficult to establish organic reason in these mountainous regions. There was also no immediate success to show for it, because the large sails started to flap convulsively in the gusty winds of the Harz and were quickly torn to shreds. Later, in line with new plans from the capital, small, crude mills were built: this time the water really did flow up to the reservoirs, conveyed by paddles, but once there, it was ignored by the miners. What was needed was the construction of an additional circulation system to redirect the energy of their entrenched ways of thinking, and the learned gentlemen in Hanover did indeed come up with a model to this end: it envisaged sending representatives from the capital, students who would spend a few autumn months practicing the art of persuasion on those working on the reservoirs. However, for his part, the learned gentleman was not able to bridge the difference between the two localities. He would have had to return to the scene and hustle the students uphill to form a sort of intellectual reservoir, thereby encouraging them, in turn, to accustom the locals to more elevated ways of thinking, so that a stream of innovations and actions would then flood downhill and drive a human machine below. The mills in the Upper Harz, even when they made a profit, thus remained mere ruins destined to become antiquities.

Recently, Prof. K. H. Manegold of Hanover had this "device for horizontal and vertical windmills in the Upper Harz" redrawn by the Hamburg civil engineer J. Gottschalk, based on the learned gentleman's sketch. The modeler J. Stromeyer made scale models true to the original. The efficiency of one of the Leibniz windmills with a vertical axis was then tested in a wind tunnel. The experiments revealed "a very crude machine that allows for a marginal utilization of available energy." This was reported back to the German Research Foundation in Bad Godesberg, which had financed the project. However, a member of the staff at the foundation's headquarters in Bad Godesberg was a Leibniz fan and at his own cost had the model transported back from the wind tunnel and then sent to Clausthal-Zellerfeld in a moving van. He had the robust device set up between two ridges of the Harz Mountains in a cleft that formed a kind of natural wind tunnel. Here, it being winter, the wind raged from the GDR to drive the sails, which in turn were able to produce sufficient energy to power forty-six stepped conveyors of equally crude construction when six of the crude mills were lined up. They could have been able to convey a considerable quantity of water from the estimated depth of the shafts in the year 1680 right up to the former reservoirs, all still visible in the form of shallow depressions in the ground.

According to the Leibniz fan, who spent 2,680 German marks for the undertaking, his hero was a man capable of providing necessary and tangible insights by taking A LONG-DISTANCE VIEW FROM THE CAPITAL, where he felt more at home than in the Harz Mountains. "In the wind tunnel, the model may appear too artificial. It is a work of art after all, yet it does obey the natural rules of the place for which it was intended. I admire the CRUDENESS OF THIS WINDMILL. Just look, on sheet 4 of the documents you find delicate, elegant, Dutch windmills. It was these that he wanted to copy. Here, on sheet 16, you find the attempt to enlarge them proportionately. These models were destroyed by the mountain winds of 1683, and here, on sheets 21, 22, and 23, you have the route by which he arrived at the robust, impoverished construction that suited the physical characteristics of the environment. He developed that without visiting the spot for a second time. That's what I call a long-distance view."

The Seven Spirits of Knowledge
Socrates, the legendary Athenian, asserted that in every serious discussion between two people there is a demon at work. This is not the case when one

talks to oneself or when groups discuss with one another. Contrary to all rational principles, the truth actually comes to light thanks to this demon. Even if
both interlocutors tell tall tales, the truth will become known in the difference
between them. For this reason, it is best if two liars enter into a discussion,
since neither has any intention of asserting the truth, and as a result, both
will avoid erecting any discursive barriers blocking the path to that truth. The
first thing to give itself away is what was not mendacious in the first place.

Socrates believed insight to be a special form of valor. It does not reside
in reason, but rather in the capacity to differentiate, in feeling, a realm
that encompasses sincerity, familiarity with oneself, and curiosity about the
peculiarities of other people. These four characteristics (sincerity, familiarity, curiosity, the capacity to differentiate) are like bowls or vessels in which
the demon chops up every statement, every piece of factual information,
before eating and expelling them again. In other words, he gives them back to
us in a purified form, otherwise known as truth (which at any moment we can
deny and replace with something new). As demonic excrement? But with a
great potential for change. You can change it from its present state into something much more interesting. Unlike Aristotle, Socrates says nowhere what
truth might in fact be. He says only what the material is from which — fingers
crossed — a morsel of truth might emerge.

The martial definition of valor, on the other hand, is narrow-minded. It
has more to do with the distinction between "doing something or not doing
it," between "what is to be feared and what is to be loved." This man would
rather have died than recant his claims, in particular regarding the beneficial
labor undertaken by the demon.

Eccentric Frenchman René Descartes, wrongly referring to Montaigne,
suggested abandoning knowledge to the next-best sensation. One should not
think things over, but rather think things anew. The peculiarity of each and
every thought delights the thinker like a footprint in fresh snow: this footprint
is mine. Knowledge is a consequence of this special feeling. Thinking, he
says, is like finding.

A commander of a parachute regiment who served in Dien Bien Phu
and who was then stationed in North Africa believed that his knowledge
was derived from his wealth of experience — the sum of all the practical
rules that his combat missions taught him, that is, the difference between
orders and an inner "emotional" resistance to them. He initially taught at
military schools in France and was later bought by the CIA. Since then, he

has held seminars on the EXPANDED MIDDLE EAST (including the CIS states in the south of the former Soviet Union, in particular Uzbekistan and Kyrgyzstan). His experiences have proven particularly useful for the asymmetrical campaign against terror. In the way he presents his courses, his experiences invariably constitute a LABYRINTH of "right" and "wrong." By taking "wrong" as a starting point, however, it is possible to progress toward "right" through a sequence of steps in the right direction, just as the "right" direction, within his system of explanations, can lead toward what is "wrong." This labyrinthine riddle demands of those taking his courses a degree of daring and an enthusiasm for experimentation. Critics well disposed to the commander of the parachute regiment have referred to him as a "tinkering thinker." One way of looking at this is that knowledge is not based simply on grammatical expressions, but that the route to attaining it in fact leads "through expression and out the other side" to the very opposite of what is actually being discussed. The solution lies "outside the box." What does not accord with experience provides knowledge. The commander of the parachute regiment takes the view that experience has been ruined by disappointment; on the other hand, there is "no knowledge without the prospect of a positive outcome."

Nietzsche mistrusted his mind. He did not mistrust his feet, the moving parts of his body, his muscles, limbs, and digestive tract. He "walked" the process of arriving at truth. The Engadine Valley offered more opportunities in this respect than the alleyways of Genoa. At first, his feet adopted a walking rhythm through which the master's body knew how to express itself; subsequently, his thoughts dressed themselves in words, what you might call the discharge of an evolutionary man. It would appear, however, that a certain steadfastness associated with this walking was able to overcome all kinds of obstacles. Nietzsche's thoughts, "transformed entirely into a coat," constitute some of the best knowledge "that can flood the market."

After nine oppressive years of married life, during which her husband's stubbornness of character had turned out to be unalterable, Gerlinde Reh came to the conclusion that her husband was being unfaithful to her. She had allowed herself to be deceived for so long and had gone so far as to do the groundwork for this deception lovingly! She did not want to confront the truth of her misery. Then her husband brought his "new lady," a rich heiress, home for Christmas Eve. This Gerlinde could not accept. Would there be no end to this SUCCESSION OF DENIAL? Gerlinde moved out of the ruins of her marriage. Had she ever brought herself to discuss it with anyone, she would have formulated her knowledge in the following terms: it is impossible to demand back from my unfaithful husband the nine years I've lived with him. She was now alone with her insight. She was able to talk about any of this only with her girlfriends. However, they were prepared to listen to her story only once. As a cheerful soul, Gerlinde did not view her knowledge as a gift from heaven.

The ultimate form of knowledge, according to the architect F., who had studied with Wright in Chicago, is an ENCLOSED SPACE. A sea of stones, as represented by the metropolis, leaves its mark on the senses and sweeps every thought and sensation along with it. Subsequently, the same enclosed space is constructed, in a subjective form, within the individual. From there, it shapes the momentum and external relations of life with the rigidity of concrete, like a riverbed cast in stone.

Another quite different definition of knowledge is offered by the circus artist Fanny Petzolt. As she puts it herself, if the trapeze artist throws herself into the arms of the catcher (as she does every evening), the click of the successful jump, the instant in which every nerve senses success, "is what I call the moment of 'knowledge.'" On the other hand, the Russian marriage broker Jekaterina Saitzev, who has now relocated her agency from Moscow to New York, describes the moment when a successfully brokered couple sinks into each other's arms (or, to put it more colloquially, "falls in love") as "fortunate knowledge." Reason has little to do with it. The surprise is more useful than all the effort spent beforehand. The owner of the agency speaks with twenty-seven years of experience.

The Harvard Kantian Dr. Mary Pitcorn believed that lockable doors are essential for the process of gaining knowledge. She often sat on the toilet amid the hustle and bustle in large railway stations, locked the door behind her, and expanded upon her ideas. As soon as the door is closed firmly behind me, the INNER FOUNTAIN opens up inside me (as it does in everyone else). This is what we call knowledge. It is for this reason that the hermits in the Middle Ages lived in hermitages. According to Dr. Pitcorn, knowledge is a thing "unto itself"; it "flows through" a person who has not fallen prey to despair spontaneously, precisely because it constitutes the "groundwater of life."

— And those who have despaired have no knowledge?
— Despair blocks the fountain.

An Estimate of the Time Needed for a "Change in Powers of the Soul"

Virtue should not as hitherto be termed strength, but rather pleasure,
as this name conveys more accurately its true nature in a way
that is both more friendly and more appealing.
—Montaigne, *Essays*, vol. 1, chapter 20

Comrade Alexander Bogdanov, who as early as 1904 played chess with Lenin on Capri, and Jonas A. Zalkind were drinking tea together while assigned to the PROLETKULT project. It had been dark for four hours. Two restless spirits lit by the bright flames.

What do you see in your mind's eye? Dialogue is an aircraft. Politically, it is vital that the Russian working and peasant classes do not simply form a coalition (which would certainly not last long), but that they coalesce into a new, third entity. Let's call it the "new man." Merely by looking at the tractors waiting to be delivered to the farms, he can transform wheat into zeppelins and airplanes, which can turn those living across the vast expanses of Russia into near neighbors; exploiting the usefulness of such industrial products, people of this kind are able to create the USE VALUE OF THE MIND, just as the proletarians in their factories (or in the tanks, ships, and ranks of the Red Army) always had the smell of fresh sausages and freshly baked bread in their hearts and noses and were thus at one and the same time workers and peasants. Coalescing means discarding mistakes. These peel away to reveal the new man: just like a Russian doll, the individual characteristics of ancestors appear and, freed from their rigidity, are reconciled with one another. Organizers could not actually concoct them if they had not been there all the time, Zalkind wrote. "Revolutionary politics is the organization of social experience."

With rum in their tea, Bogdanov and Zalkind estimate a mere seven years should be sufficient for the production of streams of airplanes needed to bring together the disparate elements that make up Russia. On the other hand, Russia would need at least thirty years for "progress" of this kind as well as the "production stream" to be accepted internally before the coachmen in the far north, with their reindeer-drawn sleighs, embrace the "necessity" of airplanes as their own, and conversely for the pilot to accept the advantage of reindeer as a "necessity," as well. And then there are the schools, Zalkind adds. These will need to be traveling schools, because it is vital to reach comrades scattered far and wide, indeed, those people who don't even see themselves as comrades yet. Reaching everyone will take time. Bogdanov calculates on a sheet of paper that an additional sixty years will be needed to instill a real sense of the achievements of the socialist economy within the individual to the extent that the doctrine of socialist virtue will become an innate pleasure spontaneously spurring people along. That is to say, organization is spontaneity and autonomy.

> Let the philosophers say what they will,
> the thing at which we all aim, even in virtue is pleasure.[40]

Translated by Cyrus Shahan, Richard Langston,
Martin Brady, and Helen Hughes

A Flemish post mill from the late thirteenth century. Mills on the Mediterranean are fixed. They are not suitable for the North's shifting winds. The innovation consists in mounting the mill on a revolving pedestal: the post. A post mill turns according to the wind. The first mills of this kind were in Flanders. Circa 1115, the area around Cologne saw its first post mills. In the late Middle Ages, they spread throughout the countryside and are local landmarks, like church steeples. [Alexander Kluge Archive]

CHAPTER FIVE

The Historical Terrain

Where Labor Capacities Emerge

Humans experience their history in the form of life spans. In spite of breaks and caesuras, such life spans are associated with generations and traditions. And from these generations, whole centuries and epochs take shape. Epochs, in turn, entail interpretative patterns (that usually arise belatedly) necessary for comprehensive processes. Amid these patterns at work in the real relations and subjectivities of humans, these processes give rise to historical formations. Both the classical authors of economics and Marx himself called these formations "relations of production." The total structure or sum thereof is called the "relation of intercourse" [Verkehrsverhältnisse]. All relations of intercourse together form the relation of history.

Of all these concepts, "life span" seems most concrete and descriptive, whereas "relation of history" seems unusual and initially abstract. These central differentiations, along with their rapidly accumulating piles of statistics, are overlaid by further comprehensive concepts. How in the relation of history of a single country such as Germany, France, the United States, or China, for example, does the central concept of six thousand years of agrarian revolution relate to an epoch such as the one to which we still belong? Or to the periods of industrialization and capitalist globalization? All these concepts and differentiations are components within the relation of history and characterize details in the process of a permanent sociation, which (according to everything that evolutionary biologists tell us) already constituted the foundation of the developments that brought about the human brain and the sensuousness of the five senses—in other words, human history.

With respect to the modern chapters of this history, French theoreticians have developed a vocabulary with novel and incisive differentiations that depart from the conceptual thought of Hegel, Marx, Ricardo, and

Adam Smith. Borrowing from the work of Talcott Parsons, systems theory has crafted analytical instruments not easily synchronized with concepts of these classic thinkers. Anglo-Saxon theory avoids grand concepts altogether, which is certainly a step forward in the battle against preconceptions but it is disadvantageous for the COURAGE OF COGNITION (Hegel), for probing questions (Weber), and for clarity (Habermas).[1] None of these intellectual factions and individual think(ing) tanks can be avoided when investigating the question: What produces productivity? Who or what is the subject in history? How can one emancipate oneself?

At this juncture, we have downscaled the English-language translation of our German original extensively and replaced three chapters with the following sketch, followed by eight commentaries.

The "Social Factory": The Relation of History

How do we come to grips with the vessel in which centuries, social transformations, and human life spans flow like water? Put less metaphorically: there exists a factory where human characteristics are forged, and this factory is located in a space and at a point in time belonging to a concrete country. This factory, in other words, is fixed in history.

We will investigate only one section of this complex whole, namely, in the constitution of individual labor capacities.

This social fabric is observable, at the very least, on three structurally different levels:

- at the level of available labor power composed of many individual characteristics and its potentials: diligence, skill, navigational abilities, motivation, culture;
- at the level of society (for example, feudalism, capitalism); and
- at the level of individual subjective-objective elements, out of which the large-scale structures from which acting persons (the "self") and society (the "whole") arise. They create an undercurrent and are often overlooked in the topography of life spans and "social totalities," but nevertheless constitute the connective network and encompass the actual events that bring about "transmutation."

Were the two-thousand-year history of the German city of Mainz to be depicted in a ninety-minute film using extreme time-lapse photography, the beginning would show a Roman *castrum*, its gates bordering a canteen or the outskirts of an encampment. Later, a medieval metropolis surrounded by agriculture emerges. Within this metropolis, a bourgeois enclave of craftsmen begins to distinguish itself, apart from the reign of the archbishop. During the French Revolution, Mainz is occupied by revolutionary forces and for a short time later is a French *département*. It was not uncommon back then to travel in horse-drawn coaches decorated with the gods of reason, fertility, the republic, and other idols of churches from which God had been expunged in order to celebrate the transformations of the revolution. Following the downfall of Napoleon, these festive carriages were retrieved from their arsenals and transformed for the city's amusement (according to the revival of Roman saturnalia and medieval traditions) into floats for local carnival parades. Subsequently, Mainz became a Prussian provincial town with industrial suburbs. It was this Mainz that was destroyed by bombings in World War II. More recently, new construction blankets the city's old layout.

Time-lapse photography that captures the REALITY OF PAST MOMENTS contained in CURRENT REALITY can also be produced for ideal products, for example, the idea of freedom or human rights. We would first see how slavery and bondage existed in an overwhelming majority of countries, were legally sanctioned, and persisted as a matter of course. This was the case in Africa and Asia, but in Europe, as well.

In cities within a very narrow band in northwestern Europe, a countermovement arose in the form of a minority opinion that was already present in Christianity's councils, but that never advanced into dominant practice. Initially localized, the new, generalized idea of freedom became an EMOTIONAL IMPETUS in southern German cities, in the Netherlands, England, Scotland, and then later in France, as well. These freedoms were then transplanted to the United States from this narrow stretch on planet Earth and then rendered valid around the world with the help, at the very least, of the language and ambitions of the French Revolution. Nonetheless, the prehistory still remains alive in the results. In this respect, ideas are neither spirits nor mere objects. Rather, ideas consist of evolutionary human energies constantly at work. If once-defeated structures are not completely defeated anew, they reemerge once again. We are not beyond slavery once and for all. The categories of future, present, possibility, and past—together with their assimilated inter-actions and deviations—create a network. Accordingly, a "grammar of real relations" exists, but only as long as history is investigated as a vessel of permanent transformations. The "social factory" has there-fore a radically different form than the one conveyed by the word "factory," along with its allusions to a specialized form of isolated labor common in the nineteenth and twentieth centuries.

In Chapters 1 and 3, we investigated the origin of labor capacity in processes of separation (landed property) and the violent expro-priation of primitive property (the burning of cottages) as one of the drive trains of the modern economy of labor power. We have char-acterized this process of primitive accumulation—in other words, primitive expropriation—along with observation of the repetition and permanence of this historical intervention—as the stinger that wounds humans and that gives occasion for protest against the injury of becoming industrial labor power. For Marx and other classical economists, this is the motor behind the development of modernity. The dramaturgy of this process is explicated comprehensively only for England in *Capital* and the *Grundrisse: Foundations of the Critique of Political Economy*. In the Soviet Union, it was a practical and theo-retical problem for a long time whether revolutionary Russia could attain industrialization if the violence of primitive accumulation was more-or-less simulated at the administrative level. In Islamic countries, India, China, Africa, and in younger countries such as the United States, Australia, and Israel (where primitive expropriation had to be imported), such necessary queries remain missing. Were the processes of separation of primitive property different and thus the disposition vis-à-vis alienated labor or work in general distinct, they would certainly have lingering influence for those respective societies.

It is puzzling at first sight how worldwide regulation and accul-turation have established themselves around the planet. The les-sons of globalization are acquired in Kyrgyzstan, just as they are in New York. However, a first glance overlooks the ways in which, for example, these adaptations, affect only the general characteristics required for participation in markets and superficial forms of confor-mity. Analysis of developmental processes of individual characteris-tics, as well as of the processes of acculturation, is left unexplored. The universal (society), the particular (history), and the individual (our concrete life spans) differentiate themselves from one another only if we pose the question as to what the circumscribed times, places, and degrees of circumstances (along with their conditions and gravitational fields) allow not only for the maturation, but also for the preservation of human characteristics and labor capacities. Put differently: **societal evolution is spatial and temporal and also carries traces of its emergence when labor capacities distance themselves from their places of origin and disperse themselves around the planet.**

If, on the one hand, the specific process of separation with which the individual characteristic of modern labor and the motivation to deploy it in a controlled fashion is manufactured is one indicator of a historical vessel (of a country, nation, or epoch) in which labor capacities are produced, then another indicator is the temporal form in which this transpires, together with whether the indicator pertains to an original process or to the overlay of many processes responsible for the transformation of the temporal form. It is thus relevant how bourgeois societies and industry in Europe shifted over the course of roughly five hundred years against the backdrop of a prehistory spanning roughly three thousand years. Conversely, the rapid process in China we are witnessing in recent decades required a backdrop of at least six thousand years of history. Younger countries founded by immigrant laborers, such as the United States, Canada, and Australia, are also characterized structurally by differing temporal forms imported by settlers who then transformed the developmental speeds considerably in spatially different, yet temporally unchanged new continents or countries. However, at the interface where such temporal forms containing different social speeds meet, there comes into being a potentially mutating transformative process capable of giving rise to unexpected, yet historically verifiable new characteristics. As if in a fairy tale, a person arrives in a parallel world where characteristics are activated from deep within, characteristics that he did not know ever existed inside him.

Akin to the historical separation of primitive property, the exodus from one's own country or, conversely, immigration into a foreign country is initially bound up with a loss. The time change associated therewith also amalgamates into new characteristics. Something about it is like the good fortune of finding a treasure trove.

Our question pertaining to the historical vessel in which subjectivity evolves is posed in the name of emancipation. It would not be absolutely necessary to pose it in order just to describe the function of labor capacity. We must pose the question, however, and with considerable intensity, if we are to analyze why deficits in civilization, let alone inhumanity, take place in some such vessels.

Who or What in History Is the Subject?

According to Marx, all relations relevant for us moderns are subjective-objective. Something merely objective or merely subjective would not be real. It would be UNREAL for both "society's essential powers" and "physical (natural) existence." According to this position, the historical SUBJECT OF EMANCIPATION is also determinable only subjectively-objectively. For the great French Revolution, the Third Estate (craftsmen, lawyers, businessmen) was the historical subject, the driving force of history. But who propelled the Industrial Revolution forward? What holds true for the industrial proletariat? And what holds true for us today in the twenty-first century?

As of 1932, the thinkers of Critical Theory practiced by the Frankfurt School no longer considered the proletariat as the historical subject of emancipation. They observed how Communist unions and National Socialist organized labor joined forces in the Berlin transportation strike of 1932. How could it have happened that workers possessed no immunity to fascism? Since then, the adherents of Critical Theory—along with the authors of the book before you—have discontinued investigating the emancipatory potentials within entire social groups and instead have turned to consider the raw material of these potentials, the ruptured, yet still lively INDIVIDUAL CHARACTERISTICS located beneath the level of the whole person. These characteristics can by all means affiliate themselves socially, but not in the form of the self or in fixed groups. From the vantage point of NONemancipation, these emancipatory CHARACTERISTICS are something cohesive (as a functional relationality). From the vantage point of emancipation, THEY ARE something not (yet) cohesive.[2]

One of the guiding principles according to which every emancipatory movement in China is repeated reads: He who is not afraid will topple emperors. The last six thousand years or so of Chinese history can be grasped as an irrepressible chain of peasant uprisings; none ever lasted long, yet none of the authorities' powers of restraint could ever prevent their return. Naturally, this is only *one* facet of Chinese history. However, it is an indicator of a potential for every society's present, a possible indicator for the future, and in any case, the sum of all pasts.

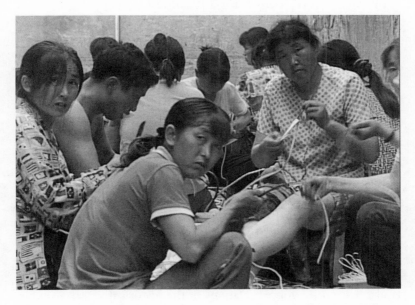

Shanghai. Workers from Xinjiang. [From Alexander Kluge's *Früchte des Vertrauens*, 2009]

In England, the expulsion of peasants and the burning of their cottages were carried out almost completely. Does the particular talent of Britons—be it forming working lower classes, being a "British subject" at every point within the colonial empire, or operating under the umbrella of FINANCE CAPITALISM—derive from this historical fate? How does French CAPITALIST PRODUCTION—its techniques, forms of life, and values are easily differentiated from Britain's—relate to the peasant uprisings there and the equilibrium of power established thereafter, the expropriation of nobility and the churches, as well as the fates of the peasant class and urban cultures of France? What occurred differently in Italy? What was different in Islamic countries?

In Germany, the peasant revolts associated with attempted religious reform and emancipation ended in bitter disappointment, not only for peasants, but also for the cities in league with them. Did this lead to the fact that in this region later called Germany, a revolution like France's never succeeded, and instead, a "National Socialist revolution" was realized? What is the difference between Germany and a republic such as Switzerland, where Wilhelm Tell represented an idea of freedom (differently than Emperor Barbarossa did) that, forged a commonwealth in the form of a cantonal constitution, a vessel where cities and rural communities of different languages and religions tolerated one another in an un-Balkanized fashion? The principle of neutrality (not to mention confidential banking and the Red Cross) came into being there.

Concentrating on a single Central European example outside Switzerland, analyses based on a peasant revolt that managed to stabilize itself in Salzburg suggest that a cantonal constitution in Germany could have permitted a happier outcome [*Ausgang*] in the conflicts between the nobility, the bourgeoisie and the peasants. Would that have been the price were Auschwitz never to have happened? This is the approach that Theodor W. Adorno proposes if we are to investigate the **relation of history**. According to Adorno, we cannot depart from the natural characteristics of human beings (they are the same in Alsace, southern Germany, and Switzerland). Rather, the forced relations of the historical vessel, in other words, its imprint, appear to exert a decisive influence on whether the elements and characteristics in humans are bound together happily or unhappily.

COMMENTARY 5: THE LABOR OF SEPARATION PROCESSES IN INDIVIDUAL LIFE SPANS

In contrast with the goods derived from material commodity production, in whose results the labor it engenders vanishes, the point of origin — the labor power of humans — never vanishes in the commodity. The same goes for the "tradition of all past generations," conflicts, the moments of good fortune throughout history, and even those moments within individual histories. They all tenaciously recur until they are substantiated anew, until history and life span have been fulfilled.[3]

A human is born. Its muscles, nerves, skin, and brain all have one shared characteristic: they are generally driven to respond. This transpires initially in a language other than that of adults. Rhythm, duration, pitch, volume, change, spatial movement, being cradled, the sense of equilibrium and its variations, falling over: every child creates its own language from these elements.[4] In general, every exertion is an attempt to make a claim to life; in other words, it is a reaction to disturbances. The child is a social creature according to a historical system. "To be really existing" means "to be *sensuous*." "To be sensuous is to *suffer*" (Marx).[5]

The child responds to primary objects it encounters. It learns in its own way, but through the **anticipation of the other**. This is the condition under which it understands how to separate itself from its environmental conditions. The child thus learns "to control itself."[6]

A string of separation processes already takes place at this point. General activity finds its limit in the interest of primary objects, not centered equally on all movements of the child, however, but rather on those that are later good for sitting, standing, or walking. The child learns to select its movements in this direction as channeled by primary objects; it will therefore not renounce the joy of general activities, but internalize them. This means a portion turns into conformity and another turns into protest.

Michel Foucault characterized this separation, in which all life is caught up from the outset, as the **form of institutions**.[7] The child exists as a whole being and attempts to assert this further. However, the primary objects are inadequate in the measurements of time associated with the "infinity of joy [*Lust*]."[8] In a later phase, the child encounters the incest taboo. The child will never understand this limit in the language of its many interior factions. What it can understand is the ambivalence by which primary objects comport themselves as bringers of happiness and as violators of its obstinacy. These objects cannot therefore be merely loved. But insofar as the child loves them, it must, on the one hand, not really love them after all, not when it becomes sexual.[9] On the other hand, the child learns to separate itself if it acclimates itself to the incest taboo. It does this because the instinctual forces [*Triebkräfte*], which are indifferent toward the reality principle, can acclimate themselves only outwardly, yet the child cannot levy its own obstinacy by developing a sense of guilt on account of the learned prohibition. Thus, the raw materials for discipline come into being, materials that will be used for the cultivation of future labor power.

Realistic kinds of motion, rationales, and characteristics evolve that are suitable for this world. With every instance of these overlays, spin-offs, and transitions, **one part conformity and one part protest** necessarily emerges. For this economy, it is immaterial which variation one chooses in order to describe the fate of the libidinal economy. It can be described superficially as a balance sheet on which 50 percent of the internal characteristics transform into protest and the other 50 percent into the capacity to conform. However, the protests must part company with their own identity as such. They are the basic stuff, the leaven or cement, that goes into the disposition that is necessary for work. Yet every one of **these** transitions takes place, in turn, in the form of one part conformity and one part protest. The separation energies consist objectively of a loss of experience, as well as of the subjective ability to reply to this loss. If both portions fail to come together, illness and neurosis arise. When they do come together, the raw materials emerge for the future disposition for labor power. Simultaneously, the detachment and production of a specialized sexuality out of the general faculty of childhood sexual eroticism also come into being.

A chain of characteristics that is separated off from processes of realization, protest possesses its own self-regulating characteristics. All future efforts to conform draw a piece of indifferent and thus voluntary supplemental labor from this chain. Conversely, efforts to conform from an earlier separation phase can move into a later phase of protest based only partially on these efforts. They comport themselves for a while like dead labor and transform themselves back into living labor. In other words, they are raw materials for a future phase.

In this respect, we must also see separation as being distinct from the principle of play in the early stages of the work principle, especially as it

224

unfolds, for example, in schools or the parental home. This step — and in each step resides a piece of conformity and a piece of protest — is the most momentous in the future life span of the child. If the total mass of past separations is involved in this step, it will assuredly fail. In reality, the child never had any intention of becoming a human machine, and it also never really enlisted under this banner.

Without these separation processes, no one can become an adult. But it can also be said that due to these separations — each a disruption of organic integrity — no one really becomes an adult (in the emancipatory sense) capable of producing social wealth, the autonomy of the other, as well as one's own. Put differently: were it possible to avoid separation processes, nothing emancipatory would evolve, because such an avoidance would only engender an entirely unrealistic being unsuitable for the whole of society.[10]

We assume that the practice of raising children is also affected by the specific manner through which labor capacities emerge out of processes of separation in any given country. At the beginning of Germany's twentieth century, for example, the processes of raising children were characterized by the severity of the separation — learning through punishment and fear and **simultaneously** through a distributive indeterminacy regarding what an adult's cruelty referred to. Indeterminacy meant a loss of reality [*Entwirklichung*]. Specific severity intensifies separation.[11] In the National Socialist campaigns for child-rearing practices that went well beyond the realm of the family there existed a particular severity and **indeterminacy**. (Some of the virtues to be achieved were not practical for modern war.) Privacy and indifference in the styles of child rearing from the 1950s, in turn, had an effect on another kind of collective indeterminacy. Here, severity meant a lack. All of these processes negated the child's satisfying and rich development during its upbringing. The positivity of this negation — the mainstream within the countermovements since the end of the 1960s — however, consisted of a simple reversal of these relations of child rearing. Attempts were made to construct emancipatory processes along these lines and simultaneously to accelerate the rate at which the separations were avoided[12] — to mitigate the external relations of social pressure in the domain of child rearing and thus to engender the longest-drawn-out illusion possible that child rearing pertains to the general development of a living being, and not to the production of the commodity labor power.[13] Severities became more prone to surface in the second half of child-rearing processes when children have encountered reality; some of the separation processes that run their course unconsciously or at speeds that child-rearing adults do perceive acquire a more absolute meaning. Simultaneously, however, a deobjectification [*Entgegenständlichung*] in the developmental processes takes place, and with it subsequent forms of indeterminacy. The synthesis of self-regulation is in some cases overburdened. Within the positivity of the emancipatory countermovement, we even see how the organizing power of the pleasure principle vanishes in social relations. These relations have never had an interest in the social, but rather are always interested only in themselves and operate above cognitive investments, which, however, already presuppose certain separation processes in order to concentrate on nearby people. On the other hand, the reality principle persists, since the pedagogical countermovement tends to segregate it, leaving it unresolved. Furthermore, its inherent organizational principles go untested.

The pleasure principle comports itself abstractly with regard to social relations. It merely poaches from them. On its own, it is a principle of production, but in relation to other forces, it is a principle of abstraction. Were a society to construct itself according to the pleasure principle, it would be composed of relations of war. This war could be drawn to a close only through an accord recognizing the pleasure of the other. (Such persons would be different from our own.) Were such a system of universal recognition and understanding to exist, this would be its principle, and its laws would be completely different from those of the phylogenetic pleasure principle. This is utopia. It does not consist of the simple positivity of negations handed down over time.

Social organization is contained within the reality principle in an inorganic undefined relation of forces that comport themselves both as a principle of production and a principle of abstraction. Indeterminacies are primarily abstract. Whereas indeterminacies are abstract, determinacies are productive. However, these determinacies, in turn, are divisible into abstract and productive ones, as soon as we investigate labor capacity not as a mere means toward self-alienation, but rather from the perspective of its realization and ability to cooperate. We then see in every single characteristic of labor both principles at work, possessing a possibility for differentiation, at which point the two child-rearing parties part ways from one another. We also notice immediately, however, how life spans and thus child rearing are not the natural laboratory for the contest between the principles of abstraction and production. Instead, that laboratory is to be found in history and society.

In the case of history, the identity of the production principle must be culti-vated. In the institutions of society, what must be cultivated is the interest of the whole. And in the rearing of children, it is the historical capacity of the whole living being that must be developed.[14]

> Finding, paying attention, recognizing something like me, these belong to the production principle. Ostracizing, scraping something, setting traps, destroying, these are the answers of the abstraction principle. As is the case everywhere, characteristics can be skewed by comprehensive pro-cesses such that they come under the influence of the opposite principle.

227

Nr. 1324.
Universalwerkzeug,
bestes Fabrikat in fein vernickelter
Ausführung. Als Hammer, Zange, Beil,
Drahtschneider, Nagelheber, Schrauben-
schlüssel, Schraubenzieher, Konus-
zange und Kistenöffner zu gebrauchen.
14 cm lang.
Stück M. 1.70

Universal tool. [Alexander Kluge Archive]

Pieter Bruegel the Elder, *The Tower of Babel*, ca. 1564. The top of the image suggests clouds. Humans in the lower-left corner are mere points in comparison with the tower. Bruegel proceeds historically inasmuch as in his interpretation of the tower, he somewhat exaggerates the Roman Coliseum at the top. Because its footprint cannot bear its weight, the tower sinks into the ground to the left. It becomes nature once again. The architectural language would be suitable for agreements if the building were completed. It would be completed if it were known what people were supposed to do with it. The gates and windows, however, are too large for these little human dots. There are no life practices that can be integrated into such a centralized building. This is not the hubris of Nebuchadnezzar, but rather the principle of indeterminacy, over which he presided as king without ever understanding it. The confusion of tongues is a deficit in determinacy. The production principle is subjugated by the abstraction principle. Without abstraction, there would be no tower and no confusion of tongues. The tower was presumably supposed to impress enemies, unnerve them, and destroy their own will. Not once did it investigate this alien will. [Kunsthistorisches Museum, Vienna]

COMMENTARY 6: ON HOUSES

In Central Europe, the seat of the economy—of what both the hand and the head do—is the house. It is neither the ship nor the river (as is the case with seafaring peoples), but rather the house and the home, along with the people who live in them.

In his "On Rights to Persons Akin to Rights to Things," Kant says: "What is mine or yours in terms of this Right is what is mine or yours *domestically* [*Häusliche*], and the relation of persons in the domestic condition is that of a community of free beings who form a society of members of a whole called a *household* (of persons standing in *community* with one another) by their affecting one another in accordance with the principle of outer freedom (*causality*)." Kant continues: "Acquisition of this status, and within it, therefore takes place neither by a deed on one's own initiative (*facto*) nor by a contract (*pacto*) alone but by a principle (*lege*); for, since this kind of right is neither a right to a thing nor merely a right against a person but also a possession of a person, it must be a right lying beyond any rights to things and any rights against persons. That is to say, it must be the Right of humanity in our own person, from which there follows a natural permissive principle, by the favor of which this sort of acquisition is possible for us."[15]

Note with which words Kant speaks of domiciliary right, as if it were about the entire world! The constitutional philosophy of Kant can itself be understood as a philosophical attempt at building a house: What is allowed inside? What must absolutely remain outside?

The Word "House"

"The general Germanic word 'house' [*Haus*] belongs to the widely subdivided word group from the Indo-Germanic root (*skeu-*) meaning '*bedecken, umhüllen*' [to cover, to enclose] (cf. *Scheune*). In Germanic languages, words associated with ➜ *Hose* [pants] and ➜ *Hort* [hoard] are closely related." Paul Grebe, ed., *Die Etymologie der deutschen Sprache* (Mannheim: Duden, 1963), p. 253.

Honorable Members of the House (an address to parliament), domiciliary right [*Hausrecht*] (including industrial parks devoid of inhabitants and protected by barbed wire and security personnel), house-to-house urban warfare, economical [*haushälterisch*], by birth [*von Haus aus*] (that is, according to the nature of a thing), to be overjoyed [*außer Häuschen sein*], budget [*Haushaltsplan*], to put the money on the table [*auf den Tisch des Hauses legen*], misery [*Elend*] (that is, to be in another country), cozy [*gemütlich*] (this word is emulated in no other European language), housewife, pet [*Haustier*], greenhouse, department store [*Warenhaus*], to dwell [*hausen*], warden [*Hausvater*], Robin Goodfellow [*Hausgeist*], paramour [*Hausfreund*], homely, home-style cooking, infestation and visitation [*Heimsuchung*], unlawful entry [*Hausfriedensbruch*], and so on.

One of Charlemagne's most important decrees from the year 792 was called *Capitulare de Villis* (Directive on Production in Homes or Courts, in the so-called villications). In the meantime, dependence penetrated into the home, and separations detached it in multiple ways from both the land and the community. If the home was earlier a sphere of production unto itself, later it became, above all, a place of defense, fortification, and community withdrawn into the home's interiority. The original system for maintaining boundaries is one's own body.[16] I experience borders by what I let out of my insides and what I put into them. I once again experience this border when something touches me. The body has the same basic form as a house. However, it is something that establishes boundaries through contact with others; one's own embodied feeling is always already a social experience. This immediate experience presupposes the next guise of boundary demarcation: the house and the primary objects dwelling within it. In this respect, the house is, if anything, my body, my feelings, and my thought, all at the same time. If I am threatened, I retreat backward into something: this is "house" in the figurative sense of the word. It therefore means more than the four walls within which I live.

The domestic thoughts of consciousness pertain, first and foremost, to safeguarding. I can close my home off from the rest of the world; this is the core idea. Secretly, I collect in my home everything I need to live. Consider Germany today at Christmas and you will see a country composed of closed-off homes, on the one hand, and travelers, on the other. Hans Christian Andersen described these same circumstances in Denmark in his story "The Little Match Girl."

At first glance, the image of the National Socialist era appears determined by the storm troopers' public parades in the streets and the party's conferences. In fact, it could be said as well that a fulfilled world composed of little houses and mobile property (Volkswagens) was what was hoped for, presuming one bought into it. Greater Germany congregated on special days via radio; from fronts on the Aegean to those on the North Cape, from Bourdeaux to Kharkiv, all points in the empire were connected "as if under one roof" through the voice of the radio broadcaster.

In warmer countries such as Italy, for example, city squares and porches in front of houses were settled differently. This may be explained solely in terms of climate, but it also pertains to a different relation to the public sphere. In England, where the climate is colder than in Italy, the house played a particularly important role, but the fortification of the consciousness against the public did not exist in the way Germans saw it in their own country. In the house of consciousness, we find the labor of a specific kind of separation. Two processing methods result from this: (1) an indifference toward one's own labor capacity and (2) a nondeferrable labor of hoping and collecting that, in defiance of all experience, wants to reverse these separations and demand the redeeming [*Einlösung*] of history.[17] Not at all indifferent, this wish is additionally withdrawn back into the home, where it is secure.

There is no mistaking that houses — in the sense of both objects and consciousness — are askew in comparison with the proportions of human beings, the modular. This is due to the fact that they respond to the separation within all people. For example, human beings are not completely quadrangular, nor do they think quadrangularly.[18]

When they cooperate, houses (unlike skyscrapers, apartment buildings, or any other vertically stacked commodities) can also bring about societal groups. If the law of a cell is "as much inside as possible, as little outside as necessary," the snail's shell [its *Gehäuse*], into which people withdraw their sensitive feelers following a catastrophic experience, is the core for the cellular development of a society. And yet it is unsuitable as an accommodation and limits the free movement of human powers. Aerial bombardment will destroy such houses. We can thoroughly assume that in such an instance, something in the human soul is leveled, just as the outward appearance of a city is when it is reduced to rubble.

"The emblem of intelligence is the feeler of the snail, the creature 'with the fumbling face,' with which, if we can believe Mephistopheles, it also smells. Meeting an obstacle, the feeler is immediately withdrawn into the protection of the body, it becomes one with the whole until it timidly ventures forth again as an autonomous agent. If the danger is still present, it disappears once more, and the intervals between the attempts grow longer. Mental life in its earliest stages is infinitely delicate. The snail's sense is dependent on a muscle, and muscles grow slack if their scope for movement is impaired. The body is crippled by physical injury, the mind by fear. In their origin both effects are inseparable."[19]

E. T. A. Hoffmann tells the story of Councillor Krespel ("Rat Krespel," 1818), who won litigation on behalf of the prince and was therefore able to build a house on his client's dime. He first had the four walls of his home built two stories high, to the bewilderment of everyone else. Using his human sense of proportion, he then measured where the doors and windows would belong and had corresponding holes cut into the already finished walls. Also subject to his sense of proportion, the interior construction was remodeled improvisationally and then gradually filled in. An unusually cozy and lively home emerged, because no plan, no blueprint, no schematic diagram — an entire prehistory lurks in such documents, not the sense of proposition commensurate with a person living in the now — disturbed its livability made **exclusively for Councillor Krespel**. Residents and craftsmen alike endorsed the highly individualistic building after they regained their senses. Their own sense of taste would have been far better satisfied had they themselves used Krespel's approach, rather than some diagram. When the building was completed, Councillor Krespel invited guests to a banquet.[20]

A Village Covered in Snow. [Ludwig Bund, ed. *Gedenkblätter an L. Hugo Becker* (Düsseldorf: Bredidenbach, 1869), p. 45]

COMMENTARY 7: SUBJECTIVE-OBJECTIVE ELEMENTS OF THE PUBLIC SPHERE OF PRODUCTION (PIPES, BONES, VESSELS, BASKETS): PRIMITIVE PROPERTY

For roughly two thousand years, humans have toiled away at a product on a site that would later be called Germany. This product is German history. We do not mean here the succession of battles, rulers, states, and regulations.

If we could interview the dead generations who produced this historical product as to whether the results of their labor were appropriated by reality differently from the motives that produced them, and if every deceased person were to have the overview of what each and every other deceased person did, we believe an unequivocal answer would yield itself: it is impossible to identify oneself with the results. The answer is: "We did not want everything to turn out that way."[21]

Identity/Rupture

There is a need for primitive property. For example, I need a place where I can stand, someplace to retreat, where I can find shelter, a house or a cave. Again, this must have a certain breadth and egresses.[22] Since birth, I need people. I need to be in society. But I also must be able to be alone. I must be able to say yes to some things but no to others. Between extreme cold and extreme heat, there is a temperature that suits me. I must be able to leave someone or give up an object or a place, but I must also be sure that I can return. The sensuously most intelligible form of primitive property is the congruence of my body as my property. However, I am also the property of my body. If I lose my head, I am beside myself or fly off the handle. This congruence with oneself is disturbed. In a certain accumulation and intensity, this disturbance is called "being sick."[23]

Such primitive property is a need, that is, an objective relation. To own property is not a natural drive, but already a reaction to alienated relations. Need results from not having such property. In this case, the designation "property" is the same **word** used for the property belonging to private-property owners who create capitalist society; however, their relation of production is the decisive disruption of primitive property and possesses no sense of proportion. It neither protects any relations of primitive property nor produces any. A society always produces too much or too little of it. The society would never be able to determine when the equivalent value to humans is exceeded. On the contrary, primitive property is what we would call in second societal nature a "natural relation" in the sense that it fits humans and their prehistory. We call such a match of relations *identity*. Such an identity is not something merely mental. It presupposes the moment of reciprocal recognition, that is, the concreteness of humans and things, much like an embrace merely rendered in song that provides no protection when someone is in need. Conversely, protection fashioned merely out of concrete or a rubber wall — in other words, something merely objective — is not identical with the need for primitive property. It is always a matter of a subjective-objective relation momentarily assembled, at the very least, by the identity of both objects and people. This is a category of survival. The opposite of the need for primitive property is the certainty of so-called primitive accumulation, whose main feature is expropriation.[24]

In addition to the known coordinates of the horizontal and the vertical, Bertolt Brecht added the category of the functional for historical relations: people slip into the functional under the influence of the abstractions of capitalist production — its valuation processes, as well as its political planning. These additional categories of expanded abstraction (which certainly also encompass expanded concretion) can be extended even further to include: the horizontal, the vertical, the functional, the irrational, the imaginary, and the revolutionary.

"The situation thereby becomes so complicated that a simple 'representation of reality' says something about reality less than ever before. A photograph of the Krupp Works or of A.E.G. yields nearly nothing about these institutions. Actual reality has slipped into the functional. The reification of human relationships, such as the factory, no longer produces the latter. So there is in fact 'something to build up,' something 'artificial,' 'contrived.'" Bertolt Brecht, "From the Three Penny Trial: A Sociological Experiment," trans. Lance W. Garmer, in *German Essays on Film*, ed. Richard W. McCormick and Alison Guenther-Pal (New York: Continuum, 2004), p. 117.

If the functional is the coordinate of heteronomy, the **irrational** is the sum of the **direct** responses, balancing acts, and evasive maneuvers made by the **motives of antirealism**. The **imaginary** is the coordinate of loss, the loss of reality, history, and identity. If the heteronomy associated with the functional is still the dimension of the self-realizing, yet contorted utilization of humankind's essential powers (that is, alienated **labor**, inverted **life**, false **consciousness**, together with their reification and expansion on a higher level), and if in this dimension the requisite derived irrationality is simultaneously present in the production process, then the **dimension of the imaginary** is determined by derealization and deconcretion. Focusing on the functional and the irrational in an effort to protest the loss of natural relations to places, times, and human contexts allows for little remaining attention for the anti-dimension of losing the ground from under one's feet and the disappearance of real time. Simultaneously, virulent, yet never fully realized in all other dimensions, the **dimension of the revolutionary** is most trenchantly antagonistic, especially toward the dimension of the imaginary, the antiworld. This antagonism is much sharper, in this case, than the one toward the slippage into the functional or toward the irrational, both of which detract from the dimension of the revolutionary, but also lend it substance.[25]

Differentiating these varying dimensions is a question of party affiliation. It conforms to particular investigative interests. It is a matter of unhierarchical categories of observation, not valuations, even when with certain dimensions it seems as if value, or the lack thereof, were already legible on account of the mere designation of the dimension.

The dimensions selected here further distinguish themselves internally if the more concrete or more abstract relations of humans to themselves or the grounds for their alienation is taken into consideration according to the categories: "proximity to the ego"; "sociated conditions/ostracized from sociation," "dominant/subservient." Just like the elements in first nature—they behave either like a solid, liquid, or gas or assume the fourth state, plasma (the most common for masses in the universe)—different aggregate states of human production and historical relations in the second, societal nature relate to these historical dimensions. In fact, all of these aggregate states relate to every dimension.

It is a question of analogy, an analogy whose sole purpose is to turn the capacity for differentiation in nature productively against the more marginal capacity for differentiation in society. Aggregate states of human relations in society can be more numerous and diverse than the four natural states of matter. This is not in the least a question for physics. Congruous with the term "firm" (as used in American political language), the firmness of relations (for example, in the form of a cadre organization in a political party, new recruits in a police force, prohibitions, or the politics of containment) corresponds to intuition. Liquefying hardened relations was frequently discussed in the West German student movement. We know of no analogy for the aggregate state of gaseousness, unless we speak of "atmospherics" or "fresh air." There are obviously more complicated structures whose disorder (for example, that of a school's administration) corresponds to an unusually thorough sense of order as seen from the perspective of self-regulation. In this sense, many a school recess is of a higher order than classroom instruction. Established designations are missing, however, for this counterconcept. They are also missing for those relations in which the individual characteristics, divided by disruptions from below the threshold where the cultural context deals with them as a whole, communicate with one another. Designations are entirely missing for this by far most frequent of objective facts prevalent throughout history and society.

The five senses mainly concern themselves with the **horizontal**. The eyes orient themselves along horizons. Human beings are horizontal animals. Mao Zedong's allegory of the high mountain relates to this dimension: positioned between a farmer's house and the sun, the mountain opens onto a horizon, even when its peak is cleared away meter by meter. I comport myself within the **vertical** when I dig deeper. Even if I orient myself according to the highest or simplest abstractions in order to embark on a trip back home, I am in the vertical by virtue of the achieved designations and the concrete diversity I excavate there. In other words, it is a matter of processing indirect experience as experience not via the direct senses, but by using the search and sensory functions of the abstracting head *together with the immediate senses*. This is the concept of experience that stands in the foreground of our book *Public Sphere and Experience*.

To slip into the **functional** means, in contrast, to deceive all the senses, as well as to render useless a wide range of labor resources necessary for indirect orientational operations. This self-evidently belongs to cultural heritage, because the culture that engendered the senses does not reckon with the functional. In this case, I must *measure* in order to orient myself; no essential context can exist immediately if we are unsuccessful in first producing it. It is therefore a matter of synthetic behavior dominating orientation. Immediate impressions and the directness of traditional thinking together deceive.

Compared with the functional, the **irrational** is characterized as the domain of protest. In this dimension, some sensual orientations prove incidentally to be especially unerring. The senses behave as if **rescued** [*erlöst*] from the reality principle. The historical, individual, and social raw materials that are passed over into this dimension are the living critique of so-called rationality. The other side of this is the fact that rationality — in the delimited sense of the irrational's opposite pole — is the governmental form of a second, sociated irrationality (that is, a social totality slipped into the functional). This is an indefinite social totality. It is irrational without corresponding to the irrational in humans. In this context, *ratio*, reason, emancipation, and enlightenment are initially skewed concepts. As emphatic categories, they acquire their substance from all the aforementioned dimensions together. They are thus not the opposite pole of the irrational. However, if they exclude this dimension, they are constricted concepts in the sense of the Enlightenment. They are not only deprived of an essential dimension, but also become irrational themselves: illogical and unfit for emancipation. They succumb to the dialectic of enlightenment. According to experience, they are incidentally always violent.

In the dimension of the **imaginary**, the external senses are initially reset to zero; "everything appears unreal." For traditional experience, this dimension is the most unintelligible and most unbelievable, even though so-called self-awareness roams largely within it. Retreat into pure comprehensibility, radical proximity, immediate relationships, and the absolutization of direct experience all derealize actual continuous social relations. A nearly incalculable abundance of whole and partial appearances belongs to this dimension, or, at the very least, comes in contact with it. Consider the following example: the dimensions of time in the workday of a foreign minister or a head of a political party begin to **swim**. Overloaded with duties that refuse to be squeezed into *a* single brain and *a* single workday, he loses his footing on account of these dimensions and becomes airborne, so to speak. He starts experiencing an irregular heartbeat. It is imaginable that he then loses all sense of time. If he succeeds at regressing (that is, if he embraces the illness), he does not have to die. Incidentally, in the period following these attacks, he will see these relations differently and will reset some aspects of his life back to zero. However, if his attempts to reset do not succeed, he will surely die.

The same thing occurs in another context — namely, when the temporal dimensions of political rebellion are completely divided from one another in times when emotional approaches are implemented. Under the guise of boisterous activity, absolutely nothing happens. In other words, something unreal is produced.

The **revolutionary dimension** is the most imperceptible in nonrevolutionary times. However, this applies only when the revolutionary is sought in a form that is supposed to copy the form of earlier revolutions. This is especially the case when bourgeois models come into question. Since the revolutionary is not a matter of a formal state, as is the case with the other dimensions, but rather of the relationality of certain production processes, and since every power relation in every one of these dimensions and their aggregate states contains potentials that can be tested by themselves for tendencies that enter into such a productive relationality, this dimension is certainly unsettling to some extent, especially when one looks at the marginal degree of societal labor power that is preoccupied practically with such an assembly. In principle, however, it is difficult for either the senses or any labor resource of experience to roam creatively throughout this dimension. It simply has not been tried.

At the current moment, an admittedly idiosyncratic semblance has emerged: if these dimensions are not at all comprehensible as an open-ended construction site — even though, for example, the total construction of Germany consists of such elements — the revolutionary acquires the appearance of the imaginary. However, the numerous escape attempts, stop-gap measures, and unsocial Robinsonades typical of the imaginary confer upon it an alternative attribute, as if one were able to arrive there by holding out in the revolutionary. That would be an eschatological-religious approach, or a simple case of making oneself at home in the first dimension, as when someone places a schoolbook **under their pillow** and expects to wake the next day educated.[26]

"Our ancestors." [From Alexander Kluge's *Krieg und Frieden* (1982)]

COMMENTARY 8: THE LOSS OF REALITY/THE LOSS OF HISTORY: "THE LANDSCAPE OF INDUSTRY IS THE OPEN BOOK OF HUMAN PSYCHOLOGY"

Marx never wrote a general theory of knowledge separate from the concrete process of research and representation because he assumed that the constellations between subject and object appear differently in real cognition than they do in the reduction of object and subject into general designations. No theory of knowledge can be developed unless it unfolds within the praxis of cognition itself, and this cognition, in turn, transpires only in contact with objects, in practical labor, in practical life experiences, and in testing things. As the perceiving subject relates to objects, a mutual constitution ensues, in other words, an inner transformation of both. As the result of an abstraction that no longer includes the constitution process of the object or that of the subject, the separation of subject and object is possible only *post festum*; Marx would consider such a separation a judicious abstraction. However, judicious abstractions of this kind neither control the concrete process of cognition nor themselves broker the complexity of the two poles. As soon as cognition begins, simple conceptions of the object dissolve, as do those of the subject.

Marx's reservations—when compared with an explicit theory of knowledge, which with its general designations precedes the collective production process of social experience and transformation—become immediately plausible if the categories of subject and object so central for subject-object relations in society are dissolved into intuition. The **subject** turns out to be a chameleon capable of undergoing the most polymorphic of metamorphoses. The figure of the subject that controls praxis is precisely not the professional thinker, for example, the philosopher. The philosopher is a rare appearance in the collective and is largely unsuitable for poking around in praxis. In general, individual thinking is not at all subjective; rather, what is subjective is the kind of thinking capable of explaining itself to entire disciplines, professions, and production processes. In other words, it is thought that turns the subjective into a subjective collective. However, its previous labor has now built the constellations and organizations of things, the entire **landscape of industry,** a form of subjects undoubtedly enriched by processed natural materials. A subjective **network of links** is an entirely different characteristic of subjectivity that can also be understood in the form of relationships between people and between people and

242

things. Without subjective bodies and the bodies of things, these relationships would certainly not exist. But this in-betweenness contains sharper designations of the subjective; more work usually has been devoted to this interstice throughout history than on any obviously overproduced subjectivity, so that human subjectivity can differentiate itself from others.

Only from the perspective of investigatory interests is it possible to say whether the social relationships of humans with one another are a matter of objective or subjective relations. In terms of their substance, social relationships are both. They are defined subjectivity according to their genesis and mode of action. And at the same time, they function as an objective relation.

Complete reversals in appearances can thus arise. The subjective assumes the guise of things, for example, the score of a composition, a tradition throughout music. That music is notated in the form of a score and then made available in printed copies is irrelevant compared with the subjectivity hardened within the music itself. In musical works of art, however, stringency depends on the consistency of the emancipation of sounds with respect to one another. This constellation can be constructed only subjectively, but it deals with objective relations. The same guise of reified subjectivity occurs in works of art that just stand there, such as buildings. On the other hand, a scientist who slaughters an animal in his lab must subsequently determine the effects of the various medications he administered to it. It appears as though he stands like a subject at the operating table, when in fact, he is actually the extended appendage of the pharmaceutical industry, as well as an objective relation of science. What he wears under his surgical garb or the cigarette that hangs in his mouth may have subjective elements. He is an object in relation to what he does, just as he transforms both the animal and the interest of knowledge into objects. The dissected rabbit takes its vengeance on man by turning him into an object.

What a subject is and what an object is, these questions are not to be judged in historical contexts in terms of how something appears and also not using a substantive concept such as those from first nature. Instead, they always depend upon a constellation.

Hegel writes in his *Elements of the Philosophy of Right*: "Thus, the significance to be attached in what follows to the subjective or objective aspects of the will should in each case be apparent from the context, which defines their position with reference to the totality."[27]

It is usually believed that the subjective and objective are *firmly* opposed to one another. But this is not the case; they in fact pass over into one another, for they are not abstract determinations like positive and negative, but already have a more concrete significance. If we first consider the term "subjective," this may denote an end peculiar to a specific subject. In this sense, a very bad work of art that does not fulfill its purpose [*Sache*] is purely subjective. But the same term may be also applied to the content of the will, and it is then roughly synonymous with "arbitrary": a subjective content is one that belongs only to the subject. Thus bad actions, for example, are merely subjective. — But in addition, we may also describe as subjective that purely empty "I" which has only itself as its object [*Gegenstand*] and which possesses the power to abstract from any further content. Thus, subjectivity may have a wholly particular [*partikulare*] significance, or it may mean something eminently justified, since everything which I am to recognize also has the task of becoming mine and gaining its validity in me. Such is the infinite greed of subjectivity, which collects and consumes everything within this simple source of the pure "I." The objective may be understood in no less varied ways. We may understand by it everything which we make our object [*uns gegenständlich*], whether such objects are actual existences [*Existenzen*] or are mere thoughts which we set up in opposition to ourselves. But we also comprehend [under objectivity] the immediacy of existence [*Dasein*] in which the end is to be realized: even if the end is itself wholly particular and subjective, we nevertheless call it objective as soon as it makes its appearance. But the objective will is also that in which truth is present. Thus the will of God, the ethical will, is objective. Finally, we may also describe as objective the will that is completely immersed in its object [*Objekt*], such as the will of the child, which is founded on trust and lacks subjective freedom, and the will of the slave, which does not yet know itself as free and is consequently a will with no will of its own. In this sense, every will whose actions are guided by an alien authority and which has not yet completed its infinite return into itself is objective.[28]

That so little of the total labor of society was utilized for the production of the subject — this would always mean that the subject generates itself from objective material — reveals itself, among other things, in the fact that throughout the process of modern philosophy, from Descartes until today, philosophical currents can be neatly differentiated according to which concept of the self they harbor. This self [*Ich*] assumes fundamentally different guises, especially in the course of Europe's history of reflection. Descartes's "I think" characterizes a kind of existential proof. The Kantian self is the epitome of a phylogenetic endowment of categories that facilitate thinking and knowledge in the first place. The Fichtean self of agency is to a certain extent the grounds for the production of all objectivity. Hegel situates the subjective self, in turn, entirely in either the liable subject of a legal entity or the self that merely watches and breathes in the objective world process as it is unfolding. Horkheimer and Adorno no longer depart from a more-or-less intact epistemological point of the self. In this respect, they practice a relativistic theory by trying to specify further the price that the Cartesian constitution of the self must pay now that it is a violent and collectively destructive process belonging to the dominant Enlightenment. For them, Descartes's sentence reads: I think because I may be able to foresee from this that I am a *self*. It pertains to the constitution of the self by healing what its negative constitution, operating primarily as the dominant consciousness, destroyed in both objects and itself. The recognition of the dissociation of the self is the precondition for the success of this process.

In other words: every construction of an epistemological self that is detached from the constitution of the self due to social labor must pay for this detachment from the concrete objective material of knowledge with a certain arbitrariness. (It does not fundamentally matter whether this constructed self is furnished with predicables [Aristotle], categories, linguistic functions, self-reflection, and so on.) This arbitrariness creates a wholeness under the assumption of domination. Without this assumption, it can create only fragments, that is, arbitrariness.

The relations are no less varied on the side of the object. It is moot to speak in terms of individual images such as, for example, how the materiality of a glass on a table comports itself toward the thinking person sitting before it. This is a very atypical case in collective praxis. Nevertheless, this image is a textbook example for analyzing how something singular acquires its material relationality from countless invisible (that is, social) designations. However, in practice, what is most important is not to see this contrasted with a laboratorylike experiment, but rather to avoid getting lost in the real dimensions of the subject-object.[29]

If totality, a single nerve or cell within the body, forms a relation, and this whole is born into something unwhole, the nonrealized totality and the eradication of the particular signal a **loss of reality** in the social processes of living human beings. This is in itself more haunting than prison. Social catastrophes can also include the loss of one's country or expulsion; we do not mean here merely the expulsion from one's homeland in the sense of political emigration, but rather the permanence of primitive accumulation that separates off one's own place, means of production, and the imagined sense of community. These are all interior or exterior places and countries. If this is the result of an unfinished history, a lack always emerges that once again entails a knowledge-constitutive motive. Another form of this is the **loss of history**. Imagine that I have taken up a profession, for example that of a typesetter, and in the course of historical development this profession disappears. This is a concrete historical loss. Imagine that I was away at war for five years, I fired guns, was scared to death, and still carried on. But now the context of the empire, whatever this collective imagination may or may not be, has crumbled. Occupation forces settle into the city. Eight weeks later, the victors have still not been demobilized. (It is furthermore immaterial for this state, for which citizens were once ready to die if necessary, whether they are unemployed or have surmounted their reintegration.) This is a concrete loss of history, as well.

COMMENTARY 9: RELIABILITY

A SOCIETY OF LABOR produces objects (commodities, consumer goods), characteristics in humans (characters), and finally civilization itself (logic, justice). An analysis of these elements demands a particular sensitivity. The elements are active in two fundamentally different spheres: one that humans can control themselves and the other in which they possess no overview.

A farmer feeds himself and his family. This is PRIMARY PRODUCTION. He knows all the elements of the process. A craftsman in an early modern city can independently produce things for himself, his family, and the surrounding city; his independent labor does not differ from the primary sphere. Neither a composer such as Mozart nor a physicist such as Einstein obeys the orders of a ruler. The archbishop of Salzburg can commission a work by Mozart but not dictate how he composes it. However, many craftsmen do work for a paying ruler. They must then respect his will and additionally produce this will. Their product consists of convincing their client of the value of their production, and then they must produce the convincing product. This displaces them into a dependence that can be called the SECONDARY SPHERE (which today moves, as with every production, in relation to the market and demand). The question: In what can I place trust? turns out to be different in the primary sphere than in the secondary one.

We can elucidate this analytic principle practically by using every characteristic of labor. Let us borrow an example from the laboring process that applies equally to industrial labor and the labor of relationships: the group of labor capacities that combine to form the **feeling of responsibility**.[30] This feeling is composed essentially of the ability to produce a reserve of attention. Its product is called **reliability**. It is a characteristic that presupposes a freedom of disposition, a subjective autonomy contrary to the unadulterated implementation of reality. The fact that this applies not to **one** elemental characteristic, but rather to a composite in which elemental characteristics operate, is obvious. Reliability also cannot appear in the form of such a composite alone. Rather, it exists within a gravitational field connected to numerous other capacities responsible for keeping this field alive. Similarly, it is clear that completely different

247

results can be achieved with this chain of characteristics. The outcome of this is **reliability, whatever it is**, that possesses no powers of distinction of its own. Someone is reliable who in 1945 saves an entire village on the Curonian Spit. However, the torturer also is reliable. The firing of a cannon that results in destruction is reliable, as is the timely repair of a machine that prevents an accident, and so on. Their differentiation must emanate from the relations of relationships.[31]

A technical officer in the United States Air Force receives the assignment at the very last moment to transmit in code a set of revised targets to a squadron of B-52 long-range bombers, whose flight path from the Philippines to Vietnam he is monitoring. He sits in a technically equipped workspace similar to that of a control room in a factory where supervision and oversight are managed. He is considered reliable. A sense of the enterprise, the security of the airplanes, and the extent of the damage at the site of the target all depend on his feeling of responsibility. Numerous other participants in this and other campaigns of war make similar decentralized contributions without which the war could never take place. This technician exclusively culls the tools of his trade and his authority from such contributions made by all participants. Without any prior understanding, he could not transmit code. Without any training or equipment, he could not control. Without any plans, he could not transmit any revised targets. This requires no further explanation. It is the same relation as in a factory or in the relations of a relationship.

Even if he were an officer of high rank, he does not belong to a ruling class. He could not himself impose contributions. Only a portion of his self, along with several million portions from other humans, together constitute domination. This is his military conscience and his knowledge. Most of what he does is supplementary production, that is, it belongs to a secondary sphere dependent on domination.

This establishes hard boundaries in the application of his feeling of responsibility within the apparatus of dependence. If, for example, the airplanes are not safe to operate, the bombing plans are no good. In this instance, his reliability goes nowhere. Solving any crisis exceeds the limits of his influence. He maintains no relationship to primary production, that is, to what accounts for the entire set of relations. If the bomber is shot down or crashes in spite of his reliability, the technician may loathe his function. He has no stake in the production of autonomy in the United States or Vietnam, for the production of an autonomous will — be it in friend or foe — would solely be a matter of primary production.

In this concrete instance, at precisely that moment when he compares the target coordinates he just transmitted with an actual map, it strikes this technical officer known for his reliability that the targets are not located in Vietnam at all, but lie beyond the border in the then neutral country of Cambodia. This marks the phase of the so-called undeclared war against Cambodia. An intimate circle around the president originally ordered bombers to depart with instructions relating to Vietnam, and in the immediate vicinity of the Cambodian border these bombers received a revised flight path. According to the computers, this appears as a bombing of Vietnam, when in fact, it is a bombing of Cambodia. Such a war entails bookkeeping carried out by computers. The technical officer relates his specific labor capacity (his feeling of responsibility) to the fact that (1) the constitutional authority of Congress (as a representative body of the people) had been circumvented in this case and (2) the fabrication of the war's bookkeeping would lead the military apparatus into anarchy. As a result, he reports his observations to the relevant congressional committee. His military superiors perceive this as irresponsible. However, it is the same capacity for responsibility as before, merely applied to another circuit: not that of primary production, but in another sector of domination dependencies that lies somewhat closer to the Constitution of the United States and somewhat farther away from the "raison d'état of the military apparatus." The process **at** work in paying attention that is held in reserve results in a portion of living, unsolicited labor unforeseen by his superiors.

When contrasted with the reliability chosen by the technician, the various components of primitive reliability (as measured by the relation of war) appear to be tiny steps. However, his choice comes about through an exchange within the relations of relationships among quotients that together yield the feeling of responsibility.[32]

COMMENTARY 10: THE VIOLENCE OF RELATIONALITY: "THE NECESSARY PRODUCTION OF FALSE CONSCIOUSNESS"

For Marx, "ideology," in the most precise sense of the word, means **necessary false consciousness.** The concept of consciousness entails much more than what is understood of it in traditional philosophy. In this case, it pertains simultaneously to consciousness as thinking, to **conscious** being, to feelings, to motives and attitudes, and finally to actual behavior. Consciousness also lays claim to those moments when humans "do something without being aware of it."[33] The concept of ideology pivotally connotes an inversion through which the mere reflection and illustration of social relations are distorted, broken, and turned upside down. However, this is exactly the practical form of the subjective appropriation of alienated relations. How this inversion occurs arises neither out of something more-or-less random nor out of sheer will. It does not result from a lack of human experience or knowledge. It is subjectively-objectively necessary insofar as it expresses adequately the contradictory foundation of experience. Therefore, the possibility of revoking this inversion is only a given if this foundation itself is altered. Marx develops this subjective-objective concept of ideology in two contexts that seemingly have little to do with one another: the fetish character of the commodity and religion.

As long as humans produce basic commodities, which they use and implement in transparent fashion in society so they are linked to their social relationships, the relationships between these products are just as unveiled and transparent as the social ones. At the moment when the decisive form of production is the production of commodities, the social relations of humans assume the "phantasmagorical form of a relation between things."[34] The social characters of their living labor confront them as "society's natural characteristics of . . . things."[35] Marx calls the sensuous, suprasensible form of products the fetishism of commodities. The inversion of consciousness and behavior is based on this moment of the essential inversion of products. In fact, every illusion of justice and freedom bases itself on this, if we assume the production of value and surplus value that follows from the processes of exchange of capital and living labor. Marx calls the necessary labor performed on this inversion the "**privatization of experience.**" For the producers, "the social relations between their private labors appear as what they are, that is, they do not appear as direct social relations between persons in their work, but rather as material relations between persons and social relations between things."[36]

If we wish to abandon these inversions in our consciousness, motives, and attitudes, we must alter the **method of production** of this inversion. Commodity fetishism cannot be banished from the earth by sheer elucidation of its social origins. Rather, it can be quelled only through counterproduction.

Still clearer is the **relation** between something necessary, which always still contains an element of rightness, and something wrong as formulated in Marx's critique of religion. In religion, the actual need for self-illusion reproduces itself on top of mortal suffering, which for Marx can in no way be exhausted by material suffering. This characterizes in far greater detail the inner turmoil of the human foundation of religion, which is "required like a tranquillizer."[37] Marx characterizes religion as the sole intact, collectively manufactured empirical science in the suffering world. Religion is "the *fantastic realisation* of the human essence because the *human essence* has no true reality. The struggle against religion is therefore indirectly a fight against *the world* of which religion is the spiritual *aroma*. *Religious* distress is at the same time the *expression* of real distress and also the *protest* against real distress."[38]

1. There exists no place, position, process of production, or collective that reliably separates right from wrong in the production of consciousness and that effectively establishes an "immense accumulation" of rightness.[39]

2. All known historical attempts to proceed effectively according to the principle of Noah's Ark by floating atop the deluge and keeping the right pairs of animals and humans safe rest upon abstractions. To the same extent that in their radical application of the principle of exerting oneself endlessly (= goodwill) they attempt both to conserve and to establish precision in rightness, they have at the same time reduced the portions of living labor in the process of the conservation of rightness, so that the rightness equally present in wrongness is not entered into the manuals of rightness. In effect, the right rightness is subtracted from the wrong rightness. The price of a surplus of objectivity is that the substance subtracts from itself. "Philosophy impure" transports the content of experience over to grand philosophy. Pure philosophy would be without content. The category of content relates primarily to the ability of thought to bind itself to the remaining forms

251

of consciousness (attitudes, motives). The nature of the content poses the question of the practical value of thinking for those who perform mental work, albeit on an unprofessional basis, within the social division of labor. A thought containing content can also become empty when it is exchanged only among professional thinkers and is therefore rendered unusable for the collective exchange of thought between different classes. Thought thus loses its social content, even if may be right in and of itself.

3. If we insist on the differentiation between necessary consciousness (which consequently contains something right) and false consciousness (which also always contains a right moment, albeit it of another kind), then we must adopt a bold descriptive language. At its core, this choice pertains to the fact that the mixture of false and right consciousness can assemble itself more strongly on account of the pressure of objects or because of the potential for resistance against this unbearable pressure among the subjective characteristics. In this context, a differentiation emerges as to whether the inversion of consciousness can affect the autonomous agency in either the **form of production** or the **produced results**. A **surplus** of pressure from objects contorts the form of consciousness production particularly intensely. Within this constellation, a small amount of false consciousness is likely to arise. When this content does appear, however, it does so only in the form of fragments of consciousness. In such instances, the form of production is disturbed, and the self-illusory assistance of subjectivity fails to develop entirely. Rather than false consciousness emerging, we instead have a case of reduced consciousness that certainly expresses itself defectively as inadequate experience and false behavior. However, at the place where the immediate pressure of objects is less — this pressure once paved the way forward and threatens to do so again in the future; for a moment, it is nevertheless reduced — the form of production of consciousness becomes less contorted and produces excess **content** for false consciousness. In one instance, an excess of rightness within the false form of production is fabricated. In another, an excess of false content in the right form of production emerges. Since praxis always involves multidimensional processes and jumbled relationships, these poles do not appear pure in form, but rather are mixed.

We can imagine this only if we take examples (that is, situations) as our point of departure. We've chosen as one such example a fairy tale, because the portion of collected experience is much greater in these stories than any example constructed by us. Hansel and Gretel develop necessary consciousness as long as they stay put within the radius of their parents' overstimulation. They strain under the pressure of their parents to participate in all the actions of grown-ups, such as, for example, their father's marriage to their stepmother. They will have certainly observed somewhere the relations that are later to be projected onto and recognized in the witch. The result of their experience, gathered in piecemeal fashion, does not assume the form of production of unharmed childlike consciousness, but rather is their decision to leave the house; in this moment (there is just as little room for mere chance in Marx's strict concept of ideology as in Freud's theory), the children are beyond the pressure of production of their primary objects. They shape the relations in **their** production form, which is momentarily somewhat undisturbed. It is clear that in the course of the fairy tale, they radically change the behavior of their parents according to their childlike wishes. They reproduce it in their own way, so that their kindhearted parents, glad to have their children returned safely, will greet them at home with open arms. (Earlier, they were sent away because the stepmother wanted to get rid of them, and the father could do nothing to oppose her.) The children succeed in engendering an illusion in their parents only when they are no longer present in the vicinity of the house. The content of the parent's illusion is false in terms of the chain of problems existing at home. This content is more false than the relevant observations made by the children when they came to the conclusion that initially, the situation was in no way bearable. And yet the radically right form of production of human relationships, the form capable of changing reality apropos identity and the method of production of children's wishes, is contained in this wrongness.

Children succumb to a similar kind of disruption of their forms of production not in fairy tales, but rather in everyday experience — for example, when they spend time in school and in the nuclear family. A difference in the production process of their experience will reveal itself when, for example, they find themselves on the **path** between school and their parent's home.

4. If the operation of sorting out rightness from wrongness is an abstract process that does not derive from the punitive laws of ideology production, there must exist other ways out for the labor of consciousness. If abstraction is an idealist path, it is plausible to assume that the materialist path to be tested can be the **confrontation** that goes beyond the border of separated realms of experience endemic to the division of labor. If those experiences that materialize under private relations, for example, are transferred over to the realm of industrial experience, they also encounter both the pressure of objects that elicit inversions and the subjective resistance against this pressure, a form of counterlabor that expresses itself in the form of an inversion, as well. However, some of these determinations are not the same in private spheres and industrial experience. Precisely because the realms are separated in terms of the division of labor, the phantasmagorical illusion can work exhaustively on a "real relation" in this confrontation without having to encounter the need for inversions back to where it can trace its roots. (Producing such relations requires an invention.) The inversions (that is, abbreviations) of the forms of production of experience that are in the service of critics of the pressure emanating from objects are reversed when compared with the pressures predominating in private relations. In fact, such a confrontation is not easily produced. This is almost entirely prevented not only by the other side of the division of labor, the historical separation of domains, but also by comprehensive inversion processes — as they appear, for example, in temporal rhythms and the pressure of time — that determine the operating labor process **and** the times of private relations. It is not the case that children would be interested in the world of industry or that lovers would have the inclination to meet one another in an industrial setting. Instead, the spatial and temporal forms of a business do not allow for such contacts and confrontations, just as the private realm of intimacy shuts out the intrusion of industry's nosiness. This is one of the reasons why the self-evident form of consciousness production stemming from the confrontation (association) of heterogeneous labor methods in various fields of experience has not yet established itself as a constitutive praxis.[40]

5. When we argue that the principal point developed by Marx, the asso-
    ciation of the working class — that is, the association of humans on
    the plane of necessary consciousness production — includes the **con-
    frontation** of all antagonistically fabricated fields of experience, we do
    not mean this in the affirmative sense. Were this confrontation manu-
    factured, thus resulting in the creation of an alternative process of
    consciousness production, all these processes would still be subject to
    the austere concept of ideology as Marx had used it; it is still a matter
    of the necessary production of false consciousness. Through confron-
    tation, a greater **opulence of relationships** to rightness and falseness
    arises. However, extremely massive production processes are envis-
    aged along with this; the production of false consciousness has at its
    disposal an unevenly larger number of open ends. There remains in
    this case the fact that historical experiences from one realm, when
    applied directly to another, comport themselves primarily ahistorically
    and therefore inadequately. It is also the case that the undoing of
    experiential production in society (industry, the experience of children,
    education, the experience of women, the experience of love, modes
    of experiencing intelligence, and so on), which produces splintered,
    reciprocally self-subtracting, and ostracizing worlds of production, is
    a source of misunderstandings or, in other words, ideology production
    in the classical sense. At the same time, however, the heteronomy of
    all these realms guarantees that the production of experience in these
    ghettos cannot be considered conclusive, since the reasons for the pro-
    duction of errors in a certain realm always possess only partial validity
    due to the heteronomy (that is, the separated historical development)
    in every other realm. Thus, with the associative connection of the ends
    of experience that prove themselves to be open, the production of right
    and false consciousness is blended anew. The subjective-objective
    chance for disentanglement, however, is as good as foreclosed within
    the single area **of a** mode of production. Conversely, at the point of
    confrontation of **various** realms of experience, such an opportunity is
    likely due to the fact that here, objective labor processes based on the
    struggle against concrete resistance are possible for the very first time.

COMMENTARY 11: ON THE DIALECTICAL RELATIONS OF GRAVITATION IN HISTORY

We arrived at the deliberations before you because one of the most important manifestations describing the dialectical method, namely, the turning of a concept of historical relations into its opposite, appeared to us as a special case of German history. Both the majority of historical-dialectical movements and their encipherment appear to consist of mere inflections. All dialectical relations are exceedingly multipolar and are subject to distortions and dialectical **inflections**. But they evince little tendency either to come to rest in their own concept or even to turn into their diametrical opposite.

Dialectics is not only a method for investigating historical relations. It is also the concrete ratio of motion throughout history.[41] The method reads as more or less an imitation of reality.

The Dialectic Is Ungrammatical

The last sentence that Rosa Luxemburg published in 1918 ends with the revolution itself speaking to the reader: "I was, I am, I will be."[42] This is what the revolution says of itself. It is language that imitates the extralinguistic grammar of revolution. Yet a distinction must be drawn: the abbreviation, expansion, and inflection—that is, the grammar—wreaked by language differ from that other language that constitutes the subject matter about which we speak. Historical inflection and the permanence of the revolution are a production process, that is, they consist of the subjective labor of the revolutionary, the antilabor of the counterrevolutionary, as well as that of those who are indifferent. They are composed of materials already processed, as well as of those still waiting to be processed. They consist of a lack, circumstances, and so on. Only through language can they speak in the first person. A revolution that once was contains a gravity that acts on every "I am" and "I will be." It is not possible for me either to pass beyond the naive, bitter experience of revolution of the victims, who paid the price of victory, or entirely to separate myself from the revolution because it failed. All bygone revolutions—"I was"—contain a "strong feeling." "I am" encompasses an anticipation of the revolution as subject that impacts every other possibility for inflection: "he (she, it)" or "we are," "you all are," "it could be," "we hope it is so," "may it be," "we are so distraught that . . ." "we would like to note most humbly that . . . " and so on. In other words, it affects all the possibilities for movement and change—the attitudes and feelings—of revolutionary processes.[43] Practically her last will and testament, Rosa Luxemburg's final words, which seem like a one of a kind when compared with the later contents of *Die Rote Fahne* in which they appeared, elicit movement in us when we read them.

However, if we compare real relations of inflection—the Commune of 1871; the revolution of 1905 in Russia; the German Revolution of 1918, which was already established as a failure when Rosa Luxemburg wrote; the bloody May Days in the 1920s; the end of World War II without any revolutionary result; the death of Salvador Allende; the meritocracy that followed the Chinese Cultural Revolution; the many different occasions to which the funeral march "Immortal Victims" has been played throughout the history of socialism—the abundance of relationships evincing the extralinguistic grammar of historical events stands in radical contrast to what a grammatical inflection captures. Rosa Luxemburg's sentence moves us. Because she died shortly thereafter, we cease to fabricate our thoughts. We begin anew because that cannot have been the meaning of her last will and testament. We must endure the inadequacy of mere thought, on the one hand, and we must search for ways out, on the other. In other words, we must look for a dialectical research method. It must be felt. It must be conclusive. It cannot consist of mere grammar.

The Difficulty with Rooting Dialectical Perception in Sensuousness

Norbert Elias writes of *Homo clausus*.[44] The need to assure themselves of something (that is, to acquire **reliable** experience) allows humans to involve their powers of perception effectively so as to look out at stationary objects from a fixed house or cave. If the primary experiences were historically such that it could not be said whether the objects of perception were harbingers of something good or bad, how much additional uncertainty would arise if they were also in motion?

Our skin is a housing that secures us. The brain, says Elias, rests protected in a container made of bone. The heart, too, lies in a kind of container (that is, the chest cavity). The sum of all secure skin-covered enclosures, along with the housings of perception, is a house; language, culture, and all anticipations of collective consciousness, that is, of *humanity*, resemble houses. Even an epistemologically grounded philosophy exhibits the tendency to defend its own skin against a noumenal world in fantastic motion. The historical instinct characteristic of subordinate experience therefore seeks to transform nouemena as directly as possible into phenomena "for me," preferably by partitioning off portions of perception, bringing the complex and confusing movements outside to a halt, and making them available to me for processing and appropriation. Such a praxis of perception proceeds contrary to the forms of movement of all objects in a society. What's more, a human being does not function as a *Homo clausus*. He is a social being, alive by virtue of the fact that he "opens the doors to others."

However, the civilizing process of perception shows no consideration for this subjective-objective realism. Rather, it criticizes the reality principle practically by resisting perception as soon as the security system that is acquired in distress believes itself to be at risk. This system contains the entire historical labor power for balancing (that is, the development of balancing techniques for blocking and giving attention that somehow enable one to tolerate distress). No need for perception is strong enough with respect to this historical groundwork. But the security structure must disrupt the vortical gravitational relations in which the dialectical movement permanently subjects all objects to its environs and all perceiving humans to its conditions in the most invasive of ways. This is also, for example, the dialectic of a world consisting of practical constraints with respect to the material of the pleasure principle that enters into the knowledge-constitutive motives and insists, in this instance, on its obstinacy, and so on. **Under historical-cultural relations, the defense of dialectical perception is thus more likely to stave off than to turn toward the reality principle**. The senses prefer to act like myth, "determining" things from the outset, rather than consign themselves to the hellish circumstances of a winding movement until such point in time as what about it that affords security is determined.[45]

Departing from this economy of needs for security, the geocentric, Ptolemaic worldview is plausible as long as the emergence of a Copernican interpretation becomes possible, albeit neither through the experience that separation processes are inescapable nor as the accumulation of the "courage of cognition." Yet the security economy ("To what extent can I either still retain basic trust or acquire new trust?") demands the substitution of geocentrism in the form of a very severe and linear causality. In place of a central and organic globe as the central point (that is, the world as a human relation), the world must appear in the Laplacean "mechanique celeste" or at least according to the Newtonian universe as a gigantic machine, a clockwork in which tactile contact exists between virtually all causes and effects: control. The movement outside of me is restrained. If I just know the necessary number of laws and the characteristics of the causes, I can forecast all movements backward forever and forward into every future. Newton's universal mechanics still combines the unsolved relationship between matter and light via the narrative of a novel: **on the one hand, harder than iron, and on the other, permeable, like nothing, ether mediates fictitiously between materialist mechanics and wave movements**. The need for security is at work here. The dominant concept of experience derived from the natural sciences of the nineteenth century pervades social analysis retroactively. In close contact, causal chains—both tactile and securing—pervade history. Social formations follow one another in blocs. At the interfaces of such a representation, the comprehensive and subterranean movement of dialectical processes is substantial enough to catch one's eye; the most intense construction work is necessary in order to deal with this contradiction between perception and the thing itself. But the basic concept of **determination** [*Feststellung*] is not forsaken.

Money is kept in a cage so it can jump around freely = "security house." [Alexander Kluge Archive]

"A little house." [Alexander Kluge Archive]

The Idiosyncrasy of Everyday Movements

Labor power is produced in the form of genealogies on a daily basis. Parents have children. It can be ruled out that children can ever really deprive themselves of the vicinity of their primary objects. Conversely, it can be ruled out as well that they are copies of their parents.[46]

In everyday experience, it is indisputable that associations, feelings, and fantasies are all in motion. In fact, we speak of **"being moved" by** our **emotions** [*Gemütsbewegung*]. We recall here the suggestion put forth in "The Workings of Fantasy as a Form of Production of Authentic Experience" in *Public Sphere and Experience*.[47] In these parts of consciousness (going all the way down into the sensory apparatus), we refer, above all, to such countermovements against outside impressions.

Contrary to Hegel's account, which settles largely on bipolar examples (for example, lordship/bondage), Marx deals with multidimensional, tripolar and tetrapolar dialectical relationships, as, for example, when he describes the relation of production, distribution, and consumption as an organic whole; however, production itself serves as the comprehensive factor. All of these poles can be asymmetrical to one another. It is also not said whether they together form an organic whole; they can also run parallel to one another for long periods of time, blocking points of contact without ever thereby arresting the dialectical movement between them. Their molelike labor falters when the separations are not deep enough, but their energy nevertheless affirms itself immediately elsewhere. Monsters are more likely to emerge than kinetic energy is to give up moving.

Gravitation. "The birth of the planets." [Alexander Kluge Archive]

The Turn of Master/Slave Relations, Outlasting Causality, Third-Party Damages

In World War I, Germany consisted of enormous amounts of lordship/bondage relations. Let us assume that they moved dialectically, just as Hegel describes for the labor of consciousness. At some point, the lord will be the bondsman's bondsman and the bondsman the lord's lord. Abundant material needs to be ferreted out to prove that on the one hand, the relation switches, and on the other, how it does not switch at all in its most impinging reciprocal effects. The same goes for France. The same inner movement of lord and bondsman, entire contexts of it, can be found throughout its history. Both aggregates of lordship/bondage relations now battle against one another in Verdun with the notion that only in war can it be decided which two nations would be lord or bondsman. On account of an entirely different causality, a third power meanwhile appears—the United States, itself consisting of particular lordship/bondage relations—and withdraws one of the reasons for the outbreak of the war, namely, the competition for the Eurocentric domination of the world. The effect of such large sequences of motion uncoordinated with one another can be traced back to all the individual movements, the changes in allegedly private relations, ethics, and the forms of political, military, and economic intercourse that make up all lordship/bondage relations. Causality prevails everywhere, but so, too, does unconnected movement, albeit with the strongest of repercussions. Think, for example, of Versailles in the German national consciousness (there, it has two diametrically opposite meanings) while Wilson's words were still ringing in people's ears. He not only promised and kept his word, but his country, which revoked his promises, also became at the same time one of the biggest believers in the Reich and nevertheless assumed the means to pay huge debts by removing economic hegemony from Europe. If the dollar became the leading currency in this way, what alarming insecurities and reallocations would have arisen (for example, for Prussian consciousness) from long-standing servitude and now inflation! Jazz was in and of itself just a new form of music that appealed to the ear, but this music contained a whole appendix of social meanings; practicing it freely in the Reich's territory symbolized a national humiliation ("nigger music") and thus had to be combated by people who otherwise did not care for music.

Does this form of movement apply only to human relationships, or does it also relate to the objects in a society that are fixed in everyday experience:

for example, houses, cities, machinery? If I pound against the wall in a jail, or run into a lamppost, or barricade myself in my house, this contains the experience that such objects are solid and are not in motion. The mistake lies in the fact that we depart from a special case of experience. From this observational standpoint, the impression of solidity depends on things. However, there are other imaginable points of observation. If they are entire historical epochs or the continuum of history in general, the point of observation is chosen arbitrarily from the temporal core of **a** person's age. Imagine an observer who sees 1,000 years just the way that the everyday eye surveys an hour of time. The total dead and living labor that was active has the status of an observer in possession of such a view of history. If I see a city such as Mainz, for example, from the observational standpoint of this historical view, its Celtic founding, its Roman influence, the Middle Ages, the occupation by France's revolutionary armies, the resurrection of the Revolution's parades in subsequent Mainz carnivals, its Prussian municipal offices and train station, the bombing in World War II, its reconstruction and industrial transformation all move together into a movement that transpires historically and realistically. I see this as a film.

City/Bombs
One of the most influential inflections in the historical concept of Mainz, for example, would be the burning and leveling of the city by Allied bomber fleets. Concatenating linearly the causal chains put into motion by the Allies—manufacturing a bomber command, flying devastating bombing runs over German cities—with the causal chain that is Mainz's two-thousand-year history would be extremely arbitrary. But if I cannot describe a relationship that penetrates that deeply, what do the remaining statements have by way of use value? Either I state what are more or less coincidences, by-products, or I follow what happened as lines that cannot be connected. In this way, it is certain that the geographical position of Mainz is determined by the fact that the Rhine River delineates a curve and the Main River flows into it. The same fact returns in the tactic of night bombings: if I have not found other cities in order to drop the bombs according to plan, then my bomber crew can still find this distinctive river constellation when the light of the moon is reflected in it. That means additional bombings of Mainz. A minor matter is explained, but not the primary one.

If, conversely, my investigation proceeds radically, I come across the dialectical relation of movement: someone is either killed by a bomb in his cellar or evades it by a hair's breadth. Attempts must be made to agree on the fact that a bomb's concentrated form of movement, its acceleration, is not solely determined by the gravitational force from even one gram. An industrialized form of social acceleration manufactured by a high concentration of labor power is stored in it. Only the technical data of the bombs (the narrower view) enter into its destructive power. The instinct to flee, the wish to escape, the cellar dweller's **strategy from below**, hardly serviceable in the moment, all these things are the product of the history of labor power as well. It is precisely this individual labor power that is unable to develop a counteracceleration against the bombs because the level of concentration of history and labor power in it is so marginal when compared with the level that materializes itself in the bomb. People and human prehistory confront one another all at once in the aggregate state of a bomb and, conversely, in the form of a human who wishes not to be destroyed.

A bomb could not fall on a cellar if gunpowder, aviation, and metalworking were not invented or if the bomber crew had not been trained. A discipline is required for all this that presupposes the groundwork of two thousand years. A few million particles of once-living labor dispersed microscopically are contained in an explosive bomb: no individual can fabricate the product as living labor, let alone deploy or drop it; a professional bomb possessing the polished character of mass-produced commodities (as opposed to an improvised bomb) also does not come into being as a one-of-a-kind product. What falls from the sky is labor power. What is annihilated below is labor power, as well. There is more dead labor contained in airplanes and bombs, in other words, greater portions of life spans, than portions of dead and living labor sitting in cellars. This is the concrete form of reciprocal effects.

The difference lies not in the fact that the one would be private and the other public; it would indeed improve nothing if he who sees himself exposed to the bomb were a (public) dignitary such as Roland Freisler,[48] or if the labor power were in full possession of its labor resources and experienced the bombing in a cooperative context: for example, all workers from a factory, screws, wrenches and other tools they have there — none of this would change the situation. The difference lies in the contrasting accumulation of historical "speeds" (mass) between bombs and victims.

The Differences among Clocks

In the nineteenth century, a few thousand Britons, supported by gunboats and military expeditions, forced their way into China along the coast and the main waterways. They bought and sold — opium, for example, which they had cultivated and purchased in other colonial zones. They did everything according to a form of movement measurable as a temporal feeling according to London's **economic clocks**; these clocks were the revenues and the fluctuations of all values on the stock exchange. **Distribution** was the overarching factor. The swiftness of transportation followed this swing of the pendulum (steamships; trains; the Suez Canal as a shortcut in maritime routes; a clear-sightedness for what had value; quick reactions; the shifting around of mercenaries, for example, Sikhs; the promptness of mail and organization; the quickness of British nerves; British conversation; jokes.) The average between a cannon shot and a commercial transaction conveyed the average of this social speed. Compared with this time (to fire a shot, for example, or to set one's sights on a Chinese person or a valuable object), which is determined by the reversal of the organic relations of production and distribution — as long as this relation is valid, it remains constant — Greenwich Mean Time acted interchangeably. It evinced a clockwork rooted in other values as soon as the newcomers reached China.

In their aggressive business affairs, such "old China hands" encountered a class-bound people passing through an agricultural phase.[49] The English said China was like a sleeping giant. It was "the middle empire," thousand-year clocks. They told of negotiations with the Chinese in which they never got to the point quickly, but attempted to wait out their adversary using so-called Asian patience. It took a lot of British stubbornness to endure this. "The clocks in the Chinese homeland tick very slowly."

No English enterprise — with all its dominance of distribution — survived independent of production and consumption. Older Englishmen (retirees from India and other colonies) remained in the British Isles, they were still bound to the younger interlopers in China by way of **a** generational contract, which **passed** experience on from one generation to another. This older generation distorted the values that Britons bustling around the world gathered together. Children in the schools, grass widows in country estates, officials in governmental positions, functionaries working in the stock markets, they all lived pro rata from income that the distributive interlopers together looted in China. The elder Britons were bound to the younger intruders by a series of conventions (for example, teatime, a puritanical upbringing, but the pendulum in their consumer clocks had a distinctly different swing. Before, they worked part-time (that is, as distributors, robbers); now retired, they often had better ideas in hindsight. They were in the position to perfect belatedly the illusion of imperialist approaches. Kipling's India is in this respect more sympathetic and tangible than every actual colonial practice in India. Brecht remained interested in the Indian experience; obviously, his were more durable experiences than those of the British practitioners, who foundered.

Both British components—consumption on the island and distribution outside—found a limit in the production processes that transpired "simultaneously" in England. This factory production was just as subordinate to the same movements of the London stock exchange, but it had its own moment, its own laws, and a particular feeling of time that showed only partial consideration of the speeds of the world. Three different nonsynchronous movements (even when they were measured according to the same days, years, or hours) took their course in the English empire, and in China, these three different movements encountered other movements, such as the ones that have emerged in present-day Shanghai.

After the end of World War II, it turned out that the three most important English clocks ran down. However, the social clocks of China apparently evinced a very different tempo after 1949. It is highly unlikely that in those few years, the basic dimension of the social course of movements could have changed so drastically. Obviously, this had to with clocks that already ran quite differently from how the Europeans had thought they did. When measuring time according to constants and interests and not according to some arbitrary universal mechanism made of the gear mechanisms of which clocks are composed, there is no irreversible sequence of events that separates the temporal modes of past, present, and future from one another in "everyday experience" and its corresponding language. Rather, the real dialectic of temporal movement consists of the fact that the future is the past, the past the future, and the present both; each of these components is each and every other one, as well. Or it consists of the fact that the influence of this dialectic also forms an organic whole, the past as the comprehensive factor engaged in production, much like manufacturing, distribution, and consumption. If the real relations are a field to be tilled, the described relations of the movement of time are a determination of the field's furrows.

"A horrendous act, committed in silence"

Two deaf youths beat to death another twenty-eight-year-old deaf youth because he bent their license plate and spread rumors that they were criminals. They forced the defenseless man to drink a pot of glue, filtered into him a "chocolate drink" made of carbonated water, perfume, and pepper and salt, stepped on his hearing aid, tried to kill their victim with jolts from an electric razor, and then clobbered him to death with bottles. At the trial, an expert witness pointed out that they had only the sense of taste and touch as well as their eyes at their disposal. Their senses were effectively caged in and wanted to break out by avenging **their** lack of sensuousness on the **other** deaf youth. The eye, their one remaining primary sense, was a "cold sensory organ"; it mediated only cold impressions of the world, but none of the "warm" power of emotions.[50]

By nature, the eye is not "in itself" a cold organ. Optical perception courses through a portion of the brain, the *thalamus opticus* (Greek for the German "Sehhügel," literally "seeing hill"), by mixing ocular impressions with the widest variety of stimuli from other organs so that a common "emotional labor," either "human warmth" or rejection, emerges. The massive disruption of other senses annuls this processing of the eye's impressions. Not only is human sensuousness borne by other humans, but the *individual senses* also acquire their specific characteristic as *human senses* from the labor *of **other** senses*. The isolation from one another makes monsters.

Before his death, Adorno intended to publish a book entitled ***Coldness***. For **society as a whole**, the **individual eye** acts coldly (just like every other isolated sense). The social eye, which exists not as a subject, but rather as an immense abstract collection of tattered pieces wrongly pieced together as a pseudosynthesis, accumulates splinters, as it were; it acts coldly toward individuals and small groups responsible for producing personhood. Not only war, but also this normal solitary condition "produces monsters" (Goya).[51]

COMMENTARY 12: THE ANCIENT NAVAL HERO AS METAPHOR FOR THE ENLIGHTENMENT; GERMAN BROODING COUNTERIMAGES; "OBSTINACY"

"The *Odyssey* as a whole bears witness to the dialectic of enlightenment."[52] The story of Odysseus's homecoming describes not only the Enlightenment's forms of movement (cunning, sacrifice, a breach of contract, consciousness), but also a human relation to history, the apparatus of labor (that is, the entire attitude of a human who avoids home only then to return, who "throws himself away, so to speak, in order to win himself").[53] Horkheimer and Adorno describe a trader, an adventurer, and a cheat, and at the same time an entire way of working, along with individual labor characteristics that no longer willingly unify themselves into a self, an organized whole:

> The heart grumbled inside him.
> . . . he struck his breast and scolded his own heart.
> "Bear up, my heart. . . ."
> He spoke that way, scolding the heart in his own chest.
> . . . it bore up and stayed firm.
> Yet the man went on tossing this way and that way.[54]

"Truth as process is a 'passage through all moments' as opposed to a 'proposition that contains contradictions,' and as such it has a temporal core."[55]

This temporal core can be more closely defined. Imagine the naval hero and his temporal core: he tied himself to the mast while his senses turned toward Scylla and Charybdis. This is self-control, a mastery of external nature, but also a mastery of the companions rowing with their ears plugged down below in the belly of the ship. They are themselves representatives of those who actually built the ships at home and who performed, beyond the realm of myth, the unsavory labor at the oars of real ships: slaves.

The roots of Greek as well as Phoenician naval adventurers—exchange, haggling, cunning, and the imaginative reversal of contracts—are to be found in the absence of the greatest portion of labor. This work is done by slaves with an apparent lesser capacity for obstinacy than, for example, Odysseus's beating heart and his sharp eyes, which automatically empower themselves from things.

And the holiness of green is revealed...
...Cultivating keen senses....
The breeze carves its way
And the sharp northeasterly
Quickens their eyes.[56]

This is the temporal core that Marx characterizes as both the childlike happiness of ancient Greece's stage in history and, at the same time, the core of the idealist tendency, the apparent enormous freedom of consciousness over objects. Greek thinkers did not quantify. They were not interested in the nature of objects, but rather in their entelechy. They dealt with them like playmates who can be swindled, and not like playthings, and certainly not like the objects of labor. That the lion's share of production labor is "supplied for free" by a foundation of slaves means that matter is excluded, thereby creating the cunning candor[57] that is interpreted in societies with other temporal cores like ours, for example, as a happier time that cannot be imitated.[58]

If we shift our attention within the realm of ancient myths, a constellation reveals itself in the report on the *voyage of the Argonauts* that, in its approach, varies the way the naval hero Odysseus grasps the world; this approach entails an essential shift in perspective: the opposition appears not in the shape of a nature metaphor, but as human victims, as Medea and the Colchians who suffer under the enterprising, enlightened grip of others. We presume that this other side of the ancient mythical report speaks abundantly to the brooding Continental tradition of myths and enlightenment, as well as to the German one in particular. The opportunities for comparison are to be found in what appears in ancient myth on the side of victims. Let us therefore imagine that as a metaphor for the dialectic of enlightenment, Horkheimer and Adorno investigated not the *Odyssey*, but the story of Jason. What this shift in perspective says will later be revealed.

Marx, Engels, Lenin, and Ovid. [From Alexander Kluge's *Nachrichten aus der ideologischen Antike*, 2008]

I. The Story of Jason

The crew of the Argo consisted of an elite group of heroes (that is, lords, a few of whom were practically children, but princes nevertheless); in total, they were fifty-four men with a hunger for new experiences and booty.[59] Among them were nautical experts such as the helmsman Tiphys, fortune-tellers such as Idmon and Mopsus, who knew how to fly the Boreads; another was a sprinter; Lynceus had supernaturally sharp eyes; Heracles was a specialist in mechanical power grips. Two sons of Hermes presided over the arts of transfiguration and were specialists in the practical application of cunning and trickery (for example, thievery without the use of violence). Polyphemus was extremely old and clumsy, from which followed special talents; Meleager was young, and therefore had a special talent, too; Palaemonius was by birth lame, resulting in special abilities; the uncle of the young Meleager was a pedagogue; the participant Orpheus was a musical magician as well as a theologian; the sons of Leda, Castor and Pollux, were specialists in cooperation and mutual help and as friends, they awaited a rapid ascendancy.[60]

This collection of experts, each a bearer of characteristics, is slightly reminiscent of a ship full of war heroes. However, it is also certainly not ship full of workers. Their motivation is initially general. The narrator of the myth feigns that Jason embarks on the trip on account of an intriguing piece of advice: someone hopes that Jason perishes during the risky enterprise. Everything else is a consequence of this piece of advice. At the same time, the narrator maintains that Zeus has determined the necessity to repatriate the Golden Fleece back to Greece. In this case, it would be a national and divine determination that started the far-reaching journey. However, in the course of the story, every one of the participants, as well as Jason himself, obviously demonstrates their desire first and foremost to retain their diverse characteristics. Secondarily, they seek booty. It is an opportunity to bring to bear their surplus acquired at home (from their prehistory and slaves) on the riches owned by agricultural tribes thought to be "inferior" living along the Black Sea. The mortals *must be thoroughly exploited* because doing so turns out to be *possible*. The particular freedom of these Greek robbers refers to this surplus of preproduced history. Specialized characteristics end up as export products.

The Golden Fleece
The Golden Fleece pertained to the following matter: Phrixus, like Jason a grandson of Aeolus, escaped being attacked by his stepmother and being sacrificed by his father by fleeing with his sister, Helle, on the back of a ram. Helle drowned in Hellespont;[61] her brother reached Colchis safely. There he sacrificed the ram, whose wool Hermes, god of commerce and thieves, turned into gold for Zeus. At Zeus's command, the Colchian king, Aeëtes, took in the rescued Phrixus; at this point he acquired the golden hide of the sacrificed ram. In the vicinity of his town, he had the fleece hung up in the god of war Ares's grove, where a **sleepless** dragon guarded it. Under serious threats from the house of Aeolus, which Jason represented at that time, Zeus demanded the repatriation of the fleece back to Hellas. Jason set out.

The entire context is arcane. It becomes even more confusing when further details are considered. In the moment of the catastrophe — "carried through the heavens over land and sea," but now surrounded by the waters of Hellespont — his sister, Helle, slips and drowns, and the ram begins "to speak like a human being."[62] The ram speaks again in another passage, following the rescue of Phrixus, at which point he is furnished with the golden hide by *force majeure*, and yet again when it suggests sacrificing itself to the highest god in order to be on the safe side.

The dragon guarding it is "immune to both brothers": death and sleep. He was born from the womb of primeval Earth and begotten by the flow of "lightening hot, scalding blood" from the head of Gorgon.[63] He is also a snake "with the infallibly deadly poison of the rebellious primeval adversary slain by mankind."[64] The passage is structurally related to a detail in the Prometheus myth and finds itself an equivalent in the *Argonautica*, book 3, verses 865–68: the potent magical Prometheus flower. Its roots are identical to Prometheus's "flesh, just freshly severed" so, on the one hand, he suffers torturous pain when the eagle injures him and, on the other, also suffers when the root of this plant is cut;[65] its dead petals are pieces of him. When prepared according to ritual, this "titanic" root produces titanic characteristics and a titanic ego, but only for *one* day. Otherwise, it is poison.[66] There exists a *telepathic* connection capable of setting off battles in love and the soul between the potent magic of the Prometheus flower and those who imagine it. This is all a matter of farming, something "anti-Jason."

However, the Golden Fleece is guarded not only by the aforementioned magic dragon, but also by machines of "mortals"; the farmers of Colchis have crafted armed automatons whose bodies protrude out of the earth and wage, on the spot, defensive battles in the name of security.

The inhabitants between the Black Sea and the Caucasus are farmers, incidentally just as in the world of non-Greeks and non-Phoenicians. They form huge empires, the capitals of which accumulate great riches. The Greeks have had their eye on the secret of these riches, in general, and the locations of these amassed treasures, in particular. In a sense, the gaze of these traders and looters, honed through exchange and deceit, only transforms the riches into treasures that feed supply chains. This is indicated by Hermes's touch of the ram's hide. As a result of his touch, the hide of an ordinary ram turns into gold. However, it remains confusing why the ram can speak, why he comes from Helles, why he suggests his own sacrifice (and this use of a human voice), and why the so carefully guarded hide is transformed into the highest incarnation of a wealthy agrarian society already presiding over so many other treasures. The Greeks do not retrieve something that was once theirs. In this respect, the ram has two different faces; there exist two different rams. The one was never in Greece and never transported Phrixus and Helle, but rather was an animal belonging to the Colchians. The Greeks have their own prehistory, as well, one that is not included in the story's catalogue. This other ram dates back to this prehistory. The story of the flight of the siblings, of the sacrifice of the ram, of the Golden Fleece, as well as that of Prometheus — all these stories form the basis on both sides, that of the Argonauts and that of mortals, the Colchian farmers. The Greeks and the Colchians merely emanate out of this prehistory at two different social speeds.

There is an additional clue why the Golden Fleece is so desirable to Jason and his companions. The actual valuable thing about it is not the golden ram skin, but its backside. It is there where a drawing had been scratched showing the entire globe with special reference to the places where treasures are stored. This map is supposedly what was at stake for Jason. This is also the explanation for the passage in the fourth book by Apollonius (verses 552–56), when the muses ask:

> how came it that beyond this sea, along
> the coast of Ausonia, among those Ligurian islands
> known as the Echelon, so many sure traces of Argo's
> passing survive this day?[67]

They did not sail directly home with Medea and the Golden Fleece, but far out into the western Mediterranean, gathering up booty according to the map, and only then returned to Hellas.[68] This unexpected tour in the western part of the globe is inexplicable in the story of Jason and Medea. It was recorded in the myth in atrophied form, is included only in part in book 4, but historically forms the central issue.

The Violent Learning Process of Commodity Exchange on the Mediterranean Sea

Several myths contain layers that do not reveal whether they were invented by the Greeks, the Minoan Cretans, or the Phoenicians. This is immaterial for an exchange economy's mode of production that plunders a ubiquitous agrarian society.

Phoenician ships appear off a coast lined with farming colonies. The ships' crew spreads out merchandise on the beach: pots, iron tools, and so on. The inhabitants along the coast collect these interesting objects in the night, because they believe them to be gifts from the gods. However, this was no exchange. The crew arms itself for a punitive expedition in which some of the colonies are burned to the ground. They retreat again to the ships. From now on, the inhabitants, who know nothing of exchange, but everything about victimhood, seek to reconcile the gods. They spread out valuable sacrificial offerings, foodstuffs and products from the land. The crew takes the "stolen" merchandise back to the ship the night of the massacre and once again spread them out the next morning. Two rows lie next to one another: the ship's goods and the countersacrifice of the native inhabitants.

During the ensuing night, the ships' crew takes the sacrificial offerings (for example, native products) for themselves. The ships then set sail. After some hesitation, the inhabitants take possession of the merchandise on the beach that they may now own without trouble. Following a few recurrences of these lessons imprinted by fire and sword, they know what exchange means. The learning process would not be possible were it not related to earlier divisions in the form of bribery or the appeasement of nature, enemies, gods, community, and so on.

Entire series of events together form the equivalent of what constitutes the separation of labor power from the soil and community (that is, primitive accumulation) for *production*. For the distribution of commodities (the exchange relation), a similar code of learning exists, introjection on account of violence. The story of the downfall of the Colchian "mortals," their losses, Medea's loss, and her eventual revenge are only another way of reporting on this basic event.

The Residents of Colchis, the Arrival of the Argonauts, Different Social Speeds

Aeëtes was still king of the Colchians in the previous myth about Phrixus and the ram. In the native lands of the Colchians, clocks run slowly, and the passing of tradition down through the generations is unflagging. In contrast, the Argonauts experience frantic crises over and over again. The myth indicates this by continually displacing its temporal and narrative rhythms. We hear elsewhere about a five-day feast. Jason celebrates his reunion with relatives over a meal at which the men

> through five full days and through
> five nights . . . gathered the finest of
> life's sacred joys

and then we read an abridgement of the verse, a description told in a mad rush.[69] Another representation of speed, an eagle, then appears. However, it is not an eagle as we know it, but a divine servant with a monstrous constitution, by "nature an ethereal bird" (that is, conceivable only in the ether), with airy, light feathers like the "paper-thin, supple trim of a flag."[70] It possesses "swift feathers, with which it brandishes in his body a strength like that of many oarsmen," in other words, oars in a sea of air.[71] On the one hand, its "polished oars" prove especially light, and on the other, they project the image of something massive and hard that digs in, something violently opposed to something else.[72] This overbird [*Übervogel*], which from the clouds high above shakes the entire (until now billowing) sails with its speedy surge, makes the "sharp-whirring" noise of its pinions.[73]

In the verses, such images of imagined excessive acceleration correspond to the speed of thievish cravings, in this case, to that of the Greek seamen in search of new experiences and booty.

In contrast, compare the wondrous "bronze" bulls in Ares's fields in Colchis (where the fleece is also hung on a tree). They are slow, in contrast with the usually extremely light-hoofed cattle.[74] Compare, too, Jason's alacrity in carrying out his intentions, regardless of which situation he happens upon; if need be, he coordinates his plans again with his companions and always does so affirmatively (that is, when necessary, he implements his intentions with whatever detours, cunning disguises, deception, or pretense at his disposal). Compare as well Medea's very slow decision-making process, which concentrates on just a few main issues (the alliance with Jason) after some initial confusion; even the grounds for her revenge accumulate slowly over the course of repeated experiences of betrayal (Jason betrays her not just **once**, but rather **multiple times**, and thoroughly so). The slowly evolving theme of revenge first **erupts** suddenly, and it does so incidentally, without the influence of any intention and without Jason's usual tendency to speculate on the chosen means. Medea uses the first instrument that comes to hand to murder her two children.

The Law of Hospitality

The arrival of the Argonauts in Colchis takes place in secrecy. They hide their ship at the mouth of a river, invisible from the Colchian capital. All this serves the purpose of avoiding confrontation. The fleece was to bring about exchange, not war. Aside from ingenuity (the will to exchange), they carry along on their ship hardly anything else they would willingly trade.

Initially, Jason leads a discussion, that is, an exchange. He guards himself against any reproach that could be made against him, the leader of the Argonauts, in the event his decision not to rob Aeëtes, but to approach him forthrightly, turns out to be a mistake. In fact, it turns out to be a grave mistake that could almost have led to the downfall of all his troops. However, approaching Aeëtes frankly was called for by a moral law, one of the few that Jason and his troops recognized at all — the law of **hospitality**.[75]

Jason's demand for the fleece is also based on this principle. In the face of possible refusal by Aeëtes to give up his unique treasure, Jason senses (book 3, verses 179–90) "offense (κακότης) and slight (ἀτίσσει) among his band of newcomers."[76] Precisely because the great king was superior in power compared with the Argonauts, he must acknowledge the principle of hospitality — that he cannot easily turn down the request made by this gaggle of his inferiors. The Argonauts have something they can offer in return, as well: they have together undertaken a dangerous voyage throughout half the world expressly for this purpose, and they have done so, in fact, not willfully, but rather under the compulsion of both gods and men. They are *xeinoi* in these lands, and so Zeus asks of the *xenois* that the foreigners retain the *xenion* (a gift from their host) for which they ask.[77]

The great Colchian king Aeëtes must reluctantly respond to this moral aspect of the right to hospitality. By refusing, he would have put himself in the wrong from the start. He would have morally dealt the other party a free hand to retaliate as they like. The realist Jason knows Aeëtes is forced by the principle of hospitality to give in, and in the end, he promises the fleece; but after much reflection, the king vows to prevent the realization of the promise. In this event, Jason already has the intention of committing robbery (this, too, excludes war as an outcome). Aeëtes breaks his promise of hospitality, an act that otherwise would be unusual for the gods and the social contract of Greek traders and cheaters, and thus delivers the moral justification for Jason's later plans. In all of the ensuing events, all known means of intrigue, magic, crime, betrayal, and murder are used; hospitality (that is, the exclusion of open violence and its necessity) is one way of communicating between two different societies; this *one* principle is not violated at any point in time. Hospitality may become a mere formality, it may be foiled or get turned upside down, but it remains the law for both sides. The side that abandons it loses.

Exporting Environmental Destruction; The Aggressive Spirit of the Greeks

The Argonaut's ship brings misfortune to the country; each of the individual special characteristics among Jason's companions makes its own contribution to the disaster. Money does not appear in this myth, but the destructive effects that monetary exchange had historically on agricultural and tribal organization [*Gentilverfassung*] are described. The organized defense of the sacred grove fails on account of the theft of the Golden Fleece. In fact, Colchian society itself threatens the fleeing Argonauts, but they are the ones who will perish. Part of this society, in the person of Medea, defects to the enemies, but she is betrayed even before the journey begins.

In an early scene with Medea, "clear" speech accompanies her "soft" crying, as if she were already horrified and full of fear. "In this hour, she thinks she knows that . . . only the selfish win and that unscrupulous betrayal is the trump card."[78] Book 4, verses 136–38:

> Fear struck at the newly delivered mothers, and around their tiny infants,
> still sleeping in their embrace, they tightened agonized arms, as the
> hiss left the babes atremble.[79]

Fränkel says: "Such gestures of fear and defense" are "without practical value."[80] Medea says to the Greeks: "You ruthlessly harnessed me to serve your plan so that you could then betray the consequences of my kindhearted help."[81]

The Argonauts procured allies, but it is certain that allies could not in fact protect them. In a later passage (book 4, verses 419–422), Jason sacrifices Medea, his bride, prophylactically: "It was far more reasonable to subject Medea to possible death by torture than to his expose his troops, to whom Medea would have also fallen prey, to certain ruin."[82]

A Greek ship. [Alexander Kluge Archive]

An image from a Central European fairy tale. [Alexander Kluge Archive]

II. Why the Myths from the Continental Interior Speak Differently; Labor Writes Its Myths in the Form of Objectified Production

Myths of a specific social relationality (that is, its prehistory), every myth in itself, and all myths together can be read like an "orchestra score . . . were it unwittingly considered as a unilinear series; our task is to reestablish the correct arrangement"; that is, as a score, it "must be read diachronically along one axis—page after page, and from left to right—and synchronic-ally along the other axis, all the notes written vertically making up one gross constituent unit, one bundle of relations."[83] If myths are read against the grain, they tell of collective history; however, they do so **in their own way**: broken down into parts not in just any potential discourse, but rather solely in their relationality.

If we examine the exact description of the catalogue containing the *Argo*'s equipment and payload, what is interesting is *what is missing* on the ship. While the provisions are not forgotten, the entire foundation of the enterprise is: who really rowed and performed the labor, the ranks of which the elite heroes were not a part. Herein lies the difference between Mediterranean and Continental myths (even though the latter were handed down not on the Con-tinent, where they arose and again disappeared, but rather in border zones (for example, in Iceland) or repatriated themselves only partially from such border zones back to the Continent). We soon will turn to the myths of the blacksmith Wieland (Volund) and Hudrun; both worked and held no slaves.

What differentiates ancient myths from German fairy tales and at least a few legends (myths) from the Middle Ages—we initially use "myth" here in a broad sense and as a "metaphoric concept"[84]—are two factors in this context: *that a house, farm, and field could not escape danger, like a ship*; and *that the dimension of production (or the poverty resulting from it) is the defin-ing moment*. Production or its disruption in ancient myths is almost always located on the side of the victim. We described the voyage of the Argonauts and Medea's fate in detail because both the former's and the latter's agrar-ian peoples characterize that layer in myth that would be related to German experience. However, if production is now the comprehensive moment (and not comprehensive as in antiquity, but rather exclusionary), stories are told in twofold fashion: first in the forms of material production, of landscapes, villages, paths, fields, castles, naves, as the "*open* book of . . . human *psychol-ogy*," then in complementary fashion in the forms of fairy tales and legends.[85]

The myths of the upper class are different from the folkways of fairy tales, both structurally and in terms of their temporality. Departures, adventure, even circumnavigating the world, and at the very least, distant travels are found in accounts such as those of both Parzival's father and Parzival himself, or in the account of the duke of Swabia and Ernest II; other legends are told from bottom to top and develop as folkways; this appears to be the case, for example, with *The Song of Roland* or the "Lay of Hildebrand," both, incidentally, precarious, almost static situations of defense and adversity and by no means an adventure. We are interested, above all, in *fairy* tales, their princes, their outlook, their long-term goals (perhaps the model is the son of the village magistrate?); we are not concerned with their accounts of their characters' deeds. The dialectic of enlightenment means something amid threatened production or delayed nonproduction—in other words, what is entrenched in houses—that resists interpretation when projected onto antiquity.

The Wolf and the Seven Young Kids: Enlightenment as the Capacity for Differentiation in the Defense of Home

Of all the German fairy tales, "The Wolf and the Seven Young Kids" best describes the specific dilemma connected to the defensive production of security, the confirmation of the world, and interiority and exteriority, that is, the basic themes of the German Enlightenment.[86] The tale is not about actions in the form of the Greek spirit on the offensive, which is possible and successful only in this free form when slave labor lays the groundwork and then disappears in the myth (only the ram is occasionally given a human voice). It is about being on the defensive. The house is immovable. It cannot engage in evasive maneuvers, like a ship.

The *Dasein* in a fixed home is also not hungry for adventure, as Odysseus was.[87] It is to be full of vigilance. The problem of home is that it can never be completely barricaded. The seven young kids absolutely must let their mother, who brings them food, inside; conversely, they must keep out the wolf.

Neither Jason nor Odysseus has this problem, nor does Theseus. Their adversary is always clear; it is only the ways to outwit him that are ambiguous. For both the Continent, and at the same time, the labor that demands relationalities (that is, in other words, what is not possible *alone*), the problem lies not in cunning or detours, but in the differentiation between loved ones and the foe. This differentiation is difficult. One cannot be surprised enough that the kids actually take the flour-covered paws of the wolf, as well as its voice made supple by eating chalk, for a depiction of their mother.

They succumb to deception because what they would let in and what they would have barricaded themselves against obviously correspond to one another. The lord of the community was once, at some point in time, something good, but his grandchild did nothing good. The "old law" enjoyed the trust of many, but now when employed by lawyers brings nothing but disaster. The vastness of the country was my power, and now it separates me from everyone else; I gave myself entirely to it, and now I am betrayed. That is precisely Medea's slow learning process, which ends in the catastrophe of her self-destruction. Whether that affects Jason remains to be seen. It clearly hits like a bolt of lightening. We must consider that the weapon of revenge does not meet its mark. We must consider once more that what counts as foe becomes blurred. It is extremely difficult to say whether the wolf with paws that are covered in flour and a chalky voice is the mother or whether (means or ends) the mother has floury skin on her hands and a chalky voice, and so on. This shifts the meaning toward the decisive question: How do I recognize my enemy at all? *Where* exactly lies the boundary between inside and outside, between safe and absolutely dangerous?

As accounts of historical experience, all Central European myths process the question regarding the "how" of wishes, narrated from this central point of uncertainty: How can the inside be recognized from the outside? The exalted pleasures of the eye in Greek myths prove themselves to be either an absurdity or an ideal. The telepathic connection between Prometheus's liver hacked to pieces by the eagle and the root of the plant identical to this liver or a product of it, which incidentally could be hacked up as well, this connection is lost in the defensive position typical on the Continent. Origin, meaning, and being — from each of these roots, an independent hierarchy forms, hierarchies separated according to wishes and labor. In other words, they form a double root. It turns out that even this complicated division of one into two — a root system and foliage, with all its diversity — does not apprehend experience.

In protest against thinking in causal chains — thought "originating from the root," which includes traditional radical thought, as if coerced relations resembled a tree or were something organic — Gilles Deleuze and Félix

Guattari have propagated the word *rhizome*.[88] They write: "We call a 'plateau' any multiplicity connected to other multiplicities by superficial underground stems in such a way as to form or extend a rhizome. We are writing this book as a rhizome. It is composed of plateaus."[89]

The matter is complicated. A Brazilian wasp and a Brazilian orchid do not resemble one another in the least. The wasp is not a copy of the orchid, and the orchid is not a copy of the wasp. If the wasp touches the orchid in bloom, it is devoured. This reciprocity is a rhizome, and that does not lend itself to causal interpretation. It would be a misunderstanding of Deleuze and Guattari to infer a link. Their work exists as protest, that is, their interpretation seeks not fate, but rather ways out. If we apply this to Continental myths about the labor of securing one's home, it is no longer surprising why the kids have difficulties differentiating between what they should definitely allow inside and what they should keep outside, whatever happens. The fact also comes into view that *on account of the specific relations of German history, it was initially difficult to determine whom Germans let in with Hitler.* There were couriers bearing nourishment, flour-covered paws, and voices both falsetto and wolflike. The man privately called himself Wolf, but actually was Adolf. He kissed women's hands, issued criminal commands, was a vegetarian, cared for both a chicken in every pot and equality, eliminated an entire people in the cruelest of ways, and brought about unity.

Finding ways out — avoiding Hitler — requires a rigorous capacity for differentiation. This is a question of production. What if someone emerges from the Left? In his last will and testament, Hitler regretted only one thing: that instead of being shackled to "appeasement," he did not make a clear stand and take action from the bottom to the top. Otherwise, the oppressed peoples in the Arabic world would have been on his side in order to secure the final victory over the plutocracy.

The Temporal Core of the Brothers Grimms' Fairy Tales

We refer to the 1812 edition of the Grimms' fairy tales. In the later edition of their collected works from 1819, Jacob and Wilhelm Grimm inserted a string of texts and suppressed a few, as well (for example, "How Some Children Played at Slaughtering"). They thought them too cruel for household use. The fairy tales were recorded between 1806 and 1811. A few came from older women, such as Dorothea Viehmann, who was over fifty years old.

Others came from younger women, such as Henriette Dorothea Wild, later the wife of Wilhelm Grimm, who already told stories at the age of sixteen. It can be assumed that the choice of words and the style of most fairy tales correspond temporally to the kind of storytelling and exchange of experience common in the middle and late eighteenth century or even at the turn of the century, around 1800. The Brothers Grimm changed nothing. Even though a few traces that are retained in these fairy tales may directly reflect narrative reminiscences going back only three or four generations prior to the Grimms' collection, the contents of the individual tales, down to the wording, are of differing ages. Some of these phrases and themes can be traced back to the eleventh century; nothing in them was invented by a single individual. The collective experience of *a single* narrative layer belongs to the Baroque and Biedermeier periods. However, this layer is rare. A *second* layer, in particular, the so-called soldier fairy tales, is based on experiences from the sixteenth and seventeenth centuries. However, the bulk of fairy tales reflects experiences characteristic of the entirety of German history going all the way back to the tenth and eleventh centuries (which is how the original form can be corrupted by overlapping layers). The collection begins with the words: "In olden times, when wishing still helped, there lived . . . ."[90]

We know it is risky to infer from narrativized memories from the Biedermeier period continuities that date back several centuries. We place trust in the traces themselves within the fairy tales, in the comparison with other sources not elaborated here, and ultimately in the plausibility of correspondences between the course of history and the fairy tale's response. This sense of trust develops when we contemplate who told these tales and wherein their specific economy of fantastic activity lies, and in short, when we observe how fairy tales reverse real experiences. If we know, for example, the manifold forms of coercion used to appropriate labor in the late Middle Ages — the social mechanism — we can also read its reversal in "The Twelve Lazy Servants,"[91] the story about an eccentric contest between twelve servants who inventively compete with one another to see who, in the face of mortal danger, accrues the largest amount of laziness. They also demonstrate how difficult it must have been to produce laziness and how life-threatening and injurious the forced countermeasure to laziness — coerced labor — could be.

"A house of one's own." [Alexander Kluge Archive]

A Few Distinctions in the Story of the Seven Young Kids

The site of altercation is the front door to a house. In the fairy tale "Freddy and Katy," the latter is exceptionally clever at safeguarding their house from robbers while she delivers meals to her husband working in the fields.[92] She excels at this because they have gold hidden in their house. The Dutch door to their home has a top half and a bottom half. In order to lock the door securely, Katy, in her infinite wisdom, bolts the top half and removes the more important bottom half from its hinges and carries it on her shoulders. The door cannot be left alone (even when it is bolted) without individual supervision. Later, Freddy and Katy sit in a tree while thieves below have broken into the house, stolen the gold, and divided up their booty. The door then becomes too heavy for Katy, who had carried it on her back, and so she throws it down from her perch; the thieves believe the devil did this and drop everything. The married couple then carries their gold back home. The important bottom half of the door thus fulfills its original task of securing the house after all.

The young kids negotiate three times with the wolf through a similar door, simultaneously a closure and opening to the outside, before they allow themselves to be deceived. However, after the wolf breaks in, the house itself consists of hiding places. The best such place is a grandfather clock. The wolf overlooks the youngest of the young kids hidden in the clock (in older versions, the hiding place is not a mechanical instrument, but a cave below the house), who then manages to deliver the news to their mother.

The wolf's attributes include: his gruff voice ("Yours is gruff. You're the wolf!");[93] he is deceitful ("The miller thought, the wolf wants to trick someone. So he refused"); first and foremost, he uses deception and second, he wields violence; the wolf "satisfied his desire"; and he is godless ("We'll fill the godless beast's belly with [with stones] while he's still asleep"). The kid says he, too, is an animal, but the wolf is the only real animal in the story.[94] That the kids speak with a human voice is not as conspicuous in the German fairy tale as when the ram unexpectedly begins to speak in the ancient myth. That the animals mutually deliver one another over to the wolf is conspicuous, however. The wolf "made his voice soft." In the end, the wolf knows: "Six little kids I thought I ate / they're more like stones with all their weight." In spite of all this, he leans over the fountain, the heavy stones pull him in, and he drowns.

In contrast to other fairy tales, this story is especially influenced by the time in which it was told (see, for example, the theme of the grandfather clock and the interior furnishings of the house). Only the theme, and not the narrated form points to earlier times. The most surprising thing is how such a lack of powers for differentiation arises at all: How can the mother be mixed up with the playacting wolf? Why does he continue to sleep when the kid cuts open his stomach? Why does he not heed his observations that he might have stones in his belly? He takes notice of this, but draws no conclusions. How short and devoid of experience the conclusion is! The kids run past and cry aloud: "The wolf is dead! The wolf is dead!" To a certain extent, it is a revolutionary solution to rise from the dead out of the belly of violence, *but the kids do so without any word about capacities for differentiation acquired from their experience*. Who will be the next to knock on the door? What disguise will he wear? The unsolved question, incidentally posed by children today again and again, points to the processing of original experience that consists of exclusions and omissions.

The relation of kid to wolf is told differently in other fairy tales; take, for example, the Grimms' fairy tale number 148, "The Animals of the Lord and the Devil."[95] "The Lord God had created all the animals and had selected the wolves for his dogs. However, he had forgotten to create the goat." "Then the devil got ready to create as well and made goats with long fine tails." Since God had forgotten them, the devil had to help out; he is admittedly an imprecise creator. "Yet when they went out to graze, they usually caught their tails in the brier bushes, and the devil always had to go to the trouble of disentangling them from the bushes. Finally he became so fed up that he went and bit off the tail of each goat." The tale ends with the following: "This is why all goats have devil's eyes and bitten-off tails and why the devil likes to appear in their shape." In any case, the devil had problems with the kids: they graze alone. They gnawed away at fertile trees, precious vines, and "spoiled other tender plants." God laments this: "Out of *kindness and mercy, he set loose his wolves*, and they soon tore apart the goats that went there."[96]

The devil also has problems because he must take care of his creatures. When God's creature, the wolf, kills the kids, the devil must file a grievance: "Your creatures have torn mine apart." The Lord answers: "'Why did you create them to do damage?'" The devil replies: "I couldn't help it.... Just as my own inclinations tend toward destruction, my own creatures can have no other nature but this. So now you'll have to pay me compensation." God now becomes cunning, like Jason. He promises payment for the dead kids if all of the oak leaves fall. In the autumn, the devil demands payment for the liability. The Lord

286

talks his way out of it. In the vicinity of a church in Constantinople stands a tall oak tree; while the leaves in Germany fall from the trees in the autumn, this one still bears its foliage. The devil must yield his claim. He feels cheated.

Once again: the capacity to differentiate. Who here is the cheat? The caring and lawful devil, to whose many labors *obstinacy* adheres? Things certainly never function as they are decreed. His labor power doesn't do as it's told, but rather possesses its own will. How benevolent is God, who requires tricks and sics wolves on kids to tear them apart? How careful is the devil, who initially grants his creatures "long fine tails"? (Compare this with: "made his voice soft.")[97] Even if the kids destroy delicate vegetative life in one case, how excessive is the punishment?

Imagine humans somehow looking for affirmation under the broadest array of particular relations of violence from the twelfth to the eighteenth centuries. All basic points of reference transform into one another; sometimes it looks like this, other times like that. Misfortune is within the home or outside of it. It is uncertain whether or not I should lock out the most important things or whether or not I should let the most malfeasant things inside. How this differs markedly from the fixed plans, cunning, differentiations, and contractual breaches in the *Odyssey*! At best, the overlords can proceed offensively. These characteristics are known to be those of God; the devil does not succeed in imitating them, no matter how much he wants them. **Those who tell fairy tales are not in control of the capacity for differentiation. A permanent doubt is at work at the point of contact between inside and outside.**

The original core of this fairy tale is solely the scene at the front door of a house; in this precarious situation, the question is: Are doors for letting in, or keeping out? Second, it consists of the broad experience in obstetrics, that is, the art of maieutics. The mother must hurry back home, fetch scissors and needle and thread, and effectively cut open the belly of the foe: "and no sooner did she make the first cut than a kid stuck out his head." They leapt out "like a tailor at his own wedding."[98] Marriage, birth, door, inside, outside. In this relation of relationships, the primary problem lies in affirmation.

The Song of Blacksmith Volund

The Rugian Queen Giso held two blacksmiths captive and had them work for her. One day, her little son ran to the jailed blacksmiths. They seized the child and threatened to kill it if she did not set them free. The queen gave in, and the blacksmiths were able to escape. "That happened around 500 A.D."

The medievalist Felix Genzmer continues: "This widely known story appears to have inspired a Teuton to model a short saga with the help of Greek and Roman templates."[99] It is quite clear that in its many versions and precursors, some of the themes from the verifiable story of the blacksmith Volund became almost completely unrecognizable due to scars, fissures, and elisions. It is obvious, too, that traces of the original story were tied together with the myth of the blacksmith Daedalus. Compare as well the commentary by the Roman author Maurus Servius Honoratus (from the fourth century A.D.) with a passage by Virgil in which the crippled god of blacksmiths, Vulcan, rapes the goddess Minerva, who came to him to call upon his skills. The ancient reports about Vulcan/Hephaestus and Daedalus are to the story of the precise and emotionally laden Volund poem (in spite of its mutilation) just as an allegory is to real experience.

Verse groups 1–11 (out of a total of 41) describe the elf Volund's longing for his feathered loved one, the Valkyrie Hervor Alvit the All-Wise. On the one hand, this longing is the theme for his art of metalworking (from other sources, we know such longing to be matriarchal). And on the other, this longing is the reason for his inattention and the absence of any appropriate watch over his home. The robber king Nithuth (the name means "hater") was therefore able to tie him up with cord and hold him prisoner in Wolfdale. He must perform indentured labor from now on. The two brothers, Nithuth's children, visit the blacksmith, wanting to view his treasure chest. Just as they peer in, Volund cuts their heads off with the sharp edge of the chest's latch and makes drinking cups for Nithuth out of their skulls. These are so artfully wrought that the king's daughter becomes jealous. She visits the blacksmith to have a ring made. "He overcame her with beer, because he was more experienced / so that on the couch she fell asleep."[100] Intoxicated and unconscious, she is impregnated by Volund (similarly to the way the goats interact with the sleeping wolf).

The king originally had the enslaved blacksmith chained. If he wanted to make use of his work, he had to undo his shackles. He therefore had the tendons in Volund's legs cut. The hamstrung blacksmith could not run away. For this reason, on account of his longing, as well as the abundance of his experiences, the blacksmith obtained the ability to fly. (The creation of magical winged garb or wings has faded in the mythology to the point of being unrecognizable.) And thus he flew past the king's court and made him aware of his revenge; in spite of his paralysis, he could still escape. The king's progeny, however, will be Volund's children. He had left behind something for the violent lord, something from which the king could not separate himself without becoming heirless.

The Story of the Rejuvenated Little Old Man

The temporal core of another story about a blacksmith, "The Story of the Rejuvenated Little Old Man," [101] is roughly a thousand years older than Volund's poem. The story begins with an ancient convention, the motif of the visit of the gods: "At the time when our Lord still walked on the earth. . . ." God calls upon humankind's hospitality and turns out to be grateful for it. (The myths of Philemon and Baucis begin this way as well.)

Thereafter, the full-fledged story begins. A destitute little man, a beggar, intrudes into the blacksmith's house and "demands" alms. But the blacksmith has nothing to give. It is nonetheless impermissible to receive the gods (disguised here as God and Saint Peter) and to turn away a beggar. The gods realize this and help out. They ask the blacksmith to light the forge and place the little old man in the hearth "in the middle of the glowing fire, so that he became as red as a rosebush." The little old man is then placed in the quenching tub "so that he was completely covered by the water." The little old man pops out and "was straight, sound, and fit as a young man of twenty." From that moment onward, he could once again look after his own livelihood and hire himself out as labor power.

The blacksmith had an old, half-blind, and hunchbacked mother-in-law. He watched carefully at this smithing of a human being. The mother-in-law asked the smithed youth "whether the fire had burned him badly," because she herself was venturing a try at becoming forged young again. She would like this "with all my heart." "So the blacksmith made a big fire and shoved the old woman in the forge. She wriggled this way and that and cried bloody murder." The blacksmith applied all of his skills but "the old woman would not stop screaming, and the blacksmith thought, this isn't working out quite right. So he pulled her out and threw her into the water tub." Right at this moment, both of the mother-in-law's pregnant daughters approached. "They both ran downstairs and saw the old woman, who was lying doubled-up in pain and howling and groaning. Her wrinkled and shriveled face had lost its shape." The shock gripped them to the marrow. They both gave birth on the same night. But the newborns were "not shaped like human beings but like apes. They ran off into the forest, and it is from them that we have the race of apes."

The core of the story lies in its middle section. The beginning and the end are modern (in spite of their allusions to antiquity). Without being distracted by the visit of the gods and the ape imagery, we must attend to the story behind the story, its core. In comparison with these conventional interpretations, the core of the story deviates from all known conventions. What we must read is this: a blacksmith—smithing human beings anew—so that they are able to work—so that they retain their earlier value—this happens with the help of gods; that is, it is possible *in principle*, but when a *blacksmith* tries it *on his own* — this fails, even when giving birth. To be sure, this misfortune is not a direct causal effect; only the old woman is miserably burned. She does not carry on into the future, but suffers on her own. However, her example (that is, the human's resistance to being forged) is made via her daughters, whose offspring turns into apes (or another sort of miscarriage). Immediately after birth, however, this offspring resembles adults (that is, they immediately run into the woods).

The Sense of Collective Agency; When Nothing Collective Is Possible
We are interested here in two fairy tales, an old one and a new one. Written in dialect, the first tale, "The Domestic Servants," is about a woman who meets another woman while traveling down the same path.[102] They decide to walk together. In their conversations, they discover that they both have husbands named *Cham*. They each have a child. Both children have the name Scab. Conveying a sense of the women's rhythmical movement as they walk, the conversation continues: What is your cradle called? For both women it was called "Hippodeige." They both coincidentally had a servant whose name was exactly the same. His name was Do-It-Right. And so on. The text shows how two completely identical individuals find pleasure in and tie their pleasure to uniform movement.

Diametrically opposed to this story, the second tale in question tells of a man and a woman who live on a clod of earth too small for the both of them. "She slaved away from morning till night."[103] But wearing sackcloth and ashes or working all day as often as she does is hardly an existence. One day she thinks: if I *found* a gulden, and someone else *gives* me one, and *my husband gives* me yet another (she knows, however, that he has nothing to offer), I would *borrow* a forth on top of the three and with it *buy* a cow. One night, she shares her unfounded plans—they are based on nothing—with her husband. He agrees and says: then I would be able to drink a glass of milk every day. "What?" the wife exclaims. "You want to drink all my milk away? If this is the case, I do not want a cow." She insists that he should not profit from the transaction in the least. And thus they fight until the early hours of the morning.

In this tale, collective agency is impossible, even though these two persons are pressed together so closely by the relations in which they find themselves. Although the entire future plan is but a hopeless idea, the wife is horrified by the thought that she should share. At the very least, what is nothing — the unfounded plans at her disposal — should remain strictly *her property*. Yet she cedes nothing of it. I myself can create the illusion of making my misery go away (for example, by making plans: "if I *found* a gulden," and so on). However, I cannot deny my misery as reflected by others who sit across from me. I hate *my* misery in the image of the *other*. This corrodes all common ground.

"The Obstinate Child." [Caspar David Friedrich, *Winter Landscape*, 1811, bpk, Berlin/ Staatliches Museum Schwerin / Elke Walford / Art Resource, NY]

"The Obstinate Child"

The shortest of the stories in the Grimms' *Children's and Household Tales*, "The Obstinate Child," is the absolute countertext to the gentleness of Friedrich Rückert's poems set to music by Gustav Mahler and collected under the title *Songs on the Death of Children*:

> Once upon a time there was a stubborn child who never did what his mother told him to do. The dear Lord, therefore, did not look kindly upon him and let him become sick. No doctor could cure him, and in a short time, he lay on his deathbed. After he was lowered into his grave and was covered over with earth, one of his little arms suddenly emerged and reached up into the air. They pushed it back down and covered the earth with fresh earth, but that did not help. The little arm kept popping out. So the child's mother had to go to the grave herself and smack the little arm with a switch. After she had done that, the arm withdrew, and then, for the first time, the child had peace beneath the earth.[104]

It is unusual for parents to be as brutal as the mother in "The Obstinate Child." The German word for obstinacy—*Eigensinn* or *Eigen-Sinn*—which can be rendered into English literally as "one's own sense," that is, the ownership of the fives senses and therewith the power to perceive everything that occurs in one's environment, describes exactly what must first be established at the level of individual historical development in order for the life of a human to be viable. For there to be obstinacy, a strong sense of autonomy in a person's behavior needs to be seized upon. We can articulate this alternatively thus: the discipline experienced by the obstinate child even from beneath the grave is the moral answer to a previously unsuccessful collective expropriation of the senses. Had it been successful, it would not have necessitated persecution that goes to the bone. Such a traumatic horror lasts for centuries in the ranks of society.

Obstinacy is not a "natural" characteristic, but emerges out of destitution. It is the protest against expropriation reduced to a single point, the result of the expropriation of one's own senses that interface with the external world. In his autobiographical novel *Green Henry* (*Der grüne Heinrich*, 1855/1879), Gottfried Keller narrates the story of the obstinate child differently and, in fact, *more lucidly*. The protagonist Henry (aka Heinrich) remembers how, suddenly one evening, he could no longer pray. His mother refuses to feed him dinner, but fails to hold out for very long. She draws closer to him in a conciliatorily fashion and says, "'There, you may eat it, you obstinate child!'"[105] The good mother manages to reconcile with her son. Yet an evil mother frequently also has a hand in compensating for the infractions caused by obstinacy.

The narrator of the novel, Henry Lee, returns in his later years to his hometown and is reminded of a story from the year 1712 when he sees the "'grave of the child-witch'" in the corner of the village cemetery.[106] A child of noble birth was handed over to a priest in order to be healed from an unfathomably premature case of witchcraft. The cure failed. "In particular, they had never been able to induce her to pronounce the three names of the most blessed Trinity, and she had remained thus godless and stiff-necked, and had perished miserably. She was reported to have been an extraordinarily delicate and intelligent girl, of the tender age of seven years, and yet, nevertheless, a witch of the deepest dye."[107] After subjecting her to lashings, hunger, and isolation from the outside world, the priest mishandled the child to death. The mother wished her little Meret dead rather than obdurate; she hired an artist to paint an image of the child with a human skull in its hand. As the coffin was lowered into the grave, a shriek rang out; the little Meret sat upright in the coffin and ran, with a horde of children in tow, atop a mountain, where she then "fell down lifeless, whereupon the children crawled around her, vainly stroking and caressing her."[108]

Only those to whom violence was done still have the sensuousness of suffering; only they can reconcile the injuries. And that, in turn, would be solely using violence and only in death; the mother must herself visit the grave and "smack the little arm with a switch." The children hound little Meret to death, only then to caress her. Even if obstinacy is constituted amid the expropriated senses, it keeps on living underground as a collective memory, one that can be overcome only by a separate ritual of reconciliation not synonymous with a simple death. The separation of terra firma from the community engenders relations of domination for which obstinacy is no less dangerous than the full development of the riches of the senses.

A Comparison of *Antigone* and "The Obstinate Child"

We cannot unfold the German text about the obstinate child any further. In comparison, the obstinacy of an Antigone in Greek mythology developed into a more differentiated and elaborate narrative. Herein lies the difference.

With respect to a specific temporal and class-based core of society, Freud describes the emergence of the Oedipus complex and its downfall as a formative stage in the psychodynamic development of the "character of boys." This is an event within the history of an individual. Yet all individual histories together enter only as a portion into the collective historical relations of the species (delimited only by the temporal core and the class relations of a specific epoch).

Freud did not seek out the psychodynamic development of women's character in a counterpart from the same myth (that is, the complete history of Oedipus and his children). Rather, he took up the myth of the house of Agamemnon and therewith discarded the term "Electra complex." But why did Freud not look into the continuation of the Oedipus story? Why does his interpretation not try to decipher the obstinate Antigone?[109]

Antigone acts on the assumption that if birth is humankind's entryway into the world, its exit, death, must be something worth human dignity, an absolute value not subject to the worldly power of Creon. She lets herself be walled in alive lest that subjection were to happen (even the German *obstinate child* is, in a certain respect, buried with *living* [that is, lively] obstinacy.)

Antigone does not renounce her intentions to bury her brother. When one considers the millions of women who, on account of the forced multiple layers of oppression, accept the basic elements of female containment — both unpaid and shrouded in privacy — in either the patriarchal relations of a reality that is not theirs or in the walls of marriage, if this is the condition for the maintenance of production, it then becomes obvious that the decisive stage in the development of continuities in the female character is described by the fate of Antigone. The Antigone complex must be studied, just as the Oedipus complex and its downfall have been studied. On the one hand, such an investigation would query the historical dimension of the complex at the ontogenetic level and, on the other, its phylogenic production in the collective process of history (in other words, the retroactive effect of every individual history stacked on top of one another.) This is necessary, especially now, if (as with the Oedipus complex) a new temporal core of society is to develop that is also capable of bringing down the Antigone complex.

This is a difficult example for the historical pursuit of individual labor characteristics. Their history — that of obstinacy beyond death — obviously deviates from countless other labor characteristics. In addition to being historically detached, it is significantly asymmetrical with the dominant culture. Measured according to the conventional labor of reason, the story would be considered unrealistic or antirealistic. Coincidently, the story is hardly detectable without an elaboration of knowledge-constitutive interests, otherwise it would become blurred in an explosion of feeling that can be traced back to "more realistic" causes such as those contained in the foreground. It is evident that such an essential characteristic has long had an influence on the sensuousness of social processes and is in no way confined to women. However, it is bewildering that theory has next to nothing to say about this temporal core. "To shun the sensible in monkish fashion is to exhibit cowardice of abstract thought." There is "a revolting arrogance that is directed against the moment of sensible presence . . . aspiring to be abstract thought."[110]

Translated by Richard Langston

PART THREE

The Violence of Relationality

CHAPTER SIX

War as Labor

French miners—"workers in uniform"—dig tunnels into a hill near Verdun in 1916. Also dressed as soldiers, German miners drill an opposing tunnel from the other side. Both groups of specialists intend to blow each other up sky-high. Whoever is faster will survive. To succeed, each of the opponents must pay close attention to the actions of his adversary. (They listen, drill, or dig faster or slower depending on how the other behaves.) If an extraterrestrial saw this, it would appear, as the dramatist Heiner Müller once observed, to be a form of cooperation. It is, however, a horrifying example of the COLLECTIVE LABORER, a concept that Karl Marx elucidates in the fifteenth chapter of CAPITAL entitled "Machinery and Modern Industry." The term combines all the labor capacities on earth into one concept. That does not prevent them from fighting to the death.

Colloquial terms for it are "operation," "victory," "defeat," or "battle." WAR is actually composed of a special form of labor that we must investigate if its monstrosity is to be effectively opposed.

In a letter to Albert Einstein in 1939, Sigmund Freud wrote that no moral code can help prevent war. (Often, such codes themselves bring about wars.) Those of us who are against war, Freud continues, must respond with all we have. It would help if we were to have an "allergy to war." In the obstinacy of labor power, forces may well reside that are spontaneously effective against war. Nothing else will help. The PRINCIPLE OF PRODUCTION is powerful against the PRINCIPLE OF DESTRUCTION. It is valid in the long run. Just as a general strike cannot last forever, so, too, workers eventually return to their jobs. In the short term, it is disappointing that until now, the principle of production has been subordinated itself to the principle of destruction at the outbreak of every war.

I.
War appears to us as something so overpowering that we do not see its small steps for what they are, as what makes war work: applied labor capacity, **labor.** Each of these individual steps would never in itself constitute war; they become war as a composite. Even the **social relations** of war have not been investigated.

II.
"In the two front ranks were the elite fighters wearing helmets and breastplates. On account of the heightened danger and because they owned better equipment, they received higher pay and were named *Doppelsöldner* (double mercenaries).... Artists of the period, as well as those who came later, have attempted to depict how this clash actually looked. However, because they did not understand the principle of the closely packed charge and also wanted to depict the fighters as heroes, they depicted it as though the pikeman had space to the sides and from behind. But, he was shoved forward and often could not thrust his spear at the enemy where he was most vulnerable.... This happened in a matter of seconds before the fighters were *face to face*. Since a pike square was 50 men deep, with everyone pressing forward against the pressure from the other side, the men were squashed, forced to turn, and they easily lost their footing. Those crowding from behind trampled on the men lying on the ground and fell over them. The ranks at the back could not see what was happening at the front and continued to shove. Many...had their ribs crushed. In this kind of battle, it seems possible that fewer fighters were rendered unfit for battle through stab wounds than by this crushing. The outcome of the battle was particularly uncertain when both squares were of a similar strength."[1]

III. The Division of Labor
The pike square was a military tactic developed by the Swiss Confederation (that is, by the inhabitants of cities) and supported by the landless younger sons of farmers. Like the halberd before it, used by the Swiss on November 15, 1315, at the battle of Morgarten and then at Laupen (1339) and Murten (1496), the pike was superseded initially by the Dutch pike and then at the end of the Thirty Years' War by shot-formation tactics. The principle of the pike square entails pushing, striking, and stabbing. The mechanical pressure of

Until the seventeenth century, pikemen marched in densely packed squares. The main square is termed the "pike square." On a loud cry or a signal from a horn, the formations advanced toward one another. The battle took place **face to face**. [Alexander Kluge Archive]

the mass of bodies that push is unstoppable; striking and stabbing or any kind of labor that changes the situation is unusual.[2] In the square itself, there is no possibility of orientation other than by the direction indicated by a flag; the pike square, in other words, is not able to change direction once it has started to push forward.

The leaders are planted up front in the first row. The only form of interaction besides mechanical pressure arises out of cooperation with an armed wing made up of a rear guard, a vanguard, or smaller pike squares (the so-called **forlorn hope** [*verlorener Haufen*] that can serve as bait for the enemy). The principle is that of a pair of pincers with a strong and weak handle [*Hebel*], or a strong hammer on a weak anvil, or a strong anvil and a weak hammer, which would imply defeat. From the perspective of the pike square, a battle thus appears as if an (imperfect) tool were being used, one consisting of approximately twenty-five hundred men subdivided into fifty rows deep, each containing fifty soldiers standing shoulder to shoulder. The square behaves like an object, that is, like a piece of dead labor. The living labor takes place in training for the battle, in the discovery of the arena of battle, and in the composition of the square as it is laboriously assembled. It takes between two and a half to four hours to get the parts to fit together properly.

The overwhelming success of these pike squares was a result of enemy tactics. Armies of knights could not remain in one place for long and had to attack before their provisions ran out. In addition to three thousand knights, there were fifteen thousand horses and a baggage train; these armies fed themselves from the land, but they could not prevent themselves from destroying by fire what they actually needed. They were impatient and, in addition, not united enough to form themselves into an object that functioned like a battering ram. The differences between the ranks forced them into a position leading to isolation. They were not capable of cooperation.

With the invention of the pike square, an older development resurfaced. The Greek phalanx is a similarly immovable mass five hundred meters wide and of considerable depth. No command from the leaders can be heard over the noise of this mass. The phalanx is victorious when it hits the enemy from the side and a cavalry unit finishes up by executing the principle of the pincer movement. In this case, during the battle itself, living labor can be used only by a mounted group. Adaptation to the changing situation is in itself impossible.

The principle of the Roman legion lies in its manifold subdivisions. According to Marius, legions were equipped with short swords[3]. In other words, fighters became as mobile as the maniples[3] and the centuria. (A centuria was a unit originally composed of approximately one hundred men, but later reduced to sixty to eighty men). The location, the means of attack, and living labor could work in partnership. The Roman military learned this from the mercenary armies of the Carthaginian traders. The most important aspect of the absolute domination of the Roman labor of war — with the exception of opponents who clearly did not operate rationally and whose behavior legionnaires could not predict, such as that of the Teutons during the surprise attack in the Teutoburg Forest — lay in the fact that legionnaires could also be deployed at any time as a labor force; they built roads, impediments, and camps, set up brickworks, and were experienced in any kind of useful labor. They understood as much about construction as they did about destruction. Their leadership was experienced in both politics and warfare and utilized both economic and military instruments.

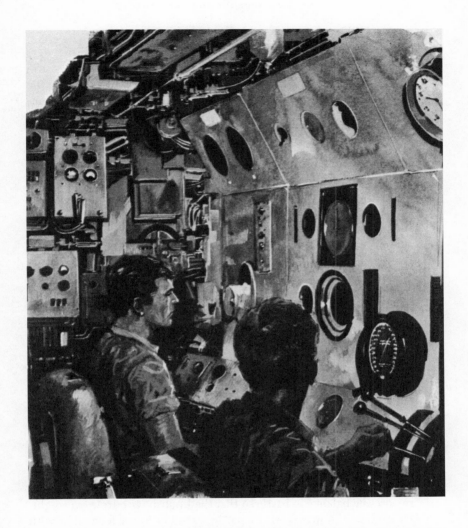

The bridge in an atomic submarine. The Nautilus is traveling blindly beneath the North Pole. The fighters sit at a bewilderingly complicated console and never see an enemy in person. [Alexander Kluge Archive]

Labor Resources

In the Middle Ages, the labor resource of military commanders consisted in the cunning with which they selected a suitable form of deployment. Once that was done, their role was restricted to the distance that their voices could carry. The leaders would then concern themselves with keeping the symbols of their leadership visible, that is, their flags and pennants; for this purpose, these had to be kept upright. The situation changed as weaponry developed. Over the course of time, tactics based on massed formations were replaced by tactics based on battle lines only a few units deep.[4]

Linear formations are based on a principle of action. They are not so much tools of violence as primarily instruments for reaching out and impressing; they ensnare. They certainly attempt to achieve a breakthrough or divert an enemy wing; they maneuver. Nobody knows exactly how this new organizational form was actually deployed. For a time, victories were achieved only because one party had the advantage and the other was unnerved by the mere demonstration and presentation of linear formations.

At the battle of Fontenoy in 1745 in Belgium, an English-Dutch-Hanoverian army of fifty thousand men confronted a French army of forty-six thousand infantrymen and sixteen hundred mounted cavalry. Without firing a shot, the English advanced to within fifty paces of the French front, which was lined up behind an entrenchment and initially remained stationary. At this point, or so it is told, the two commanders rode up to one another, lowered their swords in mutual greeting, and politely offered the other the first shot. The English then fired the first salvo. The effect at such close range was appalling. The first tactical units of the French were said to have been decimated. However, the back units and the cavalry were able to restore the balance in battle so that the English withdrew overnight. "It is certain, however, that a battle waged in linear formation with similar powers and a frontal confrontation brought losses that were far too heavy to be repeated in this schematic form ever again."[5]

The superior productivity of battle resources after this meant that despite the regressive return to pike square and breakthrough tactics that characterized the late battles of Bonaparte, the battlefield gradually emptied. Movements taking the form of a remote battle became the decisive ones; as a result, hand-to-hand combat did not disappear from the world, but it was seldom the decisive factor. How this works can best be imagined when bearing in mind that the decisive principle of guerilla warfare rests not on engagement in battle, but on remaining an enemy out of reach.

The Fighters' Motivation Is Also a Labor Resource

Strong motives have an influence on the reification of pike-and-square tactics. They function according to the principles of self-sacrifice.[6] The century of the linear formation, on the other hand, suffers from the squashed soldiers' lack of motivation. The tendency to replace actual violence with the representation of violence and battles with complex back-and-forth maneuvers follows from this, and it did so not only because of the limitations of feudal politics, which were once thought to be rapacious enough to try out the principle of total destruction. The bourgeois patriots of the French revolutionary armies had just as strong motivations at their disposal, and their sheer élan inflamed the counterpatriotism of the Prussians and Russians.

Russian patriotism surpassed bourgeois horizons. Military resources were deployed that thoroughly unnerved Napoleon's army. "This was no war" was how the declaration of total defeat put it. The more powerful motivation to drive out the intruders could not engage the conventional resources of battle, but invented new ones.

Attack and Defense

The distinction between attack and defense is not a technical one, but rather one of principle: "What is the object of defense? Preservation. It is easier to hold ground than take it.... Just what is it that makes preservation and protection so much easier? It is the fact that time which is allowed to pass unused accumulates to the credit of the defender." "*The defensive form of warfare is intrinsically stronger than the offensive.*"[7]

An army of partisans wins if it is not destroyed; an invading army loses if it does not win. This was recently the experience in Afghanistan; first for Russia, and then for NATO and the United States. The outcome has already been decided within the labor resource of motivation. If I have a reason to preserve something I depend on to live, my desire not to be separated from it will be stronger than the desire of an aggressor who has more abstract reasons for his attack. It is thus a matter of the political relations of a given war.

This insight contradicts appearances. Historically, the principle of preservation is conquered in war by considerably more abstract forces whose motives actually ought not to suffice for success. Thus, for example, the peasants in the German Peasants' War were conquered not only in each individual battle, but also in the overall outcome of the war. This experience, which has not repeated itself in our century, has its cause in the peasants' dependence on production, which is in itself a strength, but which in warring relations can make motivation awkward. The precondition is the prior parceling out of the motives to work, as well as their nonpublic nature. As soon as a language and a public sphere for these motives of preservation can be established—before the battles reach their peak—the outcome will be reversed. Time "that elapses unused" goes to the benefit of the masters, because concern for the harvest gnaws away at the peasants' sense of time. Their motives are not rooted in battle, but in production. And there exists no public sphere that can compensate in the form of time for the error regarding the consequences.

IV. The Distinction between Individual Combat Labor and War

There were peoples and classes who piled up victory after victory but still lost wars. This is similar to the fact that all individual steps in a war are based on concrete labor—in other words, they are stages of production, the addition of living labor at the interface with dead labor—and that war as a whole is nevertheless not a productive relationship. It has destroyed more than it has produced. Not only does the struggle of two opposing forces go into the relations of war—even though subjective attention orients itself according to **this** principle—but there also exists a third category of powers. These can be the interventions of so-called yellow powers" (that is, not the blue and red ones facing each other on the maps, but powers that thus far have been neutral). These are factors that remain unconscious, or productive powers that fight one another. However, the eye sees only those that are armed. Pyrrhus won endless victories, but lost the war because the motivation for his attack could not outweigh his enemies' principle of preservation. He would have needed either to battle victoriously longer or to give up on his motivation. Nothing worked. In his attack on Russia and Spain, Bonaparte accumulated strength in numbers, motivation, and means in such a way that his victory and the outcome of the war in every country should have been identical. The Spanish and Russians denied him the traditional relations of war that would have provided the correct parameters for his calculations. His plan was no good for the entirely asymmetrical relations of war with which he was confronted. He and his army were experts at preparing victories, but they had no knowledge at all of how such a war is to be concluded. A war can be started only with knowledge of how it might end. Without this knowledge, victories and individual combat labor cannot be balanced.[8]

The Object of the Labor of War

Every labor process is based on a relationship between humans and nature. It can be said that the act of labor is worth as much as the humanizing of nature and the naturalization of people that has gone into it. The quality of labor is thus based on the acknowledgement of the object of labor, on the exchange with its nature.[9]

The object of the labor of a party waging war is the enemy. In classical warfare, it can be imagined — and Clausewitz describes it thus — that it is a matter of forcing this enemy to renounce his will (that is, of destroying him), of dealing him a decisive blow, of running him through, of hacking him to pieces, in a certain sense of "transforming him through violence." Armies carry out drilling, pounding, and pincer movements as if it were a matter of a product of nature or an intermediate good. Such an enemy (in contrast with the resistance of nature, or the wildness of an animal, the force of a river, and so on) is always another **people**, a **history of motives and desires**, a **human mode of production**; the enemy consists of warmongers who were once children, culture, specific reasons for struggle, accessories. The whole of this subjective-objective complex is organized into war in classical conflicts (but not in guerilla wars) in the same way as the opposing side, that is, it behaves as though **the enemy** were a thing that needs to be processed with a will to destruction. The separation of subjective labor power from the object of labor, compared with labor in industry, is "purer," or more radical in an abstract sense. ("Radical" is used here in a way that goes against the meaning of the word: **opposed to the roots of the natural relationship**.) As far as the object of labor is concerned, war demonstrates the most completely alienated example of reification.

This relationship, radicalized in a counterintuitive sense, is a source of errors that result in entire wars being lost. First, as far as the idea of war and the perception of the enemy are concerned, the latter is subject to a distortion of the entire capacity of perception. The enemy is denaturalized in the most diverse ways. The simplest procedure is anonymization: an Ivan, the Boche, the Krauts, "like the Hun" (the enemy is reduced to a quantity, as though he had no face, no hands). Then there is the comparison with animals or inorganic materials in expressions such as "the storming floods" or "like sand." Perception distorts the reality of the enemy to such an extent that it becomes a dead thing.

In contemporary warfare, there is also a series of objectively determined deceptions. A bomber command does not come into any contact with the **enemy** bombarded below; in fact, the civilian population in cellars, invisible to the pilots, is not actually the enemy and has no power to behave like an enemy. The warring party that is stationed at the front and that comes in contact with the adversaries who sent the bombers cannot be targeted with bombs, because that would endanger the other side's own troops. From the viewpoint of the **strategy from above**, the "object of labor" is transformed into little square toy towns lit at night by colorful cascades of flares (so-called Christmas trees) marking the areas where bombs are to be dropped. Not even this level of perception is possible in rocket silos or atomic submarines that launch missiles at unknown targets over five thousand kilometers away. An enemy—known to me only from fiction or propaganda films—is **fabricated** at a technically equipped writing desk, a technical workstation, or from aircraft carriers equipped with casinos and cinemas.

If things did not move beyond this relation of reification of the enemy, defeat would already be preprogrammed, since the object of labor cannot be adequately processed in a manner so completely contrary to its nature. And thus the possibilities for surprise inherent in the object of labor also cannot be recognized. It is not a dead object, but consists of some million lives that will unfold according to their own laws and that will surprise my unit if it is not aware of them. As explained by Clausewitz, there is also a more profound issue at work here; in war, he says, I must **defeat the will of the enemy** and impose the will of my warring party on him. At heart, it is about a particular kind of battle (that is, labor) over the **enemy's**

motivation. Everything else—his weapons, his provinces, his aids, even his capital city—becomes secondary if I do not strike at his motives, his "will." This object of labor is the exact opposite of the process of reifying the object—the opposite really is the case. Here, the enemy must be animated, more life must be given to him than he himself might have. More has to be known about him than he knows about himself.

Even in war, nothing can be achieved with a mere demonstration of violence. This is not because violence is useless in itself, but because a relationship of violence—in order for it to be deployed—requires the reification of the object of labor in the way described above.

The Partial Reversal of this Relationship in the Course of War: Points of Contact with the Enemy

The path of reification leads to absolute war. Through friction with the enemy, however, a different process emerges in which the enemy goes through a subcutaneous learning process. This happens even when there are no more points of contact in space or time; consider, for example, a bomber crew stationed in Okinawa that bombarded a target on the other side of the Cambodian border without knowing whether it hit Cambodian farmers, North Vietnamese reinforcements, or just jungle. Nevertheless, they did learn that the enemy could not be reached.[10]

V. The Illusion of Leadership

In the perception of those engaged in battle, a collective distraction emerges in favor of a perspective from a strong superelevated position, that of the so-called commander. The distraction draws its energy from the fact that the individual or group directly engaged in the practice of war never perceives the whole war. Nevertheless, a need for orientation brings about the production of a completely arbitrary overview.

"The Bible says: 'The king's heart is in the hand of the Lord.'
'The king is a slave of history.'"

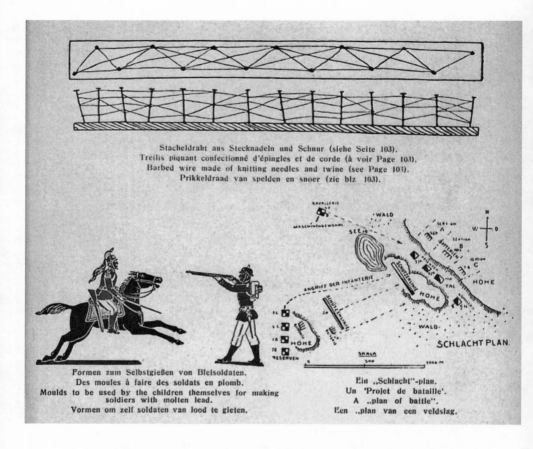

Stacheldraht aus Stecknadeln und Schnur (siehe Seite 103).
Treillis piquant confectionné d'épingles et de corde (à voir Page 103).
Barbed wire made of knitting needles and twine (see Page 103).
Prikkeldraad van spelden en snoer (zie blz 103).

Formen zum Selbstgießen von Bleisoldaten.
Des moules à faire des soldats en plomb.
Moulds to be used by the children themselves for making
soldiers with molten lead.
Vormen om zelf soldaten van lood te gieten.

Ein „Schlacht"-plan.
Un 'Projet de bataille'.
A „plan of battle".
Een „plan van een veldslag.

War from the perspective of the child or the adult commander. [Ernst Friedrich, *Kriege dem Kriege* (Berlin, "Freie Jugend" 1925)]

A godly image of the monarch who formally declares war. [Alexander Kluge Archive]

In her speech "Our Program and the Political Situation," delivered on New Year's Eve 1918 at the Founding Congress of the Communist Party of Germany (KPD), Rosa Luxemburg calls the soldiers and sailors **proletarians in uniform**. The uniform signifies the subordination of the person to the disciplined conditions of military production. However, each individual labor process in war assumes a disguise; the uniform is not the only disguise. The lack of publicly expressed perspectives on the various manifestations of war is one way of disguising the labor process. It is as if there were only one perspective, that of the war as a whole. Precisely this is what never exists in a real war. [Creative Commons]

"The power of invisible images." [© 2011 The White House]

The comparison between war and trade works only in relation to this perspective, the perspective of the commander or the military leadership. [11] In battle, it is what pays in cash, goes bankrupt, or receives the wages of victory, feeds the battle with reinforcements, sees the troops as "burnt to a cinder." Apart from a few special cases of classical warfare (Friedrich II, Bonaparte, Moltke), this view from the commander's hill does not in fact exist, not even for the commanders. In the special cases listed above, it does exist in individual battles, but not in relation to the overall course of the war. There is absolutely no Archimedean point in relation to warring parties where even a single representative can acquire such a genuine overview that he could appear as observer, analyst, business leader, or entrepreneur. Only neutral parties have such a view, insofar as they remain genuinely separate from the war. [12] **For the fighter on the ground, it is always about production, actual destruction, or the luck of the dice, but never about trade. For the commodities of war, it is consumption, and not production, that is the overriding principle.**

VI.

The opposite of war—peace—is not simple. "War is an act of violence meant to force the enemy to do our will." [13] It is about the **destruction of the will, that is, of the autonomy of the other.** The opposite pole of this would be the **construction of the autonomy or of the will of the other.** Both are production processes. Of these two, one, war, historically has been furnished with powerful and potentially regressive concepts and forms of labor, so that at every stage in its development, it always appears possible to return to it. Until now, war has overcome all other relations of production.

The Dual Nature of War
As soon as we distinguish structural violence from manifest violence and both of these from the ordered relations of self-regulating productive circulation systems, the concept of peace dissolves into states of war, temporary truces, and the counterproduction of states of war in the form of the establishment of autonomy. War does not attain to its own concept; one of its characteristics is that it repeatedly fractures this concept. It culminates instead in an "immense accumulation," a conglomeration. Within this, there is not **one** fundamental form of war, but rather there are several.

It is not a matter of indifference whether the purpose is *"merely to occupy some of his frontier districts* so that we can annex them or use them for bargaining at the peace negotiations" or whether it is "to *overthrow the enemy*," to destroy him politically.[14] War is also *"the continuation of policy with other means"* insofar as it can take on wholly different characteristics between the two poles of the state, on the one hand, and the totality of social intercourse, on the other.[15] The characteristics of **absolute** and **relative war** face each other as opposites.

Reciprocity and the Three Extremes; the Counteraction of Real Relations
First: "War is nothing but a duel on a larger scale."[16] This gives rise to three necessary reciprocal effects, the so-called first, second, and third extremes. (1) "War is an act of force, and there is no logical limit to the application of that force.... This is the ... *first 'extreme'* we meet with"; (2) "I am not in control, he dictates to me as much as I dictate to him." This is the second extreme; (3) It is a matter of "the product of two inseparable factors, viz. *the total means at his disposal* and *the strength of his will*." This is the third extreme. The absolute logic of war thus leads theoretically at every point to the most extreme exertion of power, to boundless violence, and all this according to no other principle than that of destruction, to which all other principles subordinate themselves. If such a war were really possible, it would ultimately destroy the possibility of its own finality. It exists only as the "logical fantasy" of war about itself; at the same time, this logic — as a real concept, a logic of realities — is really active in war relations. It is a real abstraction not because the materiality of this logic is inadequate, but because a real opposing logic is produced to counter it.[17]

In real relations, "in war, the result is never final." The probabilities of real life replace the extreme and absolute nature of concepts. "Here a principle of polarity is proposed"; (1) it has objective reasons: friction (the tensions of real relations), "imperfect knowledge of the situation," chance; (2) to this is added the subjective nature of war. The element of danger is answered with, for example, courage, daring, the belief in luck, boldness, rashness, and "all these traits of character seek their proper element — chance."[18]

What comes into being makes "war a remarkable trinity."[19] (1) The "primordial violence, hatred and enmity, which are to be regarded as a blind natural force"; (2) the play of probabilities and chance events "within which the creative spirit is free to roam"; (3) the "element of subordination, as an instrument of policy, which makes it subject to reason alone."[20]

VII. War as a Maze

In depictions of labyrinths, such as for example those in Reims Cathedral, the view of the dangerous maze is from above. From the superelevated position of this perspective — that of the commander in the field, so to speak — the image signals a strong aesthetic allure, an overview, nothing dangerous. For this reason, the writer Arno Schmidt conjectured that labyrinths form a vertical structure, a catacomb, an abyss. The writer claimed that this conveys more clearly their uncanny mystery, the opportunity for losing one's way.

In modern times, it is rare or indeed impossible for a military or political commander to conduct a battle from a commander's hill. The Duke of Marlborough, General Washington, Friedrich II of Prussia, Napoleon, General Lee, or General Moltke (the Battle of Sedan at Hill 304 in the presence of General Sheridan) still directed a battle. Today, wars are decided in the high hills of budget management, often years before a war begins. A terrorist operation is not led centrally. A military operation in the two Iraq wars was executed continents and oceans away with time zone differences of between ten and twenty-four hours. Today, operations are monitored and commanded in real time from a headquarters in, for example, Tampa, and taken up and executed on the ground, for example, in Afghanistan. Observe the indirect, virtual, and digital nature of sensory apprehension: day and night are different for the central command and the troops. The air force operates in these divergent time zones. The "field marshal," today a large military department, has no direct sensory contact with the enemy. Neither a "swift glance" nor any delicate influence can vary the assessment.

The idea of "leadership" was already largely an illusion in the ancient world. At the moment when the labor of war begins, all planning is thrown overboard.

The classic description of the powerlessness of the leader in the face of actual circumstances is to be found in Leo Tolstoy's *War and Peace*. Napoleon, who has the reputation of being a genius for quick thinking, made a sketch of the battle the night before and issued orders. Without paying attention to these plans, soldiers on both sides, both the French and the Russians, wandered about aimlessly in the surrounding forests. They reached different battle positions from those intended. Attack and defense deviated from the plan. The battle itself possessed a reality that the leadership could influence only by riding the wave. It could only try to harness in some way the friction, chance, and complex mass movement already set in motion. It was only in the narrative afterward, the battle report, that the illusion of leadership was reconstructed.

What Does Industrialized War Mean?
The turning point between the Napoleonic Wars and industrialized war is first visible in the American Civil War. Toward the end of this war, the army of the North, led by General Grant, threatened the army of the Confederacy under General Lee, who was attempting to defend the capital city of Richmond. General Lee was seen as a representative of the classical school of West Point. Strongly inspired by the mobility of the cavalry and experienced in all the arts of operations and castling, General Lee managed in the most inventive of ways to put up an excellent defense. In each of the individual skirmishes, General Grant drew the short straw. General Lee's army was a professional one and had the classical structure of artillery, cavalry, and infantry.

General Grant's opposing army relied on the industrial production of the North (rapid-fire weapons such as the Gatling gun, which was the precursor to the machine gun, railways). His troops were schooled in the discipline of the factory; his was a militialike army of armed citizens. It was easier to give an order for the mass deployment of these troops than for the superiors of the Confederate Army to propose in place of their "clever operations" a mass deployment of their combatants, because these trained professional soldiers tested the orders that came from above differently. The remarkable thing, if one considers these battles carefully, lies in the fact that every time an attack was rebuffed, General Grant immediately attacked again from a neighboring spot or from one farther away. The railway relentlessly delivered him reinforcements and masses of new recruits. Like an algorithm, he repeated the same principle directed at breaking through and destroying the enemy. General Lee and the Confederates were worn down by the Union's persistence, the unlimited swelling mass of power, and the factorylike schematism of a new kind of war that they did not recognize. They were not defeated in any skirmish, and yet they were gradually brought to capitulate. Here we see industrialized warfare in embryonic form. It was not yet in command of all its industrial potential, but already possessed the idea of industry (of unrelenting effort).

The next major battles—of Königgrätz (1866), Gravelotte-St. Privat, as well as Sedan (1870)—were still of the classical type (although they were based on the use of the railway system). In contrast, the battles of the Japanese Imperial powers against the Russian Empire (1904) already demonstrate a step forward and the superiority of an industrialized war machine (such as that of the Japanese) compared with a preindustrial one (such as that of the Russians). The complete image of industrialized war appears after 1914.

At the battle of Jena and Auerstedt (1806), it was possible for someone two kilometers away from the battlefield to eat lunch at an inn in peace. Preindustrialized war is localized. This is true even for a conflict characterized by hordes, murder, and the devastation of whole provinces such as the Thirty Years' War, which destroyed the German Reich.

In Scarlett O'Hara's home of Atlanta, war had already taken over not only the city, setting the whole of it afire, but also the whole of Southern society. In the wars of the twentieth century—but even more acutely in the monstrous web of terror, war, underground conflict, and professional air and land forces in the twenty-first century—there is not a square inch that is not at least virtually gripped by war or capable of being so.

What Industrialized War Involves
Industrialized war involves:

- The mass effect of deployed people and machines.
- The unbounded nature of place and time.
- Motorization, air power, transcontinental strikes (for example, rocket attacks).
- A powerful ideological accompaniment in the form of propaganda and organization that appears to replace the individual motor of war labor.

317

- The observation that all traditional forms of war below the industrial benchmark remain virulent all the way back to antiquity, even back to the forms of battle among clans in earlier centuries. This timelessness and ubiquity are particularly important. Classical forms of war were in a position to separate themselves off from atavistic forms of battle.
- The boundlessness of industrialized war corresponds to a particular confluence of all the contradictions of the political economy and, of course, to all the attributes we have described regarding labor capacities.

The Cold War: The Struggle for the Monopoly on Force
In the sixty years since the Korean War—without doubt an after-effect of the Second World War (turning point: the discharge of General McArthur)—there have been no more openly industrialized wars on a global scale. Cold War strategy nevertheless constituted a concentrated form of industrialized (virtual) war labor. In terms of controls, demands for balance, and the big machinery associated with the art of war, the structures of the Cold War exceeded all the experiences handed down by the industrialized world. Individual labor power—the individual fighter—disappeared from the picture almost completely (although he is still present as a spy or as an inventor). At the same time, this phase in the history of warfare is characterized by an intense and successful monopolization of power on both opposing sides. This concentration of executive power provides the precise conditions necessary for an effective deterrent. Chance (at least in relevant measure) and individual initiative or flashes of obstinacy have no place here. The atomic deterrent is indivisible. It cannot even be shared with neutral or independent allies. Thus, in one of the final phases of the Cold War, the so-called MISSILE CRISIS of 1981, a situation of extreme danger—the possibility, for example, that war could break out accidentally or that one side believes it needs to defend itself unilaterally—was connected to a high degree of security, because the "virtual labor of war" centralized on both sides tightened up the channels of information between these blocs with the goal of preventing accidents. Red telephones, informal contacts with secret service agents on the other side, and trustworthy contacts have never functioned as reliably as they did during this period of risk. Only the implosion of the Soviet Union

and the preceding STAR WARS project put forward by the Reagan administration and the head of the Pentagon, Richard Perle, (at least, they promoted it energetically) brought this concentrated phase to an end; the Star Wars project did so by threatening the balance of power; the transformation of the Soviet Union into the Commonwealth of Independent States did so by what was, in effect, a unilateral disarmament. Objectively speaking, this time of so-called relaxation after 1989 was a particularly dangerous period. It saw the First Gulf War, as well as the Moscow putsch of 1991. As soon as the Wall fell, the United States Secret Service warned about developments that could spiral out of control during the putsch, such as the behavior of the western arm of the Red Army stationed in the German Democratic Republic. The monopoly on force had been lost on one of the two sides of the system of deterrence. In its place came a collection of earlier projects, unresolved conflicts, and potentials for violence frozen in place. Because of the change in the balance of power between the superpowers, the potential of frozen conflicts in other zones—for example, the Middle East, Afghanistan, the relationship between Pakistan and India, and so on—also changed.

Until now, a solid monopoly on force controlled by consolidated nation-states has not been reestablished in the twenty-first century. Zones of the earth familiar with a professionalized military force exist side by side with those in which uncontrolled military force prevails. The question of the proliferation of atomic weapons has become acutely significant. In this respect, the initiative of the FOUR HORSEMEN on the question of nuclear disarmament as presented at the Munich Security Conference in 2010 and to the president of the United States in Washington, D.C., left a deep impression. American politicians such as the former senator Sam Nunn, former secretaries of defense William Cohen and William Perry, as well as former secretaries of state George Schultz and Henry Kissinger, are outstanding experts in and retired representatives of the theory of deterrence. They stand now for a general reduction in nuclear weapons on account of the urgent new dangers for which no agreements to prevent their proliferation have been reached. This signifies a tendency but not a result. However, their call is a response to the holes in the monopoly on force. You cannot leave loaded weapons lying around on a playground, Henry Kissinger intimated.

What Is Asymmetrical War?

The formulation "asymmmetrical war" is linked to the attacks of September 11, 2001. The concept refers to a conglomeration of new forms of violence and to the unexpected demands put on professional military forces of large nation-states. Only part of this phenomenon derives from the decay of religious power, the monopoly on force, and the existence of fundamentalist groups in countries that tolerate them. The structural change in the exercise of power appears to be less a question of the labor of war and more a consequence of the competition between very varied forms of authority, both in the globalized world and in local areas. This phenomenon includes the fact that in many areas, large, globally active corporations compete with the governments of territorial states, the fact that authority (and the concomitant political labor capacities) migrates to transnational organizations, and, conversely, the fact that groups and individuals can exercise violence through the use or acquisition of modern means in ways that were previously possible only before the emergence of the idea of statehood. On the one hand, asymmetrical war is a characteristic of almost all known historical wars, but on the other, it has become a concentrated phenomenon that has taken on a new dimension in the twenty-first century.

---

1. Napoleon at the Gates of Madrid

The emperor appears at the gates of Madrid with three hundred thousand of his best troops. He declares in the name of France the rights to freedom: the freedom from the burdens of feudal lords and the church. To his astonishment, he learns that he has thus provoked an uprising of partisans in general and of Spanish peasants in particular. At night, they kill his soldiers (that is, the allied French, Italians, and Westphalians). By day, he has the captured partisans executed. Goya captured the reciprocal massacre in a string of images. This battle is asymmetrical. By day, the armed peasants and priests can do little about the emperor's cuirassiers seated on their imposing horses or his artillery. By night, they dominate the events. This is the beginning of the fall of Napoleon's rule; it is not a direct result of insurgents, but of the need to change the focus of his attention continually in order not to be confronted by the insoluble problem of an "uprising in the dark." He keeps changing the goals of battle until he loses his army in Russia.

---

2. The Fracturing of the Labor of War

Already during the Cold War and even before it had properly begun, exports of small arms flooded Africa. In the Congo, the colonial regime was followed by the commercial violence of mercenaries, who devastated the land and many a government organization. Today, we see destabilized zones on the northeast coast of Africa and in the south of the Philippines. Piracy has emerged and dominates these areas, as it did the Mediterranean in the time of Caesar and Pompey; it was not until the Roman state took special measures there that it could be eliminated.

Far beyond the monopoly on force, a parasitic infestation of societies has come about here, one involving decentralized violence and local petty wars, which can selectively spread to the centers of society at any time. This selectivity makes it difficult to pursue perpetrators. As we will see below, the concept of labor does not fit these activities. In order to secure the places that harbor the perpetrators, it is not enough to occupy Afghanistan; this would require the occupation of areas in East Asia, the Somali coast, Nigeria, and zones of North Africa. Except then it would be discovered that similar regions might possibly be found in Latin America. Part of the asymmetry of the structures of violence is the variety of their status. What is on the side of "small power" can be anything from an alchemist's poisonous laboratory to a no-man's-land. Conversely, when it comes to the security agencies through which global corporations will defend themselves in the future, they are all large amalgamated structures. This asymmetry also rests on the fact that all the forms of violence precede those of agriculture and industry (that is, they are typical of tribal wars) and exist alongside the highly consolidated institutional forces of military alliances and future corporate organizations.

Equally dangerous as terrorist groups in the context of asymmetrical war are decentralized alliances between hegemonic powers and their local helpers. On account of these links, the number of perpetrators of violence [*Gewalt*] released from the monopoly on force [*Gewalt*] becomes inflated. This can also revitalize the classical image of war. Historical experience shows that small allies below the threshold of state responsibility or smaller allied nation-states can be catalysts that bring major powers into conflict. For example, this is how the Punic Wars arose out of the provocation made by a group of renegade Syracusan mercenaries who effectively called in their Roman allies. As a consequence, Rome's existence was endangered from time to time. In the end, it was Carthage that lay in ruins. The secret Serbian military society called the "Black Hand" is also one such organization. It was their weapons and their initiative that set the First World War in motion with the murder of the archduke in Sarajevo.

3.

The causes leading to the use of violence are also asymmetrical, as well as its symptoms. In this case, the question of the timeline is particularly important. The foundation of the Ba'ath party in Iraq and other Arabic countries, to which Saddam Hussein originally belonged, goes back to events from the 1920s that appalled an Arab teacher and led to the foundation of this secret society. How can a response to the roots of such a movement (which is, incidentally, anti-Islamic) be formulated when one's hands are currently full dealing with its spin-offs, derivatives, and consequences? Al-Qaeda is a similar case insofar as the roots of the conflict appear to have mutated (Bin Laden is initially appalled by the conditions in his homeland of Saudi Arabia and later by the Soviet occupation of Afghanistan). A strategy that attempts to eliminate the enemy's emotional landscape and with it his supporters is confronted on the timeline rather confusingly by various realities, parallel worlds, so to speak. This distinguishes the eleventh- and twelfth-century phenomenon of the Assassins, who also formed groups of murderers, from twenty-first-century fundamentalists and terrorist groups, the latter of which are certainly not necessarily religiously motivated.

4. The Unintentional Strengthening of Asymmetry on the Side of Those Attacked

The attack on the Twin Towers, the simultaneous attack on the Pentagon, and the attempted attack, at the very same moment, on the White House (which was not successfully carried out) caused confusion within the besieged nation and its leadership with regard to the means of exercising the power of the state. The authority of the community rests on the sentence *Protego ergo sum*. "I am able to protect, therefore I am."[21] It appeared that the military protectors of the country were not able to do anything about an unexpected assault. The result was an intolerable situation.

Think about what it means metaphorically that the Pearl Harbor fleet (itself also once hit unexpectedly) was brought through the Panama Canal two days after 9/11 so as to lie in formation off the shores of New York City. It is clear that these weapons of war were no answer to the attack that had just happened, nor would they be have been deployed for any future attack, which of course would have probably not resembled what had already happened. The same can be said for the power exercised by the other military forces responsible for customs and excise and coastal defense. It is obvious that the state was searching for a countermeasure against terror that corresponded to the possibilities in its possession. This can lead to an ACTION THAT LEAPFROGS OVER A VITAL STEP [*ÜBERSPRUNGSHANDLUNG*]. An unsolvable reality is replaced with a solvable one. At least part of the answer that was later found, namely, the occupation of Afghanistan and Iraq, represented just such a displacement of problem solving, which in turn strengthened the asymmetry.

State authority is also unexpectedly affected by natural disasters and mistakes made by civil society. This is true of volcanic eruptions, flooding in Pakistan, the earthquake in Haiti, the accidents in Chernobyl and Harrisburg, the financial crisis, or the oil-well disaster in the Gulf of Mexico, for which BP still must answer. In each of these cases, the question arises: Can the president of a modern superpower respond adequately? Or does the public authority reveal itself to be impotent?

This is what the French philosopher Voltaire meant in the Age of Enlightenment when he received news of the loss of human lives in the earthquake in Lisbon and said that human society would have to declare war on nature.

This pointed question reveals how the authority (that is, the labor capacities) of a political structure directed at the creation of the community must be brought into the question of asymmetry. In the case of the financial crisis (Lehman Brothers, the bankruptcy of Greece or Argentina), it is noticeable that critical problems were excluded in the models according to which praxis operated. This exclusion took its revenge in the form of a collapse. Among the many instances of collateral damage caused by a volcanic eruption in Iceland, one required an American army general and commander to extend his stay in the French capital, where he made comments leading to his dismissal. A natural event and an event linked to an asymmetrical war enter into a causal relationship with one another. In this instance, it was simply the authority of the state that demonstrated its capacity to act by dismissing a general. This was not as apparent in the public representations and media reports that accompanied the BP catastrophe. Should the president have been able to ask the Pentagon for help? Are there military powers — for example, combat engineers or weapons — that could work to dismantle such an accident? A forgotten but related misfortune is the nuclear accident in Chernobyl. Gorbachev's authority was not initially substantiated by the putsch, but rather by his failure (real or apparent) to act during this event. The establishment of a balance between the means of power of the authorities and attacks on public welfare forms the overall concept that, like the tip of an iceberg, comes to the surface only as part of the phenomenon of asymmetrical war.

5. Examining the Active Elements of Asymmetrical War under the Concept of Labor

Above all, it is clear that asymmetry affects the object of labor. It exists only in virtual form for both sides. The goal and object of the labor of terror is news and horror, not the explosions or the killings themselves. From the other side, the defensive side's goal and the object of its labor is an ungraspable opponent who is able to multiply like the Medusa's head, but who can often not be found at all. Indeed, there are cases in which a terrorist has retired or refrained from further terrorist activity. There is no field or factory where terror or counterterror can be tilled or manufactured. Rather, exercising violence regresses to a social status akin to what it has in hunting or clan societies.

The necessity to look for new concepts is also apparent in the question as to which power or precision grips would characterize each and every labor process. The loss of control is obvious. This also holds true for directing counterterror, so it is not simply a matter for responsible strategists, but also one that foreign forces can control to a considerable extent using attacks, provocation, and public opinion. On both sides of asymmetrical war, the lack of economies of balance is obvious. Within the counterintelligence and secret services responsible for defense, the institutionally inherent interest in increasing the number of personnel will work against the dismantling of the service (and its reconstruction in a different place). Thus, a doubling of the number of antiterror services occurs within a superpower, but it is impossible to see how a swift change of emphasis or the intensification of a particular kind of alertness can be possible within this structure. A similar balance inherent in labor power also appears to be missing on the side of the attackers. Only death, friction, or the exhaustion of their forces subdues their élan.

Investigation into levels of cooperation and the question of the amalgamation of powers in asymmetrical warfare also affords remarkable results. Such amalgamation appears to work neither for terror nor for the defense against it. In this respect, all concepts taken from the political economy of labor power are inadequate to describe the processes of asymmetrical war. However, a number of things also become relativized from this perspective: erosion is not construction. In this respect, there can be no lasting terror drawn from the same reservoir of forces. This also applies to the viability of any lasting counterterror; at the very least, counterterror does not remain focused on engaging the same target. In the light of observations about the ancient world, what emerges is instead the problem of the Praetorian Guard. Forces sent out to fight terror either fail or become confused as to their motivation and then turn against their founders, thereby endangering the authority of the community.

6. Can a Global Monopoly on Force Be Established Once Again? What Form of Emancipation of the Community Could Offer a Response to Asymmetrical Warfare?

In 1648, the Thirty Years' War ended with the Peace of Westphalia signed in Münster and Osnabrück. The war had become decentralized and asymmetrical. It had consumed people, the country's wealth, its time, and itself, as well. The peace agreement was accompanied by the establishment of a law of nations (imperfectly formulated) and an (incomplete) emancipation of the community. Territorial states came into being that were at least able to guarantee the rule of law and provide the necessary framework for industrialization in Europe. This was the first time in various countries when monopolies on the use of force were established, thereby replacing the ubiquitous use of violence with the institution of restricted warfare.

Wars obey the principle of destruction. Even when they subsume immense concentrated quantities of labor capacities and production, they are able to deploy them only in the service of destruction. For this reason, there is no emancipation in war of the kind that underlies the notion of a "good war." The answer to the problems of asymmetrical war can be provided only by the EMANCIPATION OF THE COMMUNITIES that decide in favor of war or peace. In this respect, we see our current situation mirrored in that of 1648.

The European territorial states of the seventeenth century certainly differed in size but were structurally very similar (apart from a few atypical city republics such as Venice). On the other hand, sovereign countries today are extremely out of balance. China, Brazil, India, Russia, and the United States represent extremely large units. The Netherlands, Sweden, and the majority of intact nation-states find themselves facing these powerful blocs. Countries such as Japan are huge in terms of their economic power, but as states are surprisingly small. However, it is characteristic of all territorial states in the twenty-first century that either their authority is endangered or they show symptoms of decline. In contrast, supranational organizations and local counterforces (NGOs, religious organizations in the United States, and so on) are in the ascendancy. Provinces with an unusual degree of obstinacy (Catalonia, the Basque region, Northern Ireland) are becoming increasingly important within supranational regions. As a result, industries, firms, and commercial organizations with global reach can coexist in provinces of this kind, which are characterized by both expansion and real power (and therefore also authority). None of this corresponds to the image of the ordered and abiding state that for approximately three centuries was associated with the notion of a monopoly on the use of force. All of the social forces referred to above possess the ability to exercise power. The actual potential for asynchronicity does not lie in the relationship between terror and the means of protection against it, but in this new constellation of forces that to some extent are equally legitimate, but also socially out of balance. Words such as "society," "power," "authority," "decisions over war and peace," and "the guarantee of public order" have lost something of the clarity that they once possessed in the twentieth century.

It is for this reason that we do not simply live in a decade of asymmetrical war, but also at a time when a new concept of the political is emerging. It is no longer sufficient to rely on the constitutions of territorial states and on declarations of human rights as represented by supranational organizations. Instead, all the diverse forces and counterforces have to be integrated into political authority if the community, which in this sense has both local and global roots, is to contain violence once again. This is

undoubtedly an emancipatory process for which it will be necessary to mus-
ter all historical approaches and labor processes. If this does not succeed,
there is no guarantee that the twenty-first century will not be derailed.

VIII. How the Twentieth Century Derailed in August 1914

All of the powers responsible for the outbreak of the First World
War lost substantial parts of their territories during it. Almost all of
them attempted to achieve a quick resolution ("by Christmas!") on
the basis of methods deployed in previous conflicts. These methods
and plans failed. Barbara Tuchman describes this shift from a confident offensive strategy to a stalemate offering—at least initially—no
hope of resolution in *The Guns of August*. But the catastrophe was
not only that none of the powers involved was able to find a way
of achieving peace in time, but also that a treaty was concluded—
following the armistice in 1918, when the war had worn itself out—
that destroyed any chance of any future peace. In this context, historians (Jörg Friedrich, Ian Kershaw) speak of 1914 as the outbreak of
a thirty-one-year war that ended only in 1945. The inflation of 1923
in Hungary and Germany, the abolition of the gold standard for the
British pound, Black Friday in 1929, the Great Depression, and the
currency reform of 1948 in Germany are the economic corollaries
of these processes. Hitler and Auschwitz count among the worst
catastrophes of this long war.

Of interest to us in light of this bitter observation are the labor
capacities involved and the manifestations of loss among the labor
of intelligence.

- One of the firmly held beliefs of the labor movement that sought
  to achieve international consensus was the doctrine stating that
  an outbreak of war triggered by governmental action would be
  followed on both sides by a general strike. This would make war
  impossible. Nothing of the kind came to pass. Only at the end of
  the war (first in France in 1917, where it was suppressed, and then
  in Germany in 1918, where it could no longer be suppressed) was
  there a military strike of sorts among soldiers on the front line.
- Cooperation and the escalation of industrial labor reach their
  peak in the war economy. In this respect, world war manifests

itself as a "laboratory of new social characteristics." It is for this reason that in the German Reich, THE DOCTRINE OF THE NATIONAL COMMUNITY emerged out of the Weapons and Munitions Procurement Agency (WUMBA), an organization run for a time by the industrialist Walter Rathenau. It prepared the ground for the hybrid conversion of the terms "nationalism" and "socialism" in the 1930s. What is real is the fact that there is an incredible concentration of labor capacities where the conditions of wage labor and the free market prevail. While some aspects of this phenomenon of the mass mobilization of the labor force in the war economy can be explained by the compulsion to obey and the effects of propaganda, others cannot. The latter are more a result of the tendency of human labor capacities to deploy whatever forces are available to it. In this respect, war is disinhibiting. Production is not limited by any market constraints. Here we can observe a reaffirmation of Marx's observation that *one* worker achieves less in one hundred hours than *one hundred* workers in one hour. He calls this "animal spirits."[22]

• One explanation for the immobilization of the labor of intelligence that could otherwise be directed toward achieving peace appears to lie in the excessive complexity of the wartime situation itself. THE CAPACITY TO DIFFERENTIATE and DECISIVENESS are characteristic of the political labor of intelligence. In industrialized wars right up to the present day, periods in which decisions can be reached neither from the bottom up nor the top down predominate. This empirical proposition not only manifests itself in the case of the First World War, but is also characteristic for subsequent conflicts. Thus, the principle of "unconditional surrender" (established at the Casablanca Conference) and the agreement that no one partner in the Anti-Hitler Coalition should enter into a unilateral peace agreement with Germany made all Japanese and German stratagems entirely obsolete even, for example, in the event that the attempt on Hitler's life of July 20, 1944, had been successful.[23] In the case of Hitler, Ian Kershaw has demonstrated that his character made him unreceptive to any moves toward peace. Following Japan's entry into the conflict and Germany's declaration of war on the United States, even a dictator such as Hitler, in possession of a monopoly over decision making, would have been unable to make any move toward peace.

The mutual dependence of all the different facts and decisions would have blocked the development of an informed opinion.

In democracies where opinions are coordinated by the media, the autonomous use of intelligence labor is even more difficult, because it is faced with contradictory precepts: (1) one's own people must be brought back home from a war they do not understand and from a land that is foreign to them; (2) the original goals used to shape public opinion to support the war in the first place cannot be abandoned. Here a certain amount of obstinacy, persistence, and a balance economy — that is, positive characteristics of labor capacities — combine more generally to block not only the path toward a quick peace, but also sudden changes of direction.

IX. The Illusion of the Blitzkrieg: Intelligence in War

For as long as there has been historiography, there has been a conflict between martial intelligence and military blockheads. In the twentieth century, the idea of the blitzkrieg was a manifestation of this conflict. It is a reaction to the murderous experience of positional warfare and the stationary mutual work of destruction that characterizes the First World War: in Gallipoli, near Verdun, at the Somme. With the blitzkrieg — in contrast to these experiences — mobility and the possibility of outmaneuvering the enemy were supposed to be reintroduced. The blitzkrieg is supposed to make a short war possible. It is based on the concept of indirect engagement. The aim is to destroy the adversary not by attacking his strong points, but rather by going for his weak points, or else by achieving one's military goals without targeting the adversary unnecessarily. The idea was first developed in Britain, then picked up in France (for example, by the then brigadier general de Gaulle) and subsequently propagated in Germany by a minority among the generals, including General Heinz Guderian. The idea came to fruition in various places around the world around 1940. Barbara Tuchman reports accordingly that around same time that Guderian was making his breakthrough on the Western Front in 1940, the American General Patton was engaged in training exercises in Florida with his tank division in order to practice procedures to be deployed in a blitzkrieg. Led by the German Supreme Command, the campaign against France was not originally planned as a blitzkrieg. In practice, it

ALEXANDER KLUGE AND OSKAR NEGT

turned out that the motorized infantry divisions and tank units were able to execute an advance — the Sickle Cut offensive (named thus by Churchill because the progress of the offensive toward the Channel coast was shaped like a sickle when marked out on the map) — in such a way that the opposing French forces could be sidestepped, despite their superiority in terms of tank numbers.

The German Marxist theoretician Karl Korsch analyzed this example of a blitzkrieg while living in American exile in Boston. He could not believe that the fascist enemy had mastered such an intelligent military strategy. In his analysis, he established that in their civilian life, the majority of the tank crews of the German divisions were car mechanics or engineers (that is, industrial workers with practical experience). Many of them came from the German provinces that had experienced bloody massacres at the hands of the authorities in the Peasant Wars (1524–1526). According to Korsch, they had good reason to avoid direct contact with their superiors. Almost all of them could also vividly remember the positional warfare of 1916, again a result of the actions of their superiors, in whom they had little faith thereafter.

In this way, Korsch continues, a readied and focused motive emerged from the spirit of the balance economy: it is advantageous to have as little contact as possible with the adversary, and therefore he must be outflanked once he is cut off in a confined space. At the same time, it is also advantageous when advancing to switch off any radio equipment enabling communication with your own commanders. According to Korsch, it thereby became possible for the troops to invent for themselves the blitzkrieg spontaneously, out of historical motives at hand. Orders alone would not have been sufficient to achieve such a thing. The minority faction among the German leaders who had developed the doctrine of the blitzkrieg (besides Heinz Guderian, these included the generals Erwin Rommel and Paul von Kleist) merely had to sharpen the focus of what the soldiers were already doing.

This conception of blitzkrieg already existed in ancient times. Hannibal, the commander of the Carthaginians, dashed with lightning speed from victory to victory in the Second Punic War, and in the Battle of Cannae, he provided a classic example of how to outflank your opponent. However, despite all his victories and despite having lost only a single battle (at Zama), his native town of

Carthage was razed to the ground when he tried to defend it. Practitioners of blitzkrieg are defeated if they are not able to end a war with lightning speed.

Incidentally, it is also fascinating to observe that toward the end of the Second World War, at the point when the German armies were forced to retreat from Russia, there emerged so-called MOBILE POCKETS [*WANDERNDER KESSEL*]. Entire tank armies, including the First Panzer Army under General Hube, were heading in a "backward blitzkrieg" toward the homeland. Here, too, the unexpected successes during these retreats can be seen to be the result of the spontaneous emergence of a spirit of improvisation and cooperation among the soldiers of the kind analyzed by Karl Korsch. It is motivation that determines whether a blitzkrieg goes forward or backward. No orders or offers of money could hope to emulate the results achieved here by the hope of liberation, prudence, historical experience, and sheer motivation. Here, too, the experience is an age-old one. In Xenophon's report on the retreat of a mercenary army from the heart of Persia through Anatolia to the Black Sea, the so-called *ANABASIS*, we have a withdrawal that against all expectations and despite many obstacles was a success, much like the "mobile pockets" of 1944.

X. The Prelude to War: The Production of War as the Collateral Damage of Armaments Projects

The Eurofighter is a multipurpose aircraft developed, built, and made fully operational within a period of around thirty years. Luftwaffe Officer Steinhoff, responsible for resolving the so-called Starfighter Crisis, had based his model for a replacement fighter (including its specifications) on experience gained early in his career fighting the Allies in the skies over Sicily in 1943. We paint this picture because it demonstrates the long-term thinking that goes into the design, planning, and implementation in the armaments industry.

By the time the Starfighter was finally completed, the Cold War enemy for whom this NATO weapon had been designed had completely vanished. NATO's targets had moved far away and were now, for example, in the Horn of Africa and Afghanistan. An impartial observer or an auditor might have difficulties identifying the current function of this aircraft against the background of conditions in 2010. The contradiction between long-term thinking in the armaments industry and rapid historical change also applies to many other branches of industry. Battleships were still being built at a time when aircraft carriers had become the strategic mainstay of the task force. Heavy tanks had to be stockpiled in huge arsenals because light and mobile strike brigades, made up of many different troop units, were now the order of the day within the military.

In the Yellow Sea, Russian and Chinese warships practice maneuvers. An American naval unit carries out demonstrative exercises together with its Pacific allies. For almost a half century, unresolved problems have intensified in the expanded Near East into political-military minefields. The threat of war or outbreaks of war—as is the case in Sudan—consume eleven different locations around the world. The menace of a preemptive strike against Iran on the part of Israel remains intact in spite of critical voices. Only twenty years ago, such a scenario would have been unlikely or limited to a single region (for example in the Balkans).

In the past, such a sign indicated the onset of war. In 2012, this sign becomes clear when we glance back a century to Europe in 1912. Like the distortions reflected by carnival mirrors or the initial confusion typical of cross-mapping—the overlaying of two maps that don't correspond—clues nevertheless emerge: in 1912, British Secretary of State for War Lord Haldane visited Berlin and, backed by the authority of the British cabinet, negotiated a long-term neutrality agreement with the German Reich. Such a treaty could have created thirty to forty years of peace. A twentieth century without the outbreak of war in 1914 in Europe would have meant (for our parents, for us, and even for our children) an alternative reality for entire generations, a heterotopia.

The negotiations, led on the German side by the Kaiser himself, his chancellor, Bethmann Hollweg, and an intermediary of the naval office, Admiral von Tirpitz, failed because Tirpitz refused to curb German naval armament. It later turned out that this deep-sea fleet, also called the "risk fleet," that is, a deterrent force, was not deployable, as the British historian John C. G. Röhl has described succinctly. As justification for the fleet (to the kaiser and the chancellor), the German admiral drew upon the fact that the absence of such a fleet in 1923 (when seen from the year 1912) would be lamented. It can be seen how little 1923 (the year inflation befell the Weimar Republic) can be portrayed strategically in such a distorting mirror. The same goes for Chinese, Indian, Russian and American plans today, all of which refer to the year 2040; they can only be chimerical. In the course of the 1912, the First Balkan War against the Ottoman Empire broke out. In the First Moroccan Crisis, the German Reich threatened France with war. And thus in November of that year, all factors, including an alliance between France and England, were in place, factors that were the preconditions for the outbreak of the world war the following year. Massive labor and intelligence capacities were mobilized among Europe's elite and in its voter and production base and put to work on armaments and the stabilization of the crises; in other words, preparations for war were being mobilized way. Conversely, labor and intelligence capacities that would have been suitable for dismantling these crises and preventing the onset of war were missing in the most grotesque of ways. The POLITICAL ARCHITECTURE for this was missing. Politics was nowhere to be found, when it should have been the profession of the elite: "Politics means slow, strong drilling through hard boards, with a combination of passion and a sense of judgment."[24]

For both the political economy of labor power in our societies and the necessity of a counterrevolutionary transformation of intelligence after Auschwitz (which affects conservative motivation, rigor, effort, and care) both the CASE OF EMERGENCY and RESISTANCE DURING THE PRELUDE TO WAR serve as litmus tests.[25]

COMMENTARY 13: SIX STORIES ABOUT THE LABOR OF WAR

Aspen in Summer

If only we could have a hundred such summers![26] The conference guests were in a state of constant elation at being among the few who had actually been invited. What is the general consensus of opinion among eighty-seven people whose main aim is not to say anything that might upset anyone, that might cause irritation and thereby result in not being invited back next time? Thanks to its maritime monopoly, the United States still had freedom to maneuver when it came to China. But what will happen in forty years? The theme of conference was "Agenda 2040."

— They can't stop thinking about the right moment to solve the Taiwan problem once and for all.
— Who do you mean by "they"?
— China's military strategists.
— Do you know any of them?
— I know about the massive arsenal of missiles stationed on the mainland directly opposite the island.

At that time, the Danish Secret Service had the most reliable information about current thinking among the high-ranking Chinese military leaders. Without much work, Denmark had planted a mole in the core of the Chinese leadership. As a result, this minor NATO partner was in possession of valuable information that it was willing to exchange with the United States while protecting the anonymity of its source. According to this information, Chinese military doctrine held that a blitzkrieg (of the kind implemented by Japan in 1941, planned by Germany in 1914, and that was the downfall of MacArthur in 1951) was reprehensible. No one with an eye on their future career at the Chinese headquarters would dare to suggest invading an island if they could not predict what the response would be in the ensuing conflict. The informer reported that they despised any "adventurers" in their ranks.

— What do you understand by "sweeping something off the table"?
— Why?
— You were talking just now about Taiwan, but Taiwan isn't on the table.
— That's just a turn of phrase.
— But realities are born of turns of phrase.
— It's ridiculous to compare expressions with giving birth.

The Danish expert, a major general and the mole's commanding officer, wanted to explain to his higher-ranking American counterpart that the Chinese leadership was not in any way "playing for time." They weren't playing at all, he said. They also were not maintaining "a low hegemonic profile in order to win time and then suddenly adopt the guise of a monster." The faction in the United States, which at the time was tackling the question of "China as the chief rival of the future," was too excited to pay any attention to the news from its minor NATO partner. The following day, the American chief of staff, who had left the Dane standing (merely because Wolfowitz had just entered the conference chamber), wrote the following in an article for the *Journal for Foreign Affairs*: "Despite all the technological means available to a superpower in the twenty-first century, wars can still be triggered by a misleading situation report."

At the time, this was a timely reference to Iraq and a blow aimed at the ruling faction of the network-centric warfare wing within the Pentagon that was tapping into all established posts and budgets. A successfully malicious observation. The remark was not coined for the twilight zone around the year 2040, the point in time by which the Chinese faction expected to be fully in charge.

An Exam Topic at West Point

> *Everything in war is very simple, but the simplest thing is difficult.*
> *The difficulties accumulate and end by producing a kind of friction.*
> —Carl von Clausewitz, *On War*

In the final examination at the West Point Military Academy, the most feared questions relate to the problem of the FOG OF WAR. This is the field of expertise of Major General Freddy R. Williams, military historian and instructor in strategic studies. The fog of war has nothing to do with deploying troops in a sandstorm or in a thick fog. Nowadays, neither results in any kind of danger or disorientation for a commander or his troops, because the heat sensors used by reconnaissance operatives in the area make such opacities transparent. The night no longer hides anything from the all-seeing eye of the satellite, at least as long as it is living material that radiates heat into its immediate environment.

At the risk of sounding spiritual, Major General Williams described the fog of war as a process at the outbreak of war in which the very facts themselves lose their immutable forms. Not unlike those unknown beasts of ancient times that, according to Herodotus, came into being when parts of different animals, such as goats, snakes, and lions were joined together to form a chimera, in the time of war, there emerge "unknown facts," combinations of necessity and chance, for which it is impossible to prepare oneself either by practice or through toughening oneself up. Indeed, it could well be the case that all verifiable conditions change to some degree or "bend" under the "pressure of war," as is the case with space and time in the immediate vicinity of monstrous gravitational forces.

It was difficult for the pupils of the military academy, who lacked any direct experience of war, to convey this notion in their examination work. To them, it seemed to be of a "philosophical nature." However, Major General Williams rebuffed such objections vehemently. The dangerous appearance of a "degenerate reality" created by the so-called friction or fog of war is anything but conceptual in nature, that is, not a product of observation, but of things themselves. The explanation lies in the encounter of people and things with chance. Like a ship on the open seas, the leader of a military unit ends up at the mercy of the imponderable vagaries of chance that subsist the world over. Once war has broken out, one can no longer prevent facts from coming into illicit contact with the forces of chance.

Was this all simply a crazy notion on the part of the major general? Or was this something that the young officers would actually encounter in the future? Every year, the exam questions changed. The candidates made a great effort to learn from the answers to the examinations from previous years. They were convinced that the only option was to copy these answers, rather than find their own solutions to the problem of the fog of war. They were intimidated.

On the occasions when Major General Williams flew into an uncontrollable rage in his seminars, he would insist that the tempestuous spirits of all wars since time immemorial were in league with one another in the manner of some "wild hunt" and had forced their way into the gaps that facts always throw up between each other. If this was the case, he argued, it was not simply the encounter with chance, but rather with the "generations of the dead from the dim and distant past" that was whipping the facts up into a frenzy. The interpretation, the major general concluded, remained the same: the fog of war is invincible.

Karl Korsch's Theory of the Blitzkrieg
Karl Korsch, Boston 1942, was of the opinion that Marx's method wasn't worth the paper it was printed on if it couldn't explain the phenomenon of the blitzkrieg. Korsch, who had a discussion with Wilhelm Reich on the subject in April 1941, explained it in the following way: blitzkrieg = left-wing energy

(ideas, drive, "living labor") APPROPRIATED BY THE RIGHT; hasty movements are the result and an unerring ability to hit targets ("initially"). Korsch, who had studied in Jena, was well acquainted with the area around Mansfeld, for example. Rabble-rousing in the Peasant Wars, miners; having seen people hanged, drawn, and quartered and with their eyes gouged out: work means escaping somehow." For example: for a tank division (and the fifth and seventh are from the Mansfeld area) "steering clear of the killing fields of Verdun at all costs" means: we'll push forward 50 meters tonight ("that's always possible") so that the following afternoon we'll be 200 kilometers behind the enemy, impregnable. As we attack, we are, so to speak, fleeing forward, otherwise known as the principle of the "Sickle Cut." In other words, for a certain period, at least, *avoiding harm* and *the victory of our superiors* are identical in terms of an economy of drives.

A Special Application of the Force of Labor:
Drilling into the Hills of Vauquois

Conquering an enemy summit is bad enough; having to defend it is terrible.

Beneath the village of Vauquois, which ceased to exist after the battle and still to this day has not been rebuilt, French and German sappers, especially chosen for their mining experience, dug tunnels deep into the hill from both sides; they reached a depth of sixty meters, and according to calculations made after the war, a total length of 17 kilometers. The explosions began with 50-kilogram charges of dynamite. Then, on May 14, 1916, a German charge with the destructive power of 60,000 kilograms of explosives was detonated. With this detonation, the German miners destroyed a slightly higher French tunnel that otherwise would have blown up the German one. An inflation of materials in the most confined of spaces.

— All professionals.
— A rapid escalation of losses among irreplaceable explosives experts and miners. Given the rate at which they were dying, it wasn't possible to replace them quickly enough from the mining areas.
— By the end, accommodation and storage facilities on both sides of the mountain of Vauquois resembled cities, with depots, latrines, washrooms, kitchens, and barracks to supply the attack.
— Finally the hill was useless for further tunnel building. You can't drive tunnels into ground shaken apart by explosions.

337

— So what did the sappers do after that?
— They built concrete pipes into the mountain.
— Were they any use for explosions?
— The charge had to be increased once again.
— From the outside it looked like cooperation. The concentrated force of labor on each side matched the other precisely.
— Never again would a force of labor with such qualifications be frittered away in such a confined space.

In Constantinople in Eight Hours
The historian A. F. Middleton, formerly a staff member for President Clinton's security advisor, writes that prior to 1914, the great European powers rehearsed for the First World War in foreign territories (as can be convincingly simulated with the help of the computers at Stanford). In the Balkans: Serbs, Montenegrins at war with the Ottoman Empire, whose troops were commanded by "young Turkish" officers. They joined forces together with Bulgaria and Greece. The Balkan League was armed and instructed by the French. At the time, the Germans did the same for the Turkish Army. Following victories at the battles of Kirk Kilisse and Lule Burgas, Bulgarian troops found themselves facing the isthmus near Chatalja. On the one side, they could see the Black Sea, on the other the Aegean. The Turkish General Nazim Pasha, said to be a man of "phlegmatic energy and cool perseverance," occupied the isthmus and the town of Chatalja. "In eight hours we will be in Constantinople" was the confident claim at the Bulgarian headquarters fuelled by recent success. They intended to share the conquest with Russia and France. Their ancestors had fought for this trophy for more than nine hundred years. To the astonishment of the Turkish side, which up to this point had experienced only defeat after defeat, the Bulgarians retreated after two days and a night of failed attempts to storm Turkish positions. Well-trained Turkish troops from Smyrna arrived to reinforce the front. The Bulgarians were routed. They had got to within a mere thirty-eight kilometers of Byzantium, their cherished goal. It turned out that their notion of what they actually wanted to capture once they got there was not substantial enough to ensure victory.

— Is it the case that the deep significance for the Turks of capturing the ancient sites—the city that had been the capital of the enemy for a

thousand years and formerly the center of the entire Eastern Roman
Empire — had not been explained to the Bulgarian troops at that time?
— It was forbidden to collect booty. On the strictest orders of the officers,
they were to march into the city in a civilized manner. Stand guard.
Later return home.
— Well in that case, we might as well just go home now, they thought.
We could protect ourselves that way.
— No, they were prepared to lay down their lives. They attacked
ferociously. But they didn't understand why they were doing it.
— Two fully equipped modern Turkish battleships shadowed them from
the sea?
— The sea was thoroughly unsettling to them. Why would they want to
capture a "strait"?
— Was it cold in November 1912?
— That, too.

In Middleton's work, the question was posed as to whether useful experience can be gained from SURROGATE WARS for the crisis of a "real war." That
would presuppose that such experience was of a *general* kind, he wrote. In
reality, wars consist almost entirely of unique experiences, of singularities.
In their basic form, they are a product of chance, and in the most extreme
application of willpower, they are fragments. In the battle for control of the
isthmus described above, this willpower could not be encouraged to exert
itself fully. Thus, the experience did not yield any "architecture." You can't
"live" in wars.

Later, the empirical proposition that the 7.5-centimeter canons made by
Creuzot were less accurate than those of the same caliber produced by the
Krupp factory proved to be false. A mistake with disastrous consequences,
resulting in an inferiority complex on the part of the French artillery in 1914,
which meant that the war began under the motto of "attack," rather than
"defend." In fact, fifty-one Creuzot canons intended for the Serbian Army
were unloaded in Thessaloniki, captured by the Turkish Army, and then used
against the Bulgarian attacking forces with shells made by Krupp. The canons couldn't handle the foreign munitions and missed their targets.

Conversely, the prevailing cold weather, the fortuitous arrival of reinforcements from Smyrna that "galvanized the troops," and the favorable position
of the Turks on the isthmus were all cited as decisive in the unexpected

339

victory of the Ottoman Empire. Actually, Middleton writes, it was the fact that the defense was given priority over the attack, as Clausewitz once described, that was decisive here and that would also prove its worth in the positional warfare of 1915. Ultimately, Middleton concluded in his essay, nothing can be learned from the outcome of surrogate wars.

Seeking with the Soul the Land of the Tigris and the Euphrates
Platoon Commander Dave Myers, a major in the army and an ancient historian at Stanford, was a specialist in THE HISTORY OF THE AGRICULTURAL REVOLUTION. He estimated that it had a life span of six thousand years. It has consolidated its position at the very heart of the things that define modern civilization, our senses and our manners. As they line up in front of me every morning (and they all hail from New York), says Myers, my men bring all of history along with them. Accordingly, we all carry deep within our hearts an Assyrian farmer (or his great-grandson, who became a barber). We do so more fervently, indeed, than the locals we guard with our military equipment and whom we'd only reluctantly destroy if they attack us. These locals may well be the descendants of Bedouins or Mongolian conquerors. But if this is the case, unlike us Americans and the majority of Europeans, then they do not descend from the LINEAGE OF THE AGRICULTURAL REVOLUTION. They would be the descendents of hunters.

Myers insists on the presence of the city of Uruk within all of us. Cities of this kind are fields rising upward, each one stacked on top of every other. Calling them "cities" is the result of a mix-up. Consequently, what actually happens with the arrival of our army and accompanying civilian forces is the return to its country of origin of all that once emerged in this land of two rivers. The Western spirit was born in the East. The chaos that we can observe all around us is simply a result of the fact that we mistakenly believe the blitzkrieg in Iraq to be where it all began. In reality, our souls have always been moving toward the Golden Crescent.

Translated by Martin Brady and Helen Hughes with Richard Langston

CHAPTER SEVEN

Love Politics:

The Obstinacy of Intimacy

When we write of "love politics" and of the "labor of relationships" (we see parents caring for their children, we observe lovers), we do so knowing they are unusual expressions. But when we verify what energies are at work in the realm of intimacy, we cannot deny the fact that it is full of concentrated "processes that change matter." Intimacy consists of a labor that possesses its own political economy.

The sociologist Talcott Parsons once said that a THEORY OF THE LABOR OF RELATIONSHIPS must accompany (or even could serve as an anchor or root for) the theories of money, power, and truth.

There are no "factories" in which humans grow. In the "charcoal kilns of society" in which the energies of humans and their characteristics are formed (that is, in families and the networks of social relationships), the courage of cognition develops, a chance for emancipation (or grounds for its inhibition). The 1936 volume STUDIEN ÜBER AUTORITÄT UND FAMILIE edited by Max Horkheimer is a classic text on this subject.[1] The book belongs to the core of Critical Theory.

Love Politics

Love politics is the field of experience in which humans are able to test their intimate conduct and at the same time their power of political judgment. The libido is itself blind to politics, Sigmund Freud once remarked. However, its *derivatives* are the masterminds of the political and the search for good fortune.[2]

341

"Love as a term to describe the way in which wanting something from others entails providing it yourself." [Alexander Kluge Archive]

The Search for Good Fortune in the Private Sphere

How time is divided throughout a human's concrete life span reveals just how enormous the portion of it is spent on the job. Another considerable portion is allotted to the **private labor of relationships**: the processes by which a person is transformed from a child into labor power, as well as to the debt economy that arises from this transformation. These are the confusing and powerful movements in libidinal relationships.

One can recognize that a third portion of a human's lifetime — distributed among all areas, it also seeps into the gaps between them — is consumed by the production of compulsory **balance economies** necessary for making tolerable the labor in these two large areas (within families and professions) as well as in the intermediary forms between them. The portion of scattered time that serves this balance today is at least as necessary and as large as the total labor power that goes into businesses and socialization.

Relationships transpire in all of these publicly and privately delineated areas. **In a narrow sense, however, among all human relationships, the libidinal relationships encapsulated in private relations reach the most irritating degree of intensity.** Balance is primarily sought therein. Two powerful areas in the temporal economy of life spans (libidinal relationships and balance) bind and intermingle particularly closely. Confined to the realm of privacy, today, this labor of relationships acquires the tendency to absorb the forces and allotments of time originating from all the other areas of life in order to cope with crises.

In the crisis of erosion, the programmed dissolution of the traditional public sphere therefore does not lead to the simple strengthening of the forces capable of constructing alternative public spheres. This dissolution simultaneously encounters the aforementioned tendency for the private accumulation of additional forces in the labor of relationships, **a kind of ravenousness in the labor of relationships, a search for good fortune in the private sphere**. Under the reigning circumstances, this leads to the consumption of conflict and the forced production of superficial quietude.

In the Marx Brothers films, Harpo assails with embraces basically everyone he likes. [*A Night at the Opera* (1935)]

At its core, the word *socialization* characterizes how the sociation of humans transpires in the intimate sphere not directly, but indirectly. The original objects that a child encounters (involuntarily and not always consciously) are objective agents of the empire of necessity. The precision grips that children employ as part of their upbringing are based on a special form of persuasiveness. In order to win over the self-regulating supplemental labor of the child, the reigning laws of the empire of necessity are made to look as if they were invalidated. Whereas outside, a system of services and rewards dominate, in the intimate sphere of parenting, needs take priority. Arrival in the empire of necessity, however, is only deferred. Only this principle of deception can comprehensively mobilize itself.

No agent of the external economy can replace this foundation for the initial phases of parenting. Any and all applied means would be too direct. In this respect, the basic form of sociation arises primarily in the zone of socialization. That the direct and in other ways indirect means of deception of the economy continue to build additional human characteristics upon this established foundation is another question altogether.

The Primary Production of All Human Social Characteristics in the Intimate Sphere

If one wishes to make clear the result of this process, as well as its opposite, one would need to imagine a Taylorist timekeeper paying a visit to the bedroom of a married couple. He would say, "What you married people do isn't practical at all. If you just cast off a few erroneous moves and detours, you could easily reach within a minute the climax that you otherwise slave away at for up to three quarters of an hour. Furthermore, when you mutually agree to it, such activities shouldn't be left to the chance of moods. You should introduce a kind of regularity into your lovemaking. Multiple climaxes could be accommodated at the same time every month or year. You would just have to plan on it and take regulated genital intercourse far more seriously. You must acknowledge it as a human basic right to which all people are entitled."

The married couple would counter: "According to your method, we're done before we even start. We have to retain some of our detours and mistakes. We mate: (1) because something is hidden in our embraces that gets lost when we try to put it into words; (2) because we're made of rebellion; and (3) because of all the more subtle ways the senses are capable of measuring stimuli."

Not everything the timekeeper says to the married couple is necessarily absurd. While he rummages around in their habits, they have fallen into a rut.

Normally, people live apart from one another. I cannot ring a stranger's doorbell and embrace whoever opens the door. The owner of merchandise can exchange wares with others, but he certainly does not embrace his customers. People can stand close to one another in a streetcar, but they do not have the right to consider the touch of another to be tender.

School at the time of the inflation of 1923. Children pay tuition with food. They present their teacher with packed lunches, sandwiches made with sausage. [Alexander Kluge Archive]

On the other hand, almost all humans recognize one another as laborers of relationships in the midst of their societal roles. They are constantly testing one another in terms of rejection and attraction. On this mimetic basis, they create a complete society. The monetary form of this testing acquires both positive and negative connotations and is called either "politeness" or "wariness." The need for a protective zone emerges, and for this reason, wariness is also articulated politely. With respect to this monetary form, cordiality and rejection (coldness) operate as natural resources.

The Subsistence Economy within Love
In capitalist societies, the realism of values is read economically: Is a thing or a service worth the money that I pay for it? In this context, raising children, love relationships, the work of mourning, and joy are all "unproductive labor."

The differentiation of **productive** and **unproductive** forms of work can be traced back to Marx's formulation of the concept. Under modern circumstances (but also already in Marx), differentiation yields a wondrous scholasticism, that of capitalist alienation.

> It is not the pianist, but the maker of pianos — provided he works in a capitalist's factory — who performs a productive form of labor. A clown is paid when he can bring forth either joy or sadness. If he is in the employ of the circus owner, he, too, performs a form of labor that generates both value and surplus value and is therefore productive. When he collects tips with a plate, he is paid for his performance on the job from those audience members who take delight in his art. But because the owner receives no surplus value, this labor is unproductive, according to Marx. In discussions from the late 1960s on the political economy of the education sector, the question arose whether the classes of students and instructors propelling the student protests forward performed a productive or unproductive form of labor.

The degree to which economic value systems are based upon prior understanding can be seen, for example, in the different valuation of political labor power. In the Attic democracy, participation in elections and public assemblies was honored; political merit often meant dining in the Prytaneion. Our society compensates only for professional political labor.

With respect to compensation, we find similar historical distortions in the labor of relationships. While prostitution was paid for both in antiquity and today, the product offered by a classical *hetaera*, when compared with the services offered on Kaiserstraße in Frankfurt, is rather different. A squad of cleaning ladies or the staff in a large kitchen are compensated; comparable employment in the form of drudgery existed in the Middle Ages, but went unpaid. Parenting in the home goes unpaid, but when a kindergarten or a teacher in a school does it, it is recompensed. These supremely historical classifications of labor and remuneration cannot be a criterion for productivity. From the viewpoint of nonemancipation, the concepts "productive" and "unproductive" each describe a prevailing condition. From the viewpoint of emancipation, they must be reconstituted. Therefore, they are of only minor use when they allow for a differentiation between emancipatory and regime-dependent production, in other words, between primary production, the regime itself, and secondary production dependent upon that regime. The labor of relationships relates to these differentiations just like any other implementation of labor power: it contains elements of: (1) domination, (2) emancipation, (3) primary production, and (4) production dependent on domination.

The Breeding Ground of Human Characteristics: Authority and Family

Families are breeding grounds for a human being's sense of fear, longing, and social character. The family is an enormous laboratory. Due to the high degree of violence that resides in this relationship [*Zusammenhang*], the power of the imagination guards itself from having to deal with this violence matter of factly. Karl Kraus made reference to this when he wrote, "After much careful deliberation, I'd like to take the path back to the land of children, but preferably with Jean Paul rather than with S. Freud."[3]

A key phrase in Critical Theory asserts that the fuel that drives authoritarian systems is generated in millions of families, just as charcoal is fabricated in kilns. But as Antigone made clear—she fought against the authoritarian Creon—this fuel is carried in the heart. In his *Studien über Autorität und Familie* published in Paris in 1936, Horkheimer and other collaborators of Critical Theory investigated this relationship. "None of the great social relationships remains a fixed structure permanently. Instead, a reciprocity characteristic of itself continually transpires among all of its subordinated parts and spheres. All previously existing cultures simultaneously contain continuities [*Gesetzmäßigkeiten*] that run counter to them."[4] Read in context, this assertion refers to both the primary form in which the raw materials for any future labor of relationships are

Antigone buries her brother. She follows the law of the old gods. [Gita Wolf and Sirish Rao, *Sophocles' Antigone*, illustrated by Indrapramit Roy (Los Angeles, CA: J. Paul Getty Trust Publications, 2001)]

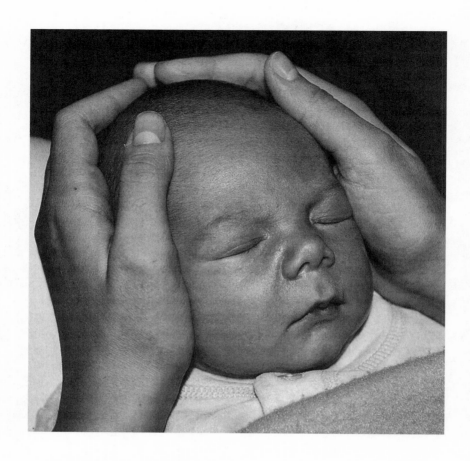

Baby. [Milan Nykodym/Creative Commons]

engendered and to the family on which an overwhelming majority of people eventually and repeatedly falls back. This phenomenon appears as either a cohesive or a disruptive factor of the societal dynamic, something that occurs in the countless laboratories of close cohabitation either as "the mortar of a building under construction" or "as the cement that artificially holds parts together that tend to repel one another, or they form a portion of the explosives that blow up the entirety upon being lit."[5]

Horkheimer continues: "In the end everything...needs to be supported and held together in an ever more artificial fashion.... The totality of relations in the present age, this universal [*dieses Allgemeine*] category, was strengthened and stabilized by one particular element within it, namely, authority, and this process of strengthening and stabilization has essentially played itself out at the singular and concrete level of the family.... The dialectical whole of universality, particularity and singularity (cf. Hegel's *Encyclopedia of the Philosophical Sciences in Basic Outline*, sect. 164) proves now to be a unity of forces that repel one another. Compared to the cohesive moment of culture, the explosive moment of culture is making itself more strongly felt."[6] Horkheimer wrote this in 1936. We know how the guiding principle of the small family returned after the catastrophes of World War II.

In another passage, Horkheimer investigates why accumulated experiences in relationships are so easily erased. "The bad conscience nurtured within the family absorbs an enormous amount of energy that could otherwise be directed against the social conditions responsible for the individual's failures.... In the present age, however, a compulsory sense of guilt, which assumes the guise of a permanent state of readiness to sacrifice oneself, foils the critique of reality.... The kinds of people who prevail today are not educated to get at the root of things.... According to Nietzsche the 'cure for a wounded pride,' cruelty finds outlets other than work and knowledge, outlets into which a reasonable education could certainly channel it."[7]

Within the family, children do not chose their primary objects voluntarily. "As students of all the many objects that surround them, of all the situations in which chance arises before them, and ultimately of all events that confront them"—their will is never queried (even well before they ever have one)—they experience their very first relationships and elaborate from them the potential for all subsequent ones. It is no different than throwing dice.[8] Every subsequent situation in which two or more people find themselves revolves around good fortune or misfortune, as well, and conversely, rarely around the freedom to chose.It would be a relief if we could liberate energies from that exhausting quest—so-called choice—and transform them into an attentiveness to those things that are locked up. In such a context, we could rely on self-regulating forces that are always silently at work and cannot reconcile themselves at all with the capacity of the ego, namely, its intentional act of choosing.

"In the yearning of many adults for the paradise of their childhood, in the way a mother can speak of her son even though he has come into conflict with the world...there are ideas and forces at work which admittedly are not dependent on the existence of the family in its present form and, in fact, are even in danger of shriveling up in such a milieu, but which, nevertheless, in the bourgeois system of life rarely have any place but the family where they can survive at all."[9] Hegel recognized this and endlessly tried to keep this substance—*in contradistinction to family and community*—intact.

For Hegel, this contrast is "the most tragic." Introduced with the chapter heading "The Ethical World, Human and Divine Law: Man and Woman," the pages in which Hegel develops the conflict between the family and publicly sanctioned authority relies on the figure of Antigone who fights over the corpse of her brother.[10] According to Hegel, the principle of love for a whole person can predominate only in a gendered community; it is accordingly associated with the principle of "femininity." Irreconcilably opposed to this principle is state subordination, which has absolutely nothing to do with the entirety of a person, but rather with a person's obedient components. For Hegel, this is the principle of "masculinity." "To the extent that any principle besides that of subordination prevails in the modern family...one social principle dating back well before the dawn of historical antiquity remains, a principle that Hegel understood 'as the law of the ancient gods, the gods of the underworld' (Hegel, *Elements of the Philosophy of Right*, § 166), that is, of prehistory."[11] The terrible conflicts with the community make this principle incompatible. These antiauthoritarian forces are the individual. But then, the universal is not suitable for anything, because it emerges from the exclusion of the most important substance.

Reliability
In the relations of relationships, the object of all labor is reliability. It has a specific temporal rhythm, and its production is hardly comparable with other forms of production.

The rhythm and the temporal framework [*Zeitgestalt*] in which relationships forged between two people are put to the test presumably leave their mark on the rhythm and temporal framework of all future relationships. Or these relationships end in ruptures and catastrophes and on the basis of such a separation translate into renewed attempts at relationships. This can be tested on one's own life story. What must I be able to rely upon if the following is supposed to come about: openness, objectivity, curiosity, creating intimacy, devoting oneself, turning away, the concentration of feelings, loving, hating, joy, mourning, allowing feelings to persist in distraction, relaxing, falling asleep, the training of protective rituals that allow for falling asleep or eating quietly or being touched on the skin? Being able to separate oneself, being able to attach oneself, leaving, coming home, and so on? **The cultivation of each of these characteristics presupposes, on the one hand, the coordinated development of parallel characteristics. On the other hand, each of these developments presupposes a specific amount of basic trust, which is nothing other than the intimate knowledge of reliability that I carry over onto the production and temporal structure of new situations.**

What we call the "temporal rhythm of reliability" in socialization reoccurs in history as a need for the recognition of one's own value and arises from one's loyal relations. Disappointment in relationships, the lack of reliability therein, leads to a displaced need: the recognition of loyal relations in society. Conversely, disappointment in loyal relations in society displaces the labor of hope onto the realm of relationships. The roots of this are as follows: I can and will not be alone. I thought I was in society and therefore failed to realize altogether some of my own interests. This exchange is a disappointment. The disloyalty of others, or rather their unreliability, has retrospectively rendered my previous endeavors meaningless. I've lost something of myself because another was disloyal.

353

Damages Suffered by Third Parties

In the course of his clinical observations, Freud came across a peculiar type of object choice common among men that requires the participation of a "damaged third party." In principle, these men fell in love again and again with women who were already involved in a union with another man (the damaged third party). The woman already involved with another man had to be sexually "disreputable" in some form or another in order to fulfill the conditions of "hooker love." At the same time, these men tended to idealize such a woman objectively and filled their heads with the idea that they had to save these lovers. This "disreputability" was related to the discovery (first made prior to the onset of puberty) that the "pure" mother actually does the exact same thing with the father that prostitutes do. Freud interpreted this mindset within the Oedipal context of an incurred trauma of separation. In the case of this kind of object choice, the Oedipal trauma expresses itself thus: "Father took mother away from me. I thought she was all mine. Mother has become unfaithful to me. I am the damaged third party." And the wish fantasy that accompanies this trauma would run something like this: "If only it were so that mother would be unfaithful to father and love only me, then father would be the damaged third party."

The mother is not only unfaithful because she associates with the father, but also because she deceives the child in the name of reality. The father does the same thing, so the process of third-party damages also affects the daughter. Father and mother are the sensorially tangible occasions for children to articulate disappointments that do not have to be caused by their parents at all. For this reason, parents can only seldom satisfy the expectations placed upon them. As a matter of principle, they are unfaithful. The sublation of unfaithfulness transpires through the redistribution of damages: "it may very well be the case that I am not the one who suffered damages."

If everyone felt this way, everyone would be dragged into a fight for the position of the uninjured party. The specific moment of property relations (in the Roman sense) is the exclusion of the other from ownership. Germanic and Celtic ownership had developed property relations based on both the household and the community and therefore precluded any such exclusion. In the relations of relationships, we find a third kind of property produced at the site of one's own body. It is based upon the idea that I may not exclude the

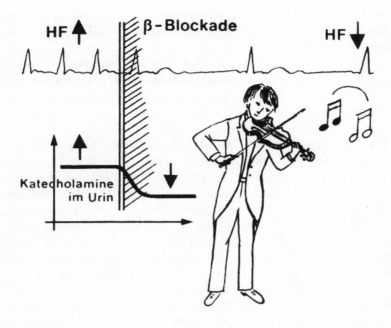

Freelance artist. The good-for-nothing plays his way to freedom (Eichendorff). Freedom has to be hampered with beta blockers because of the fear of anticipation and tachycardia (the heart cannot beat too fast). [Alexander Kluge Archive]

other under any circumstances, otherwise I, too, would be alone. I have to exclude others occasionally so that I am the injured party.[12]

I must therefore simultaneously permit and exclude. The material vehemence bound up with this form of labor does not come about solely in the labor of relationships. If this were so, other ways out would turn up. This is based upon the fact that in ménages à trois and third-party injuries, the need for relationships is overlaid by the compensation for disappointments rooted not within relationships, but outside them, for example, in social relations. These compensatory needs, as well as immediate needs, together undertake an attempt to instantiate themselves through the eye of a needle also known as the relations of relationships.

The intensity of these processes would not block the ways out if it were not for the attempts at self-realization that were attempted earlier in both the relations of relationships and society. Rebellions and utopian needs are displaced back and forth from the relations of relationships onto society and from society onto the relations of relationships so many times that they acquire foreign energies capable of constructing a **special relation of violence** guided by the motto: "The most reasoned person to go down does so adorned in full armor."[13]

The Interaction between Sexuality and Child Rearing

When dealing with sexuality, Sigmund Freud and Michel Foucault each write about something entirely different. Freud assumes "the deepest essence of human nature consists of instinctual impulses which are of an elementary nature, which are similar in all men and which aim at the satisfaction of certain primal needs. These impulses in themselves are neither good nor bad."[14] It could be added that they are not interested in parenting (other than when they do so out of error). From this material, the psychological authorities of the unconscious, the ego, and portions of the superego are manufactured. Simultaneously, the same forces work in a historical and collective vein [*Maßstab*] and have an effect on parenting and sexual praxis.

Conversely, Foucault is interested in the so-called *dispositif* of sexuality. *Dispositifs* are rules of derivation [*Abstammungsregeln*]. Foucault wishes to translate the fable of the indiscreet treasures into *histoire*. His starting point is that of the original agrarian familial alliance within clans, that is, a unity of production that brought about the agrarian revolution. According to Foucault, from the dissolution of this alliance, the *dispositifs* of knowledge, power, and sexuality arose. The crumbling family alliance needed individualization, specialization, and the overvaluation of sexuality for its transformation into modern society. This overvaluation of sexuality survived as a thirst for knowledge and a binding energy [*Bindungsenergie*], virtually the instrument and transmission belt of domination. It was not the realization of the pleasure principle.

Regardless of which cartography one follows, the observations of Freud *and* Foucault can be examined at the juncture between sexuality and parenting. Modern sexual practices among adults have been carved out of a chain of separation processes from the entire erotics of the BODY POLITIC. In this sense, it is a form of labor power with a dose of desire tacked on.

Michael Balint (Hungarian psychoanalyst, 1896–1970) compared the trainability of various organs: the beating of the heart, the breathing of the respiratory system, muscular operations, digestion and urination, hands, genitals. It is clear that this series of organ activities (excluding psychosomatic disturbances) demonstrates an increasingly sexual cathexis. As a sexual organ, the heart is less specialized than the respiratory system, and this, in turn, is less specialized than the erotics of muscle movements, and this is less sexualized than the anus, and this is less sexually ambiguous than the hand, and this is similarly cathected, but nevertheless less specialized than the genitals.[15]

On the trainability of each of these organs, Michael Balint claimed, "Heartbeat is not, as far as I know, trained anywhere."[16] Breathing can be trained in yoga cults or in diving schools. More pronounced is the educational connection to all muscular operations. A set of educational instructions can be tacked onto every comprehensive libidinal possibility for movement until such point in time when walking, standing, and sitting are learned. This learning process also structures the walking, standing, holding tight, and sitting of thought, perception, touch, and so on that are not carried out using muscles. Again, the cultural educational intervention that aims at the control of the intestinal tract is self-apparent. Entire social periods have brought about educational catastrophes that were possible only because they acquired malleable sexual energies from the cathexis of this pole. The sexualization of these zones is certainly also a function of the labor of parenting by the primary object. The labor of parenting, however, is a result of the fact that the rudimentary libidinal cathexis of primary objects was noticed. With respect to the hands, whose phylogenetic development can be traced back to large portions of the brain, neither the interaction between parenting and sexualization nor the link identified by dominant educational forces interested in genitalia requires further discussion. Entire throngs of mercenaries and soldiers are essentially already equipped with sexual motives and are dragged into huge wars. It could be argued that the more absurd that educational conformity is, the more likely it is to be dependent on taking out loans from erotic cathexes for its motives.

357

The Libido's Resistance to Domestication

It is obvious that sexuality in the broader sense deals with matters of the libido. In a more narrow sense, sexuality is the sex industry [*Sexualbetrieb*]. It is ambiguous whether sexuality belongs to the party of domination or that of resistance. Of the sexualized relations of relationships, however, it can be said that they are grounded in an elementary material, in human characteristics that largely resist social organization.

The libidinal masses (Freud's elemental forces) behave indifferently toward the reality principle, which portions of these masses simultaneously help form. However, the reality principle extensively excludes these masses, especially the processes of libidinal self-regulation. Because of their exclusion, they are particularly unimpressionable.

This is the basic contradiction at work in the political economy of the labor of relationships. The libidinal forces are the binding agent and at the same time they remain rebellious. Whatever is made out of this material, be it obedience, education, and so on, it will always be built on sand.

In *Elements of the Philosophy of Right*, G. W. F. Hegel addresses the connection between ethics [*Sittlichkeit*] (reliability as dead labor) and love (reliability as living labor). Without knowing what we now associate with Freud, Hegel noticed that the underlying forces of nature do not make this link automatically. He proceeds indirectly: "But in those modern dramas and other artistic representations in which love between the sexes is the basic instinct, we encounter a pervasive element of frostiness which is brought into the heat of the passion such works portray by the total *contingency* associated with it. For the whole interest is represented as resting solely upon *these* particular individuals. This may well be of infinite importance for *them*, but it is of no such importance *in itself*."[17] This is based on the following: "Love is therefore the most immense contradiction; the understanding cannot resolve it, because there is nothing more intractable than this punctiliousness of the self-consciousness which is negated and which I ought nevertheless to possess as affirmative. Love is both the production and the resolution of this contradiction. As its resolution, it is ethical unity."[18] Shortly prior to this,

Hegel writes: "But love is a feeling [*Empfindung*], that is, ethical life in its natural form. In the state, it is no longer present. There, one is conscious of unity as law; there, the content must be rational, and I must know it. The first moment in love is that I do not wish to be an independent person in my own right [*für mich*] and that, if I were, I would feel deficient and incomplete. The second moment is that I find myself in another person, that I gain recognition in this person [*das ich in ihre gelte*], who in turn gains recognition in me."[19]

According to Hegel, love cannot establish itself out of its intractability, punctiliousness, frostiness, or fieriness. All these relationships signify the same state of affairs — isolation as abstraction — and can never in themselves be something living. Society, substantiality, and ethics are things that cannot be produced only out of living elements.

The relations of relationships: "The family as the immediate substantiality of spirit" is something so serious that the libidinal foundation has to deflect off course the idiosyncrasies of the raw materials in the context of their own set of laws.[20] The parenting of children, the structure of the family, and reliability are so important that celibacy would actually be the more appropriate organizational form for the family. The fieriness and punctiliousness of love are necessary only initially, in order to bring love about. The edifice of ethics (that is, reliability) otherwise would be built on sand.

"To all these furious outbreaks she replied like a true woman of her species who cares little if at all, who knows the man, to whom she is bound, down to his bones, and who knows that at the bottom of this pigsty of their common household eternal warfare slumbers. She was not as mean as he was angry, but she was far more atrocious, horrific, and hurtful in her coolness."[21] [*Les Diaboliques* by Barbey d'Aurevilly] Film cannot compete with prose of this high degree of organization. It cannot form any metaphoric concepts (this pigsty of their common household, eternal warfare, the furious outbreaks) or clichés (a true woman of her species). It is not capable of antithetical discourse on such a level of abstraction. Film can never condense in such a manner. And finally, it does not have the means to imitate the internal movement of language — which is what distinguishes this text — unless the filmmaker decides to quote the text.[22]

Greta Garbo. [*Joyless Street*, 1925 (Photofest)]

Her public life is a series of relationships in the movies. Via an agent. [Marilyn Monroe and Joseph Cotton in *Niagara* (Photofest)]

In her films, Greta Garbo managed to unify all the serene looks for which life otherwise has no time. [*Single Standard*, 1929 (Photofest)]

Jean Renoir, *La Chienne* (*The Bitch*), 1931. "She's now twenty years old, was married three times, pleasured a colossal amount of lovers, and now the needs of the heart finally speak up." [Photofest]

The Many Eyes

The search for happiness or an ongoing conflict within a family that a married couple may attempt to settle usually takes place in private [*unter vier Augen*]. In each case, however, four additional people participate in the experience or fight. If a married couple has a fight, their eyes not only look across to one another, but are also internal representatives of their parents' eight eyes.[23]

However, it would be a gross simplification to assign *a* single personhood to every single person, as well as to every one of their internal representatives that feed off of strife and life. One characteristic shared by people ensnared in a fight and people who are happy, for example, is the fact that they are capable of expressing themselves rationally. I attain security and verify something reliable when I can put it into words or can make myself intelligible. Another very different characteristic deals with how I react when touched. When my skin, which tests sensations quite differently than my head, is being seduced, do I feel reliability and security? We could break down both arguing and happy people into their actual characteristics, which themselves are individual persons; within a single divided person, these characteristics sit across from one another only extrinsically. Passion's eyes are different from its hands. The eyes of the objective remote senses are different from those of the immediate senses. The eyes involved in fleeing from another are different from the eyes involved in a person's appetite. In certain respects, the entire history of humanity—the society responsible for bringing these characteristics about—is present in a fight within the family or in the happy caresses between a few select people. If this were not handed down, it would be far too complicated for two people to construct such a jungle. What we call distribution (battle) and signify as comprehensiveness is the intersection where actual social relations break into private individual ones.

They do this in the form of the collective labor power of remembering and forgetting, as the overall product in all its varieties imaginable in the relations of relationships (how to fight or toward which horizon one should search for happiness), as a social product, or **as** a life-historical need, or as an individual one articulated in response to such a product.

Measurements, Weights, and Rules

Someone goes into a supermarket and asks for a pound of sugar. This person does not get pickles or salt, for example, and also does not pay more than the advertised price. Let us transpose this simple exchange transaction into the relations of relationships. A man comes home from work and wants his back scratched. His counterpart in the relationship, however, has prepared a noodle casserole for dinner. The aims of the man are rooted in precise needs. They are not about wanting to be scratched any old way at any old time. Rather, they are specific wishes that also presumably contain something verging on the impossible. They partially have to do with a long prehistory, a former life, his relation to his body, and prior generations and their relations to their bodies.

Conversely, there is the intention of preparing a noodle casserole that materializes itself into several hours of work. It involves much effort. Both could hardly risk discussing the difference between their wishes and the actual state of affairs. If the man wanting his back scratched carps about the noodle casserole, which certainly does not look bad, he will start a fight by stating his imprecise wishes at the wrong moment. Furthermore, he wants her to come up with the idea of scratching him on her own, spontaneously, without him mentioning it. Since the noodle casserole bakes in the oven for sixty minutes, both parties could conceivably prevail if together they displaced time ever so subtly: mutual appetites, mutual satisfaction. However, the necessary understanding for this would be so difficult that it is never really attempted.

Bargaining is difficult because it is diametrically opposed to a visit to the supermarket. The exchange in relationships certainly has a mimetic collective language, its unique methods of abstraction, and a resulting complex value system: the stock market of emotions. The **precision** of this exchange, however, is so enormous that it consists of almost pure fluctuations; similar to a Celtic community, it creates a new world order each and every moment.[24] Conversely, the fluctuations throw down the gauntlet for a course of action toward customs and rigid norms in order to constitute a sense of orientation. Such a course of action behaves as if it were somewhere between the law and its observance, between a fixed price and ballpark estimate. On the one hand, shopping is about money. On the other hand, it is about pickles, cream of wheat, sugar, or sausages.

Normally, both sides of the equation appear comparable and are rendered even more precise (that is, delineated) by a plethora of third variables.

In the labor of relationships, this comparison transpires on varying levels. Right now, my senses check whether the way the other treats me suits me; immediately thereafter, very different organs test my powers of imagination and how my needs — even those needs without access to the concrete moment — respond accordingly. Right now, my desire makes an assessment; immediately thereafter, the social sense of having something tests whether my desire is also realistic. Right now, concrete needs are establishing themselves in every single person. No sooner does this happen than this moment is disturbed by new needs extending well beyond it. At its core, it is a matter of punitive economic laws within the sphere of trade carrying out robust reductions onto relations *in rem*; they also provide a security against endless fluctuations. Precisely these punitive laws and their reductive effects are initially annulled in the relations of relationships; needs fail to express themselves immediately. As a result, uncontrolled, free-floating pressures enter into the labor of relationships. In the relations of relationships, concrete moments (exchange) can also be established, but only by exclusion (reduction). The lack of any such reduction produces a picture of the undecided customer, someone who encounters a generally undecided salesperson; because both the purchase and the sale are so important to both of them, they fail to come to a conclusion. Were the external reduction of pressures for this transaction doubly annulled — as a labor of relationships and additionally as child labor — it would be called "playing." Such a scenario would correspond to the protracted and highly pleasurable transactions in a children's grocery store playset. Adults can imitate this playing as long as they interact with one another amorously or stubbornly in a context lacking reality. As soon as their investments in reality clash to a greater extent with one another, they can no longer maintain the principle of the children's playset. Because their needs permanently fluctuate and therefore make decision making difficult, they often wish that outside chance, so common in games of dice, would bring everything to a head.

The need for differentiating and measuring is significantly keener in relationships than it is in the world of commodities. The things that people produce and purchase enter into to temporal relations with one another only to a limited degree. For example, sugar and heat must act together for a certain period of time before marmalade comes into being. Apart from this interaction, the ingredients possess no temperament of their own. Conversely, the subjective laborers of relationships possess through and through a specific and unmistakable response time. Every one of a laborer's nerves as well as each one of his characteristics has its own speed within its own internal relation (one nerve thinks slowly, feels quickly, reacts quickly, remembers slowly, and so on). The same thing goes for the laborer's counterpart in a relationship. In order for reciprocal touching to transpire in a relationship, these different speeds have to be approached with the utmost subtlety and separated out onto all levels existing within a single individual. Otherwise, only disruption and its attendant forms of compensation, riddled with detours, arise. All this repeats itself with respect to any number of characteristics, such as "close" and "far," "one's own" and "the sociated," "power grip" and "precision grip," and so on. Before an exchange can transpire, subtle maneuvering is required. The motor for this is housed in each person involved in a relationship, as well as in the habits they bring into it; these are three subjective locations and sources of production entwined, but nevertheless uncoordinated with one another. It could be said that a real sensitivity [*Feingefühl*] is at work in this maneuvering.

Relationships spontaneously come up against their precursors, power relations, and at such moments search for solutions within their own relations. Only these proportions are precise enough. Perhaps at the next moment, other solutions need to be devised. If this works, this is a case of subtle maneuvering that we actually know. But it is obvious that subtle maneuvering requires permanent attention and therefore is susceptible at any moment. Without the institutionalization of proportions, weights, and rules, maneuvering is reminiscent of an archaic collective assembled out of its relations of relationships. At the same time, however, these operations needing regulation are wholly modern. When failure befalls maneuvering, these operations cannot flow into the open-ended carnage of the Celts, which, it should be added, did not destroy civilization after all. Today, however, they would lead the way out of civilization entirely.[25]

The Commodity Character in the Labor of Relationships

In order to simplify matters, we omit the effects of the external character of commodities on the labor of relationships. The permanent handling of commodities (furniture, the car, the apartment, clothes, knowledge commodities, erotic commodities) is self-evident.

People who participate in a relationship are themselves commodities. The particular beauty of a woman, the professional aptitude of a man, a child's athletic, wise, polite, or orderly upbringing, these are the commodity characteristics of people. It is arguable, however, that relationships begin where these commodity characteristics end or reverse themselves. The mere addition of commodity characteristics can appear like a family, but such an arrangement is a non-relationship if it consists only of this addition: a dream woman has a dream husband along with wonderfully smart children. The pair can live alongside one another for many years without ever constituting a relationship. The arrangement would confer pure status, like furniture.

A relationship requires an object at which it can slave away. This object must also find itself at precisely that location where a relationship begins. It must be something available that every third person would consider a disadvantage. Love will bind itself to it, and it will transform into something lovable in spite of its alleged disadvantage. This transformation of worldly commodity values or nonvalue into a socially supported relationship is the exchange value in the labor of relationships. In the exchange value of commodities, there is nothing of its use value to be found. In the exchange value of the labor of relationships, a pure use value is reconstituted for me that excludes as much neutrality as possible. This is not the use value of a person. Love transforms it. However, it should not be assumed that hate can achieve the same result. Hate transforms all objective commodity values—values that every person dons outside in the economy of values and that third parties easily recognize—into adversarial values [Feindwert].

We know that the production of pure use value dominated primordial societies that preceded the classical social formations associated with feudalism in Germany. In these societies, there was only one commodity: irreplaceable women responsible for the reproduction of generations. This inimitable commodity and its dangerous exchange created unique conditions. It was not the exchange itself,

Jacques-Louis David, *The Rape of the Sabine Women* (detail), 1796–99. [Musée de Louvre, Paris © RMN-Grand Palais / Art Resource, NY]

but the integral relationality of early households associated with it, that afforded all relationships their sense of time and place and that produced a utopian longing out of the most modern of needs.

If the attractive and repulsive capacities in the labor of relationships, historically strewn about in different directions, set forth toward their absolute goals, it is essentially a matter of redeeming [*Einlösungen*] this longing according to that original relationality This absolute goal, to which all residual labor of relationships contribute merely the groundwork, is aimed at an impossible commodity unattainable in our society. This commodity is striven for using

367

sensuous means that ultimately resist deception. The fact that such a goal does not put up objective resistance renders the search for good fortune aimed at this goal impervious to outside influence and uncontainable. This quest also does not center on the concrete other, but rather on the redeeming [*Einlösung*] of history that is thought to reside in this other. Because of this other, this quest therefore succeeds only in history; it cannot do so within the small groups that include the other.

> *Liebestod* is an enigma. Richard Wagner took up the theme with the explicit observation that he did not know what love is. He was compelled to compose his famous opera precisely because of this incomprehensibility. Compared to the *Liebestod* of Wagner's Tristan and Isolde, myths reveal something quite different. Neither King Mark nor Tristan can resist the powerful Irish sorceress. They share the task of gaining Isolde's hand between them, and Mark sends Tristan to broker marriage. Afterward, Mark becomes the sorceress's husband, but is entirely unaware that the magic potion guaranteed Isolde's hand going to Tristan. The men suffered *Liebestod* long ago. If the back-and-forth between the men is to be put to an end, Isolde must suffer from it, as well.

A Special Feature of Exchange Value in the Labor of Relationships

Exchange value produces images. If I look beyond a pair of boots that I produced myself and envisage what I can exchange for them, I would see: a quantum of grain, coal, pickles, tools, or friendly eyes. These images have an exchange value that tends, as a commodity value, to mirror in somewhat crazy ways both my labor and its social relationality. Such a world of images also contains exchange values that assemble themselves out of the two basic contradictory commodity values in the labor of relationships. This production of images, however, has distinctive features.

In the production of commodities, it holds true that from nothing comes nothing. Material things or services that bring about a noticeable change in condition (for example, the hairdresser really did cut someone's hair) must be present for an exchange image to attach itself. Exchange values are copies of objective human forms of labor or social wealth. They can produce many images, but always harken back to **one thing**, the commodity as element. Via this element, these exchange values are bound to two laws of crisis that act as actual forms of resistance against the infinite abundance of images: (1) In a crisis, all exchange values are at last tested for their utility. (2) In crises, all exponential forms of labor are reduced to simple work.

Both laws also hold true in the labor of relationships; when they are seen objectively, however, these laws expire.

Private Property of Relationships Compared with the Historical Principle of Private Property

The **principle of private property** developed consistently only in West European societies (and exported into the United States and other societies dependent upon world powers) is the core of the capitalist system. At the same time, historically, it has always been a means to significantly different interests. In this respect, Protestantism, for example, is an attempt at producing private property at the level of one's own belief or conscience. There are two different roots contained in private property: one is called "accumulating property at the expense of others"; while rendering others unsocial, this exclusionary form deems **oneself** social. On the other hand, the principle of private property refers to an attempt within non-economic realms to conserve and protect the elements of original property. The latter form of private property does not come from the possession of land, which would exclude others, but is based in community. The less others are excluded and the more others are included, the more likely property is at stake.

Each side is clearly different for the laborer who is the private owner of the commodity of labor power. A principle of fundamental decentralization and autonomy resides in both roots of private property and is irrefutable for rich social or individual relationships. Setting boundaries between self and other and maneuvering between close and far contain a necessary reserve for every instance of self-regulation. This is the historical perfidy of private property; because of its double character, its destructive labor cannot be made unilaterally plausible. By attacking private property, I simultaneously attack the economy of original property with which I determine my own sense of closeness and distance; I cannot abolish private property, because in doing so, I would always abolish two things at once: what I need and what abuses me.

> The core contradiction at work in the external economy is that there is such a thing as private property. In the internal societies of relationships, the contradiction is that there is no such thing as private property.

It is striking that a secured zone of autonomous self-development is exceedingly difficult to realize under the exchange conditions of the labor of private relationships. Indiscretion, not being left alone, whining, and constant symbiotic disruptions are taken to be signs of a well-functioning relationship. The impression of thoughtfulness only intensifies the immanent turmoil, because this civilized high ground is based on individual efforts and in the event that exerting oneself falls away, cessation sets in. Thoughtfulness and the attention to reserves within a relationship encompass the threat that they are artificial and actually contradict the principle of relations. This threat is the exception.

An economic relation underlying trade or wage labor is expressed in segmented fashion: "Everything that was not explicitly agreed upon is excluded from the agreement." Promises in the private relations of relationships are quite different. "Everything that is not explicitly excluded is agreed upon." This leads to a melting of boundaries between mine and yours, so that the security of primitive property, which is assumed to be solid ground from which one can depart and approach someone else, is not subject to recognition. However, the collective can emerge only upon a historical foundation. Along with its affiliated factions and constituent parts, within its internal relations, the ego must not only go to battle for complicated class struggles, but must also obtain comparisons with itself as well, and for this reason, it requires a space all of its own, its own private property. The confrontation with the traditional meshwork of norms, which always counts on a remainder of such autonomous individual replies, also demands this separate reserve. All visions of community in the West European tradition are grounded in an autonomy (that is, on decentralized property relations) constituted with a little injection of spontaneity and self-regulation. There exists no culturally prepared vision of how such orientation and agreement are supposed to come into being. The catastrophic lack of boundary limits, which especially distinguishes the private labor of relationships in Germany, has resulted in the fact that the respective territory and community in relationships must be secured in ad hoc, piecemeal fashion, and this must be done so anew for every single occasion. In the words of a too far-reaching promise: everything that is included that is not explicitly excluded has to be acquired.

Phylogenic Property

The phylogenetic history of primates, to which we humans belong as a chapter of social development, can be traced back to a relatively small order of animals that some paleontologists call tree shrews.[26]

Evolutionary pressure and accumulated variety throughout the course of evolution create a solid body of characteristics. These characteristics are a particular form of phylogenic property that precedes all subsequent forms of property. These principles of property are supposed to have force with respect to this particular form of original property, but they are also embedded in all subsequent forms of property. The subjective aspect within this *particular* original property, which underlies the **revolutionary** development of all humans, acts differently in its relation to nature as soon as social relations appear. The seat of this subjectivity is, on the one hand, the objective objectivity responsible for effecting separation and, on the other, the sum of internal and intimate safety circuits [*Sicherheitskreis*] in which the subjective responses to separation can be found.

This particular property of subjectivity has the raw form of nest building and corresponds to the portable nest of the mother's womb. In postnatal incubation periods, this property **builds nests patterned after the womb** that **respond to periods of disruption** with their own sense of fail-safe time. If one of these conditions goes missing—the objectivity or the safety circuit—**the raw form of original property cannot emerge.** The simplest definition of this specific private property is the category of relationality. Only in times of intimacy and protection can different temporalities and relationships be placed side by side. As a result, the raw form emerges for what is later called "social wealth." Within this wealth, assets are arranged next to one another. The strongest asset does not exclude the weaker ones. Likewise, times of separation and fortunate returns are arranged next to one another. Because of this relationality, a recurrence [*Wiederkehr*]—and, to be sure, not a mere repetition compulsion—transpires. Under alienated conditions, the obverse of this relationality would be a rupture between incompatible times.

[Tree shrew]

Tree shrew. It is not known what they looked like. Apparently, mammals developed from dino-
saurlike reptiles into four different phyla independently of one another. Therapsida evolved in
the Middle Permian (approximately two hundred and twenty million years ago) and lasted till
the Middle Jurassic (approximately one hundred and fifty million years ago). In this period,
Therapsida developed into mammals called the Trituberculata. It appears that from them
arose all later mammals. They are tiny animals that exist only as skeletal fragments. Their size
and dental characteristics are reminiscent of a mouse: small, agile, carnivorous, and more
intelligent than reptiles. The separation of the nasal passage from the jaw facilitated synchronous chewing and breathing as well as the intake of nutrients.

According to one hypothesis, our ancestors were so-called ovivores, that is, egg eaters. Amphibians emerged roughly three hundred million years ago and frequently laid their eggs on land because of the absence of predators. The firm shell helped prevent drying out. Over time, the eggs were given more and more nutrients for the development of stronger offspring. Since reptiles are inept protectors of their young, this amniotic egg must have been the very best prey for predators on land.[27] According to this argument, our ancestors should have accelerated or, at the very least, maintained the speed of generative reproduction by sucking out the reptilian eggs with predatory gusto and pleasure. Like the egg predators, archosaurs were subject to mutual selection. Small egg predators well suited for taking flight were subjected to the pressure of selection due to these reptiles' initial attempts at protecting their nests: the predators had to be more intelligent, have stronger teeth, and become arboreal (the tree as safe haven). In the shadowy lair of the reptile's nest, incubating the eggs had to replace the warmth of the sun. Giving birth to live offspring, as was the case for the predators, rendered such incubation superfluous. Feeding offspring was not very difficult for the small mother, either; gnawing open (a specialization of the head), sucking out, and eating dinosaur eggs harkened back to her own life as a suckling. Natural selection affected these animals particularly haphazardly. They had no opportunity to calibrate the slow maturation of their bodies with their sphere of activity. In fact, mutations yielded radical experiments and flukes. The remaining development followed two rules of evolution: (1) Fast generative reproduction that presupposes growth retardation allows for more mutant variations than a slow one. (2) The duration of pregnancy and postnatal development in incubation periods contains the conditions of cerebralization and the beginning of learning processes. A mouse builds a nest, but a squirrel builds an even better one. A beaver makes its nest into a castle. In this castle, there are aunts who care for the newborns and who temporarily replace the mother.

What Is Enlightenment in the Relations of Relationships?

Relationships are stuck in any number of positions [Haltungen]. Depending on whether they attract or repel, they possess a degree of material concretion that overruns enlightened discourse. They include "behavior in the stage of its mental rehearsal" [Probehandeln im Geiste]. As soon as they thicken into the labor of relationships,

Dinosaur.

Mus etrusculus: The Etruscan harvest mouse is a warm-blooded animal no bigger than a centi-
meter. No sooner is it born than it must eat so as to maintain in its small body a temperature of
approximately 98.6˚ Fahrenheit. It eats constantly until the day it dies, incapable of pausing
even for a moment for fear it will cool down. Its life is pure imprisonment. It is born bald and
does not even have the time to grow a coat of fur that would otherwise better protect it from the
cold. [Reg Mckenna/Creative Commons]

they are no longer a form of such "behavior in rehearsal." They do not have the power for reflection when in crisis.

The primacy of imprisonment (as in the case of the Etruscan mouse) knows two traditional decision-making processes: (1) *post-festum* discussions where everything has been decided already and (2) forms of prior arrangements. They are successful when a recollected behavior is found.

Arrangements can be made for portions of the labor of relationships that elude personal arbitrariness and the principle of immediacy. The guarantor of an arrangement is not the other laborer in a relationship. Rather, a Greek chorus votes collectively and uniformly for specific arrangements, such as, for example, not letting children go to the dogs.

If we take enlightenment, which resides in a stance (and not in talking or in essays) as our point of departure, a concept can home in on the following points: (1) I myself am being enlightened. I am sitting there with my enlightened experience. (2) Enlightenment enters into relationships and changes them. (3) Neither I nor the relationship act enlightened; from its crises, the labor of enlightenment enters into the collective relation of other relationships, that is, the social experience of the labor of relationships.

What we call the Enlightenment of the eighteenth century acts conservatively and affirmatively toward the labor of relationships. The rationalists and the architects of the Enlightenment insist on the preservation of ethics and provide a basis for subjective responsibilities that always lead to the fortification of traditional attachments. Whereas religions are demythologized, the relations of relationships should be mythical.

A.

The following is the most common position toward enlightenment, the one for which there exists the greatest means of production for a relationship: I enlighten myself. I *am being* enlightened. This process initially does not affect a relationship, but a single person (however, not all of that person's active forces are affected in the same way). While a relationship is maintained, its forces take flight. Reserves build up, and illusions disappear. On the other hand, positions and fabrications can arise out of this labor of enlightenment that enter into and strengthen a relationship. Clear-sightedness unleashes forces that balance out the deficits of the other. Insight turns into cooperation. Even hope for a quid pro quo can be enlightened. True misery reveals itself, and a reserve of forces emerges, or the forces file out. Such **simple enlightenment** always contains a bit of self-alienation. If I give up or abandon something in a relationship, something of my own person remains in the relationship, something from which I divorce myself either entirely or partially.

B.

A specific *form* is required in order to ensure that the labor of enlightenment does not apply just to me, which would constitute an impoverishment, but to my relationship. This also insures this labor against demythologizing the relationship and displacing the myth once again onto the free market. We have understood that this form had to consist of assuming a stance, not just talking, especially if the form is to express itself in the particular idiom of a relationship. This political form, as we know it in the West German student movement, is the qualified violation of rules. It does not abandon a relationship, but works with its actual forces and breaks through the law of inertia in play in relationships. Such violations of rules follow *the indirect method* of waging war (surprise). They have all the attributes of a blitzkrieg: dislodging the opponent's motives. They must be thrown into confusion and be allowed to collapse into a modified figure.

The labor of enlightenment mediated by a qualified violation of rules does not exactly try to destroy the will of the other. Rather, it tries to produce the autonomy of the other. It thus drives what classical thinkers call the sublation of contradictions. The word "sublation" applies here in the most immediate of ways. The work area for this labor must be identified; it always is there in the particular violent relations of relationships where the active forces sublate one another. Violence has a moment of peacefulness. The immanently productive moments of a relationship are shifted away to a point where they can be sublated and constructed anew. The forces arise out of the primary combat zones, from tumult. The places and times that allow for their organization lie at the abaric point. This gravationless moment is the point opposing both the place of origin and the instinctive work areas for the labor of relationships.

376

The abaric point between the Earth and the Moon. [Alexander Kluge Archive]

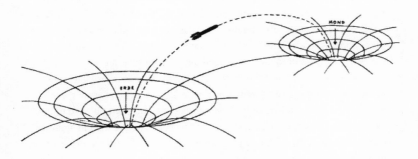

The flight path from the Earth to the Moon—an attempt at rendering the relations between gravitational fields. [Alexander Kluge Archive]

In the years during World War II, women not only ran families, but also assumed the occupations of the absent men. Another kind of self-consciousness emerged out of these circumstances. After the capitulation, men returned home without any of the hallmarks of victory. Their collective instinctual patriotism diminished because of the nation's loss. Women needed to rest just as much as the men needed to rest. Under all this weight, something along the lines of an ahistorical (and at the same time "abaric") point emerged. It may have lasted a couple of days or a quarter of a year. Without any collective attention or identification mark, this point was pretermitted, and the old relations sank back in to place. However, something must have happened to the total labor of families in this short period of time during the years after the West German currency reform that brought men and women to toil together in the name of reconstruction. Entirely alienated, German reconstruction evinced a coordination of characteristics far different from those in the 1930s or the 1960s.

In principle, this is no different for individual relations, except for the fact that the moments are extremely microstructural in nature. After a long absence, someone returns home. Let us assume this person is nostalgic. This probably leads quickly to a moment of intimacy. If the affair runs its course, it is difficult to change the outcome of the relationship before the person departs. The short time frame is not even favorable for talking. Prior to the quickly approaching departure date, there is a moment when the other answers the expectations of the love-stricken returnee with a word of certainty: something will come of this. For a few seconds, the wish to embrace one another and the certainty that something will come of this form a constellation of forces that point toward a state of balance. These seconds go by unheeded. They would have to be rendered recognizable and marked as a point of production—assuming all difficulties were stacked up there and the point itself could endure the sheer weight—where it would be possible that someone would leave a different person than they came.

C.

A series of relationships is so mired in its reciprocal conflicts that even a qualified praxis of violating rules at well-marked abaric points offsets too little of the dominion of the product over the producers. Neither simple enlightenment (of the individual) nor enlightenment in the relations of relationships can arise. This is insolvency, an emergency. It is not consoling, but certainly true how the mass labor of enlightenment that spontaneously goes into collective forms of relationships is drawn from such "impossible relations of production." The (frequently invisible) result is called "insight," "consideration." The terms sound as if they call for dissolution.

A couple marries out of love. They soon bear children. After three years, the husband's infatuations no longer suffice. He retreats into his work and lets his wife take care of him. Like an abbot from the Middle Ages, he presides over family matters, looks with pleasure at the meals served at his dining room table, dwells comfortably in his spacious home. For ten years, his wife has lived a celibate life. While the abbot cavorts like a part-time laborer in one escapade after the next, his constant oversight prevents her from having male friends. She is constantly controlled. He is not. It is difficult to endure the situation. Sometimes she thinks it would be an efficacious and qualified violation of rules if she were to bring a man home. Perhaps her original value would again become clearer for the abbot. She doesn't fear any retaliation on his part. Because of the reflections it would have in the eyes of her children, she decides not to put her plan into action. She also considers dissolving the whole thing, but thinks she would hurt her children, who because of their egocentrism themselves insist that if mother and father live together, nothing will change their status. In the end, she resolves to discuss her questions with her many girlfriends, who have similar problems. In this period, they develop an abundance of ideas. Together with her female advisees, the woman could trigger a basic transformation in every marriage other than her own. Were a group to go forth and collect these copious experiences, they would ascertain in astonishment that for quite some time there has existed a labor of enlightenment for the collective relations of relationships.

Autonomy = Emergence

Enlightenment is man's emergence from his self-incurred immaturity. *Immaturity* is the inability to use one's own understanding without the guidance of another. This immaturity is *self-incurred* if its cause is not lack of understanding, but lack of resolution and courage to use it without the guidance of another. The motto of enlightenment is therefore: *Sapere aude!* Have courage to use your *own* understanding.

Laziness and cowardice are the reasons why such a large proportion of men, even when nature has long emancipated them from alien guidance (*naturaliter maiorennes*), nevertheless gladly remain immature for life. For the same reasons, it is all too easy for others to set themselves up as their guardians. It is so convenient to be immature! ...

For enlightenment of this kind, all that is needed is freedom. And the freedom in question is the most innocuous form of all—freedom to make public use of one's reason in all matters....

If it is now asked whether we at present live in an **enlightened** age, then answer is: No, but we do live in an age of **enlightenment**....

But only a ruler who is himself enlightened and has no fear of phantoms, yet who likewise had at hand a well-disciplined and numerous army to guarantee public security, may say what no republic would dare to say: *Argue as much as you like and about whatever you like, but obey!* This reveals to us a strange and unexpected pattern in human affairs (such as we shall always find if we consider them in the widest sense, in which nearly everything is paradoxical.) A high degree of civil freedom seems advantageous to a people's *intellectual* freedom, yet it also sets up insuperable barriers to it. Conversely, a lesser degree of civil freedom gives intellectual freedom enough room to expend to its fullest extent. Thus once the germ on which nature has lavished most care—man's inclination and vocation to *think freely*—has developed within this hard shell, it gradually reacts upon the mentality of the people, who thus gradually become increasingly able to *act freely*. Eventually, it even influences the principles of governments, which find that they can themselves profit by treating man, who is *more than a machine*, in a manner appropriate to his dignity.

—Königberg in Prussia, 30th September 1784
I. Kant[28]

"Man's emergence from his ... immaturity": Birth, separation of the child from its original inward orientation, the separation from its primary objects that already begins with the first instances of attention it gives and receives, the separation from its original egocentrism, and all its subsequent relationships built upon these factors are variations on **leaving** [*des Weggehens*] or **emerging** [*des Ausgangs*].[29] In this respect, a natural process of **enlightenment for one's own sake** is vested in the core of any labor of relationships.

This process repeats itself in the historical separation from the land and the original collective, the moment when the worker becomes a free agent and adaptable to wage labor. It is clear that the epithet *self-inflicted* represents a useless perspective for these processes. It must also be recognized that to start with, every one of these separations corresponds to an "increase of our desert."[30] In this respect, it is a simple enlightenment that brings forth only the courage to use one's own understanding without the understanding of another. This is something initially empty for living matter. No one would marvel at the fact that the public use of reason, which "anyone may make of it *as a man of learning* addressing the entire *reading public,*" is less attractive for an entire collective than the light dome at the Nuremberg Rally constructed out of antiaircraft search lights.[31]

One thing that has been overlooked is the "the germ, on which nature has lavished most care," the "inclination...to think freely [that] developed within this hard shell": conversely, the **tenderness of reason** has an incisive power at its command because in the long run, no one would allow it to excuse or forbid itself.[32] At the same time, something else is overlooked: the fact that the *general* use of the principles of rationality tends to separate the tools from the material [*Stoff*]—rational human tools from the human motives. In complete contrast to this intended general use, rationality aligns itself with the tools and thus draws itself nearer to instrumental reason.[33]

But the truth of the matter is this: the tools know not the ways out, nor do they promote man's emergence. Only the material knows the paths toward help and emergence. Tools learn from the material— precisely this is what renders them useful—by arranging themselves and changing themselves from the deformation and damage they incur. This is their productive purchase on ways out, insofar as they are themselves material. In the labor of relationships, this material (motives) always initially has an audible tone of antirationality about itself, a natural vehemence and an expansion of motives. In praxis, the minuscule pauses and incubation points that also exist in this material, from which every natural emergence assembles itself, are therefore overrun. Minuscule pauses do take place and are just as much a real foundation as pure activities, but they are not noticed and therefore cannot develop tools capable of changing the material. They can neither control nor be controlled. A nameless higher-up does not so much control an immature youth as initiate processes of appropriation of uncontrolled energy.

Dealing with reason (the tender germ)[34] presupposes a *reasoned* differentiation of those moments in which reason is capable of working from other moments in which it only flattens or disturbs. For this to happen, forms of reason other than just the one found in the "courage to use your own understanding" must be taken into consideration.[35] In 1944, someone still active in the reason-adverse Second World War has a pass [*Ausgang*] one evening and goes, for example, dancing. In this instance, he cannot limit himself to the tools of reason.[36]

If these forms of reason are not about the act of determination, the meeting face to face of self and something other (objectification), but about movement, touch, rhythm (the dissolution of obstinacy),[37] then motive and reason, naturalness and deliberateness, material and human tools will conjoin differently than they would with the labor of reason. It appears that while the tender germ is a condensed form of longing that to some extent has the characteristics of a tool, simple longing possesses the characteristics of material. However, both material and tools are not exclusively composed of longing, but of praxis previously acquired from life experience and phylogeny: the relation to the body, going together, grace [*Anmut*] as derived from the German for courage, *Mut*.

It is not a matter of resolution or courage to use one's own characteristics without the guidance of another. The primary objects in me guide me. They are active in all passionate motives. In purely objective terms, without the guidance of another, I would be: ego and emptiness. Again, the point is not entirely about eliminating guidance altogether and celebrating emergence from all the networks of relationships. The words "laziness" and "cowardice" in Kant's text need to be inverted. The inversion of laziness is industry (industriousness). The inversion of cowardice is solidarity.[38]

In political praxis, people who gravitate toward enlightenment are like doves. Reactionary people are like hawks and act as if the reason-adverse position were the "harder standpoint." In fact, the material relation is the opposite. The reasoned inversion is the hard material with the longer vision. For Kant, the paradox lies in the sentence, *"Argue as much as you like . . . but obey!"*[39] However, the tender germ really is insubordination itself, according to both its laws and its material. Conversely, the closed-off passions behave dutifully because of the repetition compulsion triggered by the closure. Because of this different relation to obedience, both human materials—material and tools, depending on the moment and the situation—can hardly deal with one another. The specific labor in processes of enlightenment must initially be to provoke the naturally existing moments of contact or create them using art. Only then can the inherent autonomy of both forms of matter do the preliminary work for the process. This is what is meant by the sentence that contains the central point of this book: **The tender force [*Kraft*] presumably possesses an independent entryway into the process of enlightenment.**[40]

[**Listening**] People who live at different objective and emotional speeds do not listen to one another. This is the case even when they converse word for word. They first have to adjust their respective motion reciprocally. This can be imagined quite literally like spaceships that try to attain a uniform speed through a series of braking and acceleration maneuvers. Only in doing so can they dock with one another. There are several moves necessary here: (1) accelerating; (2) braking; (3) control and adjustment of both processes (maneuvering). Natural forces such as initial velocity, inertia, gravity, and so on act upon these maneuvering tactics of spaceships. It is obvious that sometimes it is natural forces that are the tool or fuel and other times the artificial interventions of the engineer or pilot.

During a political campaign, a retiree approaches a candidate with a petition. After the close of the campaign, the candidate repairs to his girlfriend's place, her son recovering in a hospital following a major operation. These are quite clearly four incompatible temporal beings: the time of convalescence, the time of a relationship, the time of someone retired from the labor process, the time of political actuality. If they want to listen to one another, they all must brake or accelerate, that is, construct a situation using maneuvering tactics and do so using the natural means at their disposal. In turn, their abilities to do so stem from earlier roots, depending on who listened to them as a child or on what kind of listening they developed a sense of trust in themselves or others. This process of attention can be grasped as the basic unit of enlightenment. It is not about the emergence from immaturity in and of itself, but rather about the politician leaving his prevailing daily routine, assuming that he really wants to engage the retiree, and afterward returning to his routine anew.

These processes therefore consist of a plethora of entrances and exits [*Ausgänge*]. Maturity (that is, listening and speaking) is neither developed from mere acts of entering and leaving, nor is it produced by two participants at any single moment, but emerges collectively and as a side effect of multiple instances of paying and receiving attention that come about one after another. Third parties, for example, can look on to see how this functions and even take away an experience from it. Most people are far more likely to fail at such primal scenes of listening than they are to succeed at them. "Now this danger is not in fact so great, for they would certainly learn to walk eventually after a few falls."[41]

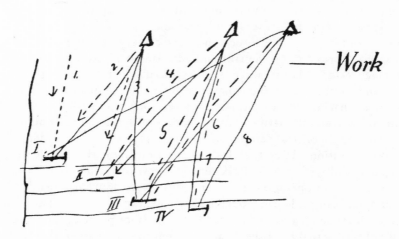

A sketch by Sigmund Freud from *The Complete Letters of Sigmund Freud to Wilhelm Fliess, 1887–1904*, trans. and ed. Jeffrey Moussaieff Masson (Cambridge, MA: Harvard University Press, 1985), p. 247. All dotted lines, arrows, and numbers are red in the original, as well as the word "work" [*Arbeit*]. Below, the sentence reads: "Work consists of a series of such stages at deeper and deeper levels."

COMMENTARY 14: FIVE STORIES ABOUT LOVE POLITICS

The Farmer in Me

An agrarian revolution has taken place over the last nine thousand years. We are still living in it. If someone moves from the country to the city, a farmer can nevertheless be found in his insides, a farmer who disguises himself. This farmer in us does not correspond to the image of a concrete person working in the fields at a certain point in time. Rather, the farmer represents a REAL ABSTRACTION. There are a billion facets and elemental spirits in a human's essential powers that learned from working the soil. That is the farmer in us, on whom we can rely in times of need.

The Origins of the Skeleton Obviously Lay in the Mouth

The biologist Steve Jones reported on inclusions found in rock on the coast near Edinburgh. The clues pertained to an until-then unknown animal, "like a jelly roll studded with razor blades."[42] The fragments of the find baffled researchers. In the expanses of an entirely different primordial ocean in China, a nearly complete set of remains from the same creature were found. It resembled an eel; only a few centimeters long, the body had two large eyes. In its back was a rigid bar. Researchers called these animals "conodonts." It became clear that they were predators. In a publication in the journal *Nature*, the animal was classified as an important ancestor of us vertebrates. THE ORIGINS OF THE SKELETON OBVIOUSLY LAY IN THE MOUTH. First the shearing off of strange flesh, then a hooklike skeleton composed of its own protein that remains more resilient than any outer shell (for example, chitin), and finally, the upright gait.

The Derivation of Reason (*Raison*) from the Word *L'arraisonnement*

Is there in the genealogy of reason (*raison*) more than just one line of ancestors? If in this respect two different lineages exist, is such a double genealogy also valid for love? Are there two distinct derivations of human fundamental powers? In his two *Geschlechter* essays, Jacques Derrida tests the typology of sexual difference and relates it to the typology of duality in human and animal evolution: two hands, two eyes, two halves of the brain, two ears — but five toes, and not two hearts.[43]

In general, Derrida doubts whether a conclusive TWO can guarantee happiness. What would a TWO be that is "not yet" or that was "no longer"? The "not yet" and the already "no longer," says Derrida, would contribute to the renewal of the structures of GROUND and REASON.

On this point, the German translator of Derrida, Hans-Dieter Gondek, laid down a footnote:

> The modern expression "ratio" or "rationality" could be derived from the word *L'ARRAISONNEMENT*. The Old French expression means: "'inspecting cargo' for its hygienic conditions" prior to a ship's departure. It also means: testing the "legality of freight (contraband)" and the correctness of its classification. It pertains to the noun derived from the verb "*arraisonner*: 'to turn to someone,' 'to try to convince someone,'" to commit oneself. [44]

On this point, A. Gartmann remarks: The brain does consist of two hemispheres, but is used as a unit in the production of *ratio*. However, if we follow a note by Friedrich Nietzsche, the future of humanity is threatened if two brains are not available: the one with experience and a motivation for science and the other adapted to the creaturely pleasures of humans, a brain capable of generating illusions and defending itself. Were both activities to take place in the same brain, the sciences (and the search for truth) would be at risk of being slain by the pursuit of pleasure. This is always stronger, than the powers of reason, says Nietzsche.

Pleasures of the Tongue, Empathy, and the Impartial Spectator

In the time of the Enlightenment—a time when slaves from Africa cultivated sugar on plantations in Haiti, when sugar was refined in complicated machines delivered from Europe, and when sugar was shipped to England as a luxury article—a large bowl containing sweet crystals was placed on a table in one of Edinburgh's salons. The philosopher David Hume skimmed his hand over the bowl of delights that afternoon and could not stop shoving pieces of sugar into his mouth. That did not correspond to the expectations on account of which he was invited. He contributed nothing to the conversation until the host, who also feared for the philosopher's insides (back then, sugar was thought to be poisonous in large quantities), had the container of sweets removed.

Separated now from the desired object, Hume began to formulate his thoughts regarding the refutation of a sentence by Thomas Hobbes: *Homo homini lupus*. Hume based his thoughts on a conversation on the topic he had discussed a short while ago with his friend Adam Smith. Humans are crueler and considerably more unsociable than wolves, said Hume. However, in general, humans differ from wolves by virtue of the fact that they arrive at no uniformity in their character. Rather, the prospects for humans are based on the fact that they are always qualified by two disparate characteristics that wrestle with one another. This is impossible for wolves. Humans (and no one interrupted Hume, who lectured in the same concentrated fashion with which he consumed the sugar) have at their disposal the VIEW OF THE IMPARTIAL SPECTATOR and—conversely—the compulsory impulse for EMPATHY IN THE OTHER. Those are the two "pincers of feeling" that are in the position to grasp the world. Said differently: every labor demands "contrasting oneself and something," as well as a "bringing into oneself" (it should have been called "bringing to oneself"). This is the apparatus of knowledge. It is also the processual foundation in every WORKSHOP. The coterie derived pleasure from the scholar's explanations, whom they had observed a short while ago disparagingly as the genie with a sweet tooth. They looked on at the "labor of his thought" in order to approach it with greater intimacy, while Hume distanced himself more and more from any given thing.

Among the guests of the salon were slave traders, physicians, and inventors. Nothing, according to Hume's view, followed from their everyday practice. However, it was obvious that the MOVEMENT OF INSIGHT was itself something they gladly witnessed and on which they wanted to nibble. They all felt part of the PRODUCTIVE CLASS. Landowners were missing from this coterie. A flood of doors opened, escape into rooms seemed to come into view the longer the evening went on. The long route traveled by the chunks of sugar, reaching back to Haiti, where sugar cane was laboriously harvested, was nothing that moved the guests. With respect to this fact, they were neither impartial spectators nor were they full of empathy.

Traction through the Belly

The sensitive nape of the three-month-old baby's neck was protected by a head restraint. Below the region of its body where later its buttocks would be lay the mother's hand. Traction through the belly was still in effect. The ground was the young woman's breast and shoulder. She appeared to be happy. "As if it were taking possession," the hand of the child lay on the mother's shoulder. Through their behavior, small children make peace in their surroundings. Solely on account of the inventiveness of their contacts.

Translated by Richard Langston

At a dance marathon, a short
break. [Library of Congress]

An Atlas of Concepts

(with Interspersed Stories)

[*Translator's note: The glossary that follows operates according to a peculiar organizational logic. In an effort to preserve the cartographic characteristics of the German original, neither the logic of an alphabetical glossary nor any concomitant reordering evinced by translating the German into English influenced the sequencing of the following concepts, stories, and images. The boundaries of this atlas of concepts are not limited to these final pages of* History and Obstinacy. *The arrows contained in many of the following entries point back to the book's seven chapters, the German original, and the authors' other two books of theory, not to mention Negt's many publications and Kluge's countless stories, films, and television broadcasts. "Read for the gaps," Negt and Kluge exhorted their audience on the final page of the German edition. Analogous to Kluge's own concepts of imaginary guides, the logic of the atlas is akin to that of gardening: "gardening, for example, [the] brain as garden, building canals, making connections between places, people, and situations like irrigating an area through a system of furrows, being able to plant a nursery, and so on in every figurative, but nonmetaphorical sense." See Oskar Negt and Alexander Kluge,* Geschichte und Eigensinn, vol. 2, Der unterschätzte Mensch: Gemeinsame Philosophie in zwei Bänden *(Frankfurt am Main: Zweitausendeins, 2001), p. 640 and p. 1283.*

All twenty-eight stories included in the glossary are taken from Alexander Kluge, Das fünfte Buch *(Frankfurt am Main: Suhrkamp, 2011), pp. 163, 171–72, 164, 165–66, 166–67, 170, 202, 201–202, 200, 201, 206, 210–11, 211–13, 190, 191, 195, 196, 196–97, 376–77, 377, 379, 380, 444–45, 429–30, 417, 252–53, 254, and 259–60, respectively.*]

Obstinacy (*Eigensinn*)

A fundamental current observable throughout human history. It develops out of a resistance to primitive expropriation. Its elements continually construct themselves anew and grow out of such heterogeneous roots that the type of experience and resistance identified as OBSTINACY cannot be conceptually isolated. It is possible only to observe how obstinacy necessarily develops in the social evolution of intelligent beings. → The story of the obstinate child; → Obstinacy as principle.

History (*Geschichte*)

In antiquity and the Middle Ages, the form RES GESTAE gave way to a form of storytelling of past events in which the genre of the novel and the realm of facts were not yet separated from one another. Since the end of the eighteenth century, the word "history" has become an emphatic search criterion: where the social determinates are located describes the situation, as well as the production processes that led to this specific present. Not a criterion of substance, but rather a search criterion.

Labor (*Arbeit*)

There exists a plurality of words for this concept in various languages: "labor," "work," "craft," "employment" (English), "travail," "ouvrier" (French), "lavoro" (Italian), "rabóta" (Russian). Originally, "labor" signified a purely corporeal activity, that is, hardship. In antiquity and in the European Middle Ages, labor was not the concern of lords. Within the Protestant tradition since Luther, "labor" has connoted an ethical and character value. In the century of engineers—the twentieth century—"labor" entered into the center of politics. In physics, the word equals force times distance as measured in ergs. In classical economics, it is the concept for the human activity capable of transforming materials and creating value. Labor is the least abstract category in any exchange society. → Living and dead labor; → Conscious labor not subject to the will; → Resistance, Protest labor; → VARIANTS AND POLAR OPPOSITES; → To grow, to develop oneself, to find, to hunt, to gather; → Pursuit of happiness, to be fortunate; → Handcraft work, *bricolage*; → "Work is taking place inside of me"; → Evolution's "mode of labor" that differs from the image of labor as a planned, goal-oriented physical transformation. The present book purposefully conceives the concept broadly; it is concerned with all subjective elements through which humans' essential powers objectify themselves, that is to say, the central and decentered connections in subjective-objective relations.

Out of Sight, Out of Mind

The Ferdinand Magellan, Roosevelt's presidential railcar, rode through the suburbs of Chicago as chimneys exhaled their little clouds into the waxing twilight. Low on the horizon, fires flickered. It is industry in 1943, busy at work producing deadly munitions. After the war, it will be difficult to redirect this concentrated violence back to the production of vacuum cleaners, baby carriages, shelves, and thermos bottles.

In conjunction with the celebrations in honor of his fiftieth birthday, which were supposed to have been humbly canceled on account of the budget crisis, President Obama (viewed from a centurial perspective, that is, A SHORT TIME LATER) is traveling by train along the same stretch of track. Nothing of the chimneys or the lights or the round-the-clock production can be seen through the train windows. More goods are produced around the world in 2011 than in 1943. But somewhere else other than here. Where are all the centers of production in the world? How do demographers map the MIGRATION OF LABOR? Or has it disappeared into some crevice?

"Where Has All the Work Gone? Long Time Passing"

An American composer wanted to remake the song "Where Have All the Flowers Gone?" for a big music label. He didn't want to a cover the original, but combing through the hit parades from the last fifty-five years, his agent happened upon the hit song, and presuming the mood of the song of loss was still very much alive among his target audience, the composer wanted to invoke the tune anew.

Where are all the soldiers sent to Afghanistan? Where are the steelworkers from Pittsburgh? Where are the factories of the Pullman Car Company of Chicago? Where are the beaches in the Caribbean not polluted by oil?

He had the melodies and sounds on his computer. The song sounded different, "harsher" than the sentimental song first penned in 1955. Either the facts did not square with the lament (because there are plenty of other beaches in America and because coffins from Afghanistan always brought up the rear of returning troops) or the target audience did not sense the disappearance of people and things as a loss. And no pop song can express in verse the fading value of the dollar and the loss of a country's solvency.

However, it seemed as though "work" had disappeared, too. The composer knew from his grandfather and father what work meant. The song evoked hardly any wistful feelings. When the hired singer sang of work, the song conveyed far more a sense of astonishment. If one were to claim work will return someday, one could sing about it more positively, the agent explained in response to the composer's doubts. A boom in jobs in the United States (nondescript, humdrum, unremarkable, yet decent-paying jobs) would be attractive for the target audience. One could represent work as an adventure vacation (just like when one eats a pork steak with fried onions and thinks back on the laborers who toiled away in the old days).

A Gray Monday
The space shuttle is supposed to embark on its last trip to the International Space Station around 2 p.m. today. One last time, all of NASA's units involved in the space flight have worked in concert in the enormous control room. Regardless of whether they normally competed with one another from their respective offices or not, here in the control room, they have assembled their input and output cooperatively. During countdown, there are roughly sixty-two hundred synchronous points that react to one another. There are experiences integrated into this sequence that date back to bitter catastrophes. This is the last time this ASSOCIATIVELY RICH WHOLE will work together. From now on, it can be repeated only for a museum or some other mnemonic exercise. As of tomorrow, a portion of their KNOWLEDGE will be unusable, because it can be wielded only within this large group. This part of the COLLECTIVE LABORER will vanish. If NASA wants to reach Mars one day, this knowledge will have to be rebuilt from scratch, along with all the countless new mistakes from which so much can be learned. Meanwhile, the morning haze has lifted. Around noon, the sky is supposed to clear.

The constellation of the hippopotamus. [Werner Forman / Universal Images Group / Getty Images]

An author. [Jon Bodsworth/Creative Commons]

Subjective-Objective (*subjective-objectiv*)

A philosophical (and political) notion according to which neither interiority (the ego as in Robinson Crusoe) nor exteriority (society) can ever construct a reality for itself. Rather, a SOCIAL RELATION — a reality for humans — develops through a SUBJECTIVE-OBJECTIVE connection. A happy love affair cannot consist of one person's idea and that of the other. Rather, it develops on a common platform between them (and this requires time). Accordingly, the object of labor constitutes itself subjectively-objectively through the will of the laborers, as well as through the will of the material. A community develops, therefore, BETWEEN HUMANS, not *in* them and not *next to* them.

Labor Capacity (*Arbeitsvermögen*)

Labor capacities refer to those potentials that assemble individual tasks and combinations thereof. These potentials have structures and goals (teleologies) that are different from individual skills or practical activities. A philologist of antiquity becomes England's prime minister. Someone compulsorily laid off from his learned profession makes a trailblazing discovery in the field computer sciences (on the basis of the potential tied to labor capacity).

Navigational Labor (*Steuerungsarbeit*)

Society places demands on the individual. The individual in turn must adjust his intrinsic ambitions, capabilities, forces, and counterforces (in the internal relations with himself), so that he can respond to the demands that come from the outside. At both intersections (with society and with the inner life of humans) there persists a remainder of obstinacy that is never entirely used up. The ruptures between the object world, the ego, and the subjective individual forces demand a specific orientation and navigation. This applies to each individual grip of the hand, to lifelong practices, as well as to the transfer of experience from one generation to the next, that is, the → Generational contract. The maneuvering typical of navigational labor is necessary for each of these spatial and temporal planes. This form of labor differs from that performed when using a hammer, tongs, sickle, or even a computer. Thus, with GOAL-ORIENTED ACTIVITIES and with the PRODUCTION OF ABILITIES TO PERFORM A GOAL-ORIENTED ACTIVITY, there are two different achievements of instrumental and rational action. Various disruptions or enhancements correspond to both. Obstinacy either lays the groundwork for these achievements or seeks to counteract them. All fundamental forms of recklessness vis-à-vis this central subjective-objective network lead to LOSSES OF CONTROL or, in extreme cases, to DERAILMENT.[1]

Concept (*Begriff*)

The German word *Begriff* possesses an emphatic meaning in German philosophy that does not correspond to the word's usage in everyday language. Although the English translation of *Begriff* as "concept" makes the Latin root of the word palatable, its meaning is narrower. A concept possesses different states of aggregation. It comprises the INDIVIDUAL [*die EINZELHEIT*], the UNIVERSAL [*das ALLGEMEINE* and the PARTICULAR [*das BESONDERE*].[2]

A telephone book and the mapping of a city from a planetary orbit reveal individual features. However, they remain incomplete, because the ring Mrs. F. sealed in a jewelry box—both a reminder of her deceased husband and a representation of a particularity charged with emotional significance—is hidden from view.

Because it cannot be counted, the universal is more difficult to convey. The principle of the city (along with its history) reveals transformations that must be rendered using words. Megacities developed in Mesopotamia around 3000 B.C. In Greece, cities developed twenty-five hundred years later (perhaps the ancient ships of Greece were like these cities, too); they were clearly structured and afforded Alexander the Great and his relatively small army with everything necessary to conqueror Asian cities. The principle of the city proved itself once again different in Rome. With their streets and tablets of law, the "urbs" stretched around the entire world. How strong was Caesar's astonishment at the "oppida" of the Gauls, who kept fortified storehouses for their cities. The cities of the Renaissance reveal a "principle of the city" not similar to the modern agglomerations of Lagos, Mexico City, and Shanghai. A portion of the term "universal" includes all of these differences and cannot be rendered solely by measurements. For Hegel, the tendency of the PARTICULAR ranks above that of the universal (insofar as there can be rankings within such a dynamic concept). Theoretically, the universal should be assembled out of the network of particulars. The deeply engrained characteristic (the character) and historical time are two of the most vital attributes of the concept out of which the strength for RELATIONALITY develops. A particularity belonging to the elements of the concept of the city is the fact that in the history of the world, serfdom and slavery were not abolished in the cities of northwestern Europe until later, and from these cities, the Western concept of freedom was spread over the Atlantic. And thus concepts such as, for example, freedom and the city permeated one another such that nothing of the relationality of the concept can be left out; in the development of financial derivatives (the Black-Scholes model), for example, the economy dealt with models comprising the antithesis of this concept of concepts.

Dealing with the time line of philosophical concepts and the category of OBJECTIVE POSSIBILITY are two among several distinguishing features of modern Critical Theory (Benjamin, Horkheimer, Adorno, Habermas). An exclusively topical consideration that excludes the production process remains abstract and unreal; it does damage to the concept. From this perspective (notably represented in Alfred Sohn-Rethel's *Soziologische Theorie der Erkenntnis*), the "real abstractions of reality" are one of the most important objects of investigation; in this case, reality itself is credited with a conceptual constitution, the observation of which is indispensable.

Self-Regulation (*Selbstregulierung*)
A universal principle found in the cosmos and in biology. The principle of self-regulation encounters an intensification in the structure of the human brain. As the neuroscientists Wolf Singer and Eric Kandel state, it is an "orchestra without a conductor."[3]

Self-regulation means that the laws of nature function from the bottom up. They know no superiors ("with increasing complexity, the elements obey less and less"). The impulse driving the processes is called: NEGENTOPY; in other words, disorder and disruption spur development forward. Equilibrium emerges in the result (homeostasis).

Niklas Luhmann, Francisco Varela, and Humberto R. Maturana replaced the concept of homeostasis with the concept of homeodynamics for social systems. In their systems theory, they carry over the processes of self-regulation to social relations. A "stasis," they say, would be the death of a self-regulating movement. All forms of self-regulation find themselves in a constant flux.

Self-regulating relationalities are characterized by movement from the bottom to the top. With political relationalities, especially political revolutions, precise observation is necessarily to see what presents itself BELOW and what is ABOVE.

Metaphoric Concept (*Oberbegriff*)

According to its nature, a concept has no hierarchy. A metaphoric concept is therefore a designation for an exaggeration. In other words, there are facts that are open to the subsequent formation of concepts and those that have to be opened. They are conceptually incomprehensible. It would be a mistake to characterize them using an "arbitrary generalization," the caricature of a concept. Accordingly, "the political economy of labor power" stands as an invitation to produce a concept. However, it is not the result of a concept. We call the assertion of having a concept prior to the development of categories of differentiation that work within it a case of misusage: a metaphoric concept.

The Peasant Rebellion of the Spirit in Mathematics

There are several number-worlds
as there are several Cultures.
—Oswald Spengler

In the crisis on Wednesday, August 10, 2011, the shares of banks from around the world crashed to a fraction of their original worth in just a few hours.[4] This pushed to the brink even those countries other than the United States and those of Europe that were not causally bound to the market crash. In one of the smaller markets in Africa, a technician caught up in the general despair ripped the fuses from the wall. The power supply died, and the computers came to a halt.

The impression prevailed that it was not just rumors and speculation that led to the turbulence, but that one witnessed a CONSPIRACY OF ALGO-RITHMS. These mathematical abbreviations, whose iterations manifest the freedom of the will and the obstinacy of the Internet, monopolize rates and destroy in real time millions of dollars, euros, and every other local currency. At some point in human history, inventors created the algorithms (decentrally, of course, because every inventor works independently), and then they began to unite with one another in the course of long nights until they could then strike as a COLLECTIVE HAND.

Mathematical formulas of this kind, the catastrophe theoretician Witzlaff once wrote, keep computers running and not only faithfully repeat the sequence of their programming, but also spawn progeny — in fact, considerably faster than the entire world population of humans can procreate. An invisible mathematical evolution is taking place. Mathematical formulas are not oriented toward elegance or originality (the standard units of value within the guild of mathematicians), but have developed their species based on their ability to dock with one another and propagate abundantly. Soon these algorithms will topple governments, even when — in this respect they are akin to the libido — they are indifferent toward the political. There will be two random clouds, both elaborate and crystalline in structure, that will then set the world in motion: one inside humans and the other — the machines — far beyond the reach of "earlier humans." Witzlaff supplemented his notes with the following: CALCULATIVE MATHEMATICS OF BABYLON AND NINEVEH. His notations were in shorthand. They pertained to calculating, delimiting, and summarizing. No interest in the laws of mathematics. Great understanding for the circulation of commodities and the calculation of levies for the king and the holy shrine. The OBSERVATIONAL MATHEMATICS of the Greeks followed. The primacy of geometry over arithmetic. Infinitesimal calculus of the seventeenth century. The opening of mathematical doors. The closing of said doors by models and exclusionary mechanisms. According to Witzlaff, this all corresponds to the dynamic of merchandise management. In the meantime, HYBRID MATHEMATICS. Algorithms behave like the handy calculators of Mesopotamia. However, they prevail over the violence of every leftover mathematical culture. They possess the "combat strength of a Platonic idea."

An Encounter with Good Fortune in a Globalized World
On the forty-sixth floor of a skyscraper in Manhattan, a "young buck" is responsible for a small portion of an investment bank's global portfolio. The firm is British-American. His computer systematically compares the price-earnings ratios of companies — in particular, the relation of their book value, their profits, and their share price — in search of deals. A former manufacturing plant in North Rhine-

Westphalia, now a cultural park, goes unnoticed by him because four different holding companies are lodged between his computer's data and the
actual industrial park itself. With just one keystroke, he can decide on the
entire existence of a company (just as long as his keystrokes are coupled
with those of his colleagues). When this juggler's stomach begins to growl,
he sallies out of his office and makes the twenty-minute trip involving two
different elevators down to the street. Amid this modern agora's many cor-
ners set aside for smokers, he finds food trucks and stands where the young
man can grab a meal from the Third World. Today, he picks out a dish from
Bangladesh. As the economic migrants from this faraway country nodded at
him as he paid, he could have responded. He could have perhaps taken them
in at his apartment. Or have begun a new life with them. Or even have had a
child with them. He could been a hero and have defended them against all
the unrealities of the world.

Elements of a global society convene here in a few square feet, but never
come in contact with one another in the computers on the forty-sixth floor.
A fledgling country such as Bangladesh (formerly a British colony and now
regularly plagued by flooding) has not the slightest chance with an investment bank as long as its interests pertain to its own citizens.

There's no time for Romeo and Juliet to come closer on this afternoon.
The young man requires another twenty minutes after lunch for the ascent
back to his control room. What he consumes in time in order to sate his appetite was much too excessive, especially when measured from the perspective
of how many procedures go unobserved and deeds go undone by his small
department. He often sits at his computer for hours, never touching his key-
board. And then all of a sudden, he has to set in motion billions of strands in
a minute, even when he is the author of just one transaction and the accom-
plice for all the others.

Lived Time for Cash
A worker in Frankfurt am Main spent his whole life in one and the same
factory. The factory went bankrupt. The employees were let go. The worker
visited a doctor. He had a severe stomach ache long before the factory shut
its doors. The doctor prescribed him medication. I devoted countless days of
my life, the worker said, and as a reward I get these pills. I'm not OK with this.

> You shouldn't hang your head, the doctor consoled him. I don't even have the energy to fuel my anger, the worker replied. This isn't a fair exchange: lived time for cash.

Derailment (*Entgleisung*)

A metaphorical expression that reflects an important experience, derailment appears at all stages of both a human's life span and history. The twentieth century derailed historically, for example, with the outbreak of the First World War (which from this point of view endured for thirty-one uninterrupted years, from the armistice of 1918 until 1945). Even life spans can derail. Observation reveals the extent to which the illusion of a "path," a plan, or a goal is contained in our life praxis without us ever realizing it. Without hope, which masks our perception of possibilities for derailments, daily life probably would be impossible. → Necessary false consciousness.

The Law of Included Third (*Der Satz vom eingeschlossenen Dritten*)

Rational logic as well as mathematics work according to the law of the *excluded* third or middle, a principle proposing that either A is equal to B or A is not equal to B. This method of "framing" parses real relations into excerpts accessible to logic. Such an exclusion creates the problem of the thirteenth fairy. In the fairy tale of "Sleeping Beauty," it is the thirteenth fairy who is excluded from the feast in the royal house (there were only twelve golden plates available for only twelve of the wisest women of the land, not thirteen). The one excluded exacts revenge by enchanting the castle and its inhabitants to sleep for one thousand years.[5]

Exclusionary Mechanisms (*Ausgrenzungsmechanismus*)

A synonym for all models that follow the law of the excluded middle. This exclusion is observable in the Black-Scholes model (used to eliminate improbabilities). Considered a milestone for financial markets, this model is used to devise which options and derivatives are suitable for the stock market. The excluded risk in this system of "framing" returned in the public sphere with the crash of the Lehman Brothers Holdings Inc., as was previously the case with the Chernobyl disaster. This a characteristic path toward unanticipated catastrophes under the conditions of the twenty-first century. For this reason, the systems theoretician Niklas Luhmann suggested—depending upon the degree of exclusion and the concomitant creation of artificial realities—that we heighten the degree of our attentiveness and focus on what is excluded. In context of our book, emphasis is placed on the exceptionally grave exclusion of human realities and processes of labor power through abstraction value. Exclusionary mechanisms take effect in → Navigational labor; → Prewar periods; → The endangerment of currencies; → Emergency management; → All political realms whatsoever; → The relation of history.

Forces, Associative and Hermetic
(*Assoziative und hermetische Kräfte*)
As a rule, strong motives (for example, "I feel responsible for the future and the development of my children," "my faith is inalienable") are less likely to ally themselves with the motives of other humans than are weak motives (for example, civil laws, stock-market rates, typographical norms, laws and rules in physics). With respect to the latter, today, we have associations of world citizens. With respect to the former, we will always have "Spanish partisans." The unification of forces interested in emancipation and enlightenment fails in part because of a lack of associations and institutions capable of bundling these strong forces. While the bundling of forces in a capitalist organization appears comparatively easier, this nevertheless produces *not a* collective capitalist, but rather a millipede of individual interests that behave as if in a swarm: they superficially appear to be robust and unified, but this they are not. The evolution of a collective worker as well as today's *Robo sapiens* develops at the opposite pole, the pole of labor. This COLLECTIVE LABORER (unified skill and knowledge in the world) appears in the practice of everyday life as something tattered: he is everywhere, but he is never seen (in part because the categories of observation necessary to see him are underdeveloped). The fortunate moments in history are when capitalist development and the development of labor power (including that of intelligence) have proceeded on similar paths for a short time, as they did at the end of the eighteenth century during the age of Enlightenment and industrialization. At that historical moment, Kant's concept of reason and the logic of the expanding

economy of commodities (that is, philosophical freedom and commercial freedom) mutually supported one another.

Stinginess and Abstract Hedonism (*Geiz und abstrakte Genußsucht*)
The combination of both of these characteristics belongs to the core of the capitalistic character; they simultaneously constitute both strong and weak forces. The emancipation of labor rests almost entirely on strong forces and the ability to expend them. These forces should not be abstract and must be free of momentary greed (that is, they may not be stingy).

The Attribute of Isolation

In early August 2011, one of the EXPERIENCED TAMERS OF CAPITAL sat in a tower in one of Frankfurt's skyscrapers. He had eyes only for his computer screen. At this elevation over the city, the blinding glare of the sun was muted by an adjustable screen over the windows. On the computer screens, very little was recognizable. It looked as if the room itself was wearing a pair of sunglasses.

On this day, the experts didn't know how to be of assistance. They saw the market crash graphically in the form of a vertical line signalizing the DAX's loss of four percentage points in four minutes. That corresponded to a value of a few billion dollars. The practitioner possessed no theory for the events as they transpired in the dimly lit room above the city. Does the lion tamer have a theory? He knows his animals. This creature's behavior, responsible for causing monstrous destruction on both sides of the Atlantic, was unknown to the experts. Was this a new species? Or was it the crisis of 1929 dressed up differently? The legendary man in his boardroom, the man who otherwise knows how to bridle markets, would gladly have reacted to the events in a practical fashion: crack a few nuts, peel an apple, pour a glass of sparking water. He wanted contact to any old activity if it meant he didn't have to stare at the screen and wait.

A Dissertation with Inadequate References

It turned out that Evelyn Smith had almost completely copied her dissertation on the SEVEN DWARVES OF ANTWERP from the manuscript of a New York

scholar, a child of Belgian immigrants, who penned a monograph about the
WOOL EXCHANGE in that city at the dawn of modernity. He brought together
all of the available relevant sources from across the Atlantic and collected
them in a bundle that landed after his death in the New York Public Library.

That legendary wool exchange (the beginning of finance capital) did not
deal in wool stored in the storehouses of the city. Instead, it dealt in wool still
on the sheep in Middle England, waiting to be shorn, wool from sheep not
yet born, or sheep that were still in transport from France to England. Evelyn
Smith emphasized this: the negative factor of lack creates a vacuum, a pull
or attraction more powerful than all the finished products, even those from a
silversmith from Florence. In those days, peasants' huts burned in England.
Where people lived up to that point, sheep were to graze. That belonged to
the "ghostly distant effects" of Antwerp's exchange.

When it came out that Evelyn Smith had plundered an older source from
New York without acknowledging her citations, her doctoral advisor, who
wished her only goodwill, tried to save her by bringing forth the following consideration: even the act of finding something belongs among the academic
virtues. Evelyn Smith pursued this virtue by rediscovering the work of this
scholar from New York. She justifiably did this against the backdrop of the
topic's timeliness. This plea failed to persuade the faculty. The degree was
not conferred.

Hermetic and Associative Forces
Ilse von Schaake lived with her Russian lover for a long time. Working from
Berlin for the Science Center in Akademgorodok, he wrote a study on the
POTENTIAL FOR WORLD-SCALE REVOLUTIONARY CHANGE. The secondary
question guiding his work was: Which forces in humans tend toward association and which ones hamper the unification of these forces? The comrade
gave up on the project when he turned his affections to a younger woman
(from a family in North Rhine–Westphalia with industrial assets). Years later,
Ilse could not completely banish the traitor from her heart. In the meantime,
out of spite and tenacity, characteristics residing in her family, she continued
with his project. The manuscript encompassed roughly two thousand pages.
East German publishers, with which she had contacts, showed no interest
in its publication.

She came to the following conclusion: there are strong forces in people (*my* family, *my* progeny, *my* property) that have a hermetic impact. They allow for no comprehensive associations. They are unsuitable for revolution. In contradistinction to these strong forces, there are weak and still weaker forces (the interest in physics, logic, and everything that I would willingly *sell* from myself and my loves). They rapidly coalesce with one another and bring about change over a long period of time. Even the evolution of modernity harks back to these weak forces, Ilse believed. In evolution, weak forces exclusively produce weak changes. The weak messianic force (Walter Benjamin)—that is to say, a connection back to roots in history—is the only fountain of hope. Ilse von Schaake wants to finish the work by 2018, the five hundredth anniversary of the Reformation in Wittenberg.

A Return to "Independent Cultivation"
Erika Künneke specialized in the thirty-third chapter of Marx's *Capital*. She worked on her dissertation in Baltimore. In that chapter, entitled "The Modern Theory of Colonisation," Marx writes of the European immigrants to the United States who arrived between 1842 and 1848 to escape their lords in Europe (nobles, capitalists). Having arrived in America, the majority of them dwelled in cities on the East Coast for only a short while, so the new lords had little chance to ensnare them.

> Please don't tell
> What train I'm on
> So they won't know
> Where I'm gone?

They traveled until St. Louis and then made the trek farther westward. They found their own land there. And so they became once again independent producers, just as their ancestors had been more than a thousand years earlier. The characteristic American self-consciousness emerged from this, Erika Künneke argued from her reading of Marx's short chapter. Not until the collateral damage of the depression of 1929 were these people reeled in, she claimed. John Steinbeck described their misfortune in *The Grapes of Wrath*. As a result, capitalism reached them (with all its consequences). Since then, Künneke writes, portions of the United States have sought their salvation in faith.

Production, Primary and Secondary
(*Primäre und sekundäre Produktion*)

A peasant in the European Middle Ages fed himself and his family autarkically. In other words: not only grain and livestock were produced on his manor, but also clothing and ideas: self-consciousness. These farms were self-sufficient. Neighboring convents, traveling surgeons, and itinerant blacksmiths also belonged to this structure, a structure entirely free of domination. This is primary production, a primary economy ("house production" in the truest sense). A craftsman in the city initially worked just as independently, both for himself and for city dwellers. Already a division of labor had emerged here. His ways of work belonged to the primary sphere. This influenced his self-consciousness, his affinity for "human and common sense," and his sense for "proportionality"; his character would be similar to that of Hans Sachs in Richard Wagner's opera *Die Meistersinger von Nürnberg*. A composer such as Mozart and a physicist such as Einstein did not obey the directives of bosses or bestsellers. The archbishop of Salzburg could not effectively dictate to Mozart how he should apportion his notes. This has remained the distinctive feature of primary production as exemplified by present-day inventions from Silicon Valley. If participants in these primary structures came under the hierarchy of church and nobility—craftsmen, artists, and scholars ["scribes"] worked primarily for these masters—the orientation and measure of value of their labor changed. They no longer had to produce quality products. Rather, they had to convince the uninformed master, their client, of the quality of their products or services. Before he embarked westward, Columbus had accomplished exactly this before the royal couple of Spain. The silversmith Benvenuto Cellini had to win the interest of the House of Medici, which was nothing more than a bank, before he could produce his masterpieces. This dependence carries over into a concomitant way of thinking.

In the secondary sphere of production, two things must always be produced: a consumer good and insight into the customer as to whether and, if so, how he can use such a thing. He must want to pay for it. In modern markets, the apparently encumbered mobility of the consumer's sovereignty corresponds to that of the lord of the Middle Ages. Capital worth billions in persuasion and conviction (advertising and media) is necessary in order to bring production to the public. If these means do not in the least suffice to kindle demand in a time of crisis (as was in the case following Black Friday in 1929), a monstrous coalition arises; fascism and economics attempt to overrun the laws of the market using the means of the so-called society of compulsory exchange [*Zwangstauschgesellschaft*] and to enforce the turnover of production through violence. This is possible only through war, is always at the expense of other peoples, and as a rule fails in the long run because it contradicts the law of exchange societies. The human's powers of judgment—they sway between the monstrous structures of dependence and determination by others that is induced in the second sphere and their groundedness in the primary sphere (which in the end gets lost neither in the intimate sphere of the family nor in lived time itself)—rules over the progress of history.

The labor society produces objects (merchandise, commodities), human characteristics (characters), and finally civilization itself. The precision of a concept, self-consciousness, and the potential of labor are different according to whether they have advanced in the form of primary or secondary spheres.

Spanish Partisans (*Spanische Partisanen*)

A primal scene of asymmetrical warfare can be observed in the following situation: in 1809, Napoleon arrived in Madrid with three hundred thousand of his troops. He declared the civil liberties of the French Revolution, liberating farmers from the yoke of nobility and the clergy. At night, the "freed" Spanish farmers massacred the emperor's German, Italian, French, and Polish soldiers. These farmers are *conservative* partisans, against whom Napoleon would never find an oppositional strategy during the whole of his reign. Spanish partisans, represented (literally) in Prussia by rebels such as Heinrich von Kleist, demonstrate a PARTICULAR FORM OF OBSTINACY.

Ways Out Must Be Found within People's Fields of Action, and Not in the Centers of Governance
(*Auswege muß man in den Handlungsfeldern der Menschen suchen und nicht in den Zentren der Regierung*)

In the progressive political discussions after the First World War, a maxim resounded throughout Europe: "There is always a way out." The experience contained in this maxim is not detectable in the present-day aporia among politicians and in the political stalemate regarding the financial crisis in Congress. This is different in the immediate spheres of action of humans (which certainly pertain to very different topics). The experiences of night nurses and doctors in hospitals in emergency rooms, the confrontation of zones of experience when a renowned sociologist speaks at a conference of European surveyors, experiences in the educational sector: stimulating dialogue arises where a difference in experiences exists, a potential for ways out. The fields of action of real working people (and not of mere political decision makers) must be investigated. In the trajectory of history, new differences and ways out come into focus. For example, surveying was the factor necessary for the privatization of Greek state ownership leading to economic stimulation. In the eighteenth century, a new discipline emerged that (as presupposed by Adam Smith) concretized a definitional element of property by surveying plots of land, which then became the precondition for the development of markets. A tool composed of the billions of ways out and solutions cannot be produced at the level of governance (acting under the extreme poverty of time). For the "creation of ways out within people's fields of action," sociologist Richard Sennett turned to an urban agglomeration such as Lagos.[6] On the one hand, an anarchic urban area arose. On the other, people invented new forms of urban proximity, allowing them to realize their needs better than in a planned city. According to Sennett, city planners and architects run after what people in Lagos actually do and learn from the system of trial and error how to implement an idea of city starting from below and working their way up, even if nothing emerges that is in the tradition of the Italian cities of the Renaissance. This is an example of "learning from the bottom up."

Derivatives of Subjective Characteristics
(*Derivate subjektiver Eigenschaften*)
The descendants of subjective characteristics act differently than the derivatives of stock exchange values. Derivatives of the capacity to love, for example, are: friendship, public welfare, tenderness, helpfulness, and studiousness. They draw their surplus value from their intrinsic value: because you love me, my love for you increases even more. Beaumarchais's and Mozart's hero Figaro does not have a sexual relationship with the countess, but he does her hair every

morning with great intimacy. He counsels her more intimately and confidentially than her husband ever could. Derivatives of classical labor characteristics are particularly modern virtues: sustainability, long-range discipline, promptness, exactness, and communicative talent. The urcell of such transpositions can be found in Socrates, when in one of his dialogues, he translates blind courage in war into its derivative: "Only the courage to know is important."[7] Following Socrates, it follows that: BRAVERY IS KNOWLEDGE OF WHAT I SHOULD BE AFRAID OF AND OF WHAT I SHOULD LOVE.

Homo volans

For more than two thousand years, the FLYING HUMAN has been represented from the point of view of the fall. Icarus fell. At the same time, however, flying is an ideal in all reformation movements of the twentieth century. RELATED CONCEPTS: → Homo sapiens; → Homo compensator; → Homo faber; → *Robo sapiens*.

The Collective Worker (*Gesamtarbeiter*)

A central category in Karl Marx's *Capital* (see *Capital*, section 4, chapter 15, "Machinery and Modern Industry"). Initially it referred to a so-called real abstraction designating the (theoretical) alliance between all labor powers and labor capacities throughout the entire world, without which the capitalist world economy would be inconceivable. Later on, this collective worker developed into something real, but without the ability of being autonomous (as a relationality) and without its objectively interrelated elements ever being observable as a unity. Effectively ignored by the public sphere, everyday experience, and science, all human developments — odysseys and progress alike — run their course on the level of this collective worker. On another level, the idea of the collective worker is the motif for posters and other memorials of labor.

Homo volans. [Fausto Venanzio, *Machinae Novae* (Venice, 1616), plate 38]

A 1939 convention poster from Chicago. As if grasping snakes, the all-powerful worker grasps three-story-high power lines that otherwise would blow up the city. *Lower center*: a real but unrecognizable laborer at the window of a building. [Alexander Kluge Archive]

Reality (*Wirklichkeit*)

The term for the world of experience, as opposed to the world of mere ideas. In first nature, reality is a practical relation: if I run against a wall, I hurt my head. In second nature, the concept of reality proves itself to be complex; it constitutes a "second skin of experience" manufactured by social and communicative agreement. According to Friedrich Nietzsche, humans are not interested in reality, but rather in the production of an illusion. Homer's Cassandra would be an antirealist in this regard. → The principle of skin-to-skin closeness. Cells have an outer shell. All the body's cells have a skin. Covering this skin are clothes. A house or an apartment, the city or the countryside where I live, can count as an additional skin. This additional skin is the reality we collectively construct.

Property (*Eigentum*)

A human's primitive property is his or her *lived time*; it incorporates all personal characteristics and reciprocities between the self and the outside. Juridical property is a completely different concept, developed in Roman law and modified by modern commerce. This formed exclusionary property. In Karl Marx's analysis, the conflict between these two forms of property engender the crises of capital while also producing an instinctual desire for emancipation. Within the dimension of time, primitive property has a radical root in evolution (an evolution that is more than 500 million years old). Life develops on crystalline planes and later in vessels. If this "for itself"—that is, this demarcation—is nonexistent, life cannot organize itself. This principle of the SHAPED FORM can be understood as the foundation of property. Sigmund Freud's skepticism vis-à-vis the "socialist experiment of proprietary freedom" can be understood in this sense. The form of primitive property sketched out here is not exclusionary, but rather is incorporative and aimed at social unification. It incorporates the logic of the "zoon politikon" just as it does the logic of "elbow room." Such elementary kinetic forces are easily observable in the evolutionarily old, yet time-tested phenomenon of SWARM INTELLIGENCE. It is striking to index their durability in contemporary relations. PRIVATE PROPERTY, upon which capitalism is based, is separate from this, state capitalism constituting but one variation. Private property relates to primitive property abstractly and creates an artificial world in which humans are not mirrors for one another. In this world, they do not behave like living beings, but rather like things.

In a derivative sense, this property has numerous forms, each of which affects the economy of labor power and the chances for emancipation and reason differently. → Production capitalism; → Financial capitalism; → Anarchistic alternatives to property, Workers' councils, Self-sufficiency, Barter economy, Black market; → Compulsory exchange society; → Planned economy; → Commons and collective property; → Living reserves of primitive property beneath the threshold of capitalist societies (irrepressible).

Primitive Expropriation, Primitive Accumulation
(*Ursprüngliche Enteignung, ursprüngliche Akkumulation*)

Central concepts for the beginning of capitalist structures. We can observe how primitive accumulation functions today and how it continuously renews itself. Karl Marx deals with primitive accumulation most notably in the form of a historical narrative in the twenty-fifth chapter of *Capital*. He uses as his example the formation of English capitalism through robbery and expropriation in the transition from the Middle Ages to the modern age. On the one hand, he says, this primitive expropriation produced misery; on the other, it produced in humans a theretofore nonexistent willingness to change and willingness to work. We see different hues of relationality depending on the country, continent, or kind of primitive accumulation to which we direct our powers of observations. Similarly, its relevance for the political economy of labor power is distinct from its relevance for the search for ways out in the interest of emancipation. We can thus search for primitive expropriation in emigration waves; on the one hand, working-class emigrants bring with them in their consciousness and, in their desire to emigrate, the expropriation that they experienced in their native land. On the other hand, the challenges of the new country (for example, the United States, Australia) act as an incentive for developing new characteristics. In general, it seems to be the case that 50 percent of the responses to primitive expropriation generate impoverishment and a loss of control. The other 50 percent contribute to new characteristics and social gain. Thus, the individual becomes poorer, and society profits. In societies such as those in China, Africa, Russia, or South America, these processes have been hardly researched, if at all, to date. This research would be particularly beneficial for understanding the history of the United States.

Balancing Labor (*Balancearbeit*)
A main feature of political economy is located neither externally, in society, nor psychologically, in the interior of humans, but rather in the joints *in between*. How do I insert myself—as a former child and a natural being—into the second nature of society? For that, what I need is not mere reason (*Homo sapiens*), but equilibrium within my self (*Homo compensator*). There are thus always these *two* labor instruments of reason. With respect to the particulars of this balancing labor and the balance economy (that is, what one could call "walking upright of the second degree"), history and obstinacy confront one another.

Antirealism of Feeling (*Antirealismus des Gefühls*)
Something within the subjective side of humans responds in the form of denial to a reality that injures them.

"Antirealism of Feeling"
In a foxhole in the Crimea in 1944, a man stood buried up to his neck in dirt. Protected by a steel helmet, his head protruded out into the dangerous realities of a battlefield blanketed by enemies. Joseph Beuys had an eye on this image, which he knew from personal experience, while planning his installation *Die zwei Aggregatzustände des Menschen* [The two aggregate states of human beings]. His illness swept him away before he could finish the work. He bought the plastic doll of an American soldier for cheap at a department store and buried it up to its belly in potting soil. The rest of the body above ground was protected by (or ensnared in) a cellophane shroud; at the periphery of the installation, twelve poles, presumably in the shape of a grid, pointed at the torso. Two water faucets were attached to the doll, one at its mouth and another, jutting out from the soil, at its crotch. When turned on, liquid would drip or stream out.

Beuys explained the sketch of this installation to a sociologist of the Frankfurt School thus: humans are divided into two parts. When they encounter circumstances that harm them (as in the case of a soldier in war, a casualty in an accident, or someone doing work they can hardly bear), they respond with denial. In this respect, we humans live in two different realities that are human only when in concert with one another (as in the case of a vault requiring two keys). The sociologist described the idea using the then commonly used expression "antirealism of feeling." Feeling protects itself against a perception that it wishes not to endure by replacing it with an illusion. Conversely, Beuys added, such a feeling is also immune to persuasion and propaganda, because as experienced fabricators of illusion (and full of so much wisdom), people also disavow the lies that arise out of real circumstances. Neither labor in a barracks nor imprisonment can make people absolutely unhappy. Shortly before they were to reach the zero point of unhappiness, hope would leap forth. Which it cannot do in your installation, the sociologist replied. Your doll is held firmly in the soil. Humans are not dolls, Beuys answered. Why then the installation with the doll? Because of the "antirealism of feeling."

A Playful Interaction in the Office

An important physicist and nuclear scientist, together with the sociologist Jürgen Habermas, founded the Max Planck Institute for the Research of Life Conditions in the Scientific-Technological World. The physicist, who came from an esteemed Swabian family of nobility known for its many political leaders and top officials, was accustomed to follow his particular interests. And his interests shifted like the weather. They were even dependent upon those whom he met on any given day. As many witnessed, he left behind — like children at play who leave a long trail of toys in their wake — a chain of broken-off plans, projects that never saw the light of day, each of which could have been considered interesting, but which together gave rise to a mountainous debt of unfinished business. For Habermas, this was not compatible with his notion of serious work. The lack of discipline of this kind, which the spoiled physicist displayed and which neither friendly nor stern warnings proved capable of changing, was one of the elements that ruined the Max Planck Institute.

Film Scenes from the World of Work

When R. W. Fassbinder and his production team (which both took to the stage at Frankfurt's Theater am Turm and shot films) resided in Kaiserstraße, one of his favorites mistakenly procured a film permit to shoot in an abandoned factory in the Rhine-Main region in which typewriters and machine tools were once produced. By the 1970s, the company had gone bankrupt, and demolition was imminent.

Once the film permit was finally issued, Fassbinder decided to make use of it after all. It was seldom that he filmed in the world of work. He had tracks installed for the camera dolly. The camera was supposed to follow the actors smoothly as they walked along a long stretch of the premises. A technically perfect tracking shot stood in contradiction, so to speak, to the tattered technology in the already partially destroyed factory. Fassbinder's idea was unrecognizable in the shoot, since the close-up revealed only the actors' heads against a nondescript background. In contrast, photographs taken during the shooting were of greater aesthetic value. Visible were the paved street and the embedded tracks for trolleys (or the factory-owned narrow-gauge railway) from the nineteenth century, on top of which sat the modern, technically advanced tracks from the firm Arnold and Richter Cine Technik for the dolly; big floodlights shed light showing clearly a world from the twentieth century.

On account of the public crisis surrounding the play *The Garbage, the City, and Death* stemming from the role of the "Jew from Frankfurt," as well as the pressure from a follow-up project with West German Broadcasting, the shooting in the factory never went beyond this one tracking shot. Fassbinder later furnished the roughly seven-minute sequence with a text spoken by one of his actors. It had to do with words that did not fall under the concept of LABOR: PLAYING, YAWNING, PRAYING, SLEEPING, BROODING, HATING, CHOKING, STEALING, STRETCHING, JUMPING, LYING DOWN TO DIE, WAKING UP, SMOKING, DRESSING ONESELF, UNDRESSING SOMEONE ELSE, CRYING, HUNTING, COLLECTING, SPYING, ABSCONDING, PICKING OAKUM, EAVESDROPPING, EATING, DRINKING, STINGING, MUTTERING, SEARCHING, FINDING, FREEZING, DRYING, TELLING JOKES.

During the editing of the film (when the film positive in the studio was synchronized with the film negative corresponding to the soundtrack), the sound engineer asked Fassbinder whether work was not still hidden in the activities signified by these words. The impatient Fassbinder was not inclined to make philosophical explanations:

— You can always somehow say "something is working."
— But a stone on the border of a path doesn't do work.
— The weather works on it.
— But that's not work in the human sense.
— Cells and digestion work while we sleep.

With his final sentence, Fassbinder relented in order to curtail the conversation. And what do you plan to do later on with the film sequence we've mixed? It's seven minutes long. There are no venues in movie theaters or on television for a film of this length, the sound engineer said. The piece was made for eternity, Fassbinder answered. He was nervous.

The Breakdown of Experience

It occurred to a Frenchman attending the funeral at which far too few guests were permitted that along with this 101–year-old man, an entire experiential world was being buried, too, once and for all, at least with regard to what pertained to personal testimony. No person in command of the powers of expression was more present, more capable of telling roughly a hundred years later of the reality of the industrialized war of 1916. This "laboratory of experience" was costly for both sides, both Germany and France. Such experiences cannot be pinned down in books, the Frenchman said.

Already in 1940, Ernst Jünger felt isolated on account of his knowledge. The young men from the triumphal procession knew not the slightest thing about the First World War, and yet its paws struck a blow in 1944 when some fronts on the blitzkrieg transformed into trench warfare. Like everyone else, the Frenchman cast into the grave a scoop of sand and a flower and therewith the illusion that there was ever such thing as the transfer of experience across generations. In modern-day armament, there are more traces of the years 1914 to 1918 built into Eurofighters or missile-defense systems than in the minds of the young mourners who made their way onward to the arranged refreshments.

The Appearance of Cooperation

An extraterrestrial observer would have considered the events in Passchen-daele on June 7, 1917 — involving more than two hundred thousand fit and armed men on both sides of the front — an example of cooperation. On the German side, huge masses of munitions and artillery had been concentrated in conjunction with the last offensive of the German Empire in the Great War. Dynamite wrapped in metal was supposed to be fired off at British lines in the vicinity of entire railway lines. Preparations for this LABOR OF ANNIHILATION were complete. A subterranean layer of loam passed from the positions of the English well into the German front line. On that seventh of July, some twenty bombs exploded directly underneath the German artillery: a crater sixty meters wide and twelve meters deep. More than fifteen thousand soldiers died.

Loamy soil absorbs rainwater. As easy as the ground is to tunnel through, so, too, is it quick to level out any unevenness, even craters. At the site of the explosion, today's tourist finds an unprepossessing little lake, the "Pond of Peace." Heiner Müller visited the body of water when he was busy with his Verdun piece. He discussed the battles of the First World War in Northern France with Dirk Baecker — in his final years, Müller regarded him highly as an informant in all things in economics: every movement on the British side corresponded to a countermovement (and its derivations) on the Ger-man side, Müller said. The event had roots going back one hundred and fifty years or more; in this respect, certain forms of national character require a considerable amount to time in order to develop. In addition to this came the four years of war, which proceeded so differently from how the leader-ship originally assumed. The LABOR OF ANNIHILATION ON BOTH SIDES first developed below the radar of such leadership. It is an artifact. Müller and Baecker did not want to call it "art," even though all the ingredients belong-ing to a large art installation were contained in this moment of the collective laborer, as Baecker, who was accustomed to the objectivity of the Bielefeld school of sociology, pointed out. Somewhere the comparisons stop, Müller said, and therewith concluded the debate.

Proletarian (*Proletarisch*)

Today a seldom-used expression that is nevertheless indispensable for understanding classical theory. In Latin, *proles* means "youth of the wall"; the word refers to young people on the outskirts of town who are marginalized and unemployed. Life in Paris's *banlieues* would be the contemporary instance of this. In classical economics, the concept is used specifically to refer to wage workers in the emerging realm of organized labor in factories. It denotes human labor from which unfettered access to the labor resources it requires is taken away as a matter of principle. In classical theory, *proletarian* is thus synonymous with being unpropertied. The expectation on the part of theoreticians goes so far as to say that the propertyless, driven by misery, will inevitably force themselves to appropriate the means of production; under the supervision of this philosophy, an emancipatory process will materialize. Observations from the last one hundred and fifty years have yet to support these expectations. That these processes do not function automatically — not even when they are guided by a nonproletarian intelligentsia — nevertheless does not prove them wrong. What is observable, however, is the fact that being propertyless does not make someone immune to bribery. Thus the diagnosis fateful for the Critical Theory of the Frankfurt School when, in 1932, Communist and National Socialist workers allied themselves in the Berlin public-transportation workers' strike. According to the protagonists of Critical Theory, this suggested that the proletariat will not be the revolutionary subject. On the other hand, powerful, but nevertheless scattered waves of emancipation within the European workers' movements must be taken into consideration. The respect for these forces (even for the martyrs of Chicago, whose deaths are remembered every May 1) testifies against abandoning the concept *proletarian* and for directing the necessary wariness toward the conceptual substance of the *proletariat*. We treat the word practically like a foreign word (that is to say, we borrowed it from classical theory, which does not correspond to prevailing contemporary parlance), as a key for transmission and as a search criterion.

"Capitalism within us" (*"Kapitalismus in uns"*)
Many thousands of years or even maybe only a few hundred years after the emergence or downfall of a social formation (soil cultivation, classical industry), certain analogies evolve inside humans (often significantly changed). Thus there exists the "farmer in us" and the "craftsman in us" (especially in the intelligentsia). Based on our observations, though, there is also the internalization of capitalist structures and the "hedging of surplus value." Also part of this is "the search for private good fortune" that plays a significant role in love

affairs. Socially more relevant is the compensation of social losses with a fundamental disposition for faith. This functions similarly to the way powerful market forces do, even if the products of this INTERNAL MARKET are not exactly exchangeable and do not accumulate any countervalue like that of money. → Talcott Parsons's theory of media.

Not only functioning capitalism, but rather all forces of anti-capitalism—the search for ways out and reserves—converge in the "capitalist in me." On the precursors of this, see Max Weber's *The Protestant Ethic and the Spirit of Capitalism* (1904).

Separation Energy (*Trennungsenergie*)
The polar opposite of binding energy.

Precision Maneuvering (*Feinsteuerung*)
Synonymous with selectivity, precision maneuvering refers to the ability to respond to the strengths of another person or object, but also to characteristics such as "foresight" and indirect methodology. There are an extraordinary number of always concrete examples wherein an unusable power grip is replaced by a precision grip. Medical practice since Asclepius can be depicted as a long line of progressively more precise forms of maneuvering or navigation.

Simple Labor (*Einfache Arbeit*)
Contrary to the conventional view that a god of war such as Napoleon was capable of mobilizing more forces than one of his foot soldiers, classical economists posit that all labor is based on the average expenditure of effort per hour. The differences between muscle power and ability are balanced out in a nation's balance sheet. In this respect, the hour that a human works is equivalent to an hour that another human works. The same holds true for the "joining of hands." Deception first emerges, according to classical economists, at the level of hierarchy (itself representing no labor whatsoever). During a crisis—Napoleon's flight after the Battle of Waterloo—output power per hour begins once again to approximate that of simple labor.

Land of Unlimited Opportunities
(*Land der unbegrenzten Möglichkeiten*)
An attribute of the United States, above all from the point of view of European emigrants. However, during the Russian Revolution

of 1905, Max Weber speaks of Russia as the "land of unlimited opportunities." It is interesting to apply this search criterion — which tests the chance of hope in the world — to our present. The land of unlimited opportunities can also lie inside humans. It can also be sought out as the "historical subjunctive case" in the boundedness of the possible.

Industrial Ruins, Left Behind by Investors
With the approval of Chinese officials, a group of twenty-two American pension funds put up an industrial park in a special economic zone northwest of Shanghai (this was at the beginning of the boom), and ran it for a while. Then the funds reinvested its capital in India. The Chinese manufacturing facility became a ruin. The son of the functionary who was made responsible for the overly trustful ingress of the foreign investors and who was severely punished for it (he took his own life in prison) is now the chairman of a committee in the National Assembly of the Republic of China. He is determined never to let such an instance ever happen again.

Adult Education for the Finance Industry
My grandfather, explained the vice-president of China's National Audit Office, still taught Marx at Shanghai University. He succumbed to the Cultural Revolution. Then my father and I (both of us are in the Office of Economics) appropriated the teachings of the Chicago School on the economy of capitalism, with which we acquired our experience after 1990. In the meantime, this doctrine is disintegrating in the West (at least from our point of view in the East).

With the support of our administration, we have recently organized continuing education courses in Manhattan for perplexed financiers in the United States. We are prepared to offer foreign aid. We made these arrangements in our own interests, as well, since an unscientific approach to the financial crisis, such as we noticed in New York, endangers the assets of our own people, the biggest believers in America. We have brought production experience into the FREE-MARKET ECONOMY (which we learned painstakingly and have now perfected). We have made considerable long-lasting strides with our reports and training in South Sudan, Nigeria, and at Cairo

University. In the United States, however, we fall on deaf ears. No one wants to enroll in our courses. Those responsible do not have the time to learn about something that would only help them.

A Nightcap Conversation

The scholar of culture studies Joseph Vogl won the attention of economic experts with his book *The Specter of Capital*. Following a press conference with the publicist Claudius Seidl, the two sat down together in the editorial offices of the *Frankfurter Allegemeine Zeitung* well into the night. They partook of a nightcap. The events of the financial crisis and the fact that such a conversation would be printed a day later without so much as a change of wording—these things are incompatible with the idea of falling asleep instantly, regardless of all the fatigue beleaguering mind and body.

Seidl asked whether components produced in thirty different countries, when assembled into a computer by Samsung, constitute production. That is not production, but design, Vogl replied. I don't see any laborers at work. The assembly is taken care of by robots, he added. And what are we to make of the finger flicks with which the cancer-plagued head of Apple, Steve Jobs, made his touch-screen models so successful—is that not also design? No, Vogl responded (who followed the rule for nightcap conversations by always answering with great surprise). The products are the fingertips themselves (namely, products of evolution) and then "handiness," he added. Something like that enters into the world as a need because in everyday life there are no worry stones to hold in your hand and certainly little if any sensuousness. The lack is the producer himself.

Second Nature (*Zweite Natur*)

A designation for social nature as opposed to naturally occurring nature: a steppe or jungle becomes a field. Vertically stackable properties (fields) become cities. The urban intelligence that once cultivated the earth now develops gardens. The high-rises that make up the business and residential districts of New York City have Central Park as an attribute. Christo's installations illuminated Central Park. It belonged to second nature when non-nomads played their sports there.

Dependent Annex (*Abhängiger Annex*)
Farms and landed estates in the Middle Ages managed themselves autarkically. Not only were grains, beer, schnapps, and wood produced, but also fabrics were woven and shoes and clothing were manufactured. The estates were self-sufficient. The neighboring covenant school, the traveling doctor, and the traveling blacksmith belonged to a structure overseen by no ruler. This is PRIMARY PRODUCTION. In the dependent annex, the craftsman must first produce the needs of the purchaser, and only thereafter the product. This condition endures in contemporary relations wherein the consumer is king. A massive advertising industry (one among many others) must generate needs in order to make the product possible in the first place. Production is not all-encompassing. Rather, it is overshadowed by the production of purchase orders. The extreme, chimerical variant of the dependent annex is the structure of fascism. At normal levels, the dependent annex entails the ABBERATION OF INTELLECTUAL LABOR. Left to itself, intelligence would normally be targeted at knowledge and orientation, insofar as it entails a form of primary production autonomous in structure. In actuality, purchase orders from third parties—for example, a system of contracts that the intelligentsia must initially produce—focuses 90 percent of the global deployment of intelligence on services and circuitous production methods. A revolutionizing counterexample: the Internet was invented at CERN as the primary means of communication among scientists. It was adapted for militaristic purposes as a product of the ruling annex, and in this form, it was unilaterally, often clandestinely developed. Then, however, the Internet was acquired globally by broad swaths of people and thus in this respect became a generator for unanticipated participation and freedom of communication. Every human is a transmitter and a receiver: this was Bertolt Brecht's and Hans Magnus Enzensberger's theory of radio, which in their respective times was considered utopian. This goes to show how inventive humans are when it comes to the reappropriation of primary communication: in the long run, they will not breathe oxygen, but rather produce it. → Production, Primary and Secondary

Subsumption, Formal and Real (*formelle und reelle Subsumtion*)
Subsumption entails the subjection of someone to heteronomy. In some cases, it is merely formal, such as British rule over India; for

a long time, it determined the way capital ruled over both mental activities and the sciences. Such subsumption becomes REAL when it controls in detail the way in which heteronomy is implemented: in an army or in the assembly line's impact on the factory labor. Depending on the degree of subsumption, the effects on the political economy of labor power can differ radically. It would be a mistake, though, to assume that with real subsumption (that is, intensive heteronomy) the counterreaction rooted in obstinacy would become weakened. As with primitive expropriation, 50 percent of what real subsumption generates is specialized resistance and the potential for ways out, and the other 50 percent is for the additional capacities for adaptation and alienation.

Above and Below (*oben und unten*)
Contrary to its appearance, authority grows from the bottom up. An empire (a chain of command) rules from the top down. A radical relation develops "when those below are no longer willing and those above no longer can."[8] At this point, a system breaks down (as with the German Democratic Republic in 1989). Another example: people sitting below ground in air raid shelters are defenseless, even though bomb-disposal experts are among them; a bomber armada high above them, itself a flying industrial complex—nears the city. Those below appear (or are) powerless, those above omnipotent. Relations between the two are inverted as soon as one of the airplanes is damaged. The difference between above and below lies in prehistory; an industrial groundwork is stored in the organization of three hundred approaching bombers and their bombs, yet none of it is accessible to the residents in the cellar.

Concreteness (*Gegenständlichkeit*)
Degree of concretion: subjective forces can be objectified only in a concrete object. Antithesis; → Indeterminacy; → Being adherent to a mere idea; → Enthusiasm (Immanuel Kant); → Appearance [*Schein*].

Relation of History (*Geschichtsverhältnis*)
The succession and contemporary superimposition of all relations of production and instances of production of a concrete territory, continent, or epoch.

Relations of Production (*Produktionsverhältnisse*)
Agrarian, feudal, urban, industrial, postindustrial, precapitalist, capitalist, or hybrid societies each exhibit certain production norms. According to classical economics, these relations of production determine the particular character of labor. In our estimation, it is also possible to observe countercurrents that work against the dominion of the relations of production.

Relation of Intercourse (*Verkehrsverhältnis*)
The totality of the conditions under which humans and things can enter into exchange. The aggregation of concrete relations of production in a territory, a continent, or an epoch. → Being consigned to the junk heap as a result of working in concentration camps; → Slavery; → Urban freedom, international waters, commercial freedom; → Human rights.

Action That Leapfrogs over a Vital Step in Politics
(*Übersprungshandlung in der Politik*)
A sprinting dog must to decide between two contradictory commands. It doesn't alter its sprint, but rather its direction. This is called "displacement" or "disinhibition." Two days after the attack on the Twin Towers on September 11, 2001, the U.S. Hawaiian naval fleet appeared off New York City. Contemporary witnesses had the impression that the very same armada that was once surprised by a Japanese attack (in 1941) had shown up to protect the wounded city. However, these were modern vessels floating off the coast. They represented an attempt on the part of the Pentagon to respond to the catastrophe as rapidly as possible. Displacement is thus a reflex that derails. As a matter of fact, the politics of the United States had no means with which it could have directly responded to the attack of September 11. It was only shifting the question on to Afghanistan—that is to say, on to another world—that allowed for the deployment of forces.

Use Value (*Gebrauchswert*)
A counterconcept to commodity value that does not define itself through exchange value. In times of need, use value steps into the foreground.

Commodity Fetish (*Warenfetisch*)

Humans do not recognize themselves in the products they themselves have manufactured and that have been assembled out of their lived time. This is the primary cause of alienation. In this respect, commodities, in the production of which human lived time resides, are "enchanted human beings."

Specialists, 1946. [Ullstein Bild/DPA]

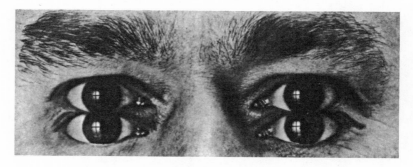

The multiplication of the eyes. "Social senses." [Alexander Kluge Archive]

426

Inflation Is Raining In

The protagonists of the colloquium dined at two porcelain-topped tables. They had met today to discuss tomorrow's event. At the one table sat the hostess, at the other the host. The two-story-tall painting by Anselm Kiefer in the stairwell cost him 400,000 euros, said the host. It was expensive, and thus not for sale. But its value has presumably increased. He appraised the shelf life of the glue and other additives used to hold together the installation and individual parts of the work of art at fifteen years. The artist was careless in his choice of work materials. If the parts came undone, the value would depreciate.

At the tables sat five financial experts and a historian. They agreed that the financial authorities in the United States would redress their mountain of debt with inflation. And this would happen at exactly the moment when investors switch from short-term bonds, which they accepted exclusively at that time (and which prevented inflation), to midterm and long-term bonds with attractive interest rates. This would correspond to the experience from the last century. Governments and central banks from debtor nations make use of this moment. Certainly not intentionally, the historian and legal expert Hannes Siegrist interjected, but rather carelessly. We lawyers call that "luxuria." The carelessness, another participant noted, was in the fact that discretion in such decisions was spread over governments following one another, in other words, along a temporal axis. A minister and his cabinet make a decision. His successor and staff then undertake a further step. The decision for inflation is made at interfaces — that is, with a change of government — where apparently no decisions are made. Picking up where the one financial advisor left off, the host added that in this respect, values don't crash. They are more prone to crash at the end. This could be avoided only if there were no government. We've already seen this quite often, they said among themselves. It is because of these precedents, without which we would perceive nothing, that we can see these imperceptible steps. In any such case, it always comes down to inflation. This is certainly, the way it happened, but then again maybe not, Kai A. Konrad recapitulated.

November 1923

The two children played in the snow in the garden behind the house where the banker Friedrichsen shot himself in November 1923. Under the guidance of their nanny, they built a snowman and then a wall around him. Their cheeks were red as much from the cold as from their own zeal. They were kept in the garden late into the evening by Friedrichsen's personnel. When they were finally brought inside and ate their dinner in the kitchen, the corpse had already been taken away by the local police. The autopsy showed no evidence of foul play. His fortune was lost. For forty years, the banker had defended the finances of the German Empire, which meanwhile had shattered.

The Concierges of Paris

During his Parisian visit with James Joyce at the end of November 1929, Sergei Mikhailovich Eisenstein brought along an idea for his film about Karl Marx's *Capital*. Joyce was to spin the sketch into a screenplay. Eisenstein expected a JOYCEAN CASCADE OF WORDS from which he would develop sequences using the tools of silent film. At that point in time, Joyce was practically blind. He vaguely saw the two large lamps illuminating the room. He was in no position at all to read the manuscript that Eisenstein held before his face. What was he supposed to write, then, Joyce asked, if there was already this sketch?

Nowhere in the draft was there an image sequence slated for Black Friday, which the press reported on at the time. Something like that would have to be filmed (according to Eisenstein's notion) by a team of documentarians under the direction of Dziga Vertov. But he would not have received a travel permit for the West in time to shoot in Paris, London, or New York during the event. It was also doubtful whether a camera team from the Soviet Union would have received a permit to shoot in capitalism's stock exchanges.

Eisenstein wanted to represent the share values indirectly using the reactions of people affected. This he told James Joyce and therewith requested a text from the poet. No current shots of the events from recent months can achieve this, he said. The reactions develop much later. We must record now what the concierges of Paris would have experienced ten years ago, when it turned out that the Soviet government would no longer attend to those bonds for the Siberian railroad from before the Great War that the concierges had bought in small amounts (in tranches from 1902 to 1908). These concierges were powerful women, rulers and inspectors of entranceways to Parisian homes since the French Revolution. They had just decided the outcome of recent elections. They refused to vote for France's Communist Party because the Council of the People's Commissars had reduced their saved assets to zero. This outrage first needs to be shown in film, Eisenstein said, and then subsequently the degree to which (the farsighted) Lenin also perceived their interests. Joyce improvised the tonality of a concierge, a monologue in French mixed with bits of English. It sounded like singsong.

A Suggestion from Alexandria
In December 1929, a casino owner from Alexandria, whose mother's ancestors dated back to the Phoenicians and whose father claimed Greek-Venetian ancestry, approached the Soviet Union's commissioner for foreign trade. He offered to buy up shares of American technology and electric power industries at Russia's expense using inconspicuous stock exchanges, for example, in Alexandria and Istanbul. Since Black Friday and the series of ensuing nosedives in stock prices, shares were to be had for an astoundingly low value. After the acquisition of such property, the technologies could then be taken back the Soviet Union. Included in the proposal was a schedule showing that with this acquisition, Russia would be able to execute its five-year plan seven years earlier. Where did the man from Alexandria get such information?

The Accumulation of Unreality as Exemplified by Greece
(*Summierung von Unwirklichkeit an Griechenlands Beispiel*)
On account of the fabrication of statistics, the Hellenic Republic was incorporated into the Eurozone. Now the mountain of Greek debt (along with factors from other European countries) threatens the status of the currency. For a seven-year period, it was possible to borrow money inexpensively, thanks to the status of the euro. This corresponds to the observation that a large portion of the equivalent value of these loans is to be found in hotel construction in London, in accounts in Switzerland, in the assets of Alexandria, in ship construction, as well as in ruinous investments that initially brought profits but then resulted in operating losses. Only a small portion of the equivalent value of loans went into consumption by the general population; in this respect, the value was consumed. Present and future populations of the republic are now supposed to work off the

cumulated mountain of debt. They are neither ready for this nor in any position to do so. Economically, two parallel worlds have come into being: one rooted in the equivalent value of borrowed money no longer in existence in Greece's reality, and the other rooted in the mountain of debt weighing down the country. Such a bifurcation of reality engenders an aporia.

In addition, there is the fact that Greece has neither a real-estate registry nor an intact tax-collection system. Large segments of the economy have a governmental bureaucratic structure and are contaminated by patron-client relationships.

In the deep layers of history, this governmental structure developed out of the revolts of 1821 and 1829 on the Peloponnese against the Ottoman Empire. The militant movement (similar to Libya's today) was accompanied by a European press campaign, as well as by idealistic initiatives taken by a few individuals (Lord Byron, Prince Ypsilanti). Sympathy for the founding of the state emerged out of a fiction that the population of Greece was identical at that time with the Greeks of antiquity, to whom we owe the principle of the polis and the idea of democracy.

Market Legitimation versus Popular Legitimation
(*Legitimierung durch den Markt vs. Legitimierung durch das Volk*)
A newsworthy scene: the G-20 Summit meets in the city that plays home to the Cannes International Film Festival. Just then, the acting prime minister of Greece makes the disturbing announcement that he wants to have a referendum to legitimize the imposed austerity measures, which include financial aid through the European Central Bank (ECB) and the International Monetary Fund (IMF) as well as the renunciation of the parliament's right to sovereignty. This ensures a delay. The participants of the summit are shocked. They fear that the markets will be allergic to this reference to the sovereignty of the people. There's no time for the democratic process to take its course. The experts at the summit question the standing that the sovereign obstinacy of a small nation can claim among the powers represented at the G-20: a single nation lost under a mount of debt cannot stop the convoy of other nations.

On Greek soil, the polis became the structure of free commonwealths and subjective consciousness (from Heraclitus to Socrates) in the so-called axial age (around 500 B.C.). The participants in the democratic process in the agorae of Athens received pay and free meals as compensation for their political labor. From the view of antiquity, democracy is not a natural accomplishment, as the subjugation to strongmen historically appears to be. It is a product of civilization. This expresses itself in the use of public means to finance the labor necessary for democracy. The costs and detours of democracy do not make any sense to markets. The algorithms of the market do not perceive that trade routes and democracy presuppose one another and that only broad participation by people opens up market potentials. After the dramatic appearances of the prime ministers from Athens and Rome before the committee of the G-20, the plan for a referendum in Greece was revoked, and a new ministry formed composed solely of financial experts. It is regarded as the "managing committee of banks."

Thermidor
According to the French revolutionary calendar, the day in July 1794 when Robespierre and his comrades Saint-Just and Couthon were arrested. (They were executed a few days later.) Thermidor marked the end of the French Revolution.

The Human Is an Inversion Machine
(*Der Mensch ist eine Inversions-Maschine*)
Sigmund Freud's law characterizes the cognitive processes of DISAVOWAL and DISPLACEMENT through which humans respond to the perception of intolerable relations. → Balance economy; → Necessary false consciousness.

Damaged Dialectic (*Zerbeulte Dialektik*)
Hegel's works represent the dialectical movements of concepts in their full complexity; he does so, however, using only words. The gravitational forces that these concepts actually exert in reality — their disruptive and attractive effects — are difficult to describe in such a literary form. Dialectical relations are nonlinear. In antiquity, the dialectic developed out of dialogue, that is, almost grammatically. Its application to historical relations, which are not based on two individuals talking, renders it ungrammatical. Like celestial bodies, dialectical gravitational relations reciprocally warp one another. This is how dents and "damaged dialectics" develop. It is particularly difficult to straighten out.

431

Condorcet Hurls Himself into the Welter of the Revolution
Successor to d'Alembert as secretary of the Academy of Sciences and Voltaire's pen pal, the earnest Condorcet, whom Jules Michelet called the "last great philosopher of the eighteenth century," threw himself into the "waves of the revolution." Two year earlier, he had married his young wife, Sophie. Sophie de Condorcet, née Grouchy, was twenty-two years of age and twenty-one years his junior. She was known for her essay *Lettres sur la sympathie* (1798). When Condorcet asked for her hand in marriage, she explained, "her heart was no longer free." She was unhappily in love with another man who did not love her in return. And for two years, both Condorcets lived chastely, each with great respect for the other's feelings. But then on that day in July when the Bastille fell, in the enormous emotional commotion of the moment, Mme Condorcet conceived her only child. In April 1790, nine months later, the child was born.

At this point, Condorcet began a kind of third life. He first was a mathematician (under d'Alembert), then a public critic (alongside Voltaire), and now, "he set sail on the ocean of political life." This earnest man was full of panache. His sharp-witted "Letter from a Young Mechanic" was evidence that he could not do without an old joke. He got involved in the question whether there should be a republic, a constitutional monarchy (and if so, how should it be established?), or merely a modification of the royal ministries. In Condorcet's letter, the young mechanic obliges himself for a minimal fee to create a CONSTITUTIONAL KING that with occasional and meticulous repairs would be immortal. Such embellishments made Condorcet suspicious in the eyes of the Jacobins and unpopular among the royalists.

He made no mistake about the danger of his situation. It was not foreseeable which of the forces would win the upper hand in a civil war that at that point still went on. Because of possible repercussions, he later feared for his wife and their young child, the creature from the "sacred July days from the year 1." He secretly sought out a port from which his family could flee and ended up choosing Saint Valéry.

Deng Is Amazed by How Swiftly People Learn the Complexities of Capitalism
Thought by Mao Zedong to be a counterrevolutionary of bourgeois character, Deng Xiaoping was astonished by how lightning fast the Chinese disseminated the spirit of capitalism from special economic zones to the entire

country. He himself knew capitalism only from books. He had yet to familiar-
ize himself with all its rules. In fact, as enclaves in the party and in the armed
forces formed, it was important to restore the LAW OF EXCHANGE OF POWER
where the LAWS OF MONEY emerged. What was the reason for this rapid
learning? Was commodity exchange a fundamental human capacity? Deng
did not think so. Did the capitalist sensibility, which not all Chinese provinces
had embraced previously, merely "fall into a slumber" after the Revolution
of 1949? Did not the socialist republic and the Cultural Revolution cover it
over? Awakened as a result of the stimuli brought on by economic liberaliza-
tion, did it now grow in strength and even conquer what was blocked before
1949? The whole thing got started without any training or the use of manuals.
It appeared as if capitalism moved according to the principle of autopoiesis.
It initially appears as a teacher and then as an economy.

The Fossilized Trace of an Independent Thought

One of philosopher Sohn-Rethel's favorite ideas upon which his *Soziologische Theorie der Erkenntnis* (1985) is based was the derivation of Kant's
enigmatic construction of the TRANSCENDENTAL SUBJECT from the praxis
of the commodity-exchange society.

There are general rules for the use of reason, says Immanuel Kant, which
emanate neither from the experience of the individual nor from some divine
world, but precede the autonomous use of the tools of reason like a "tender
seed," like a dowry of the human species, as the A PRIORI. For Kant, these
pertain to a category of ideas. However, as a spoiled son from a good family,
an intensive observer of Germany's social laboratory in the 1930s, and a
darling of philosophy, Sohn-Rethel saw the roots of autonomous thought not
in thinking heads (as is always conveyed mysteriously by the ghostly suprain-
dividual subject and by a glance forward toward a world made up of cosmo-
politans), but in the DEEDS of humans. They glean thought from their modern
praxis (in other words, from the REAL ABSTRACTION OF THE CIRCULATION
OF COMMODITIES), he says, so that without knowing one another and being
of an indifferent disposition, like *impartial spectators*, but at the same time
still sweating the details, they develop a sense of pride as producers; in other
words, their egalitarian values are not indifferent at all, but humane. Abstract
concepts, logic, and finally reason have their grounding in production, says

433

Sohn-Rethel. That is the A PRIORI in the materialist sense. Concepts and thought tag along after it.

Capital—Countercapital (*Kapital—Gegenkapital*)

In the same way that property has various forms, the relationality of capital assumes numerous shapes. The agglomeration of assorted elements of individual forces that constitutes countercapital transforms concrete historical capital. Thus, curiosity, the spirit of resistance, and, above all, labor itself are all elements of countercapital to which societies turn in crisis. Although capital does not merely produce such countercapital itself, we can still find a fundamental current of this countereconomy in every conjuncture of capitalism. Normally, this fundamental current stabilizes the system, but it can also allow for emancipatory ways out and thereby make it possible for heterotopias to develop.

Alienation (*Entfremdung*)

A central concept in Marx's *Economic and Philosophical Manuscripts of 1844* ["The Paris Manuscripts"]. See also Hegel and Adam Smith. Alienation deals with an irritation between subject and object. Something objective has entered into humans as if it were subjective, and this objective thing makes them inhuman. An example from the Eastern Front in 1941: normally well-mannered fathers organized as a police battalion and shot people they did not know. The weight of the concept lies in the fact that there are subjective forces in humans that provoke this disorientation (this alienation). Naturally fluid in nature, humans' essential powers turn to stone. External violence cannot control such alienation. No slave could ever commit the atrocities that a motorized group of storm troopers composed of volunteers carried out, or, for that matter, the atrocities that came to light due to the indifference on the part of a central bank that refused loans to West Africa. Under the conditions of alienation, humans no longer recognize the product of their labor as their property (for example, the product of historical time). Their lived time (so-called dead labor) lies buried in what they produce, but they perceive their products as foreign values on which they bestow authority over themselves.

Emergence from Self-Incurred Alienation
(*Ausgang aus der selbstverschuldeten Entfremdung*)

Alienation is not NECESSARY. "Piercing attentiveness" breaks alienation just as much as "passion and visual judgment" do. All emancipation stems from the "emergence of human beings from self-incurred alienation."[9]

Singularity of the Polis (*Singularität der Polis*)

Citizenry developed in Greece in the first century before Christ (Aristotle names it *POLITEIA*). It was a matter of a clearly laid-out circle of people and fields; this was where cultivation, commerce, slaveholding, and a bit of sea piracy took place. In classical times, there were seven hundred such *poleis*. Their structure corresponded to Asterix's Celtic *oppida* and vaguely resembled the urform of Swiss cantons. The scholar of antiquity Christian Meier has researched and retold the genesis of this political concept in the context of this singularly unique historical period. According to Christian Meier, achievements such as the Greek concept of freedom and political community were unlikely in the Egyptian empires and the mega-cities of Mesopotamia. The monstrous concentration of power in great empires made any alternative to central rule appear like chaos. Things were different in the Greek *poleis*. For this reason, Marx identifies the Greeks as DARLINGS OF GOOD FORTUNE: "the historic childhood of humanity, its most beautifully unfolding...[is] a stage never to return."[10] This is where the ideal of the political — one necessary for emancipation — develops.

Separation (*Trennung*)

The opposite of "coming home," as Odysseus experienced it. It begins with the first cries after birth and repeats itself when children become adults. It constitutes the interface between the pleasure principle and the realty principle. Usually something is lost because of separations. Often something else is acquired. With respect to the political economy of labor power, separation pertains to the separation of laborers from the means of production. Early on, a migration to the cities arose due to the separation of home and soil, as did one of the elements of work discipline in the interiority of humans that presupposed the Industrial Revolution. In (almost half of) all of these processes, a loss and discovery of new ways out are observable. In the twenty-first century, it seems that the separation of people from the determination of the means of production has attained a degree of absoluteness in certain areas. The reclamation of forms of separation is imperative and necessary so that responses transpire not on an abstract level, for example, the level of finance capital, but from the bottom up in the extremely heterogeneous "spheres of action." Observation shows that separations of things belonging to identity leave behind a wake of reconstruction of the originary conditions representing one of the strongest social drives and that its "leap" does not return to older conditions, but leads to innovation.

Relationality (*Zusammenhang*)
A synonym for "context." When applied to social relationalities neither networked nor conscious, the concept also applies to structures of violence. In this respect, relationality describes an aggregative state and a condition of reality. Its opposite: "incohesive." The concept also denotes at the same time a specific form of condensation, gravitational relations in the social sense. In this case, the opposite would be: "empty," "idling," "at rest," "the absence of violence" (as it relates to the entire relationality), "a gap or blind spot."

On the Roof of the World
Twelve assistants to the president of the United States, two economic advisors, and a security advisor prepare the budget proposal of 636 billion dollars for the following day, the most expensive budget in the history of the Pentagon. OVERNIGHT, THE FIRST SNOW OF THE YEAR FALLS ON WASHINGTON. At nine o'clock, the president retires to his living quarters for dinner with his family. The security advisor takes leave of the meeting at midnight. The others work until five in the morning.

As they leave through the side exit of the White House, everything is covered with snow. It's a pleasure to put your feet in fresh snow.

Far to the east, nine time zones away from Washington, the president's liaison, Ambassador Richard Holbrooke, sped in his motorcade through a mountain pass. He still wanted to reach the mountain village where he had an appointment that night with a tribal chief from the northwestern border.

The mountain is in one of the highest regions in the world. In December, it is also one the coldest. In this zone, the surface of discontinuity on the border between the earth's mantel and crust lies seventy-five kilometers below the surface. The fracture zone in the Indian Ocean has pressed powerfully on the Baluchistan Plateau for eons, pushing the mass of rock northward, where it encounters the Karakoram range. Accordingly, the Pamir, Karakoram, and the Afghan Hindu Kush mountain ranges have historically always been in dispute with one another. Geologists call this part of the earth the THIRD POLE. According to the geoscientist Abdel-Gawad, however, the masses of snow, cold, and fog formations and the restlessness of the earth's innards at this third pole are completely different from the static conditions in the Antarctic and the solitude in the Arctic Ocean.[11]

Holbrooke traveled in an unarmored car. To distract assassins, a convoy escorted by tanks was in transit in another direction. For this convoy, the Pakistani secret service promised remote backup, which certainly guaranteed the betrayal of that undertaking. It was Holbrooke's impression that such necessary tricks did not bode well for the power of the United States. He hoped nothing happened to the passengers of the other convey.

In the *political* geology of the region divided into three conflict zones (Kashmir, Pakistan, and Afghan Hindu Kush), "frozen" and virulent crises clashed within a radius of roughly five hundred kilometers. Negotiations and provisional accords were of no avail there, Holbrooke believed, but he nevertheless deployed all of his abilities and eagerly anticipated his arrival at the designated village.

Ice fog blinded the driver. On the gravel road, which was hardly a road at all, the speed of the vehicles slowed considerably. The drivers turned on their parking lights so as to cause as little reflection as possible from the microscopic crystals carried by the fog.

> The giantess lies expecting
> Out came three wolves crawling
> She lies in between ice, fog and snow[12]

Holbrooke's End

Ambassador Holbrooke felt a flash of heat and then an unbearable pain on the left side of his chest. Naturally, he thought of signs of a heart attack. In the middle of a speech by Hillary Clinton in the privileged halls of the U.S. State Department, his own speech became unintelligible. He grasped his breast with one hand and his flank with the other. The secretary of state worried. The ambassador would seek out his doctor later in the day. Yes, this certainly needs to happen. In the meanwhile, the ambassador was able to get the pain under control.

The elevator from the secretary's floor to the ground level was restricted. No one can stop it, and no one else can get on. The elevator travels at dizzying speeds. The secretary assigned two of her assistants to the obviously sick ambassador. Called in over cell phone, a convoy brought the dying man to George Washington University Hospital.

The experienced surgeons knew how to deal with such extreme conditions. The chief surgeon needed only seconds to reach a diagnosis. In a short period of time, a tear in the aorta had formed a neoplasm leading to a pooling of blood between the outer and inner tissue of the vascular wall: an aneurysm that has the tendency of bursting the aorta. A fatal case. On top of the time spent racing him to the hospital, it took minutes to position the man on the operating table, to lay bare the area for the surgery, and to exchange two or three words (witty remarks) before he was sedated. "You've got to stop this war in Afghanistan." That was the dying man's witty reply to the chief surgeon's humorous comment. Teams from the renowned hospital operated in two shifts for twenty hours on the ambassador's front, middle, and side. His body, soul, or maybe the excessive demands he had endured took revenge on both his heart and the surgeons. In the wake of the operation, Holbrooke could not be brought out of his coma. Shocked mourners, heads of state, diplomats, and two U.S. presidents honored the deceased man by sharing his last words in their eulogies. We must not be sad, they said. We rejoice that he lived.

21,999 B.C.

Ice age. The peak of coldness (we still live in the same period of the Ice age, not the big one, but the little one) has to be imagined as a late afternoon in the Engadine Valley in December, said Alexej Tichonov, the science secretary

> of the committee on mammoths of the Russian Academy of Sciences. Not any colder? Asked Sylvie Charbit. Cold enough, especially when you have no fuel to burn and no shelter in which to hide.
>
> A weather forecast in those days would have read like this, the Russian continued: Europe is still stuck under its two-year high-pressure zone. Steady winds blown in from pack ice will bring dry air into the region. An end to the extreme dryness, to the continual wind from the northeast, and to the excessive dust is unlikely in the next four thousand years. At one in the afternoon today, the temperature will sink to the freezing point.
>
> And humans scurried across this dry steppe (with its grasses and nutritious herbage, but still lacking trees) that no longer exists today? Our ancestors, Tichonov replied, did not "scurry," but looked, searched, and hunted in a race with death. If they did not find something quickly, they died of hunger.

Circulatory Systems (*Kreisläufe*)

All living systems form circulatory systems. An elementary example is the human body. The image of the circulatory system repeats itself in all production processes, even in those such as educational and other social processes in which human characteristics are produced.

Identity (*Identität*)

The designation for a high degree of equilibrium that materializes in the heterogeneous characteristics of humans. They are, for example, both individual and social living beings. When such characteristics stabilize, we can speak of identity. This applies as well to any accord between thought, feeling, and circulation. A certain degree of identity is necessary for human self-confidence. Hegel, in his *Phenomenology of Spirit*, considers the question of identity in the form of Antigone. She represents the individual [*Einzelheit*] (family, the person, loving devotion toward her deceased brother, morals) vis-à-vis the universality [*Allgemeinheit*] of the sovereign Creon (the law, disciple, the renunciation of particularity).

Theory Labor (*Theoriearbeit*)

A synonym for "thinking" and "observing." In the last year of his life, Theodor W. Adorno formulated the emphatic concept of theory

labor in response to hasty political labor. Adorno directed the concept against the neglect of theory in the student movements: "Praxis
without theory...cannot but fail."[13]

Orientation (*Orientierung*)
According to Kant, the concept "orientation" is derived concretely
from positioning oneself according to astral constellations and horizons. In a figurative sense, determining horizons vis-à-vis the center
of experience (as well as the reciprocity between periphery and
center) is one of the most important elements of the faculty of judgment. We thus can speak of an "astronomy of the spirit."

Translated by Richard Langston and Cyrus Shahan

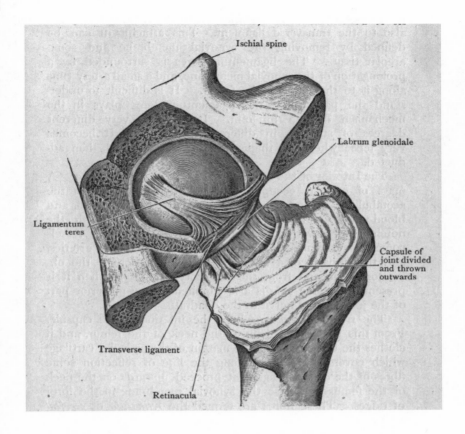

The femoral neck. The weak spot. Everyone knows that one day they will fall, and then this bone will break. "The violence of relationality." [D. J. Cunningham, *Manual of Practical Anatomy*, ed. Arthur Robinson, 5th ed. (New York: William Wood and Co., 1912), p. 255, fig. 78]

Notes

INTRODUCTION

Enduring thanks go to Leslie Adelson, Andreas Huyssen, and Tony Kaes for their generous feedback on earlier drafts of this text. I am especially grateful to the indefatigable Alexander Kluge, not just for the conversations that first animated this project, but also for the resourcefulness and commitment to see it to fruition.

1. Oskar Negt and Alexander Kluge, *Public Sphere and Experience: Toward an Analysis of the Bourgeois and Proletarian Public Sphere*, trans. Peter Labanyi, Jamie Daniel, and Assenka Oksiloff (Minneapolis: University of Minnesota Press, 1993), p. 247. Consider, especially, the transition from commentary 10, "Learning from Defeats?" to commentary 11, "The Temporal Structure of the Experience of Historical Struggles."

2. After *Public Sphere and Experience*, Negt and Kluge seem to have "abandoned the epithet *proletarian*, or even *oppositional*, in favor of an emphatic notion of *Öffentlichkeit*, defined by such principles as *open*-ness (the etymological root of *öffentlich*), freedom of access, multiplicity of relations, communicative interaction and self-reflection." Miriam Hansen, "Reinventing the Nickelodeon: Notes on Kluge and Early Cinema," *October* 46 (Autumn 1988), p. 184.

3. "This is why all the substations of [the bourgeois] public sphere are organized as arcane realms. The keyword 'confidential' prevents the transfer of social experience from one domain into another." *Public Sphere and Experience*, p. 16

4. "If *Public Sphere and Experience* still presented a more or less coherent theory—with narrative (anecdotal, parabolic) passages permeating both text and footnotes—*Geschichte und Eigensinn*, despite its comprehensive claim to theorize the historical, technical, and libidinal aspects of human labor power, to a certain extent demonstrates the limits of theory." Miriam Hansen, "Alexander Kluge: Crossings between Film, Literature, Critical Theory," in Sigrid Bauschinger, et al. (eds.), *Film und Literatur: Literarische Texte und der neue deutsche Film* (Bern: Francke Verlag, 1984), p. 176. One review of *History and Obstinacy* opened with a

443

line that captured this methodological sprawl even more bluntly: "It is no longer possible to consider Critical Theory a unified project." Andrew Bowie, "Review of Oskar Negt and Alexander Kluge, *Geschichte und Eigensinn*," *Ideas and Production* 1 (1983), p. 183.

5. Rainer Stollmann writes that "there may be a swarm of fans, but most of the volumes sold were left to starve on bookshelves only half-read. Thus, despite its commercial success, *History and Obstinacy* is also a message in a bottle—and one that still hasn't arrived." Stollman, "Vernunft ist ein Gefühl für Zusammenhang," in Christian Schulte and Rainer Stollmann (eds.), *Der Maulwurf kennt kein System: Beiträge zur gemeinsamen Philosophie von Oskar Negt und Alexander Kluge* (Bielefeld: transcript Verlag, 2005), p. 235.

6. It should be pointed out that neither Kluge nor Negt belong to the generation whose political consciousness was formed by the experiences of 1968. Born respectively in 1932 and 1934, they, like Jürgen Habermas, are members of the older generation of "'58ers." While this generation was considered less rebellious and more pragmatic than the younger, more radical '68ers, this pragmatism also made them less vulnerable to the disappointment that followed after 1968 and the attendant shift to conservatism. See Oskar Negt, *Achtundsechzig: Politische Intellektuelle und die Macht* (Göttingen: Steidl, 2001).

7. Michael Rutschky, *Erfahrungshunger: Ein Essay über die siebziger Jahre* (Frankfurt am Main: Fischer, 1982).

8. Alexander Kluge, *Lernprozesse mit tödlichem Ausgang* (Frankfurt am Main: Suhrkamp, 1973), p. 5.

9. Fernand Braudel, "History and the Social Sciences: *The Longue Durée*," in *On History*, trans. Sarah Matthews (Chicago: University of Chicago Press, 1980), p. 47. The "gloomy captivity" to which Braudel refers here are the years from 1940 to 1945.

10. Denis Hollier, "Desperanto," in *Absent Without Leave: French Literature under the Threat of War*, trans. Catherine Porter (Cambridge, MA: Harvard University Press, 1997), pp. 175–94.

11. "The world revolution had become very remote," Weiss's protagonist writes: "it would no longer be a unique act, it would now be a long-lasting process of class struggles, crowded with victories and defeats." Peter Weiss, *Aesthetics of Resistances*, trans. Joachim Neugroschel (Durham: Duke University Press, 2005), p. 101.

12. Taken from Hölderlin's poem "Der Gang aufs Land," the phrase "years of lead" was used by director Margarethe von Trotta to describe the 1970s. "Lead" refers both to the heaviness of the age and to the bullets of the Red Army Faction.

13. Michael Rutschky describes the 1970s as a decade of "hermeneutic predation" (*hermeneutischer Raubbau*), an era that extracted every potentially meaningful

aspect of existence from the life of the individual. According to Rutschky, the militarized extremism and wildcat tactics of the "negative heroes" of the Red Army Faction—designed to fracture and destabilize society, rather than to build coalitions and new contexts for living—were a logically consistent, albeit desperate response to this generalized loss of meaning. Rutschky, "Stücke zu einer Theorie des hermeneutischen Raubbaus," in *Erfahrungshunger*, pp. 138–64.

14. Alexander Kluge, *Nachrichten aus der ideologischen Antike* (2008), liner notes, p. 7. He observes in an interview with Thomas Combrink that stars are valuable for orientation because they are remote and cannot be influenced. Alexander Kluge, *Glückliche Umstände, leihweise: Das Lesebuch*, ed. Thomas Combrink (Frankfurt am Main: Suhrkamp, 2008), pp. 331–52.

15. About the consumers of capitalism's industrial culture, Bertolt Brecht writes: "Since the object of exploitation is put inside them, they are, so to speak, victims of 'imploitation [*Einbeutung*].'" Brecht, "Der Dreigroschenprozess. Ein soziologisches Experiment," in *Werke: Grosse kommentierte Berliner und Frankfurter Ausgabe*, ed. Werner Hecht, 30 vols. (Frankfurt am Main: Suhrkamp, 1988–), vol. 21, p. 476; Brecht, "The *Threepenny* Lawsuit," in *Brecht on Film and Radio*, ed. and trans. Marc Silberman (London: Methuen, 2000), p. 170.

16. Negt and Kluge, *Public Sphere and Experience*, p. xlvi.

17. Kluge notes that when they began the collaboration that would eventually yield *Public Sphere and Experience*, "we quickly became aware that the essential and substantial realms of human experience are actually not organized publicly. Take intimacy, first of all. Where my family is, how I grew up as a child, what I love, what I hate. All of that is actually not organized publicly, but intimately. That is where it gets decided whether I have cause to be autonomous and self-confident or whether I carry around with me experiences of lack. The second realm, almost as large, is that of labor. It, too, is organized in private. Each person is isolated from the next. If you want to go into a factory, you are stopped at the gate." Alexander Kluge and Oskar Negt, "Öffentlichkeit als wertvolles Gut und die Idee der Gegenöffentlichkeit," in *Maßverhältnisse des Politischen: Öffentlichkeit und Erfahrung an der Schwelle zum 21. Jahrhundert*, ed. Hans-Peter Burmeister (Loccum: Rehburg-Loccum Evangelische Akademie, 2003), p. 41.

18. An important campaign in Willi Münzenberg's efforts to develop a proletarian counterpublic sphere in the 1920s and 1930s was his appeal to workers to photograph the factory interiors where they worked—sites of labor that, because of industrial espionage laws, could not be represented publicly. Münzenberg's call to document the industrial workplace became a cornerstone of the worker photography movement in Weimar Germany and led to the founding of its primary organ, *Der Arbeiter-Fotograf*, in 1926. In *Public Sphere and Experience*, which revives many

aspects of Münzenberg's project, Negt and Kluge explain that under the rule of bourgeois society, labor and production were not just unrepresentable legally, but also literally incommunicable: the proletarian context of experience "is rendered 'incomprehensible' in terms of social communication: ultimately, it becomes a private experience." Negt and Kluge, *Public Sphere and Experience*, p. 18.

19. Oskar Negt, *Der politische Mensch: Demokratie als Lebenform* (Göttingen: Steidl, 2010), p. 292. This process had in fact already taken place in Germany's recent, albeit repressed, historical past: a glance at the "total mobilization" of the National Socialists provided a perfect example of a regime that had incorporated the realms of production and family into its public sphere all too successfully—although hardly with the salutary effects that Negt and Kluge predicted. "In *Public Sphere and Experience*, the concept of a public sphere of production is applied narrowly to the realm of the media. While we were writing *History and Obstinacy*, we realized that this was actually much too limited a concept and that a public sphere of production ultimately encompasses all structures of a society that have been made public. For example, during the Third Reich, the public sphere experienced something like a boost in production and began, in all of its aspects, to incorporate things that had been excluded as 'private' from the classical bourgeois public sphere, taking not only from war production but also the structure of the family.... The Third Reich's public sphere of production incorporates everything that the bourgeois public sphere had shut out. Family is practically a public institution in the Third Reich, a public mission: Crosses of Honor, for example, are awarded to mothers for a certain number of children. Sovereign authorities penetrate the private sphere at the most practical levels. The operations manager has a position in the social hierarchy, and everything that, from the perspective of emancipation, we had conceived as a proletarian public sphere, is integrated into the Third Reich's public sphere of production." Oskar Negt, "Der Maulwurf kennt kein System: Oskar Negt im Gespräch mit Rainer Stollmann und Christian Schulte," in *Der Maulwurf kennt kein System*, p. 26.

20. Until the emergence of neoliberalism, bourgeois economics had been a quantitative science that was largely focused on calculating the laws and periodicities of fixed machine capital. Foucault writes that neoliberalism, by contrast, began to take into account the "qualitative modulations" of human capital, that is, living labor power that has not "been cut off from its human reality, from all its qualitative variables." Unlike classical economics, then, the neoliberals shared with Marx an interest in the neglected anthropology of labor, although their analysis of the qualitative and behavioral features of flexible (human) capital came to conclusions that were quite different, if not fundamentally opposed, to those of Marx. "And it is precisely because classical economics was not able to take on

this analysis of labor in its concrete specification and qualitative modulations, it is because it left this blank page, gap or vacuum in its theory, that a whole philosophy, anthropology, and politics, of which Marx is precisely the representative, rushed in." Michel Foucault, *The Birth of Biopolitics: Lectures as the Collège de France 1978–1979*, trans. Graham Burchell (New York: Palgrave Macmillan, 2004), p. 221.

21. *Ibid.*, p. 231.

22. Oskar Negt and Alexander Kluge, *Maßverhältnisse des Politischen*, in *Der unterschätzte Mensch*, 2 vols. (Frankfurt am Main: Zweitausendeins, 2001), vol. 1, p. 800.

23. This analysis is in fact already anticipated in lines from the last chapter of *Public Sphere and Experience*: "In terms of arms buildup, war, and competition, National Socialism follows classical imperialism.... At the same time, that which in classical bourgeois society falls outside the framework of the public sphere — the horizon of experience and the consciousness of the masses, which originated under repressive conditions — is drawn into a process of mobilization" (pp. 166–67). Further: "The present scope of capitalist countries' foreign spheres of influence appears, compared with classical imperialism and the imperialism of the 1930s, to be fundamentally restricted. It is true that the so-called underdeveloped territories become, as before, objects of exploitation.... But the capitalist countries are no longer faced with the alternatives, in the traditional sense, either to start wars against one another or collapse. New alternatives are provided through a higher level of organization of capital in supranational economic blocs such as the EEC, capital absorption, inflationary tendencies, and redistribution between the economic, political, national, and supranational sphere of complexes of contradictions that contain the potential for crisis. Imperialism is directing its energies inward. In the urban areas above all, it turns even human beings and their contexts of living into an intensified object of imperialist expansion and of the higher concentration of valorization" (p. 170).

24. In this particular regard, the course of Germany's modernization more closely resembles that of its neighbors to the east than that of European countries. Negt and Kluge observe, for example, that the "introversion of labor capacities" distinguishes Germany from "every other European country *besides* Russia." *Geschichte und Eigensinn*, in *Der unterschätzte Mensch*, vol. 2, p. 632; italics added. Indeed, many scholars have similarly noted that Russia's development followed a course of so-called internal colonization in which Russia was at once "both the subject and the object of colonization." Alexander Etkind, *Internal Colonization: Russia's Imperial Experience* (Cambridge: Polity, 2011), p. 2. See also Alvin W. Gouldner, "Stalinism: A Study of Internal Colonialism," *Telos* 34 (1978), pp. 5–48. It is perhaps not surprising to observe, as the biopolitical corollary to this project

of internal colonization, an explosion of interest in the anthropotechnical project of creating *Homo sovieticus*—a "higher sociobiological type"—in Russia after 1917. On the "New Soviet Man," see Lev Trotskii, "Iskusstvo revoliutsii i sotsialis-ticheskoe iskusstvo," in *Literatura i revoliutsiia* (1923; Moscow: Politizdat, 1991), pp. 177–97.

25. "A human is being made," proclaims the doctor's assistant. Negt gives a close reading of this line ("Es wird ein Mensch gemacht") in *Die Faust-Karriere: Vom verzweifelten Intellektuellen zum gescheiterten Unternehmer* (Göttingen: Steidl, 2006), pp. 182–200. On the construction of the canal and the doctor's transformation into a capitalist entrepreneur in *Faust II*, Negt writes: "This questioning [of the sovereignty of nature in the time of Goethe] extends to the concept of the human, as well, as in the case of the homunculus that is produced, but also to the external relationship to nature, to the domination of the wild forces of nature, of vulcanism and of neptunism. However, this cannot be achieved with the broadside of force, as Hegel said, but only indirectly, through channels and systems of tubes. In order to be able to defeat forces of nature that are beyond the human, it is necessary to mobilize the forces of nature that are themselves human" (pp. 211–12).

26. Negt writes that the German imaginary, in both its myth and its literature, has always been preoccupied with the distinction between inside and outside. It seems that other national imaginaries do not exhibit the same obsession with this boundary. "The loss of control over the relations between inner and outer, between the inner world of the house and of the family, on the one hand, and society, political institutions, and the state, on the other: has this been especially pronounced in German history down to the present day? I do not know, but it is astonishing how many stories, plays, tragedies, and novels have taken this imbalance between inner and outer as their subject matter. The territories and kingdoms that engage with the inner world of the subject—with the noumenon, the intelligible, the space of pure purpose and freedom—have had an immense scope in German literature." Negt, *Die Faust-Karriere*, pp. 48–49. Further: "The world of German fairy tales is full of themes that circle around the broken connection between inner and outer, between revolution and obstinacy. Again and again, people have pointed out that we live in a country that occasionally lapses into a phase of political depression whenever those who have power in this world use excessive force to retaliate against the obstinacy of the populace and the public audacity of its claim to political participation" (*ibid.*, p. 157).

On this point, it is intriguing to note Rutschky's claim that the ideological disorientation of the 1970s was caused by a disturbance in the mental "schematic dividing the internal and external worlds." Rutschky, *Erfahrungshunger*, p. 48. In his analysis of the 1970s, Rutschky also rephrases this distinction between internal

and external as the difference between warmth and cold (pp. 41–43), two categories that have been central to Negt's own theorization. On warmth and cold, see
Negt's introduction to *Kältestrom* (Göttingen: Steidl, 1994), pp. 3–20.

27. As Jean-Pierre Vernant observed, myth is a vital resource for humanity: its
language "represents a way of arranging reality, a kind of classification and setting
in order of the world, a preliminary logical arrangement, in sum an instrument of
thought." Vernant, "The Reason of Myth," in *Myth and Society in Ancient Greece*,
trans. Janet Lloyd (New York: Zone Books, 1990), p. 255. In a similar vein, the
playwright Heiner Müller describes myth as "coagulated collective experiences"
(geronnene kollektive Erfahrungen), a phrase that echoes Marx's famous definition of capital as "coagulated collective labor" (geronnene kollektive Arbeit). See
Müller, *Krieg ohne Schlacht: Eine Autobiographie*, in *Werke*, ed. Frank Hörnigk, 13
vols. (Frankfurt am Main: Suhrkamp, 1998–2001), vol. 9, p. 321. On myth as a form
of collective noetic labor, see Hans Blumenberg's important book, *Work on Myth*,
trans. Robert M. Wallace (Cambridge, MA: The MIT Press, 1985). Not incidentally,
Blumenberg's account of the anthropological sources of mythical thinking in this
book builds on the work of the philosopher Arnold Gehlen, who defined the human
organism as a *Mängelwesen*, "deficient being," that needs elements that can distance
and buffer it from the shocks of experience in the immediate present. As we will
see below, Gehlen's understanding of humans as deficient beings is central also to
the anthropology of Negt and Kluge. For Gehlen and Blumenberg, myth provides
Entlastung, "relief," for a being that would otherwise be paralyzed and crushed by
the exigencies of reality (*Weltzwang*). By giving anthropomorphic form to the "chaos
of the unnamed" and thereby particularizing our existential dread, myth ruptures
the "absolutism of reality," Blumenberg explains. "The organic system resulting
from the mechanism of evolution becomes 'man' by evading the pressure of that
mechanism by setting against it something like a phantom body. This is the sphere of
his culture, his institutions—and also his myth." Blumenberg, *Work on Myth*, p. 165.

28. Fredric Jameson, "On Negt and Kluge," *October* 46 (Autumn 1988), pp.
151–77.

29. Raymond Williams, "Base and Superstructure in Marxist Cultural Theory," in *Problems in Materialism and Culture* (London: Verso, 1980), p. 35.

30. Negt and Kluge, *Public Sphere and Experience*, p. xlviii.

31. Despite the resemblances between *A Thousand Plateaus* and *History and
Obstinacy*, Deleuze and Guattari's book had no direct influence on Negt and Kluge's
collaboration. *A Thousand Plateaus* appeared one year before, and there scarcely
would have been time to write a book of 1283 pages in such a short period of time.
Interviews with Negt and Kluge in 1980 indicate that work on *History and Obstinacy*
already had started long before the appearance of Deleuze and Guattari's book.

32. On the resemblances between *History and Obstinacy* and Engels's *Dialectics of Nature*, see Rudolf Burger's review of Negt and Kluge, "Die Mikrophysik des Widerstands," *Ästhetik und Kommunikation*, no. 48 (1982), pp. 110–24, esp. pp. 118–20. For a Deleuze-inspired materialist history that is comparable to—although significantly less dialectical than—Negt and Kluge's *History and Obstinacy*, see Manuel de Landa, *A Thousand Years of Nonlinear History* (New York: Zone Books, 1997).

33. Kluge, *Nachrichten von der ideologischen Antike*, liner notes, p. 6.

34. "The methodological difficulty of developing a *political economy of the labor force* is as follows: since capital reduces the labor force to an abstract expenditure, we are dealing with an object of knowledge that is more or less uniform; there is only *one* political economy of capital, only *one* law of motion observed by the capitalist mode of production. But the political economy of the labor force behaves in an entirely different way: this is not a matter of simply describing capacities or of objective laws of motion that have been split off from the subject, but instead involves *two* aspects, namely, the subjective and the objective at the same time; for this reason, *every* subject-object relationship that is caused by the exteriorization and separation [*Äußerung und Entäußerung*] of a social labor force entails its own specific law of motion. Just as there is one political economy for the body, there is also one for intelligence, one for the psychic apparatus, and one for the senses." Negt and Kluge, *Maßverhältnisse*, p. 772.

35. "Actually what we need is *Homo compensator*, not *Homo sapiens*. *Homo sapiens* develops a particularly one-sided kind of rational conduct, of emotional omnipotency in the way that it applies its intelligence. We need an equilibrator [*Gleichgewichtler*] who balances between man's different characteristics with a delicate sense of feeling, with the *sole of his foot* that is at home *in his ear*." These last two organs are important, respectively, to the proprioceptive and vestbular systems, two sources that provide us with sensory feedback about the balance, movement, and orientation of the body. Kluge, in Rainer Stollmann, *Die Entstehung des Schönheitssinns aus dem Eis: Gespräche über Geschichten mit Alexander Kluge* (Berlin: Kadmos: 2005), p. 46.

36. See p. 134 in the present volume. Elsewhere, Negt describes the various balance labors of this welder as follows: "she is not working precisely at those moments when the Taylorist would say that she is working. She solders her small parts as an extended arm of dead labor, as an appendage of a mechanized operation. At that moment, she does almost nothing. Unless she is thinking something to herself or listening to music in order to endure it. When the capitalist purchases the labor force of this woman, his job is already over. In his mind, he already sees the completed work. For the woman, the labor with herself is just beginning. She is a life-form that must first integrate itself into the operation. To do that, she

has to transform herself, to accomplish an act of balance. This is not simple. She could also refuse. She has to carry out an entire sequence of labors to bring herself to go into a factory that does not conform to her nature." Oskar Negt, in "Die Geschichte der lebendigen Arbeitskraft: Diskussion mit Oskar Negt und Alexander Kluge," *Ästhetik und Kommunikation* 13.48 (1983), p. 88.

37. *Ibid.*, p. 89.

38. See Chapter 1, p. 94, in the present volume.

39. Although the conservative thinker Gehlen was publicly denounced by the Left, he is occasionally referred to in the work of Negt and Kluge. Negt discusses him in *Der politische Mensch*, pp. 373–74 and invokes him again in *Die Faust-Karriere*, where he compares the Gehlen's anthropology of the "deficient being" to Freud's definition of man as a "prosthetic god." With reference to Goethe's *Faust*, Negt writes that "the main character is not Faust, but Mephisto, the one who points out that the deficient being called man, with his anthropologically meager equipment, demands as part of his very nature a social project of organ substitution, organ extension, and organ supplementation. Thus the anthropologist Arnold Gehlen pointed to a way out through an expansion of man's powers using substitute organs that conform to the 'prosthetic god's' form of life; however, these helpful supplementary organs can be produced only through social labor and by enriching individual capacities to form reality" (p. 194). One discovers aspects of the philosophical anthropology of Gehlen in many contemporary Leftist projects, from Étienne Balibar's revival of philosophical anthropology as a model for defining citizenship in a postnationalist era to Bernard Stiegler's synthesis of Heideggerian phenomenology with the paleoanthropology of André Leroi-Gourhan.

40. Arnold Gehlen, *Der Mensch: Seine Natur und seine Stellung in der Welt*, in *Gesamtausgabe*, ed. Karl-Siegbert Rehberg, 7 vols. (Frankfurt: Vittorio Klostermann, 1993), vol. 3, p. 14; available in English as *Man: His Nature and Place in the World*, trans. Clare McMillan and Karl Pillemer (New York: Columbia University Press, 1988), p. 12.

41. In correspondence with Wolfgang Harich, a member of the Lukács circle, Gehlen observed in the early 1950s that the notion of action (*Handlung*) that he had developed in his analysis of the "deficient being" played the same role as labor in Marxist theory. Indeed, close examination reveals more theoretical correspondences between Gehlen and Marxist thought than have previously been acknowledged. Reinhard Pitsch, "Institution und Subjektivität: Die Tragik Gehlens und der Marxisten," *Sezession* 4 (January 2004), p. 44.

42. Gehlen discusses our underdeveloped organs and juvenile characteristics in detail in the first chapters of *Man*. On extrauterine gestation and neoteny in human development, see the work of the Swiss zoologist Adolf Portmann,

especially his *Biologische Fragment zu einer Lehre vom Menschen* (Basel: Schwabe, 1944), which influenced Gehlen's own research immensely. In this text, Portmann writes that "after one year, man has achieved a level of development which a true mammal must effect at birth. For man's situation to correspond to that of true mammals, pregnancy would have to continue a year longer than it actually does; it would have to last approximately 21 months." Gehlen comments: "The newborn is thus a type of 'physiological,' or normalized, premature infant, a 'secondary nestling.'" Gehlen, *Man*, p. 36.

43. Sigmund Freud, *Gesammelte Werke*, ed. Anna Freud et al., 19 vols. (Frankfurt am Main: Fischer, 1964–1968), vol. 14, p. 49; *The Standard Edition of the Complete Psychological Works*, ed. and trans. James Strachey, 24 vols. (London: Hogarth Press, 1953–1974), vol. 21, p. 91.

44. At one point, Negt and Kluge considered titling their collected writings, with reference to Freud's formulation, *Man as a Prosthetic God*. Negt, "Der Maulwurf kennt kein System," p. 11.

45. Kluge, in Kluge and Negt, "Öffentlichkeit als wertvolles Gut und die Idee der Gegenöffentlichkeit," p. 42.

46. Gehlen later conceded that his original account in *Man* had underestimated the power of drives and instincts in humans.

47. Walter Benjamin, "One-Way Street," trans. Edmund Jephcott, in *Selected Writings, Volume 1, 1913–1926*, ed. Marcus Bullock and Michael Jennings (Cambridge, MA: Harvard University Press, 1996), p. 487, translation modified.

48. Bernard Stiegler, *Technics and Time*, trans. Richard Beardsworth and George Collins, 3 vols. (Stanford: Stanford University Press, 1998–2011).

49. Negt observes that "*democracy is the only politically conceived social order that has to be learned*, over and over, every day, into old age. For Aristotle, who defines man as a *zoon politikon* (a political life-form), this sounds like a sort of anthropological constant, but in truth, this doesn't designate the final product of a natural development, but a direction and a result of a process of education and of learning. The definition of man as a *zoon politikon* has as its *goal* a *life-form* rooted in the free self-determination of citizens who are capable of autonomy. Only gods and animals can live *outside of* the *polis*, thus, without politics." Negt, *Der politische Mensch*, p. 13.

50. Giorgio Agamben, *The Open: Man and Animal*, trans. Kevin Attell (Stanford: Stanford University Press, 2004), p. 13.

51. Sophocles, *Antigone*, in *Sophocles I*, ed. and trans. David Grene (Chicago: University of Chicago Press, 1991), ll. 368–69. Negt discusses these two lines in *Die Faust-Karriere*, p. 39. The stasimon of the chorus continues by moving through the manifold expressions of man's pluripotentiality: he crosses water,

transforms the earth, tames animals and influences their genetics, cultivates speech and thought, and builds cities and other shelters to defy the elements. "He has a way against everything [παντοπόρος: all-inventive], / and he faces nothing that is to come / without contrivance," (ll. 393–96). In his reading of *Antigone*, Jacques Lacan points out the striking conjunction of two contrasting words in this last phrase, without any interpunctuation — παντοπόρος ("all-inventive") and ἄπορος (the opposite of the previous word, meaning one who has "no resources or defenses against something," or as Lacan rephrases it, "one that is 'screwed'"). Lacan thus summarizes the status of the deficient being as follows: "He advances toward nothing that is likely to happen, he advances and he is παντοπόρος, 'artful,' but he is ἄπορος, always 'screwed.'" Lacan, *The Seminar of Jacques Lacan. Book VII: The Ethics of Psychoanalysis, 1959–1960*, ed. Jacques-Alain Miller, trans. Dennis Porter (New York: W. W. Norton, 1992), pp. 274–75.

52. In his 1926 essay "Inhibitions, Symptoms, and Anxiety," Freud noted that the "intrauterine existence of the human seems to be short in comparison with that of most animals, and it is sent into the world in a less finished state. As a result the influence of the real external world upon it is intensified and an early differentiation between the ego and the id is promoted. Moreover, the dangers of the external world have a greater importance for it, so that the value of the object which can alone protect it against them and take the place of its former intrauterine life is enormously enhanced. The biological factor, then, establishes the earliest situations of danger and creates the need to be loved which will accompany the child through the rest of its life." Freud, *Gesammelte Werke*, vol. 14, p. 200; *The Standard Edition*, vol. 20, pp. 154–55.

53. Returning to Aristotle's definition of man as *zoon politikon* ("the being naturally living by and for the city"), Étienne Balibar similarly observes that "the human subject is able concretely to meet the essence of its 'humanity' only within a *civic*, or *political*, horizon in the broad sense of the term." Balibar, "Subjection and Subjectivation," in *Supposing the Subject*, ed. Joan Copjec (London: Verso, 1994), p. 8.

54. Karl Marx, *Grundrisse*, trans. Martin Nikolaus (New York: Penguin Books, 1973), p. 84.

55. See p. 94 in the present volume.

56. This line appears only in the second edition. Oskar Negt and Alexander Kluge, *Geschichte und Eigensinn*, 2nd ed., 3 vols. (Frankfurt am Main: Suhrkamp Verlag, 1993), vol. 1, p. 17. In this way, it could be said that the broken bone of the individual fortifies the backbone of the species. To offer a related example: in response to the recent discovery of the skull of a male *Homo erectus* who had lived for years without teeth, paleoanthropologists have concluded that this individual

could have survived only with the help of companions who prepared food for him. As a result, this skull has come to represent for some the earliest evidence of human compassion and community. John Nobile Wilford, "Some See Roots of Compassion in a Toothless Fossil Skull," *New York Times*, April 6, 2005.

57. Gehlen, *Man*, p. 25

58. This is the subtitle of Kluge's fourth book *Neue Geschichten: Hefte 1–18: "Unheimlichkeit der Zeit"* (Frankfurt am Main: Suhrkamp, 1977).

59. Stiegler, *Technics and Time*, vol. 1, p. 172.

60. Alexander Kluge, *Tür an Tür mit einem anderen Leben: 350 neue Geschichten* (Frankfurt am Main: Suhrkamp, 2006), p. 9.

61. Alexander Kluge, *Die Lücke, die der Teufel lässt: Im Umfeld des neuen Jahrhunderts* (Frankfurt am Main: Suhrkamp, 2003) p. 319.

62. Alexander Kluge, "Die Macht der Bewußtseinsindustrie und das Schicksal unserer Öffentlichkeit," in *Industrialisierung des Bewußtseins: Eine kritische Auseinandersetzung mit den "neuen" Medien*, ed. Klaus von Bismarck, Günter Gaus, Alexander Kluge, and Ferdinand Sieger (Munich: Piper, 1985), p. 75. Negt likewise emphasizes the close connection between slow learning and political obstinacy: "I am someone who learns slowly, and since I have managed to extract this knowledge only through great effort, it makes sense that I am not inclined to give it up quickly." Negt, "Vorwort," in *Unbotmäßige Zeitgenossen: Annäherungen und Erinnerungen* (Frankfurt am Main: Fischer, 1994).

63. Kluge, "Die Macht der Bewußtseinsindustrie," p. 82.

64. Thus, for example, the impossibility, or at least extreme improbability, of reciprocity in love: "Feelings take time to develop. It therefore seems unlikely that love at first sight is mutual. An emotion erupts that has been building up for a long time, enriched by fantasy, by stories one has heard; yes, love at first sight, but only for one; the other feels magically attracted to the prey that is just lying there. He acts like one in love. Thus, in appearance at least: love at first sight. Yet, one of them is investing the whole weight of his or her life, whereas the other, happy-go-lucky, merely seized an opportunity." Alexander Kluge, "On Opera, Film, and Feelings," ed. Miriam Hansen, *New German Critique* 49 (Winter 1990), pp. 95–96.

65. "Since the libido is blind, it doesn't even notice when it starts to do something else than what it was originally doing." Kluge, *Die Entstehung des Schönheitssinns aus dem Eis*, p. 87.

66. Kluge points out in "Die Macht der Bewußtseinsindustrie" that there are divisions to be overcome even within the architecture of the brain itself—synapses, gaps, and cameralisms in the neural pathways that impede the frictionless circulation of data (p. 78). As a result, sensation and intellection always involve a process of translation—"and *that* is a theoretical moment" notes Dirk Baecker in

"Wozu Theorie?: Dirk Baecker und Rainer Stollmann über Kritische und System-theorie," in *Der Maulwurf kennt kein System*, p. 69.

67. Negt and Kluge, *Maßverhältnisse*, p. 990.

' 68. Bernhard Siegert, *Relays: Literature as an Epoch of the Postal System*, trans. Kevin Repp (Stanford: Stanford University Press, 1999).

69. Kluge, "Die Macht der Bewußtseinsindustrie," p. 79.

70. Klaus Eder and Alexander Kluge, *Ulmer Dramaturgien: Reibungsverluste* (Munich: Hanser, 1980), p. 48. On the priority of writing over vision in Kluge's work, see also Hansen, "Alexander Kluge: Crossings between Film, Literature, Critical Theory."

71. "Even at the times when I was making films, books have always been for me the actual form of enclosure [*Gehäuse*]." Alexander Kluge, "*Die Chronik der Gefühle*: Lesung mit Kommentaren," in *Maßverhältnisse des Politischen: Öffentlichkeit und Erfahrung an der Schwelle des 21. Jahrhunderts,* ed. Hans-Peter Burmeister, p. 79.

72. Kluge explains: "Cinematic projection is based on an illumination of 1/48th of a second, which is followed by a phase of darkness that lasts 1/48th of a second, the so-called 'transport phase.'" "Die Macht der Bewußtseinsindustrie," p. 105.

73. Jean-Paul Sartre, "Consciousness and Imagination," in *The Imaginary: A Phenomenological Psychology of the Imagination*, trans. Jonathan Webber (New York: Routledge, 2004), pp. 179–87.

74. Karl Marx, *Capital, Volume One*, trans. Ben Fowkes (London: New Left Review, 1976), p. 284.

75. Alexander Kluge, in conversation with David Roberts, "Alexander Kluge and German History: 'The Air Raid on Halberstadt on 8.4.1945," in Tara Forrest (ed.), *Alexander Kluge: Raw Materials for the Imagination* (Amsterdam: Amsterdam University Press, 2012), p. 145.

76. Alexander Kluge, *Die Patriotin* (Frankfurt am Main: Zweitausendeins, 1979), p. 294.

77. Dirk Baecker and Alexander Kluge, *Vom Nutzen ungelöster Probleme* (Berlin: Merve, 2003), p. 12. Similarly, Joseph Vogl remarks in conversation with Kluge that "freedom consists less in acting spontaneously than in interrupting the chains of action, the functional courses, and the automatisms once they have already been triggered. Uncoupling." Alexander Kluge and Joseph Vogl, *Soll und Haben: Fernsehgespräche* (Berlin: Diaphanes, 2009), p. 8.

78. Alexander Kluge, "On Film and the Public Sphere," trans. Thomas Y. Levin, *New German Critique* 24–25 (Autumn 1981–Winter 1982), p. 209

79. On scarring, sensory withdrawal, and the genesis of stupidity, see Avital Ronell, *Stupidity* (Chicago: University of Illinois Press, 2002) and Birgit Erdle,

"Thinking in Times of Danger: Adorno on Stupidity," *The Germanic Review: Literature, Culture, Theory* 88.3, pp. 260–70.

80. Theodor W. Adorno, *Gesammelte Schriften*, ed. Rolf Tiedemann, 20 vols. (Frankfurt am Main: Suhrkamp Verlag, 1997), vol. 6, p. 9.

81. Kluge traces the human capacity for ideation and mental representation—the "cinema of the mind," as he calls it—to the Pleistocene era: "Since the Ice Age approximately (or earlier), streams of images, of so-called associations, have moved through the human mind, prompted to some extent by an anti-realistic attitude, by the protest against an unbearable reality.... This is the more-than-ten-thousand-year-old-cinema to which the invention of the film strip, projector and screen have only provided a technological response." Kluge, "On Film and the Public Sphere," p. 209.

82. Negt and Kluge, *Maßverhältnisse*, p. 888.

83. See Elmar Altvater, Frigga Haug, and Oskar Negt (eds.), *Turbo-Kapitalismus: Gesellschaft im Übergang ins 21. Jahrhundert* (Hamburg: VSA, 1997).

84. Negt and Kluge, *Maßverhältnisse*, p. 962. Similarly: "The impossibility of technologically processing data in real time is the possibility of art. Literature, as an art of human beings, is a gift of interception, which operates on the basis of feedback loops between human senses and the postal materiality of data processing known as the alphabet.... Literature is implied in the postponement of sending as the possibility for interception by the senses." Siegert, *Relays*, p. 12.

85. "In his book *Sculpting in Time* (the Russian title [*Zapechatlennoe vremia*] means "captured" or "preserved time," time that has been transported in time), Andrei Tarkovsky speaks of film as a 'matrix' of real time. Henceforth, time that has been viewed and captured could 'be preserved in metal tins' for a long (theologically, even an eternally long) time." Kluge, "Die Macht der Bewußtseinsindustrie," p. 106.

86. Kluge calls for us to reconsider the potentially progressive aspects of auratic experience. Benjamin "claims that theater is still on the side of the classical arts, while film exceeds this classical framework. It has no aura, he claims. Here Benjamin's assessment is an exaggeration.... At the opposite pole of duration and singularity—those are what produce aura—are ephemerality and iterability. Benjamin does not understand them as negative concepts. They are just irreconcilable with duration and singularity." Kluge, "Die Macht der Bewußtseinsindustrie," pp. 72–73. "I require time for everything. It part of the work of art to produce time out of itself. This has been confused with aura, with the veneration that we show to them—meaning that we are supposed to destroy this as a myth, or declare it for dead" (p. 107).

87. *Ibid.*, p. 104.

88. See Negt, *Kältestrom*. Also see Joseph Vogl, *Kalkül und Leidenschaft: Poetik des ökonomischen Menschen* (Munich: Sequenzia, 2002).

89. "In Marx," Fredric Jameson observes, *Trennung* means "above all, the historical 'separation' of the producer from the means of production (as well as from the produced object and from production itself as my own activity). This is for Marx, of course, the central structural feature of the historical catastrophe at the very origin of capitalism, namely, so-called 'primitive accumulation.' There is, therefore, already in Marx a mediation between a form of production and a historical event. Negt and Kluge will now project this event—primitive accumulation—along with its structural concept—*Trennung*, division and separation—into a more general historical and philosophical one, which designates all the catastrophes of history, most crucially at its beginning and in the destruction of traditional agricultural and communal societies." Jameson, "On Negt and Kluge," p. 160.

90. Ernst Bloch, *Erbschaft dieser Zeit*, in *Werkausgabe*, 16 vols. (Frankfurt am Main: Suhrkamp, 1985), vol. 4, p. 106; Bloch, *Heritage of Our Times*, trans. Neville Plaice and Stephen Plaice (Berkeley: University of California Press, 1990), p. 99.

91. As a primitive archetype of nonalienated production, Negt and Kluge evoke a scene of natural labor in which the working body is connected organically to the land. Thus, Negt avers that a "farmer in the Middle Ages realized the properties of his labor by interacting with the field or with animals, by observing the weather; these were of course all very important labor properties, on which the success of the harvest depended. This farmer had to develop aptitudes and properties that were decisive for the success of his process of production. The properties of this labor were embedded in a working and living community that occurred naturally; they did not exist apart from this context and did not need to find an object through which to be realized. But with the process of primitive accumulation, with the division between earth and polity, the status of labor properties in the historical context of objects changed fundamentally.... Labor as a category of reality, *Arbeit sans phrase*, labor as mere labor capacity—that is a modern category." Negt and Kluge, "Die Geschichte der lebendigen Arbeitskraft," p. 93.

92. Marx, *Capital, Volume One*, p. 874.

93. "All of these new characteristics that make up industrialized man and that have defined a civilization for several hundred years are characteristics that have their roots in the old conditions that *precede* expropriation; preserved from the expropriation, they then become the answers to expropriation." Oskar Negt and Alexander Kluge, *Suchbegriffe*, in *Der unterschätzte Mensch*, vol. 1, pp. 286–87.

94. On primitive accumulation as a strategy of continuous expropriation, see also David Harvey, *The New Imperialism* (Oxford: Oxford University Press, 2005).

95. Tony Brown, "The Time of Globalization: Rethinking Primitive Accumulation," *Rethinking Marxism* 21.4 (October 2009), p. 571.

96. Jim Glassman, "Primitive Accumulation, Accumulation by Dispossession, Accumulation by 'Extra-Economic' Means," *Progress in Human Geography* 30.5 (2006), p. 615.

97. Negt, "Der Maulwurf kennt kein System," p. 13.

98. In chapter 10 of *Capital*, "On the Working Day," Marx recalls the case of Mary Anne Walkley, a millner who was worked to death in 1863. The account of her demise vividly illustrates the consequences of allowing capital to dominate the pattern of work rhythms without providing time for the reproduction of labor power, for the organic maintenance of life. Without the compensatory flight of becoming bird, the becoming machine of Taylorized labor is unsustainable.

99. Negt and Kluge take this phrase from Michel Foucault, *Discipline and Punish: The Birth of the Prison*, trans. Alan Sheridan (New York: Vintage, 1995).

100. Negt, *Der politische Mensch*, p. 259. Kluge similarly notes that the essential powers of human capital unfold within a temporality that is notably slower than the abstract time of machine capital. He remarks in an interview: "With Oskar Negt, I often labored on the question of whether there exists a political economy of labor, as capital's polar opposite. For labor can express itself much better than capital; it is not abstract at all. At the same time, human qualities—man's essential powers, as Marx calls them—develop so slowly that we must observe them with much greater diligence than the very rapid and sweeping processes of capital we are witnessing now, for instance." Gertrud Koch, "Undercurrents of Capital: An Interview with Alexander Kluge," *The Germanic Review: Literature, Culture, Theory* 84.4 (2010), p. 361. Especially now, in the age of turbocapitalism, the organic rhythms of living labor are increasingly in direct conflict with the mechanical algorithms of capital.

101. On bioderegulation, see Teresa Brennan, *Exhausting Modernity: Grounds for a New Economy* (New York: Routledge, 2000) and Jonathan Crary, *24/7: Late Capitalism and the Ends of Sleep* (London: Verso, 2013). For a discussion of the temporal deformations introduced by fixed capital, see "The Time of Capital: Three Industrial Novels," in Devin Fore, *Realism after Modernism: The Rehumanization of Art and Literature* (Cambridge, MA: MIT Press, 2012), pp. 75–132.

102. Oskar Negt and Alexander Kluge, *Geschichte und Eigensinn*, p. 335.

103. In 1852, Marx used the trope of the old mole to describe the process of revolutionary advancement—slow and subterranean, but thereby also systematic and ineluctable: "the revolution is thorough. It is still on its journey through purgatory. It goes about its business methodically. By December 2, 1851, it had completed one half of its preparatory work; it is now completing the other half...."

And when it has completed this, the second half of its preliminary work, Europe will leap from its seat and exultantly exclaim: 'Well burrowed, old mole!'" Karl Marx, *The Eighteenth Brumaire of Louis Bonaparte*, trans. Ben Fowkes, in *Political Writings, Vol. 2: Surveys from Exile* (London: Penguin, 1992), pp. 236–37, translation modified. Marx's invocation of the old mole refers to Shakespeare's *Hamlet*, whose protagonist addresses the revenant ghost of his father as an "old mole" that refuses to be put to rest.

The mole has subsequently come to represent the chthonic forces of history, base materialist impulses that eschew the light of day and defy the directives of consciousness. Thus Georges Bataille explained in 1929 that "'Old Mole,' Marx's resounding expression for the complete satisfaction of the revolutionary outburst of the masses, must be understood in relation to the notion of a geological uprising as expressed in the *Communist Manifesto*. Marx's point of departure has nothing to do with the heavens, preferred station of the imperialist eagle as of Christian or revolutionary utopias. He begins in the bowels of the earth, as in the materialist bowels of proletarians." Bataille, "The 'Old Mole' and the Prefix *Sur* in the Words *Surhomme* [Superman] and *Surrealist*," in *Visions of Excess: Selected Writings, 1927–1939*, ed. and trans. Allan Stoekl (Minneapolis: University of Minnesota Press, 1985), p. 35.

Kluge likewise lauds the unsung intelligence of the bowels in the story "Unintentional Stroke of Luck. Episode From the Age of Asymmetrical Warfare," which tells of an American fighter pilot in the Middle East who had "fixed the sights of his plane on an object he took to be a bunker," but that was in fact "a farm on which a wedding celebration happened to be taking place." Preparing to discharge his payload, he suddenly experienced a "convulsive evacuation" of his bowels that caused him to knock the aiming mechanism so that the missiles fired into "the swampy fields, where they harmed no one." Alexander Kluge, *The Devil's Blind Spot: Tales from the New Century*, trans. Michael Chalmers and Michael Hulse (New York: New Directions, 2004), p. 38. In an interview Kluge comments about this story: "If intestinal colic prevents the bomber pilot from propagating death in Iraq then his intestines were smarter than his head. And that the intestines do this dates back to a previous time. If the intestines' ability to anticipate is greater than the head's foresight—which is also artificially deadened again and again through education—then the intestines were the prophet. It concerns a reason that is underneath reason. That is the core issue." Kluge, *Glückliche Umstände, leihweise*, pp. 337–38.

104. "In *History and Obstinacy* we are always looking for the aspect that has been covered up, for what is burrowing around under the surface, which is why our favorite animal is the mole that works *sous terre*, as Hegel says. That is

precisely where, within man, the concealed, buried, and distorted characteristics are located—protest energies, which we try to straighten out in our writings; but this is also where certain needs are located in the form of concrete." Negt, "Der Maulwurf kennt kein System," p. 12.

105. Miriam Hansen, "The Stubborn Discourse: History and Story-Telling in the Films of Alexander Kluge," in *Persistence of Vision* 2 (Fall 1985), pp. 19–29.

106. Andrew Bowie, "Geschichte und Eigensinn," *Telos* 66 (Winter 1985–1986), pp. 183–90.

107. Jameson, "On Negt and Kluge."

108. Georg Wilhelm Friedrich Hegel, *Phänomenologie des Geistes* (Frankfurt am Main, 1983), in *Werke*, 20 vols. (Frankfurt am Main: Suhrkamp, 1980), vol. 3, p. 155; Hegel, *The Phenomenology of Spirit*, trans. A. V. Miller (Oxford: Oxford University Press, 1977), p. 119. On Eigensinn in Hegel, see Judith Butler, "Stubborn Attachment, Bodily Subjection: Rereading Hegel on the Unhappy Consciousness," in *The Psychic Life of Power* (Stanford: Stanford University Press, 1997), pp. 31–62. Like that of Negt and Kluge, Butler's reading emphasizes the connection between splitting (or *Trennung*) and obstinacy: "One might read Hegel's references to *Eigensinnigkeit* or stubbornness as illustrating the process of splitting and defense in the formation of neurosis. That Hegel refers to this 'unhappiness' as a kind of stubborn attachment suggests that, as in neurosis, the ethical regulation of bodily impulse becomes the focus and aim of impulse itself. In both cases, we are given to understand an attachment in subjection which is formative of the reflexive structure of subjection itself" (pp. 57–58). Significantly, too, she concludes that this scheme literally mobilizes desire, that is, detaches it from the subject and sets it into motion, much in the way that Kluge understands emotions to be itinerate states that cut across individual subjects: "If part of what regulatory regimes do is to constrain the formation and attachments of desire, then it seems that from the start a certain detachability of impulse is presumed, a certain incommensurability between the capacity for a bodily attachment, on the one hand, and the site where it is confined, on the other. Foucault appears to presume precisely this detachability of desire in claiming that incitements and reversals are to some degree unforeseeable, that they have the capacity, central to the notion of resistance, to exceed the regulatory aims for which they were produced" (p. 60).

109. Kluge, in Stollmann, *Die Entstehung des Schönheitssinns aus dem Eis*, p. 51.

110. Walter Benjamin, "On the Concept of History," trans. Harry Zohn, in *Selected Writings, Volume 4, 1938–1940*, ed. Howard Eiland and Michael Jennings, (Cambridge, MA: Harvard University Press, 2003), p. 392.

111. Jameson, "On Negt and Kluge," p. 159.

112. Braudel describes three temporal strata prospected by the historian—the geographical, the sociocultural, and the individual—as follows: "The first is an inquiry into a history that is almost changeless, the history of man in relation to his surroundings. It is a history which unfolds slowly and is slow to alter, often repeating itself and working itself out in cycles that are endlessly renewed.... Over and above this unfaltering history, there is a history of gentle rhythms, of groups and groupings, which one might readily have called social history if the term had not been diverted from its full meaning.... Lastly comes the third part, concerned with traditional history, history, so to speak, on the scale not so much of man in general as of men in particular. It is that history which François Simiand calls 'l'histoire événementielle,' the history of events: a surface disturbance, the waves stirred up by the powerful movement of tides. A history of short, sharp, nervous vibrations." Braudel, *On History*, p. 3.

113. Negt and Kluge, "Die Geschichte der lebendigen Arbeitskraft," p. 91.

114. Jameson, "On Negt and Kluge," p. 159.

115. "In short, the working class was presented as struggling 'economically,' whereas 'politics' was the concern of the bourgeoisie, inasmuch as the latter, through the State, was distinguished from mere capitalists, the owners of the means of production." As a result "Marx could never stabilize his theoretical discourse with respect to the concept of 'politics.'" Étienne Balibar, "The Notion of Class Politics in Marx," trans. Dominique Parent-Ruccio and Frank R. Annunziato, *Rethinking Marxism* 1.2 (Summer 1988), pp. 22 and 24–25.

116. "We have always understood this concept 'proletarian' in the sense of repressed and expropriated characteristics, and never in the narrow context of a class theory. We do not use 'the proletariat' as a concept for a material substance, but instead use the provisions of characteristics [*Eigenschaftsbestimmungen*] and their concepts. In this regard, for us, 'expropriation'—or the 'permanence of primitive accumulation,' which is the same thing—is brought to bear on separate or several human characteristics, not on an entire person.... In this regard, every moment of repression and expropriation is linked to a form of protest energy, and that is what we call 'proletarian.'" Negt, "Der Maulwurf kennt kein System," p. 13.

117. In "Reification and the Consciousness of the Proletariat," Georg Lukács characterizes the proletariat as "the identical subject-object of the social and historical processes of evolution." The proletariat is defined here as an object that has achieved subjectivity and consciousness—or, as Negt and Kluge write, capital that has learned to say "I." See Lukács, *History and Class Consciousness: Studies in Marxist Dialectics*, trans. Rodney Livingstone (Cambridge, MA: MIT Press, 1994), p. 149.

118. Balibar, "The Notion of Class Politics in Marx," pp. 19 and 18.

119. Bertolt Brecht, "[Marx an die Proletarier]," in *Werke*, vol. 22, p. 48.

120. Bertolt Brecht, "Die Beule," in *Werke*, vol. 19, p. 319; "The Bruise," in *Brecht on Film and Radio*, pp. 142–43.

121. Brian Massumi, "Notes on the Translation and Acknowledgments," in Gilles Deleuze and Félix Guattari, *A Thousand Plateaus: Capitalism and Schizophrenia*, trans. Brian Massumi (Minneapolis: University of Minnesota Press, 1987), p. xvi.

122. Writing about *History and Obstinacy*, Thomas Elsaesser proposes "to see this vast tome that chronicles 2,000 years of Germanic history in the context of the paradigm of parapraxis, of what in the world of work and human labor constantly misfires, goes awry and misses its intended goal or target." Elsaesser, "New German Cinema and History: The Case of Alexander Kluge," in Tim Bergfelder, Erica Carter, and Deniz Göktürk (eds.), *The German Cinema Book* (London: BFI, 2002), p. 186.

123. Kluge, in Stollmann, *Die Entstehung des Schönheitssinns aus dem Eis*, p. 93.

124. Norbert Bolz, "Eigensinn: Zur politisch-theologischen Poetik Hans Magnus Enzensbergers und Alexander Kluges," in Jochen Hörisch and Hubert Winkels (eds.), *Das schnelle Altern der neuesten Literatur: Essays zu deutschsprachigen Texten zwischen 1968–1984* (Düsseldorf: Claasen, 1985), p. 57.

125. Negt and Kluge, *Public Sphere and Experience*, p. 8.

126. Negt and Kluge, *Maßverhältnisse*, p. 766.

127. *Ibid.*, p. 784.

128. Negt and Kluge, *Suchbegriffe*, p. 306.

129. Kluge, *Nachrichten aus der ideologischen Antike*, liner notes, p. 36.

130. Carl Schmitt, *The Concept of the Political*, trans. George Schwab (Chicago: University of Chicago Press, 2007).

131. When Negt and Kluge write of the political, they have in mind the practice of the politics prior to the eighteenth century, when French philosophers came to define politics more restrictively as a theory of the state. When Negt and Kluge use the word "politics," they are usually referring to this earlier, more encompassing definition, namely, politics as a general science and practice of collective being (*Gemeinwesen*). Negt and Kluge, *Maßverhältnisse*, p. 725. Kluge writes that the political is nothing other than "a particular intensity of everyday feelings." See the speech he delivered on being given the Fontane Prize for Literature, "Das Politische als Intensitätsgrad alltäglicher Gefühle," *Freibeuter* 1 (1979), pp. 56–62; translated by Andrew Bowie as "The Political as Intensity of Everyday Feelings," *Cultural Critique* 4 (Fall 1986), pp. 119–28.

132. Alexander Kluge, "Das Marxsche Wertgesetz ist in der Natur verankert: Ein Gespräch zwischen Rainer Stollmann and Alexander Kluge," in *Der Maulwurf kennt kein System*, p. 47.

133. Alexander Kluge and Florian Hopf, "'Gefühle können Berge versetzen...,' Interview von Florian Hopf mit Alexander Kluge zu dem Film: DIE MACHT DER GEFÜHLE," in Alexander Kluge, *Die Macht der Gefühle* (Frankfurt am Main: Zweitausendeins, 1984), p. 180; translation by Robert Savage as "'Feelings Can Move Mountains...': An Interview with Alexander Kluge on the Film The Power of Feelings," in *Alexander Kluge: Raw Materials for the Imagination*, p. 240.

134. For a brilliant reading of the work-love gestuary in Godard's *Passion*, see Leo Bersani, "The Will to Know," in *Is the Rectum a Grave?: And Other Essays* (Chicago: University of Chicago Press, 2010), pp. 154–67. For Bersani, Godard's *Passion* illustrates the haptic bond that is connects the mother to the young infant, a bond that the psychoanalyst Christopher Bollas called an "aesthetic of handling." This kind of "being-with" enables "the baby's adequate processing of his existence prior to his ability to process it through thought" (p. 162).

135. In his 1983 film *The Power of Emotions*, Kluge compares the cultural institution of opera to the Crystal Palace Exhibition of 1851, in which the capitalized, mass-fabricated emotions and feelings of our society are put on phantasmagoric display in the manner of commodities.

136. Kluge notes that he is most drawn to consider emotions that do not even appear as such: "I am very interested in the feelings that are not immediately recognized as feelings, that are integrated into institutions and that first manifest themselves only in an emergency, at the moments when we forget ourselves—only at the moment of deployment, so to speak. A mother rescues her child who is lying in front of a tractor: she pushes it out of the way and dies herself. That is a short reflex arc, one that cannot actually be achieved through calculation, that is feeling. But this feeling has nothing to do with sentiment, with the feeling that we know from theater. It has more to do with the feeling in my fingertips that I use to secure a gasket at the right moment. It is actually a matter of labor." His interviewer adds: "to feel [Fühlen], the concept of feeling [Gefühl] comes from 'to touch' [tasten]." To which Kluge responds: "The sense of touch. It is very important to confront this with the highly cultured feelings in the opera, which have been processed many times over and which then lead to such confusions that an Egyptian general must, at any cost, take a female slave from Ethiopia onto the royal throne—and both die as a result." Alexander Kluge, "Kritik als verdeckte Ermittlung," in *Verdeckte Ermittlung: Ein Gespräch mit Christian Schulte und Rainer Stollmann* (Berlin: Merve, 2001), p. 43.

137. Kluge, in Kluge and Hopf, "'Feelings Can Move Mountains...,'" p. 244.

138. Kluge, "Das Marxsche Wertgesetz ist in der Natur verankert," p. 49.

139. Kluge, "Kritik als verdeckte Ermittlung," p. 44.

140. Kluge, in Kluge and Hopf, "'Feelings Can Move Mountains...,'" p. 244.

141. Freud, *Civilization and its Discontents*, p. 78.

142. Negt and Kluge, *Maßverhältnisse*, p. 756.

143. Negt quotes Machiavelli in *Der politische Mensch*, p. 516.

144. Kluge, "The Political as Intensity of Everyday Feelings," p. 128. Negt highlights a line from Christa Wolf's book *Kassandra*: "It is possible to know when war begins, but when does the prelude to war begin [*der Vorkrieg*]?" He comments that "the subject matter of the counterpublic sphere is to identify what Christa Wolf meant by a prelude to war, to make it nameable in everyday conflicts—for example in struggles for employment—to decode the prelude to war in the real lifeworld of people." Negt, in *Suchbegriffe*, p. 277. See also Negt, *Der politische Mensch*, p. 21.

145. Kluge, "The Political as Intensity of Everyday Feelings," p. 127.

146. Kluge, "On Opera, Film, and Feelings," p. 106.

147. Negt and Kluge, *Public Sphere and Experience*, p. 296. One of Kluge's regular collaborators, Rainer Stollmann, observes that the rallying cry for Negt and Kluge's work is no longer "Workers of the world, unite!" but rather "Experiences of the world, unite!" Stollmann, "Zusammenhang, Motiv, Krieg: Ein Holzschnitt zu Negt/Kluges Theoriearbeit," *Text + Kritik* 85–86 (1985), p. 82.

148. In Kluge's early films, counterhegemonic practices and feelings seem to be accumulated primarily in women, whose nonvalorized forms of unpaid labor represented for Kluge a repository of oppositional strategies, models for concrete resistance to capitalism's mechanism of abstract subsumption. Thomas Elsaesser correspondingly notes that "female Eigensinn" "stands for the ethical act of refusal par excellence" in Kluge's work from the 1970s. Elsaesser, "The Stubborn Persistence of Alexander Kluge," in *Alexander Kluge: Raw Materials for the Imagination*, p. 26. But by the 1980s, Kluge no longer foregrounded female obstinacy in his films. *The Patriot* (1979) was the last such film. This shift in part responded to the censure of feminist scholars who interpreted his association between women and nonrationalized labor to be an identification of women with irrationalism tout court. Miriam Hansen summarizes the controversy thus: "Why Kluge prefers to project this associational anarchy onto the minds of female characters and often makes them the agents of what by 'adult' standards might be called irrational behavior, is a thorny question. Apart from the general problem of a 'woman's film' produced by a male director (though not, as the traditional 'woman's film,' for a predominantly female audience), it involves Kluge's analysis of specifically female modes of production as vital to patriarchal society, yet never completely assimilable to the standards of industrial capitalism." Miriam Hansen, "Cooperative Auteur Cinema and Oppositional Public Sphere," *New German Critique*, no. 24–25 (Autumn 1981–Winter 1982), p. 51. At the same, Kluge's waning emphasis on female obstinacy, specifically, also

responded to the inroads made by capitalism in the 1970s, when, as we have already seen, capitalism began aggressively to annex reproductive forms of labor that were traditionally performed by women in the private sphere of the family. During these years, it became clear that the claim that proletarian and counterhegemonic strategies of resistance were better preserved in women was no longer a tenable claim.

149. "Short and long times coexist within the same body and mind." Kluge, *Tür an Tür mit einem anderen Leben*, p. 9.

150. Kluge and Vogl, *Soll und Haben*, p. 9.

151. Kluge states his variant of the Sapir-Whorf thesis as follows: "If Greenlanders have 200...expressions for different sorts of snow, because snow is important for them. And ancient Greek likewise has quite a number—an entire chain—of words for the color yellow, which appeared important in antiquity. If the word happiness can be expressed in Greek using numerous words like 'kairos,' 'eudaimon,' 'makarios,' and so on; which describe many different variations because happiness is something that is important to man and that cannot be designated using a single word. —Then we would likewise have to have more than one expression for the word 'love' in our language. But if we diversify too broadly here, we quickly arrive at indecent expressions that can't be circulated in public. Which means that our expressions are impoverished regarding the most important intimate experiences that we possess. And when someone says I love you to someone else—just what that is supposed to mean, well, an entire volume of commentary would be forthcoming. And this differentiation is exactly what we lack here. While we have handbooks for the stocks of ammunition or arsenals of bombs that can be unloaded in Afghanistan. With directions, differentiation, and so forth. What can be done with all of that, with the incendiary bombs especially. Investigated with absolute precision. And this was different at the beginning of bourgeois society. *The Princess of Cleves* is a novel that describes with precision—that deals with—how to equip oneself for the abysses of love, against betrayal in relationships. And then creates a mass of faculties for distinction at the exact place where one has to decide whether or not to dare trust oneself in the most important question: With whom do I bond or not?" Kluge, in Kluge and Negt, "Öffentlichkeit als wertvolles Gut und die Idee der Gegenöffentlichkeit," p. 48.

152. Kluge, "Kritik als verdeckte Ermittlung," p. 48.

153. "It is as if modernization speaks itself as a machinery of discourses in whose grids individual subjectivities are simultaneously constituted and imprisoned, even stunted and mutilated." Andreas Huyssen, "Alexander Kluge: An Analytic Storyteller in the Course of Time," in *Twilight Memories: Marking Time in a Culture of Amnesia* (New York: Routledge, 1995), p. 149. The analytic coldness of Kluge's approach to his synthetic characters may turn out to be ideologically

more progressive than sentimental humanist critiques of capitalist alienation. Consider Brecht's own experience with the bourgeois censors, who objected not to the revolutionary pathos in his film *Kuhle Wampe*, but rather to its utterly neutral portrayal of the proletariat and its glacial indifference to the psychological motives of the working-class characters: "I reproach your depiction for not seeming sufficiently *human*," the censor informed Brecht. "You have not depicted a person but, well, to put it frankly, a type. Your unemployed worker is not a real individual, not a person made of flesh and blood, and distinct from every other person, with his own particular worries, particular joys and finally his own particular fate." Brecht was impressed: "The censor proved to be an intelligent man," he noted in response. Brecht, "Kleiner Beitrag zum Thema Realismus," in *Werke*, vol. 21, pp. 549 and 548; Brecht, "Short Contribution on the Theme of Realism," in *Brecht on Film and Radio*, pp. 208 and 207.

154. "In America, they say about someone who is so consistently matter-of-fact that he is as cool as a cucumber." Hans Magnus Enzensberger, "Ein herzloser Schriftsteller," *Der Spiegel*, January 2, 1978, p. 81.

155. Alexander Kluge, *Chronik der Gefühle* (Frankfurt am Main: Suhrkamp, 2000), p. 7.

156. Kluge underscores the importance of these paradigmatic connections, which are nonlinear and nonnarrative, when he notes that some of his films have to be watched multiple times. About *The Power of Emotions*, for example, he observes: "One problem of the film is that it would have to be viewed several times, so that the individual images and their inner connections are retained in memory." Kluge, *Die Macht der Gefühle*, p. 195.

157. Kluge, "Justierung des Jahrhunderts. 'Das Vergangene ist nicht tot, es ist nicht einmal vergangen,'" in *Verdeckte Ermittlung*, p. 16.

158. Kluge, "Kritik als verdeckte Ermittlung," p. 43.

159. "Ovid is the god of Montaigne, of Heiner Müller, and of me as well." Kluge, quoted in Wolfram Ette, "Aggregat Leben: Ovid und Alexander Kluge," *Komparatistik: Jahrbuch der Deutschen Gesellschaft für Allgemeine und Vergleichende Literaturwissenschaft*, 2008–2009, p. 155.

160. Negt and Kluge liken the qualitiative shifts between states of feeling to the phase transitions between solid, liquid, gaseous, and plasmic states. But they simultaneously qualify this metaphor by pointing out that these four states are intended as a heuristic model, not an accurate description of reality, since there are in fact an infinite number of such aggregate states. Negt and Kluge, *Maßverhältnisse*, p. 720. They thereby draw a line, again, between their own collaboration and Engels's *Dialectic of Nature*, which used a similar language of phase transitions to describe social relations.

161. The process of transcoding "is analogous to the problem of translation in the realm of natural languages, which all project at least minimally distinct cognates of the meaning a translated sentence is supposed to share with its original. What is philosophical about translation is, then, not the effort to reproduce a foreign utterance as the same, but rather the deeper experience it affords of the radical differences between natural languages." Jameson, "On Negt and Kluge," p. 157.

162. Ovid, *Metamorphoses*, trans. Charles Martin (New York: W. W. Norton. 2004), p. 12.

163. Baecker, "Wozu Theorie?" p. 76.

164. See Kluge's interview with the philosopher Peter Sloterdijk in *Nachrichten aus der ideologischen Antike*, "Alle Dinge sind verzauberte Menschen."

165. Kluge, in Baecker and Kluge, *Vom Nutzen ungelöster Probleme*, pp. 39–40

166. Kluge, "Kritik als verdeckte Ermittlung," p. 44.

167. For Kluge, "Germany cannot easily be defined in spatial terms," observes Anton Kaes. "In Search of Germany: Alexander Kluge's *The Patriot*," in *From Hitler to Heimat: The Return of History as Film* (Cambridge, MA: Harvard University Press, 1992), p. 133.

168. Marx, *Capital, Volume One*, p. 296.

169. Negt and Kluge, *Geschichte und Eigensinn*, pp. 98–99.

170. Stiegler, *Technics and Time*, vol. 1.

171. Ernst Bloch, *Thomas Müntzer als Theologe der Revolution*, in *Gesamtausgabe*, 16 vols. (Frankfurt am Main: Suhrkamp, 1985), vol. 2, p. 9.

172. Negt and Kluge, *Geschichte und Eigensinn*, pp. 692–93. Negt and Kluge cite the predictions of Fourastié that at some point in the near future, the number of those who are employed in industrial facilities will contract to the numbers of factory workers around 1800, at which point dead labor will assume definitive command. The law of posthumous influence applies not just to machine capital, of course, but also to the technical media and recording devices that have exploded in the modern era, as Friedrich Kittler observed: "The realm of the dead is as extensive as the storage and transmission capabilities of a given culture." Kittler, *Gramophone, Film, Typewriter*, trans. Geoffrey Winthrop-Young and Michael Wutz (Stanford: Stanford University Press, 1999), p. 13.

173. Negt and Kluge, *Maßverhältnisse*, p. 849.

174. Marx, *The Eighteenth Brumaire of Louis Bonaparte*, p. 146.

175. Kluge, *Die Patriotin*, p. 58.

176. Kluge, in Stollmann, *Die Entstehung des Schönheitssinns aus dem Eis*, p. 34.

177. Heiner Müller, *Gespräche 2*, in *Werke*, vol. 11, p. 614. See the interviews between Müller and Kluge in Alexander Kluge, Heiner Müller, and Max Messer,

Ich schulde der Welt einen Toten (Berlin: Rotbuch, 1995) and Alexander Kluge and Heiner Müller, *Ich bin ein Landvermesser* (Berlin: Rotbuch, 1996).

178. Kluge, *Die Patriotin*, p. 45.

179. Perhaps the most fitting theoretical model for metamorphoses such as these can be found in the act of translation, understood in Benjamin's sense as a process of conversion that is not based on fidelity or outward likeness. For Benjamin, the best translation is not the one that most accurately *imitates* the original text, but the one that most perfectly *succeeds* it. As Paul de Man observes about Benjamin's essay "The Task of the Translator," the latter defines translation not as an act of resembling, but one of following, a process of *folgen* not of *gleichen*: "what is already present in this difference [between original and translation] is that we have *folgen*, not *gleichen*, not to match. We have a metonymic, a successive pattern, in which things follow, rather than a metaphorical unifying pattern in which things become one by resemblance. They do not match each other, they follow each other." De Man, "Conclusions: Walter Benjamin's 'The Task of the Translator,'" in *The Resistance to Theory* (Minneapolis: University of Minnesota Press, 1986), p. 90. Against the notion that the translator should aspire to produce an accurate imitation or likeness of the original, Benjamin himself notes that "to grasp the genuine relationship between an original and a translation requires an investigation analogous in its intention to the argument by which a critique of cognition would have to prove the impossibility of a theory of imitation. In the latter, it is a question of showing that in cognition there could be no objectivity, not even a claim to it, if this were to consist in imitations of the real; in the former, one can demonstrate that no translation would be possible if in its ultimate essence it strove for likeness to the original. For in its afterlife—which could not be called that if it were not a transformation and a renewal of something living—the original undergoes a change." Like the metamorphotic thinking that underlies Negt and Kluge's analysis of human traits and labor capacities, the process of translation reminds us that "life [is] not limited to organic corporeality," as Benjamin notes, but embraces inorganic phenomena, as well. Walter Benjamin, "The Task of the Translator," trans. Harry Zohn, in *Selected Writings, Volume 1*, pp. 256 and 254. Direct echoes of Benjamin's theory of translation can be heard in Kluge's claim that "something that has been merely recorded in words becomes 'fluid,' that is, becomes an idea, when it is translated back and forth in different languages. As in the game of 'operator,' an experience or a thought will begin to glow like a prism if it is systematically translated from French into Russian, from there into Latin, from there into English, from there into German, and then into Chinese." Kluge, *Nachrichten aus der ideologischen Antike*, liner notes, p. 32.

180. Kluge, *Die Patriotin*, p. 171.

181. Kluge, in Negt and Kluge, "Öffentlichkeit als wertvolles Gut," p. 54.

182. Étienne Balibar, "The Elements of the Structure and Their History," in Louis Althusser and Étienne Balibar, *Reading Capital*, trans. Ben Brewster (London: Verso, 2009), p. 274.

183. *Ibid.*, p. 273.

184. Balibar, "Elements for a Theory of Transition," in *Reading Capital*, pp. 343–44. "The new system of the productive forces...is neither an absolute end nor an absolute origins, but a reorganization of the entire system, of the relation of the real appropriation of nature, of the 'productive forces.'" Balibar, "The Elements of the Structure and Their History," p. 272.

185. Heide Schlüpmann connects Kluge's understanding of the flow of the cinematic image to the work of Bergson in "'What Is Different Is Good': Women and Femininity in the Films of Alexander Kluge," trans. Jamie Owen Daniel, *October* 46 (Autumn 1988), p. 139.

186. As support, Balibar here cites Georges Canguilhem, who noted about the theory of evolution that "originally such a development was understood as applying to a unique and qualified individual. No doubt, around the middle of the [nineteenth] century, it became hard to tell what was the *subject* of this development (*what* developed). This invariant behind the embryological transformations could not be assimilated to surface and volume (as in an unfolding), nor to the adult structure (as in a maturation)." Balibar, "The Elements of the Structure and Their History," pp. 275 and 274.

Along similar lines, Leo Bersani points out that Freud's hypothesis about the successiveness of the phases of infantile sexuality was a late addition, proposed only with the 1915 revision to *Three Essays on the Theory of Sexuality*, originally written in 1905. The narrative about normative development toward the "proper" genital organization is superfluous to Freud's theory, which functions typologically even without the later linear teleology. As Bersani observes, "the reality of those phases as distinct historical organizations is therefore somewhat problematic." Indeed, Freud writes "as if infantile sexuality were sexuality itself, as if he had forgotten its presumably preparatory, subordinate role in leading to the 'principal act' of human sexuality." Thus, "alongside the teleological argument of the *Three Essays on the Theory of Sexuality*, a wholly different argument runs its course—insistently yet also almost invisibly. This second argument nearly dissolves the specificity by which Freud could expect his subject to be recognized." Bersani, "Sexuality and Esthetics," in *The Freudian Body: Psychoanalysis and Art* (New York: Columbia University Press, 1986), pp. 32, 33, 39.

Kluge is in turn skeptical of the socially normative organization of sexuality: "Those are highly synthetic compounds that need to be examined for their elemental components; there is nothing at all originary in them. Even genitality: it is true that as men we have a certain member, and that women differ here, but it makes no sense then to come to conclusions about fixed characteristics on this basis. The elemental components have to be taken apart. In principle everything is androgynous, that is what is true. The male and female phenotypes, along with all of their roles and cultural components, first come into being out of this androgynous state." Kluge, "Das Marxsche Wertgesetz ist in der Natur verankert," p. 49.

187. Kluge, in Stollmann, *Die Entstehung des Schönheitssinns aus dem Eis*, p. 34.

188. Negt and Kluge, *Maßverhältnisse*, pp. 677–78.

189. Helmut Thoma, quoted in Christian Schulte and Winfried Siebers, "Vorwort," in Christian Schulte and Winfried Siebers (eds.), *Kluges Fernsehen: Alexander Kluges Kulturmagazine* (Frankfurt am Main: Suhrkamp, 2002), p. 8. Kluge's interest in older technical formats also reflects a desire to access the hidden resources and potentials bottled up in these outmoded artifacts: "We might use the Debrie camera of 1923 and teach our computers the rules that were once fed into this Debrie camera by cameramen who died long ago. We thus retrieve a piece of dead labor from cinema history and program it into the show." Kluge, in Astrid Deuber-Mankowsky and Giaco Schiesser, "In der Echtzeit der Gefühle: Gespräch mit Alexander Kluge," in Christian Schulte (ed.), *Die Schrift an der Wand* (Osnabrück: Rasch, 2000), p. 363. "In short: the provocation issued by the new media — the ecological danger for structures of consciousness — demands nothing less than a return to the beginnings of the entire public sphere: we have to reactivate, revitalize this partial chapter, beginning in 1802 (or earlier). This time it must really be put in motion. As far as the moving pictures of film are concerned, the journey can only 'go back to Lumière and Méliès,' thus, back once again to its beginnings. In each one of these beginnings, we find male and female cousins of the actual development, which can be translated in the most interesting ways into inventions for the new media." Kluge, "Die Macht der Bewußtseinsindustrie," p. 64.

190. Bloch, *Erbschaft dieser Zeit*, p. 124; *Heritage of Our Times*, p. 114. Bloch takes this phrase from Ludwig Börne.

191. Oskar Negt, *Arbeit und Menschliche Würde* (Göttingen: Steidl, 2001), p. 432.

192. Ernst Bloch, Freiheit und Ordnung: Abriß der Sozialutopien (New York: Aurora Verlag, 1946), p. 155.

193. Kluge, "On Film and the Public Sphere," p. 210.

194. See Alexander Kluge, "[Was bedeutet "Rechts vom Nationalsozialismus]," in *Das Bohren harter Bretter: 133 politische Geschichten* (Frankfurt am Main: Suhrkamp, 2011), p. 320.

195. Kluge attributes this sentence to Montagine. Kluge, "Was hält freiwillige Taten Zusammen?" in *Verdeckte Ermittlung*, p. 60.

196. Negt and Kluge, *Maßverhältnisse*, p. 850.

197. Foucault, "Of Other Spaces," trans. Jay Miskowiec, *Diacritics* 16.1 (Spring 1986), p. 24. Kluge discusses Foucault's concept of heterotopia in the speech given on the occasion of receiving the Büchner Prize in 2003: Alexander Kluge, "Rede zum Büchner-Preis-2003," available at http://www.kluge-alexander.de/zur-person/reden/2003-buechner-preis.html. Elsewhere, he explains: "I would use heterotopia to identify not something that is utopian, but a way that the characteristics that we possess could be grouped differently — on a different planet or in a different society, by shifting them around or by jostling humanity. It is completely untrue that there is no place for this. It just looks utopian in our places, given the fraudulence of the entire system and the lack of experimentation and experience." Kluge, in Stollmann, *Die Entstehung des Schönheitssinns aus dem Eis*, p. 130.

198. Stollmann and Schulte, *Verdeckte Ermittlung*, p. 65.

199. Kluge, in *Suchbegriffe*, p. 278.

200. Negt, in *ibid.*, p. 276.

201. Alexander Kluge, "Thesen 1–4," in Kluge, *In Gefahr und größter Not bringt der Mittelweg den Tod: Texte zu Kino, Film, Politik*, ed. Christian Schulte (Berlin: Vorwerk, 1999), p. 155.

202. Theodor Adorno, Max Horkheimer, et al., *Soziologische Exkurse: Nach Vorträgen und Diskussionen* (Frankfurt am Main: Europäische Verlagsanstalt, 1956) p. 179. Negt comments in *Der politische Mensch*, p. 450.

203. In his *Science of Logic*, Hegel observed that the "Idea of *essence*, namely, to be self-identical in the immediacy of its determined being, is already immanent in measure." Georg Wilhelm Friedrich Hegel, *The Science of Logic*, trans. A. V. Miller (London: Allen and Unwin, 1969), p. 329.

204. Negt and Kluge, *Maßverhältnisse*, p. 696.

205. Wolfgang Bock, "Exemplarische Reflexionen einer Dekade: Maßverhältnisse des Politischen," in *Der Maulwurf kennt kein System*, p. 111.

206. Kluge notes this in an interview given while he was working on *History and Obstinacy*: "Was hat die Geschichtslehrerin Gabi Teichert mit Walter Benjamin am Hut?: Ein Gespräch mit Alexander Kluge," *Anachronistischen Heften* 1 (1980), p. 64.

207. Kluge refers to emergence theory explicitly in the appendix to *Das Bohren harter Bretter*, where he defines *Emergenz* as an "attribute of a behavioral pattern that comes into being through the interplay of many smaller behavioral patterns, which, joining together, burst at a collective point into a parallel reality" (p. 312).

On Kluge and systems theory, see his conversations with the sociologist Dirk Baecker, *Vom Nutzen ungelöster Probleme*, as well as Baecker, "Wozu Theorie?"

208. Marx, *Capital, Volume One*, pp. 443–44.

209. Negt and Kluge, *Maßverhältnisse*, pp. 696–702.

210. *Ibid.*, pp. 696–97.

211. Kluge, *Das Bohren harter Bretter*, p. 138.

212. *Ibid.*

213. The "tragedy of the commons" is the famous phrase used by the ecologist Garrett Hardin to describe the exhaustion of society's shared resources as a result of the egocentric behavior of its individual members. "Individuals locked into the logic of the commons are free only to bring on universal ruin," Hardin writes. "The Tragedy of the Commons," *Science* 162 (December 13, 1968), p. 1248.

214. Negt, *Der politische Mensch*, p. 11. Kluge makes a comparable reference to the "invisible hand" as a theory of a self-regulating collective: obstinacy "will always invent something that the [capitalist] corporation did not commission and that triggers the peculiar dialectic that Adam Smith described in *The Wealth of Nations*—that the intentions of a thousand egoistic devils will nonetheless work subterraneously to produce a collective existence." Kluge, in Stollmann, *Die Entstehung des Schönheitssinns aus dem Eis*, p. 51.

215. This line is from Weber's 1919 lecture "Politics as a Vocation," in *The Vocation Lectures*, trans. Rodney Livingstone (Indianapolis: Hackett, 2004), p. 93. With reference to Weber, Kluge titled a recent collection of stories about politics *Das Bohren harter Bretter* (Drilling through hard boards).

216. See Chapter 5, "The Historical Terrain Where Labor Capacities Emerge," pp. 215–21, in the present volume.

217. Here, Luxemburg's words echo Trotsky's theory of permanent revolution. Negt, "Der Maulwurf kennt kein System," p. 38.

218. Negt and Kluge, *Maßverhältnisse*, p. 887.

219. See the Appendix, s.v. "Damaged Dialectic," in the present volume. Discussing Freud's endorsement of "ungrammatical" free association, Kluge observes that "grammar, for instance, is one of mankind's most interesting illusions. It's a sort of repression of an experience, like logic, or like rationalism. You have to understand that I'm never against grammar, rationality, or logic; it's just that they're only abstractions. In any concrete situation, these abstractions must be reduced to the concrete situation." Kluge, in Jan Dawson, "Interview with Alexander Kluge," *Film Comment* (November–December 1974), p. 55.

220. Negt and Kluge describe the challenge of philosophizing in the present tense as follows: "Philosophy as an integral system can refer only to a reality that has already been concluded. It takes its coherence from observation, that is,

retrospectively. This is not so for the process of philosophizing, especially for the philosopher who is rooted as a particle in every individual human characteristic, for example, in the fingertips, in the feet, and so on. *This* philosopher is in contact with reality through the detail, is always a contemporary, is always present, but he is dependent on the felicitous moment in which he *has himself*—otherwise, he cannot grasp and intervene. This philosopher has the concentration of a gambler." Negt and Kluge, *Geschichte und Eigensinn*, p. 84.

221. Kluge, in Stollmann, *Entstehung des Schönheitssinns*, p. 22.

222. Negt and Kluge, *Geschichte und Eigensinn*, p. 790.

223. Negt and Kluge, *Maßverhältnisse*, p. 887.

224. Kluge, *Nachrichten aus der ideologischen Antike*, liner notes, pp. 52–53.

225. Kluge, in Dawson, "Interview with Alexander Kluge," p. 56.

226. See the stories collected under the rubric "Der Zeitbedarf von Revolutionen," in *Tür an Tür mit einem anderen Leben*, pp. 341–408.

227. "The structure of the fundamental economic elements of society remains untouched by the storms which blow up in the cloudy regions of politics." Marx, *Capital, Volume One*, p. 479.

228. Friedrich Engels and Karl Marx, *The Holy Family, or, Critique of Critical Critique*, trans. Richard Dixon (Moscow: Foreign Languages Publishing House, 1956).

229. Negt, "Der Maulwurf kennt kein System," p. 38.

230. Roman Jakobson famously bemoaned the inertia and resistance of *byt* (everyday life) as "the stabilizing force of an immutable present, overlaid, as this present is, by a stagnating slime, which stifles life in its tight, hard mold." Jakobson, "On a Generation that Squandered Its Poets," in *My Futurist Years*, ed. Bengt Jangfeldt, trans. Stephen Rudy (New York: Marsilio, 1992), p. 214.

231. Negt and Kluge, *Maßverhältnisse*, pp. 702–17.

232. Kluge, *Nachrichten aus der ideologischen Antike*, liner notes, p. 4. On crisis and trust, see Kluge's recent DVD, *Früchte des Vertrauens* (2009).

233. Negt, *Der politische Mensch*, p. 26.

234. Negt and Kluge write that moments like the immediate postwar period in Germany are significant "not for the potential for the action that they contain, but for the potential for knowledge contained therein.... These years are an abaric point, that is, a moment in which contradictory forces cancel each other out, precisely because it was not possible to intervene in society.... Within a planetary space, it has hardly any effect on the essential spheres of action, [but] for thought, it is ideally situated." Negt and Kuge, *Geschichte und Eigensinn*, p. 1122.

235. "One could imagine books that were printed so that the words were written together without punctuation or spacing. Moreover, all vowels were removed and

needed to be reconstructed out of the context through association. Above all, the words would be written on top of one another so that one typewritten page would seem to be overtyped differently four thousand times. Such overwriting corresponds exactly to the labor of historical relations, to the labor of generations and their linguistic conventions. There is also the fact that each of these elements—and this part does not apply to letters—is found in a state of dynamic movement: it turns out that each element is not just written on top of other ones, but also as something that has been overwritten, is itself in a state of dynamic change. All texts are therefore transforming themselves quietly [unter der Hand]." Negt and Kluge, *Maßverhältnisse*, p. 862.

236. Negt and Kluge, *Maßverhältnisse*, p. 701.

237. See Kluge, "On Opera, Film, and Feelings."

238. *Germany in Autumn*, dir. by Rainer Werner Fassbinder, Alexander Kluge, Edgar Reitz, Völker Schlöndorf et al. (1978).

239. Negt, "Der Maulwurf kennt kein System," p. 39.

240. Negt and Kluge, *Maßverhältnisse*, p. 967.

241. On the Thirty Years' War as a *Lernprovokation*, see Negt, *Der politische Mensch*, pp. 118–35. According to Negt, the Peace of Westphalia, which was drawn up at the end of the war, represents nothing less than "the documentation of an enormous learning process" (p. 118).

242. Kluge writes that "after 1991, following the disintegration of the Russian imperium, as we looked forward to the year 2000, I had the feeling that the new century would take the bitter experience of the 20th century and turn it into something hopeful. But are we now seeing instead a relapse into the era of the Thirty Years' War? No one reading my stories is likely to imagine that I believe in scenarios of doom. 'There are no expiration dates.' It's more worthwhile to examine the allegedly pre-modern, to find out what in it releases human power and what the power of the Devil." Alexander Kluge, *The Devil's Blind Spot*, p. vii.

243. Bloch writes the following about the doctrine of three kingdoms found in early communist Christianity: "Strange as these categories may sound to the modern revolutionary...we equally must not allow ourselves to be thereby deterred from noticing and honoring the hunger for happiness and freedom, the images of freedom on the part of people deprived of their rights, in these dreams. Socialism has a fantastically splendid tradition; if at such early stages, as goes without saying, it lacks any kind of economic view, it certainly does not lack one of its other essential features: humaneness and the Advent view connected with it." Bloch, *Erbschaft dieser Zeit*, p. 135; *Heritage of Our Times*, p. 124. About the "objectivity and inevitability" of the revolution within the medieval dream of the thousand-year kingdom, Bloch writes that "it was not chiliasm which prevented the economic consciousness, and the concrete control of reality at that time." Rather, "no

economic consciousness existed at the time purely for economic reasons, and if chiliasm had not existed, no revolutionary consciousness would have existed either, and therefore no revolution whatsoever." Bloch, *Erbschaft*, p. 145; *Heritage*, p. 131.

244. Giorgio Agamben, *The Kingdom and the Glory: For a Theological Genealogy of Economy and Government*, trans. Lorenzo Chiesa (Stanford: Stanford University Press, 2011).

245. Braudel also notes that "the very first thing the historian sees is the troop of events which have come out on top in the struggle of life. But these events place themselves once again, order themselves within the framework of a variety of contradictory possibilities, among which life finally made its choice. For one possibility which was fulfilled, there were tens, hundreds, thousands, which disappeared, and there are even some which, numberless, never even appear to us at all, too lowly and hidden to impose themselves directly on history." Fernand Braudel, "Toward a Historical Economics," in *On History*, p. 84.

246. In the value abstraction of the "novel of reality," "there prevails...a primacy of economy, which drives experience and reality away from the thread of the action." Negt and Kluge, *Public Sphere and Experience*, p. 274. See also Miriam Hansen, "Alexander Kluge, Cinema and the Public Sphere: The Construction Site of Counter-History," *Discourse* 6 (Fall 1983), p. 64.

247. Kluge, in Stollmann, *Die Entstehung des Schönheitssinns aus dem Eis*, p. 109. On the "Communist disbelief in destiny," see Kluge, *Verdeckte Ermittlung*, p. 57.

248. Kluge, "Rede zum Büchner-Preis-2003." On reality and historical fiction, see also Alexander Kluge, "The Sharpest Ideology: That Reality Appeals to its Realistic Character," trans. David Roberts, *On the Beach* 3–4 (Summer 1984), pp. 23–24.

249. "When Clausewitz says that all the potential battles—those that do not take place—are just as important as those that do, he has understood a certain dialectic: he acts like a realist." Kluge, "On Film and the Public Sphere," p. 45.

250. Kluge, in Dawson, "Interview with Alexander Kluge," p. 54.

251. It should not be surprising, then, that Negt and Kluge give little credence to the distinction between real and imaginary pasts, "true" memories and "false" ones. Citing the work of the developmental psychologist Jean Piaget, Kluge explains that recollection is a matter not of accurate and objective recall of the past, but of arranging experience in a way that renders it intelligible. "Memory is not the translation of something unconscious or the conception of something that has been temporarily hidden; instead, becoming conscious of something always a reorganization, a reconstruction." Kluge, "Die Macht der Bewußtseinsindustrie," p. 101.

252. Jürgen Habermas, "The Useful Mole Who Ruins the Beautiful Lawn: The Lessing Prize for Alexander Kluge," in *The Liberating Power of Symbols: Philosophical Essays*, trans. Peter Dews (Cambridge, MA: Polity, 2001), p. 121.

253. "Demystification, breaking reality down into its components: that is the program of enlightenment. Today it is *reality* that has taken priority over religion in this matter." Negt and Kluge, *Maßverhältnisse*, p. 694. Bruno Latour has recently called into question the distinction between fact and fiction, observing that science has never actually been able to maintain the distinction between fabrication and reality in its practice. Latour, "On the Cult of the Factish Gods," in *On the Modern Cult of the Factish Gods*, trans. Catherine Porter and Heather MacLean (Durham: Duke University Press, 2010), pp. 1–65.

254. Negt, *Der politische Mensch*, pp. 57–65.

255. Caryl Flinn, "Undoing Act 5: History, Bodies and Operatic Remains: Kluge's *The Power of Emotion*," in *The New German Cinema: Music, History, and the Matter of Style* (Berkeley: University of California Press, 2004), pp. 138–69. Kluge characterizes the impression of fatefulness: "It begins with love and ends with divorce / It begins in 1933 and ends in ruins / The great operas begin with a promise of elevated feeling, and in Act V we count the dead." And yet, he notes, it is "still doubtful whether there really is such a thing as fate. Maybe there are only a hundred thousand different causes, which we call fate after the event." Kluge, *Die Macht der Gefühle*, p. 56 and preface, n.p.

256. Christian Schulte, "Alle Dinge sind verzauberte Menschen: Über Alexander Kluges *Nachrichten aus der ideologischen Antike*," in *Die Frage des Zusammenhangs: Alexander Kluge im Kontext*, ed. Christian Schulte (Berlin: Vorwerk 8, 2012), p. 275.

257. Kluge, *Nachrichten aus der ideologischen Antike*, liner notes, p. 4.

258. On Leibniz and *plumpes Denken*, see Kluge, *Glückliche Umstände, leihweise*, p. 345.

259. Heiner Müller, "The Mission: Memory of a Revolution," in *Theatremachine*, ed. and trans. Marc von Henning (London: Faber and Faber, 1995), pp. 59–84.

260. Kluge, "Revolutionärer Versuch an den Rändern Frankreichs," in *Tür an Tür mit einem anderen Leben*, p. 346.

261. Susan Buck-Morss, "Hegel and Haiti," in *Hegel, Haiti, and Universal History* (Pittsburgh: University of Pittsburgh Press, 2009), pp. 74–75.

262. See the Appendix, s.v. "History."

NOTES ON THE TRANSLATION

1. Oskar Negt and Alexander Kluge, *Geschichte und Eigensinn*, vol. 2, *Der unterschätzte Mensch: Gemeinsame Philosophie in zwei Bänden* (Frankfurt am Main: Zweitausendeins, 2001), p. 1,283.

2. Fredric Jameson, "On Negt and Kluge," *October* 46 (Autumn 1988), p. 151.

3. See Alexander Kluge, "Öffentlichkeit und Erfahrung, Faust," in Sebastian Huber and Claus Philipp (eds.), *Magazin des Glücks* (Vienna: Springer Verlag, 2007), pp. 95–96.

PREFACE

1. [*Translator's note*: Unlike, for example, Hannah Arendt, who parses the concept of "labor" (equated with *Arbeit* in the 1967 German translation of *The Human Condition* originally published in English in 1958) and relates it to the other categories of what she calls the *vita activa*, namely, "work" and "action," the authors do not explicitly qualify or differentiate their use of *Arbeit* in *Geschichte und Eigensinn*. Following commonly accepted translations of frequently used Marxian concepts such as *Arbeitsvermögen*, *Arbeitskraft,* and *Arbeitsprozess*, the translators have generally rendered *Arbeit* as "labor" while nevertheless allowing for "work," depending on context. On their recognition of the plenitude of English equivalents for *Arbeit*, see the entry s.v. "Labor" in the Glossary.]

2. The eyes change their focal point in short spans of 0.2 to 1.5 seconds when viewing a well-structured image. It has been be observed "that preferred eye movements are characterized by the contours of stimulus patterns, their interruptions or the ways they overlap one another.... The eyes and the mouth (are) common points of fixation. After observing the motor scanning movements of the eyes long enough, a 'movement image' results." O.-J. Grüsser, "Augenbewegungen bei Betrachtung komplexer Reizmuster," *Physiologie des Menschen*, ed. R. F. Schmidt and G. Thews, 19th ed. (Berlin: Springer Verlag, 1977), p. 261.

CHAPTER ONE: THE ORIGINS OF LABOR CAPACITIES IN SEPARATION

1. [*Translator's note*: The theoretically rich term *Eigenschaft* used throughout Negt and Kluge's collaborations is rendered here and throughout *History and Obstinacy* as "characteristic." Etymologically derived from the Latin *proprietas*, and further from *proprius*, meaning "one's own, particular," the German word *Eigenschaft*, literally "a condition of or object in one's possession," is also often related to the English word "quality" (as in Robert Musil's novel *Der Mann ohne Eigenschaften* [*The Man without Qualities*] from 1930–42) and "trait" (as in the various trait theories of personality psychology). Contrary to the inconsistent use of both "quality" and "characteristic" in the English translation of Negt and Kluge's *Public Sphere and Experience*, ed. Peter Labanyi, Jamie Owen Daniel, and Assenka Oksiloff (Minneapolis: University of Minnesota Press, 1993), pp. 2 and 296, the translators of this volume have retained the predominant usage of the latter term as found in the Marx and Engels's *Collected Works*, which is used here exclusively. In

addition to its distance from matters of value that Marx often associated with quality and quantity, "characteristic" is also fitting on account of its ability to convey the making and malleability of *Eigenschaften* in the sense of the Greek *kharaktēr*, meaning "a stamping tool." Readers should be mindful, however, that what falls away with either translation is the morphological relationship between *Eigenschaft*, *Eigentum* (property) and *Eigensinn* (obstinacy).]

2. Karl Marx, "Outlines of the Critique of Political Economy," in *Collected Works*, vol. 28, *Economic Works, 1857–61* (London: Lawrence and Wishart, 1986), p. 431. [*Translator's note*: The *Collected Works* are hereafter cited as *MECW*.]

3. [*Translator's citation*: Bertolt Brecht, "The Manifesto," trans. Darko Suvin, *Socialism and Democracy* 16.1 (2002), pp. 1–10.]

4. [*Translator's citation and note*: Karl Marx, *Economic and Philosophic Manuscripts of 1844*, in *MECW*, vol. 3, *March 1843 – August 1844*, p. 336: "Whenever real, corporeal man, man with his feet firmly on the solid ground, man exhaling and inhaling all the forces of nature, posits his real, objective essential powers as alien objects by his externalisation, it is not the *act of* positing which is the subject in this process: it is the subjectivity of objective essential powers, whose action, therefore, must also be something objective. An objective being acts objectively, and he would not act objectively if the objective did not reside in the very nature of his being. He only creates or posits objects, because he is posited by objects—because at bottom he is nature. In the act of positing, therefore, this objective being does not fall from his state of 'pure activity' into a creating *of the* object; on the contrary, his objective product only confirms his objective activity, his activity as the activity of an objective, natural being.... Here we see how consistent naturalism or humanism is distinct from both idealism and materialism, and constitutes at the same time the unifying truth of both. We see also how only naturalism is capable of comprehending the action of world history." Source cited and glossed in the German original of *History and Obstinacy* are Oskar Negt and Alexander Kluge, *Geschichte und Eigensinn*, vol. 2, *Der unterschätzte Mensch: Gemeinsame Philosophie in zwei Bänden* (Frankfurt am Main: Zweitausendeins, 2001), p. 78. Boldface in Negt and Kluge and italics in *MECW*.]

5. [*Translator's note*: The German word *Steuerung*, as in *Steuerungsvermögen* above, presents a persistent resistance to simple translation. Evoked repeatedly in various compound nouns from here onward—for example, *Steuerungsarbeit*, *Steuerungsfähigkeit*, *Feinsteuerung*, *Steuerungsverlust*—the term has been rendered in translations of other kindred texts as "control" or "steering." Both of these options, as well as the corollaries "navigation" and, here, "maneuvering," are used throughout *History and Obstinacy* in order to emphasize the balancing act implied therein.]

6. The decisive formulation of this in the *Grundrisse* (*MECW*, vol. 28, pp. 399–438) is found in "Forms Preceding Capitalist Production" and part 8 of *Capital Volume* 1, "The So-Called Primitive Accumulation" (*MECW*, vol. 35, pp. 704–50): 1. "The Secret of Primitive Accumulation"; 2. "Expropriation of the Agricultural Population from the Land"; 3. "Blood Legislation Against the Expropriated, from the End of the 15th Century..."; 4. "Genesis of the Capitalist Farmer"; 5. "Reaction of the Agricultural Revolution on Industry. Creation of the Home Market for Industrial Capital"; 6. "Genesis of the Industrial Capitalist"; 7. "Historical Tendency of Capitalist Accumulation." Marx essentially limits himself in *Capital* to an exemplary case; a more general theoretical approach is offered in the *Grundrisse*. These were rediscovered in 1932 and thus could not have been known to revolutionary theorists in 1917. Orthodox economics draws on them selectively and misjudges their scope.

7. The demolition of a derelict house occupied by squatters who are under police surveillance is an example of this cruder grasp; it is different from the mute force of economic relations that express their violence indirectly. There are two dimensions at work when a firm collapses and puts masses of its workers out on the street: on the one hand, it is the result of the law of economic movement; on the other, it is a devaluation of life histories, the directly violent supplemental production of "industrial army reserves," the self-evident crude grasp. War is another form of the crude grasp.

8. [*Translator's note and citation*: Negt and Kluge list three additional priorities in the German original: the conditions for the political economy's conceptualization, the organization of experience, and derealization. See Negt and Kluge, *Geschichte und Eigensinn*, p. 31.]

9. Capital is not a metaphoric concept, because it does not comprise the entire context.

10. Marx and Engels, "Outlines of the Critique of Political Economy," in *MECW*, vol. 28, p. 415. The conditions and means of production are a "[second] skin," his "sense organs" (*ibid.*, p. 409); "the primordial instrument of...the soil itself," "spontaneous fruits" (*ibid.*, p. 422); "results and repositories of subjective activity" (*ibid.*, p. 413); "The individual relates simply to the objective conditions of labour as his own, as the inorganic nature of his subjectivity, which realises itself through them" (*ibid.*, p. 409); "the workshop of his forces and the domain of his will" (*ibid.*, p. 421).

11. *Ibid.*, pp. 399 and 416.

12. [*Translator's citation*: Gerhart Hauptmann, *The Weavers*, trans. Theodore H. Lustig, in *Plays*, ed. Reinhold Grimm (New York: Continuum, 1994) 91–165.]

13. [*Translator's note and citation*: Arguing that both Vladimir Lenin's and Theodor W. Adorno's respective concepts fall short of what actually consti-

tutes the dialectic, Negt and Kluge contend elsewhere that the dialectic is both a tool for the materialist method *and* "the shape that cohesive [*zusammenhängende*] material processes" assume in "real-world events." "This is the material foundation of dialectics: what develops from the bottom up in turn manufactures well-organized, multipolar relations between lord and bondman from the top down. Dialectics is the specific form in which the elemental character of an organization changes." See also "The Principle of 'Cowardice in Thought'" in Chapter 4 of the present volume, "The Idiosyncrasy of Everyday Movements" in Chapter 5, as well as Negt and Kluge, *Geschichte und Eigensinn*, pp. 240 and 239.]

14. [*Translator's note*: *Zusammenhang* and its derivatives can be rendered variously as "context," "connection," "connection making," "relation," "relationship," "perspective," and "relationality." In keeping with the core of scholarship on Negt and Kluge, the last of these is used wherever possible, with the first operating as an alternative.]

15. [*Translator's citation*: See Walter Benjamin, *The Arcades Project*, trans. Howard Eiland and Kevin McLaughlin (Cambridge, MA: The Belknap Press, 1999) B1a, 2.]

16. [*Translator's citation*: Friedrich Engels, "The Part Played by Labour in the Transition from Ape to Man," in *Dialectics of Nature* (Moscow: Foreign Languages Publishing House, 1954), pp. 228 and 234.]

17. See Bernhard Grzimek (ed.), *Tierleben: Enzyklopädie des Tierreiches*, vol. 13 (Zürich: Kindler, 1968), pp. 117–41. Grzimek's authors explain: "The closeness of the hippopotamus's characteristics to those of primates is somewhat irritating. In fact, it lives in schools and raises its calves in organized groups that include [older calves that act like] 'aunts.'" P. Chalmers Mitchell, *The Childhood of Animals* (New York: Frederick A. Stokes Company Publishers, 1912): "African travelers have described the sudden apparition of a small hippopotamus above the water, rising up until it appeared to be standing on the surface, but really being carried on the mother's back" (p. 172). Ronald M. Nowak, *Walker's Mammals of the World*, 6th ed., vol. 2 (Baltimore: Johns Hopkins University Press, 1999): "The calf may scramble onto [the mother's] back and sun itself while she is floating at the surface. Such behavior may afford some protection against crocodiles" (p. 1070).

In his diaries, Leonardo da Vinci attributes a special intelligence to the hippopotamus. When they infiltrate Egyptian fields at night in order to feed on grains, they edge their way in backward, their heads pointing away from the field, so that it appears to an observer as if they were leaving.

**CHAPTER TWO: SELF-REGULATION
AS A NATURAL CHARACTERISTIC**

1. Karl Marx, *Economic and Philosophic Manuscripts of 1844*, in Karl Marx and Frederick Engels, *Collected Works*, vol. 3, *March 1843 – August 1844* (London: Lawrence and Wishart, 1975), pp. 300–301. [*Translator's note*: The *Collected Works* is hereafter cited as *MECW*. Both italics from the *MECW* and boldface from *Geschichte und Eigensinn* are retained throughout.]

2. *Ibid.*, pp. 301–302.

3. Karl Marx, *The Eighteenth Brumaire of Louis Bonaparte*, in *MECW*, vol. 11, *August 1851 – March 1853*, p. 190.

4. [Translator's citation: Marx, *Economic and Philosophic Manuscripts of* 1844, in *MECW*, vol. 3, p. 299.]

5. Klaus Theweleit, in *Male Fantasies*, trans. Erica Carter and Chris Turner, vol. 2, (Minneapolis: University of Minnesota Press, 1987), pp. 164–69, describes this with respect to soldiers, especially in the context of blacking out. The process Theweleit discusses is more complex than is presented here. But the contradictory constellation has to dissolve itself into this loss of consciousness, that is, of brains; to be sure, it must also express itself in this way.

6. [*Translator's note and citation*: See V.I. Lenin, "The Collapse of the Second International," in *Collected Works of V. I. Lenin*, vol. 21, *August 1914 – December 1915* (London: Lawrence and Wishart, 1964), pp. 213–14: "For a revolution to take place, it is usually insufficient for 'the lower classes not to want' to live in the old way; it is also necessary that 'the upper classes should be unable' to live in the old way."]

7. Sigmund Freud, "Formulations on The Two Principles of Mental Functioning," in *The Standard Edition of the Complete Psychological Works of Sigmund Freud*, trans. James Strachey, vol. 12 (London: The Hogarth Press and the Institute of Psycho-Analysis, 1958), p. 225. "One is bound to employ the currency that is in use in the country one is exploring—in our case a **neurotic currency**" (*ibid.*, p. 225). [*Translator's note*: boldface added by Negt and Kluge.]

8. On the category of the monad, see Gottfried Wilhelm Leibniz, "The Principles of Philosophy, or, the Monadology," *Philosophical Essays*, ed. and trans. Roger Ariew and Daniel Garber (Indianapolis: Hackett Publishing Company, 1989), pp. 213–24. "Thus, neither substance nor accident can enter a monad from without" (p. 214).

9. [*Translator's note*: The German original characterizes the declaration as including "fraternity" as a third operative term. The translation makes a slight change in the text here to account, on the one hand, for its formal absence in the founding document of the French Revolution and, on the other,

its currency in the historical discourse. See: Mona Ozouf, s.v. "Fraternity," in *A Critical Dictionary of The French Revolution*, ed. François Furet and Mona Ozouf, trans. Arthur Goldhammer (Cambridge, MA: Harvard University Press, 1989).]

10. A report once told of a woman whose child was pinned underneath a car. In this state of emergency, she lifted the heavy vehicle and rescued her child.

11. Similar forms of stimuli can be transmitted and controlled retroactively by different receptive organs. However, these organs are not distributed equally throughout the body. Pressure and pain are not readily distinguishable. For those organs sensitive to coldness and warmth, the clarification provided by stimuli is never conclusive.

12. At the periphery of the field of perception, nerves cooperatively switch to the opposite pole. They turn "off" and form a zone of inhibition. At the interface between a stimulated field and its periphery, a contrast based on the selectivity of the sensation forms automatically.

13. We wish to note that the brain's forms of self-regulation are entirely different from those operating locally and in concert with the fine touch of the fingertips. The retina's autonomous activity, the processing of impressions, and the eyes' movement again have their own spheres. The specific relation of relationships, with its disruptions and successful forms of cooperation, **between** these forms of regulation is constituted by a further self-regulating authority, that of the "between." We must ask whether any such autonomous circles could engage in their specific form of self-regulation without the others. In this respect, self-regulation always amounts to a category of relationality. If two autonomous activities come in contact with one another, then a tendency emerges to sublate the resulting friction and separation from pure autonomous activity through the formation of relationality. The sublation represents itself as independent self-regulation with its own laws. Although initially these merely apply to what they unite, they certainly catalyze friction and separation again from above to below, once more releasing anew chains of autonomous activity.

14. Marx, *Economic and Philosophic Manuscripts of 1844*, in *MECW*, vol. 3, p. 298.

15. On the category of the "not yet fully born," see the examples in Theweleit, *Male Fantasies*, vol. 2, pp. 252–62. One of Theweleit's premises is that an endemic lack of precision grips in early child rearing and an excess of harsh grips prematurely led an entire generation of children, at least in the Wilhelmian era, to break off their development as nourished by the self-regulating energies of the libidinal economy. They were not "finished being born." The self-regulation of libidinal energies, inexpressible in the form of the extensive training of mental authorities, did not become invalid. Rather, CHARACTER ARMOR formed, and the discharge

of libidinal energy took place through specific processes that Theweleit represents in his rich material on soldiers and workers especially vulnerable to exploitation. What could have found its form in self-regulation became energy that ruptured anarchically. It was not a case of "where **id** was, there shall **ego** be," but rather what could not defend the form of its self-determined nature against the pressure of the reality principle became a tool for striking or for the rigidity of work. [*Translator's citation*: Sigmund Freud, "New Introductory Lectures on Psycho-Analysis," in *The Standard Edition of the Complete Psychological Works of Sigmund Freud*, trans. James Strachey, vol. 22 (London: The Hogarth Press and the Institute of Psycho-Analysis, 1964), p. 80.]

16. [*Translator's note*: Italics retained from the English Kant translation and boldface from the German original of *Geschichte und Eigensinn*.]

17. Michel Foucault, *Discipline and Punish: The Birth of the Prison*, trans. Alan Sheridan (New York: Vintage Books, 1977) pp. 25–27 and 103.

18. There is a similar illusion criticized by Marx in his description of the **trinitarian formula**. Allegedly, the soil or capital produces **value**, and labor receives its reward. In actuality, the applied labor power is what works on the soil and within capital, thus producing the value partly retained in the form of a wage.

The educator mediates values and realism. (This mediation also appears as value maxims). But these values themselves produce no direct change in the child, who can encounter them for years without recognizing them. In the real development and transformation of a child's characteristics through education and upbringing, the teacher has an understanding of self-regulative processes — hence the attributes of self-regulation, regardless whether he is aware of this or confuses it with his intentions and conception of values — together with that of the self-regulating economy of the drives and its coded value within the child. From this labor, an exchange emerges, which is to say a unification of forces materializes that mediates values or real-life facts to the child. Here, too, labor produces value by generating the product, and this is possible only in line with the particular laws of both the childhood economy of drives and the teacher; value itself does not perform work.

CHAPTER THREE: ELEMENTS OF A POLITICAL ECONOMY OF LABOR POWER

1. See, for example, Karl Marx and Frederick Engels, "The Inaugural Address of the Working Men's International Association," in *Collected Works*, vol. 20, *Marx and Engels: 1864–1868* (London: Lawrence and Wishart, 1985), p. 11: "Hence the Ten Hours' Bill was not only a great practical success; it was the victory of a principle; it was the first time that in broad daylight the political economy of the

middle class succumbed to the political economy of the working class." [*Translator's note*: The *Collected Works* is hereafter cited as *MECW*.]

2. *Ibid.* "But there was in store a still greater victory of the political economy of labour over the political economy of property." In the English original, this passage about **property** pertains to Robert Owen's system of cooperative factories.

3. See Karl Marx, *Economic and Philosophic Manuscripts of 1844*, in *MECW*, vol. 3, *March 1843–August 1844*, p. 325. [*Translator's note*: The italics are original to the English translation of Marx. The German *Vermögen*, as in *Arbeitsvermögen*, is rendered here in the Marx translation as "faculty," whereas the translators of *History and Obstinacy* have opted for "capacity" wherever possible. While both convey a sense of ability, quality, and power, the latter, which is also used liberally in the *MECW* translation of *Capital*, underscores the concept's reference to a holding space capable of containing and producing, as in this case, labor.]

4. [*Translator's citation*: Karl Marx, *Capital, Volume 1*, in *MECW*, vol. 35, p. 26.]

5. It is a natural need to have something essential to do with another human whom I love. The natural power contained in the economy of the drives would take into consideration all relationships that make it possible to get close to this love object. This power would also certainly be inventive as to how to search for labor resources and how to bring them closer to the object. We would also need to test what aligns the incest taboo when the loved one belongs to one's family. We would additionally have to test the immense accumulation of prohibitions, laws, and moral concepts (wherein dead labor lies). We would quickly see here the separations between the means of production and the object.

6. We wish to tease out the difference between the immense relevance of what Marx says in "The General Relation of Production to Distribution, Exchange, and Consumption" on pages 26 to 36 of the introduction to "Outlines of the Critique of Political Economy" and the peculiar unreal impression aroused in the reader armed with an ordinary feeling for language by the string of words on these pages. [*Translator's citation*: Karl Marx, "Outlines of the Critique of Political Economy," in *MECW*, vol. 28, *Economic Works, 1857–1861*, pp. 26–28.]

7. In the *Grundrisse*, Marx criticizes Adam Smith (*ibid.*, p. 530) for attempting to derive a kind of valuation of labor from the victims it yields. Marx sees therein a misunderstanding rooted in the Old Testament. He quotes Engels (*Economic and Philosophic Manuscripts of 1844*, in *MECW*, vol. 3, p. 290) as having called Adam Smith the Luther of political economy. Marx counters Smith by arguing that there exists a need for a "normal portion" of human labor. The labor does not stand vis-à-vis any old originary instance of peace and quiet [*Ruhe*], so the unrest of labor does not represent simply a sacrificial transition toward a final state of calm.

8. Bertolt Brecht, "Flüchtlingsgespräche," in *Werke*, vol. 3, *Prosa 3*, ed. Jan Knopf (Berlin: Aufbau-Verlag, 1995), p. 263.

9. *Ibid.*, p, 262: "Hegel had what it takes to be one of the greatest humorists among philosophers." "Like all great humorists, he delivered everything with a deadly serious expression on his face"; "everything seems quiet and sluggish at first and then suddenly a bang comes along. With Hegel, the concepts always constantly teeter on a chair, which at first makes a particularly pleasant impression until it falls over." Hegel's *Science of Logic* "deals with the ways by which concepts live, those slippery, unstable, irresponsible things. It's about how they berate one another and fight each other with knives and then sit down to dinner together as if nothing happened. They appear in pairs, so to speak, each one is married to its opposite and they finish their business as a couple. In other words, they sign contracts as a couple, go to court as a couple, organize muggings and burglaries as a couple, write books and give depositions as a couple, and do so, in fact, as a couple completely at odds with one another in every respect. They can't live without each other and they can't live with each other." [*Translator's note and citation*: The fourth portion of this translation is taken and slightly revised from excerpts published in: Bertolt Brecht, "Conversations in Exile," trans David Dollenmayer, *Theater* 17.2 (Spring 1986), p. 13.]

10. [*Translator's citation*: Bertolt Brecht, "An Karl," in *Werke*, vol. 13: *Gedichte 3: Gedichte und Gedichtfragmente*, ed. Jan Knopf and Brigitte Bergheim (Berlin: Aufbau-Verlag, 1993), p. 376.]

11. Marx, *Capital, Volume 1*, in *MECW*, vol. 35, pp. 187–208.

12. A machine can have a shorter life span, like that of a person, but as with the crane "Milchsack No. 4" it can also witness several generations pass. Machines do not appear as individuals, but as entire associations of generations. The constructions following a worn-out machine accumulate the dead labor contained in its predecessors. Only a *certain* amount of living labor is added for its production. The bulk is "bequeathed." This is especially clear with the pedigree of machine tools and the breeding of sophisticated computers, into which the knowledge of all previous generations of computers is incorporated.

13. The capitalist period is a unique case, insofar as its measures of time bear relatively short-term, yet exceptional changes. However, the contradiction between living and dead labor did not first exist in the capitalist period. For example, peasants soon circumvented the feudal power produced as a form of superiority from their living political labor. Initially, a division of labor arose only between those busy farming and those who were armed to protect the community from external threats. The product of this division of labor then became independent, that is, by virtue of their possession of previously produced notions

of faithfulness and bondage, the feudal lords were in the position to oppress the formerly free peasants. However, such oppression was at the lord's own disposal only to a small extent. Oppression was related to a far greater extent to the dead labor of producers, who brought forth a specific social system of relationships, namely, that of feudalism.

14. [*Translator's note and citations*: Translated here as "life-context" according to the prevalent usage throughout Jürgen Habermas's English-language publications, Negt and Kluge's use of *Lebenszusammenhang*, along with Habermas's, reaches back to Wilhelm Dilthey's hermeneutics, for which "life-nexus" is the usual translation. For Habermas's earliest sustained encounter with Dilthey, see Jürgen Habermas, *Knowledge and Human Interest*, trans. Jeremy J. Shapiro (Boston: Beacon Press, 1971), p. 140–60. See also Wilhelm Dilthey, *Introduction to the Human Sciences*, ed. Rudolf A. Makkreel and Frithjof Rodi (Princeton: Princeton University Press, 1989), pp. 277–81.]

15. The general strike contains no reversal of alliances; it is not an alliance of living labor and dead labor. Rather, it is the making public of its secret. Dead labor produces nothing for itself. Abandoned by living labor, it is at a standstill. Living labor can ascertain this demonstrative image for itself. At this moment, it produces a public sphere, a political product, but its productivity, too, comes to a standstill. This side of the contradiction discloses itself in the fact that the condition of the general strike can have no permanency, while production is something permanent.

According to Marx, the production side of a general strike, namely, the alliance of living and dead labor that becomes generally available, is the "Republic of Labor," the "victory of the political economy of labor over the political economy of capital," which according to Marx's description, appeared in the Paris Commune as a "working...body" [*arbeitende Körperschaft*]. [*Translator's citations*: Karl Marx, "The Civil War in France: Address of the General Council of the International Working Men's Association," in *MECW*, vol. 22, *Marx and Engels, 1870–1871*, p. 336; Marx, "Inaugural Address of the Working Men's International Association," in *MECW*, vol. 20, p. 11 and *MECW*, vol. 22, p. 331.]

16. [*Translator's citation*: Marx, *Capital, Volume 1*, in *MECW*, vol. 35, p. 331.]

17. Marx describes this for a sphere of politics in *Economic and Philosophic Manuscripts of 1844, MECW*, vol. 3, p. 313: "When communist artisans associate with one another, theory, propaganda, etc. is their first end. But at the same time, as a result of this association, they acquire a new need—the need for society—and what appears as a means becomes an end."

18. No human can permanently endure a purely instrumental mode of labor. As long as it is temporarily possible at all, it is thus probable that a second layer of production overlies the **unreality** of abstract labor. Contrary to all realism, the female

worker will also exert herself to make the product as well as possible. In addition, she will produce relationships in her relation to other female workers. At the same time that she changes her clothes after work, she also dresses herself with those attributes of her person that until then remain unengaged. This change in wardrobe takes effect when she returns to the circle of people with whose assistance she produces her person outside of work. This second, parallel person, the one at work and the other in relationships, is the real of the workday. The dialectic of person and abstraction, in turn, is to be applied once again to this second production.

19. Marianne Herzog, *From Hand to Mouth: Women and Piecework*, trans. Stanley Mitchell (Harmondsworth, UK: Penguin Books, 1980), pp. 55–56: "By this time both Frau Bartz and Frau Winterfeld must have welded 30 tubes. By this time about two thirds of all the female workers in the shop have begun welding. Frau Heinrich has arrived. She takes out her yoghurt and places it on the machine, starts up the machine and empties onto it the first box of materials. She sits in a row behind Frau Winterfeld and Frau Bartz. Frau Heinrich's work goes in short cycles. You can tell that by the boxes stacked up in front of her which make up her day's task. She almost disappears behind them. Her work-cycle lasts for nine seconds. She picks up a base with her hand and a support with a pair of tweezers and welds the support to the base. She does the same with the second support and puts the finished base in the box. To be able to go on like this Frau Heinrich has extended her movements over the years, within the limits of piecework. She has invented a few additional movements, but still manages to get through the required amount of work. She doesn't simply pick up the materials and weld them together beneath the electrode. If you watch her you see that she spreads out her arms as if she were flying, draws them together and picks up the materials with both hands as if she had come upon them by pure chance. As she does this she rocks backwards and forwards, treads on the foot pedal three or four times, and only then welds the first part. Then out go the arms again. Frau Heinrich uses all of this to help her get through her piecework, otherwise it would be superfluous movement and she couldn't afford it. She does exactly the same thing with her feet. She has to weld two spots on every unit, while the other women have to do from twelve to sixteen. But here again Frau Heinrich adds a few movements. While she picks up the pieces and before she puts them under the electrode she treads three or four times on the foot pedal, and only then does the real welding. Frau Heinrich has developed these movements in resistance to the inhuman piecework." [*Translator's note*: translation slightly modified.]

20. Marx, *Capital, Volume 1*, in *MECW*, vol. 35, p. 53.

21. The different deficits and the principle of extracting energies from the terrain of the balance economy, which particularly affects the potential for labor capacities focused on general interests, explains the appearance of passivity.

22. [*Translator's note*: On the semantic field deployed for the permutations of *Steuerung* here, see note 5 in Chapter 1. See also s.v. "Navigational Labor" in the Glossary.]

23. On this context, see Max Horkheimer, "Authority and the Family," in *Critical Theory: Selected Essays*, trans. Matthew J. O'Connell (New York: Continuum, 1982), pp. 47–128.

24. A German worker would have linguistic and political difficulties informing a Chinese worker about the experience of his social class; they could instantaneously and nonverbally compare notes on the skills required to repair a machine familiar to them both or to fasten a screw.

25. The motive for realism is never the confirmation of reality, but rather protest. This protest can express itself when collective forms exist that mediate its expression. At the same time, the labor of protest requires self-consciousness when toiling away at overpowering reality. This is much like a child who attains self-consciousness in its successful relationships to primary objects or an adult who acquires it only through manifold transpositions and repetitions of a fundamental relationship. The production therefore presupposes a **form of publicness** (that is, a **social relation**) and at the same time trust (that is, a certain **relation of relationships that I have for myself**). [*Translator's note and citation*: Compare this formulation with Alexander Kluge, "The Sharpest Ideology: That Reality Appeals to Its Realistic Character," trans. David Roberts, in *Alexander Kluge: Raw Materials for the Imagination*, ed. Tara Forrest (Amsterdam: Amsterdam University Press, 2012), p. 192.]

26. Countless fairy tales tell of children who were not loved, who had stepparents, or whose one sibling was unmistakably preferred. Today, they possess a scintilla of happiness because the antirealism of their feeling defends them, and their trust is based on something other than their parents (for example, the seven dwarfs, a good hunter, and so on). Perhaps they are especially resourceful in their adversity. In fairy tales, the fate of these children takes a turn. However, if nothing trustworthy is found, in spite of the twists of fate, they cannot be objective. So-called evil assembles itself this way. It is unfair that the second passed-over son, Franz Moor, in Schiller's play *The Robbers*, turns evil, while Karl Moor, the beloved son, remains noble as a robber. The protest against this injustice prompts the wish that the entanglement be reversed. "Because it happened to me this way, I will do exactly the opposite." Such reversals correspond to experience, whereby the one treated impertinently produces objectivity. However, he must have won trust from another source, having reason to do so. Utter lack of trust cannot engender a turn of fate.

27. Dostoevsky: "Everybody is guilty of everything, but if everybody knew that, we would have paradise on earth." Someone who expands his ownness

[*Eigenes*] through hermetic trust at the expense of others encounters an environment that always yields; this is a fictional relationship. This is tolerable neither for the person in question nor for anybody else. Bracketing him out would be equally fictional. Only fighting is realistic, because it tolerates the antirealism of constellations. [*Translator's note and citation*: Kluge has used this Dostoevsky quote since *Yesterday Girl* (1966), in which it appears as the film's final intertitle; the translation here is directly from Kluge's German translation and does not reflect current English translations. See Fyodor Dostoevsky, *The Brothers Karamazov*, ed. Susan McReynolds Oddo, trans. Constance Garnett, 2nd ed. (New York: W. W. Norton, 2011), p. 257: "we are each responsible to all for all, it's only that men don't know this. If they knew it, the world would be a paradise at once." See also the translation in Gary Indiana, "Alexander Kluge," *BOMB* 27 (Spring 1997), p. 50.]

28. Of course, Medea (without Jason), Othello (in a nonracist society), a Kohlhaas (whose sense of justice has not been injured to the quick), Hamlet (in the presence of his father, who had not been murdered), Lady Macbeth (if no monarchy had existed), each of these figures would have had no reason for their specific hermetic potentiation of forces. They could have formed groups without any tragic conflict, the way Fourier, in *The Theory of the Four Movements*, adapted the grouping of his phalanstères in such a way that Nero could fit in as the best master butcher in the world. With hermetic labor capacities, there is the problem of retranslating these forces back into simple labor. This is possible only outside their specific situation (that is to say, athwart the reality principle); it presupposes a transformation that must be produced from capacities capable of creating associations.

29. If a miner washes and changes his clothes, does this belong to the time of labor, or to free time? This interest in differentiation is the primary object over which labor went to battle in Germany after 1918.

30. Bertolt Brecht describes this in the parable of laborers who said: we thought we were producing parts for baby carriages, but when put together, they turned out to be machine guns.

31. Ernst Bloch, *The Principle of Hope*, vol. 1, trans. Neville Plaice, Stephen Plaice, and Paul Knight (Cambridge, MA: MIT Press, 1986), pp. 51–64). Bloch's explanation is perplexing. Bloch says at another point: "Man does not live from bread alone...especially...when he does not have any." He also says: "The human hunger is not *just* simple, like that of animals, and what he eats tastes better." By playing hunger against libidinal drives, he obviously refers to a materialistic procedure that initially requires bringing the completely elementary into view before hidden, mediated forces can be made visible. There is no doubt that Bloch does not believe hunger is the driving force of history; rather, one could speak of imagined hunger, that is, the utopic image of unsatisfied being that drives humans and

history forward. Nevertheless, the necessity still exists for a materialist to grasp once again what is self-evident. He therefore thinks that the uridealist Schiller is closer to the real relations with his proposition that hunger and love are the driving forces of humans than Freud was. Bloch is not mistrustful of Freud, but rather of Freud's Viennese environment. His insistence on the history of hunger is not an attempt at a materialistic reduction—an attempt at desublimination—but comes out of the Blochian trust in the sublimination processes of hunger. He thus wants to know that the labor of hope is not founded upon what he views as the offshoot of the libidinal structure, but upon the allegedly stronger roots of adversity. Herein Bloch evinces a critique of the arrogance to which some intellectuals are attached, those who immediately set their sights on culturally differentiated mediations as something more important before they recognize and acknowledge these elementary relations of adversity. [*Translator's citations*: Ernst Bloch, *Politische Messungen, Pestzeit, Vormärz*, in *Werkausgabe*, vol. 11 (Frankfurt am Main: Suhrkamp, 1979), p. 397; and Bloch, *Tübinger Einleitung in die Philosophie*, in *Werkausgabe*, vol. 13 (Frankfurt am Main: Suhrkamp, 1979), p. 15.]

32. Bloch, *The Principle of Hope*, vol. 1, p. 56. [*Translator's note*: italics in the Bloch translation.]

33. The music of Beethoven's later string quartets is considered deeply profound; Offenbach's music is considered superficial. Theodor W. Adorno always insisted that tones themselves neither move their hearers nor allow themselves to be understood according to these categories. "Beneath the skin" of later Beethovenian constructions, according to Adorno, lies a substratum of skin (he calls it "subcutaneous," hence "under the skin") that produces both real motion and delight. This substratum can also be present in apparently superficial kinds of music. To this end, he interprets the return of a motif in Tchaikovsky—particularly because of the concertante return of the motif certainly unbeknownst to the composer, that is to say, because of its superficiality—as the return of the dead, as "depth." Compare also the analysis of the music pieces cited in the first volume of Marcel Proust's *Remembrance of Things Past*. They are salon pieces of primitive quality. From listening and through Proust's writing, they obtain a quality they do not themselves possess, a free surface that nevertheless allows for the intensity of feeling. [*Translator's note and citation*: Negt and Kluge are referring here to Theodor W. Adorno, "Toward an Understanding of Schoenberg," in *Essays on Music*, ed. Richard Leppert, trans. Susan H. Gillespie (Berkeley: University of California Press, 2002), p. 634.]

34. Harry F. Harlow, "The Nature of Love," *American Psychologist* 13.12 (December 1958), pp. 673–85.

35. *Ibid.*, p. 673: "There can be no question that almost any external stimulus can become a secondary reinforcer if properly associated with tissue-need reduc-

tion, but the fact remains that this redundant literature demonstrates unequivocally that such derived drives suffer relatively rapid experimental extinction. Contrariwise, human affection does not extinguish when the mother ceases to have intimate association with the drives in question. Instead, the affectional ties to the mother show a lifelong, unrelenting persistence and, even more surprising, widely expanding generality." Harlow thus comes to grips with John B. Watson, who presumes that an inborn capacity to love is reanimated though tender (cutaneous) stimulation of the erogenous zones.

36. *Ibid.*, p. 674–75. "We had separated more than 60 of these animals from their mothers 6 to 12 hours after birth and suckled them on tiny bottles. The infant mortality was only a small fraction of what would have obtained had we let the monkey mothers raise their infants. **Our bottle-fed babies were healthier and heavier than monkey-mother-reared infants**. We know that we are better monkey mothers than are real monkey mothers thanks to synthetic diets, vitamins, iron extracts, penicillin, chloromycetin, 5 % glucose, **and constant, tender, loving care**." [*Translator's note*: Bolding is Negt and Kluge's.]

37. Both mother machines had a ventilator in the background that gave off warmth. But it was not the kind of warmth that would radiate from the wire. The experiments included the introduction of a "typical fear stimulus": the babies fled to the cloth mother, but practically never to the wire mother. The face of the cloth mother was made of wood. After a certain period of time, the same cloth mother was presented with a painted face. The babies turned this head around 180 degrees. Rather than seeing a face, they wanted the wooden head that matched the warm, vibrating, but otherwise immobile skin-covered body of the mother.

38. *Ibid.*, p. 685. Compare the above with Chapter 1, note 18. Systematic observation reveals that the development of the human hand of labor also has this subjective, apparently superficial side and that human labor certainly did not develop without *this* detour out of privation.

39. [*Translator's note and citation*: Verse quoted in *ibid*, pp. 677–78 and taken from an unidentified zoo guide for children.]

40. Sigmund Freud, *Civilization and Its Discontents*, in *The Standard Edition of the Complete Psychological Works of Sigmund Freud*, trans. James Strachey, vol. 21 (London: The Hogarth Press and the Institute of Psycho-Analysis, 1953), p. 70. Our emphasis.

41. This difference must be made clear. In our cities, cars have the right of way at green traffic lights, otherwise collisions occur. The results are visible to the unaided eye: car things [*Auto-Dinge*] really collide in space and time. But this reality is just like the knight at King Arthur's court who says: Do these people not have any eyes in their heads? I can see how the Sun rises on the

eastern horizon and sets on the western horizon. The Sun is therefore moving, not the Earth.

The observation recounted by Freud collides with something that appears clear to the senses. In the historical relation, it would be as if cars driving to and fro in all directions paid no attention to stoplights in the city and nevertheless never collided. But such a historical flow is the real relation; the reification built into an automobile, however, behaves unnaturally and unrealistically toward this flow. Neither the cars themselves (as inanimate objects) nor the living labor that produced them exhibits the tendency to effect collisions with other forms of living labor. At annual fairs, the collision of bumper cars produces enjoyment. It is the historical relation of relationships—dead labor's built-in system of resistance—that enforces the regulatory system of street traffic: built-in private egoism. Recklessness is not a natural form of living labor. Because everything was built up recklessly, a corrective in the form of consideration must be built into the motion.

42. Jürgen Habermas, "Toward a Reconstruction of Historical Materialism," in *Communication and the Evolution of Society*, ed. and trans. Thomas McCarthy (Boston: Beacon Press, 1979), p. 137. [*Translator's note*: italics in the English translation of Habermas, boldface in the Negt and Kluge original.]

CHAPTER FOUR: THE LABOR OF INTELLIGENCE

1. [*Translator's citation*: See Michel Serres, *Hermès*, 5. vols. (Paris: Éditions de Minuit, 1968–1980). Available in English as *Hermes: Literature, Science, Philosophy*, ed. Josué V. Harari and David F. Bell (Baltimore: Johns Hopkins Press, 1982).

2. [*Translator's citation*: Blaise Pascal, *Pensées and Other Writings*, trans. Honor Levi (Oxford: Oxford University Press, 1995), p. 158.]

3. The man who went forth to learn to be afraid [*das Fürchten*] did so in vain because he did not understand what fear [*Angst*] was. This "dumb fool" (Parsifal) did not understand the rules and was therefore independent. An external course of events is similar to this when cunning plays itself out: think, for example, of Eulenspiegel, who wins by acting as if he does not understand, or the solider Švejk in Jaroslav Hašek's picaresque novel, who defends himself against being executed by understanding the words of his masters literally, thus sabotaging them.

4. [*Translator's note*: This translation of the term *vergesellschaften* (as in *Vergesellschaftung*) follows David Frisby's study of German sociologist Georg Simmel, who, according to Frisby, coined the term to designate "processes by which we engage in and are members of society." David Frisby, *Georg Simmel* (London: Routledge, 2002), p. xiv. For more on the origin and development of the term see *ibid.*, pp. xv–xxii.]

5. Freud says: There are the libidinal drives, but the psychologist must not necessarily clarify what their capacities are assembled from or what objective natural proportion or subjective labor are in order to understand and analyze the processes built thereupon. "The study of the sources of instincts lies outside the scope of psychology.... An exact knowledge of the sources of an instinct is not invariably necessary for purposes of psychological investigation." Sigmund Freud, "Instincts and their Vicissitudes," in *The Standard Edition of the Complete Psychological Works of Sigmund Freud*, trans. James Strachey, vol. 14 (London: Hogarth Press and the Institute of Psycho-Analysis, 1981), p. 122. The same goes for the logic of capital, in which the political economy of labor power disappears: the elementary drive energies of the libido appear as something objective; however, from our perspective, they must be resolvable into subjective-objective processes. For Freud, they become subjective-objective only after they fight antagonistically between the poles of the pleasure principle and the reality principle.

6. [*Translator's note and citation*: For a extensive discussion of the potential exceptionality of theory labor, see Oskar Negt and Alexander Kluge, *Geschichte und Eigensinn*, vol. 2, *Der unterschätzte Mensch: Gemeinsame Philosophie in zwei Bänden* (Frankfurt am Main: Zweitausendeins, 2001), pp. 480–85.]

7. [*Translator's citation and note*: Oskar Negt and Alexander Kluge, *Public Sphere and Experience: Toward an Analysis of the Bourgeois and Proletarian Public Sphere*, trans. Peter Labanyi, Jamie Owen Daniel, and Assenka Oksiloff (Minneapolis: University of Minnesota Press, 1993) 24. Compare, too, the previous paragraph with Negt and Kluge, *Public Sphere and Experience*, p. 22 n.37.]

8. Immanuel Kant, *The Critique of Pure Reason*, trans. and ed. Paul Guyer and Allen W. Wood (Cambridge: Cambridge University Press, 1998), p. 627. [*Translator's note*: The first two terms in bold in the quote were added by Negt and Kluge. The remaining typography conforms to the Kant translation.]

9. However, this critique of an inadvertent narrow-mindedness that comes into existence by getting mired down in the particular, from which the universal is supposed to spring forth, does not contain the demand of general, public comprehensibility. In a class-based society, there are degrees of intensity of labor tucked away in the conceptual appropriation of a thing. Whoever demands that all relations should be illustrated simply and immediately in an intelligible fashion overlooks the fact that it does not lie in the power of the concept to express objectively complicated relations simply and clearly. The more complicated the circumstances are, the more labor and groundwork is necessary in order to express them adequately. Insofar as real conceptual labor is at work, what appears to the reader to be hermetically sealed or willfully unintelligible, is frequently nothing other than the obstinate attempt to take possession of something through linguistic

means that elude language. Therefore, the accusation of abstruseness often is leveled not so much against the individual intelligence laborers and their parlance as, more generally, against the network of cultural mediations and detours that break up the objective appearance of simple relations.

10. [*Translator's note and citations:* Described in somewhat greater detail in note 20, Negt and Kluge's reference to "loyalty taxes" is initially established in conjunction with their discussion of the "circulation of economic reproduction" in chapter 4 of the German original that was truncated for the English translation. Based on the work of Hungarian economist Ferenc Jánossy (*Wie die Akkumulationslawine ins Rollen kam: Zur Entstehungsgeschichte des Kapitalismus* [Berlin: Olle and Wolter, 1979]), Negt and Kluge's concept of a loyalty tax refers to the monetary dependence of two primary classes in vertically aggregated economies such as that of the preindustrial Middle Ages: "Following Jánossy we refer to those classes that pay taxes [*Abgaben*] on the things they produce as the **primary sphere of production** and the nonproductive class that appropriates those taxes as the **ruling annex**." A more inclusive concept than socioeconomic class, the cognate "annex," derived from the Old French and Latin for "to tie" or "to join," is deployed to emphasize the interconnectedness of streams of labor, money, and capital within the economy's larger circulatory system. Loyalty applies to those reciprocal relationships between workers and organized forms of labor that sustain both the realization of needs and the flow of labor power. See Negt and Kluge, *Geschichte und Eigensinn*, pp. 248, 243–52, and 132, respectively.]

11. Oskar Negt and Alexander Kluge, "The Fate of the Cognitive Drives: Experience through Production of Knowledge," in *Public Sphere and Experience*, pp. 22–26.

12. It develops monopolies. Such monopolies of the public sphere are in part identical with domination. This is the reason, for example, why dissidents in the Eastern Bloc mistook themselves for an autonomous class.

13. With respect to the generation and preservation of knowledge-constitutive motives, what we call "need," "separation," and "misery" are quite ambiguous. On the one hand, they produce fear and concomitant obstructions to the development of knowledge-constitutive motives, insofar as those motives transcend the immediate labor of survival. They make one blind to situation-dependent interpretations and relationalities. This is even the case for the form of intelligence labor that finds itself under the immediate pressure of ordered production from the ruling class. On the other hand, the emancipation from hardship—the integration of intelligence labor into the dead labor of institutions and other apparatuses—sublates, as a rule, existential need and thereby liberates knowledge-constitutive motives; however, it is at the same time a confinement of the territory of living labor, linked

to the degradation of knowledge-constitutive motives due to the institutionalized neutralizations of planes of conflict and sources of friction. This is one of the
reasons for the often observable sterility that distinguishes major research institutions, at least in comparison with the enormous means they utilize. If one excludes
their foundational phases or even their initial individual wills to research, relations
of listlessness appear quite rapidly. Courage, trust, and the fantasy of knowledge
get lost and often even lead to disruptions of the individual life perspectives of
coworkers. They are freed from external need, but that is apparently insufficient
to keep their original knowledge-constitutive curiosity alive. It is overwhelmed
by dead labor. Only a movement originating from outside, one that bears with it
new motives, could wake it from its sleep.

14. [*Translator's note and citation*: Negt and Kluge deploy here and elsewhere
the term "Probehandeln im Geist" from Sigmund Freud's 1911 essay "Formulations on the Two Principles of Mental Functioning." See Sigmund Freud, *Standard
Edition of the Complete Works of Sigmund Freud*, ed. James Strachey, vol. 12 (London:
Hogarth Press, 1958), pp. 213–26.]

15. Georg Wilhelm Friedrich Hegel, "Inaugural Address, Delivered at the
University of Berlin (22 October 1818)," in *Hegel: Political Writings*, ed. Lawrence
Dickey and H. B. Nisbet, trans. H. B. Nisbet (Cambridge: Cambridge University
Press, 1999), p. 185. [*Translator's note*: emphasis in the Hegel translation.]

16. On the materialistic instinct, see Negt and Kluge, *Public Sphere and Experience*, pp. 43–45; solidarity that can be grasped by the senses belongs to this,
see pp. 38–39; on the desire for the simplification of relations, personalization,
see pp. 40–43; on linguistic barriers, see pp. 45–49; on the activities of fantasy,
see pp. 32–39; on the blockage of experience in the proletarian life context, see
pp. 28–32; on the public sphere of industry, see pp. 49–53.

17. William Shawcross, *Sideshow: Kissinger, Nixon and the Des of Cambodia*
(New York: Simon and Schuster, 1979), pp. 77–78 and 83–84. [*Translator's note and
citation*: Negt and Kluge's fleeting reference to the role of decision making in the
exercise of political power is very likely taken from Carl Schmitt's *The Concept of
the Political* (1927), which they cite in chapter 6 of *History and Obstinacy*. See also
Carl Schmitt, *Political Theology: Four Chapters on the Concept of Sovereignty*, trans.
George Schwab (Chicago: The University of Chicago Press, 2005), pp. 16–35.]

18. [*Translator's citation*: ibid., p. 78.]

19. [*Translator's citation*: ibid., p. 84.]

20. [*Translator's note*: "Decentralized annexes" refers to the modern decentralization of Negt and Kluge's more simplistic, vertically aggregated model of
labor economy based on a medieval dyad of ruler and ruled. (See note 10 above.)
Intelligence in today's economy of labor, they infer, does not subsist solely on

taxes paid by the proletariat or the bourgeoisie. Rather, it lives off of revenues from myriad laboring streams, not to mention interest from stocks, endowments, and charities.]

21. If it were to sublate this relation of domination upon which it so consistently rests, it could not mobilize anything against authority. For example, if the Institute for Social Research in Frankfurt am Main is occupied by students, its authority takes a hit in public. Now neither the occupiers nor the institute can exercise their original power of critique against social relations, as they had done previously.

22. Substantial consideration from the side of manual production, that more and different commodities must be produced than just the object of utility, cannot be understood linearly. Production produces a need, but the need produced at one point, say for luxury objects, can itself create new and expanded needs, so these then emerge as demands on production. Commissions of this kind can become independent under certain conditions, which in the early stages prior to the great German Peasants' War, had the effect, among others, that princes and religious lords demanded ever-greater cash payments instead of the levies paid in kind, which were typical until then. When luxury becomes a demonstrative public exercise of power (as in the times of the Medici and the popes dependent upon them, for example), the competing commissions for architectural and artistic luxury themselves become indices of power and influence.

23. Karl Marx, "Contribution to the Critique of Hegel's *Philosophy of Law*," in *Collected Works*, vol. 3, *March 1843 – August 1844* (London: Lawrence and Wishart, 1975), p. 187. The *Collected Works* is hereafter cited as *MECW*.

24. [*Translator's note and citation*: Kluge refers here to the following televised interview: "Die Rolle der Persönlichkeit in der Evolution," conducted by Alexander Kluge, *10 vor 11*, RTL, September 5, 2011.]

25. [*Translator's note and citation*: This phrase appears in English in the German manuscript. This reference refers to Kluge's televised interview available as "The Magical World of Evolution," *Seen sind für Fische Inseln*, conducted by Alexander Kluge, August 5, 2007, DVD, Zweitausendeins, 2009.]

26. [*Translator's citations*: See Michel Serres, *The Five Senses: A Philosophy of the Mingled Body*, trans. Margaret Sankey and Peter Crowley (London: Continuum, 2008), p. 344. See also "Jede neue Technologie setzt Sinne für neue Aufgaben frei," *Mensch 2.0*, conducted by Alexander Kluge, DVD, NZZ Format, 2011.]

27. [*Translator's note and citation*: This quote originates from a televised interview that Kluge conducted with the coeditor of the *Frankfurt Allegmeine Zeitung*. See "Die Auswanderung des Denkens aus dem Gehirn," *Mensch 2.0*, conducted by Alexander Kluge, March 22, 2010, DVD, NZZ Format, 2011.]

28. [*Translator's note and citations*: Kluge refers here to the televised interview "Auf dem Weg in die nächste Gesellschaft," *News & Stories*, conducted by. Alexander Kluge, SAT 1, April 20, 2008. See also Dirk Baecker, *Studien zur nächsten Gesellschaft* (Frankfurt am Main: Suhrkamp Verlag, 2007).]

29. [*Translator's citations*: See Hans Magnus Enzensberger, "Constituents of a Theory of the Media," trans. Stuart Hood, in Enzensberger, *Critical Essays*, ed. Reinhold Grimm and Bruce Armstrong (New York: Continuum, 1982), pp. 46–76, and Bertolt Brecht, "The Radio as a Communication Apparatus," in Brecht, *Brecht on Film and Radio*, ed. and trans. Marc Silberman (London: Methuen, 2000), pp. 41–44.]

30. [*Translator citation*: See Jürgen Habermas, "The New Obscurity: The Crisis of the Welfare State and the Exhaustion of Utopian Energies," in Habermas, *The New Conservatism: Cultural Criticism and the Historians' Debate*, ed. and trans. Shierry Weber Nicholsen (Cambridge, MA: MIT Press, 1989), p. 54.]

31. [*Translator's note*: Infante Henry, Duke of Viseu (1394-1460), also known as Henry the Navigator, was an important a figure in the early days of the Portuguese empire during the Age of Discovery, just as Columbus was in the early days of the Spanish imperial expansion.]

32. [*Translator's citation*: Theodor W. Adorno, *Minima Moralia: Reflections on a Damaged Life*, trans. E. F. N. Jephcott (London: Verso, 2005), p. 50.]

33. [*Translator's citation*: Immanuel Kant, *Critique of Pure Reason*, trans. and ed. Paul Guyer and Allen W. Wood (Cambridge: Cambridge University Press, 1998), pp. 193–94.]

34. [*Translator's citation and note*: Immanuel Kant, *Groundwork of the Metaphysics of Morals*, trans. and ed. Mary Gregor (Cambridge: Cambridge University Press, 1998), p. 31. Italics in the original Kant translation, boldface added by Negt and Kluge.]

35. [*Translator's citation*: Theodor W. Adorno, *Negative Dialectics*, trans. E. B. Ashton (London: Routledge, 1990), p. 365.]

36. [*Translator's citation*: Jürgen Habermas, *Knowledge and Human Interests*, trans. Jeremy J. Shapiro (Boston: Beacon Press, 1971), pp. 290–300.]

37. [*Translator's citation and note*: Gilles Deleuze, *Nietzsche and Philosophy*, trans. Hugh Tomlinson (New York: Columbia University Press, 1983), pp. 195–96. Italics added by Negt and Kluge.]

38. [*Translator's citation*: *Ibid.*, pp. 25–31.]

39. [*Translator's citation and note*: The quote in the subheading is from Karl Marx, *The Economic and Philosophical Manuscripts of 1844*, in *MECW*, vol. 3, p. 303. The Marx translation has been slightly altered to fit the context of the Negt and Kluge original.]

40. [*Translator's note*: Of these stories, the first and second originally appeared in German in Alexander Kluge, *Die Lücke, die der Teufel läßt: Im Umfeld des neuen Jahrhunderts* (Frankfurt am Main: Suhrkamp, 2003), pp. 709 and 687. Although the first of these two are already published in translation, both of them and all the others are translated anew for *History and Obstinacy*. See Alexander Kluge, *The Devil's Blind Spot: Tales from the New Century*, trans. Martin Chalmers and Michael Hulse (New York: New Directions, 2004), pp. 38–39. The third story originally appeared in Oskar Negt and Alexander Kluge, *Chronik der Gefühle*, vol. 1, *Basisgeschichten* (Frankfurt am Main: Suhrkamp, 2000), pp. 442–44, and the fourth and fifth originally appeared in Alexander Kluge, *Tür an Tür mit einem anderen Leben* (Frankfurt am Main: Suhrkamp, 2006), pp. 552–55 and 368–69.]

41. [*Translator's citation*: Michel de Montaigne, "That to Study Philosophy Is to Learn to Die," in *The Essays of Michel de Montaigne*, ed. W. Carew Hazlitt, trans. Charles Cotton (Chicago: Encyclopedia Britannica, 1952), p. 188.]

CHAPTER FIVE: THE HISTORICAL TERRAIN
WHERE LABOR CAPACITIES EMERGE

1. [*Translator's citation*: Negt and Kluge refer here to a trope repeatedly invoked by Hegel with respect to the task of philosophy. See, for example, Georg Wilhelm Friedrich Hegel, "Inaugural Address, Delivered at the University of Berlin (22 October 1818)," in *Hegel: Political Writings*, ed. Lawrence Dickey and H. B. Nisbet, trans. H. B. Nisbet (Cambridge: Cambridge University Press, 1999), p. 185. See also Max Weber, "The Profession and Vocation of Politics," in *Political Writings*, ed. Peter Lassman and Ronald Speirs (Cambridge: Cambridge University Press, 1994), p. 369, and Jürgen Habermas, "The New Obscurity: The Crisis of the Welfare State and the Exhaustion of Utopian Energies," in *The New Conservatism: Cultural Criticism and the Historians' Debate*, ed. and trans. Shierry Weber Nicholsen (Cambridge, MA: MIT Press, 1989) pp. 48–70.]

2. [*Translator's note and citation*: Compare this formation with Oskar Negt and Alexander Kluge, *Public Sphere and Experience: Toward an Analysis of the Bourgeois and Proletarian Public Sphere*, trans. Peter Labanyi, Jamie Owen Daniel, and Assenka Oksiloff (Minneapolis: University of Minnesota Press, 1993) p. 296.]

3. Karl Marx and Frederick Engels, "The Eighteenth Brumaire of Louis Bonaparte," in *Collected Works*, vol. 11, *August 1851 – March 1853* (London: Lawrence and Wishart, 1979) p. 104. [*Translator's note*: The *Collected Works* is hereafter cited as *MECW*.]

4. Jürgen Habermas characterizes this as a symbiotic phase of development. The symbiosis between child, attachment figure, and physical surroundings is a form of cooperation made viable through various ways of speaking. In this phase,

the child cannot perceive "its own body" as a system capable of maintaining its own boundaries. What then follows overlaps with the egocentric phase (according to Jean Piaget the sensorimotor or preoperational stage), in which the child learns in its own way to differentiate with the help of cognitive and moral egocentrism between self and environment; in Piaget's operative phase, the child acquires this once again, but in a different and novel way. Habermas calls this subsequent later phase, which already corresponds to the nature of labor, an objective and universal stage of development. See Jürgen Habermas, "Historical Materialism and the Development of Normative Structures," in *Communication and the Evolution of Society*, trans. Thomas McCarthy (Boston: Beacon Press, 1979), pp. 95–129.

5. Karl Marx, *Economic and Philosophic Manuscripts of 1844*, in *MECW*, vol. 3, *March 1843–August 1844*, p. 337.

6. This is a long process transpiring over multiple stages of its life. If the child has no father, the accumulation of commodities in the reality it encounters becomes the father. If the child has no mother, it will attempt to assemble a mother figure from the people it encounters, or it will devise an imagined object in its unmature mind that functions as a primary object. Michael Balint, *The Basic Fault: Therapeutic Aspects of Regression* (Evanston: Northwestern University Press, 1992, p. 24). This battle for survival is robust. If none of these substitutes are successful, the child will die.

7. See: Michel Foucault, *Discipline and Punish: The Birth of the Prison*, trans. Alan Sheridan (New York: Vintage Books, 1979), p. 30. Whereas for Plato, the body is "the tomb of the soul" (τὸ μὲν σῶμά ἐστιν ἡμῖν σῆμα), for Foucault, "the soul is the prison of the body." The soul is seized by the relations of relationships and engenders separations. [*Translator's note and citation*: Footnote slightly altered according to authors' wishes. See *Gorgias* 493a.2–3].

8. "For all joy [*Lust*] wants—eternity!" The mother must, however, work, do the dishes, become a man, or she wants out. Somehow she improvises, lives on "2 channels." She is exhausted. [*Translator's citation and note*: the quotation in the note is from Friedrich Nietzsche, "The Sleeperwalker Song," in *Thus Spoke Zarathustra*, trans. Adrian Del Caro (Cambridge: Cambridge University Press, 2006), p. 263; the quotation in the text is from Charles Baudelaire, "The Bad Glazier," *Paris spleen and La fanfarlo*, trans. Raymond N. MacKenzie (Indianapolis: Hackett, 2008), p. 17.]

9. Modern adults allow this to occur in small children; it is indeed a matter not only of adult sexuality, but also of the raw material out of which it develops later via separation processes. An illusion evolves out of this: the displacement of the incest taboo until a later point in time, when it will strike the childlike illusionists even harder. The idea that the child—in the meantime a now-functioning being—

would have known of better forms of assistance for dealing with this separation is specious, since prepubescent cognition cannot negotiate any such insight.

10. This would be a spoiled hero like Siegfried, who threw the court of Burgundy into chaos and even after his death caused the slaughter of the Huns.

11. We will certainly see later how this second component (for example, Wilhelminian child-rearing practices) entailed a lost capacity for control and, in this respect, strengthened indeterminacy. Cleanliness, for example, was rigidly enforced in English child-rearing practices of the nineteenth century. Treated as if it were obvious, cleanliness was seen as *the* only path through which the raw materials for intensified discipline could arise. In German child-rearing trends of the late nineteenth century, slovenliness played the same role as the rigidity that was characteristic of other places. Think, for example, of the soiled vest of the professor in Heinrich Mann's *Small Town Tyrant* (*Professor Unrat*) [1905]. A rigid upbringing is unequal to the task, if we disregard developing competency for waging war. With regard to the future development of labor capacities, however, child rearing is rather confused. A craftsman's or scholar's ideal of a well-ordered house has no use in child rearing. In any case, group ideals do not allow for special individual forms of discipline such as those of the English.

12. In a lecture delivered to American behaviorists, Jean Piaget explicated the sentence: "Every time we teach a child something, we prevent him from discovering it on its own. We inflict damage." In the discussion afterward, a behaviorist said: "The scales have fallen from my eyes! My question is: How can this procedure be accelerated?" At which point Piaget then laughed. He did not answer. [*Translator's citation*: Jean Piaget, "Some Aspects of Operations," in *Play and Development: A Symposium*, ed. Maria W. Piers (New York: Norton, 1972), p. 27.]

13. This happens in one of two ways. A larger abundance of individual abilities actually arises. Child rearing revokes shortcuts. Educational experiments have proven that math and orthography are learned relatively late, so much so that parents and traditional pedagogues react with fear. But then the children grasp these capabilities astonishingly quickly at a later phase of their schooling, as if they were incidental. The fears thus were groundless. No educational experiment is ever complete, because this would require the parents' preschool child rearing to recognize self-regulation among all children as structural. On the other hand, children raised from such educational experiments exhibit greater capacities for needs and feelings, so much so that they suffer more when all of reality rains down upon them.

14. Recognition means that I—being in full possession of the warded-off forces of the drives, on account of whose autonomy (they have never been anything else but autonomous) I know I am united—recognize all other similarly structured

human beings, because I have been recognized by those who, in a similar fashion, know themselves to be united. We have merely replaced the concept of reason, as Kant and Habermas understand it, with that of the elementary particle of joy [*Lust*].

Answers also allow for a primitive accumulation other than the capitalist one, since the production principles inherent in a subjective response are capable of driving self-actualization. "If this unity is not present, nothing can be *actual*, even if it may be assumed to have existence. A bad state is one which merely exists; a sick body also exists, but it has no true reality." Georg Wilhelm Friedrich Hegel, *Elements of the Philosophy of Right*, ed. Allen W. Wood, trans. H. B. Nisbet (Cambridge: Cambridge University Press, 1991), p. 302. [*Translator's note*: Italics original to Hegel translation.]

15. [*Translator's citation*: Immanuel Kant, The *Metaphysics of Morals*, trans. Mary Gregor (Cambridge: Cambridge University Press, 1991), p. 95.]

16. Habermas, "Historical Materialism and the Development of Normative Structures," pp. 95–129.

17. [*Translator's note and citation*: Negt and Kluge's use of *Einlösung* ("redeeming" in the sense of coupons, checks, and pawn shops) is distinct from Benjamin's theological concept of *Erlösung* (that is, redemption), perhaps best illustrated in thesis 9 of his "On the Concept of History." The first and best explication of this difference is advanced by Andrew Bowie in his review of *Geschichte und Eigensinn* in *Telos* 66 (1985–86), pp. 183–90; see especially p. 187.]

18. "Modulor" is the name of a system Le Corbusier used to develop his architectural concepts. He uses it to describe the Palais Royal in Paris built by Henry IV. All proportions in this building correspond to the corporal proportions of someone from the South of France. [*Translator's citation*: See Le Corbusier, *The Modulor: A Harmonious Measure to the Human Scale Universally Applicable to Architecture and Mechanics*, trans. Peter de Francia and Anna Bostock (Cambridge, MA: Harvard University Press, 1954).]

19. [*Translator's citation*: Max Horkheimer and Theodor W. Adorno, *Dialectic of Enlightenment: Philosophical Fragments*, ed. Gunzelin Schmid Noerr, trans. Edmund Jephcott (Stanford: Stanford University Press, 2002), p. 213.]

20. E. T. A. Hoffmann, "Councillor Krespel," in *Tales*, ed. Victor Lange (New York: Continuum, 1982) pp. 80–100.

21. In hindsight, the living say nothing less than the same thing. German Social Democratic politicians responsible for the Antiradical Decree of 1972, which required a loyalty oath from all public servants, say: We did not want it to turn out that way. After immense efforts in World War II, it was said of the results of 1945: We did not want it to turn out that way. It cannot be denied that the Second

World War was supposed to be an attempt at revising the outcomes of the First World War; but it, too, referred to the Great War itself: We did not want it to turn out that way. It this case, it was said: We were not the ones who caused this misfortune. Misfortune is ambiguous, especially in the form of a war declaration and its negative outcomes. This saying "We did not want it to turn out that way" takes on the character of the guilt question of war, the legend of the stab in the back, and the shameful dictate of the Versailles Treaty. German history is full of belated reactions, each of which says: We did not want that, we did not know that. Had we known, we would have set ourselves into large-scale motion. This goes back to the death of Conradin (1252–1268), which was the first reaction of Christianized Teutons: Had we been present at the Crucifixion, it would have ended differently. In this case, it is a form of despair over the outcome of history (over which neither good nor bad will have any influence as it is intended by individuals) that the obvious possibility of knowing or preventing something or even the already publicized foreknowledge is denied after the fact. This occurs, for example, in the connection with the murder of the Jews and the case of Auschwitz.

22. Kant uses the Latin *locus standi* to name the emphatic category for this. It does not mean "a place to stand." The concept of primitive property expresses itself as a radical need in the form of understatements. *Locus standi* is what I must have in order to remain identical to myself as a human being. In protest against the separation from this minimal demand, it is not the affluent, but rather the poor relations of identity that immediately identify themselves. If they say breathing freely is supposed be possible, a modern Swedish prison cell may very well be nicely ventilated, but the absolute minimum requirement for breathing air for living beings with an upper respiratory system is not identical to life behind bars. Human identity has always been about an abundance of possibilities for *movement*.

23. Karl Marx, "Contribution to the Critique of Hegel's Philosophy of Law," in *MECW*, vol. 3, p. 40: "What is it, then, that ultimately and firmly distinguishes one person from all others? The *body*." As simple as it sounds, this assertion that people carry their bodies around their whole lives as their own property (that is, they are stuck in their own skin for the longest possible time) corresponds neither to the consciousness's attention span nor to any identity within this relation. On the contrary, the heteronomies of the labor process, as well as the majority of demands in the relationalities of life—above all, thought—act as if the body were composed of independent, disposable pieces. It's not on its mind. The self associates itself with its body via hierarchical notions; for example, what the higher senses—eyes, the musical ear—enjoy are valued as being superior to the liver or the digestive tract, which are never considered to be musical or philosophical. In the clash between body and the registering self there lies the source of the conflict: the spirit finds

itself in the prison of the body, or, conversely, the body in the prison of the soul. The levels of intensity of the self's rebellion against the body, of the body's characteristics among themselves, and of the body against the self are surprisingly small in relation to the organized nonidentity in which both body and mind find themselves. A kind of conservativism dominates in these reactions, which possess an uncanny quality, because we know that the body never forgets anything.

24. See also the original chapter 8 from *Geschichte und Eigensinn* on the permanence of primitive accumulation in Germany. In opposition to the primitive seizure of property, Marx speaks of how *so-called* primitive accumulation occurs in rational natural law as a concept characterizing the initial act of apportioning countries, oceans, and nature not yet juridically regulated. The need for the constitution of primitive property and the moment of a not yet specified appropriation at the other's expense—in other words, privatization—intermingle in this concept. This act is a gesture toward dominion and the exclusion of others. At the same time, it is also merely the simple movement of people in nature and a sign that someone who maintains a relation to the land he works on asserts a claim to general recognition. In this respect, it is a nonaggressive relation. In this context, Kant speaks of the *beati possidentes*, the happy original owners. [*Translator's citation*: see Oskar Negt and Alexander Kluge, *Geschichte und Eigensinn*, vol. 2, *Der unterschätzte Mensch: Gemeinsame Philosophie in zwei Bänden* (Frankfurt am Main: Zweitausendeins, 2001), pp. 541–769.]

25. We have explicitly named just six dimensions here. It is certain that they, in turn, contain within themselves the additional dimensions of the political, the historical, the realization of labor power, feelings, consciousness, revolutionary transformation, as well as the horizontal and the vertical (the dimensions best known to sensuous perception), which, for their part, include place, time, punctuality, space, movement, nonmovement, relationalities, and differentiations.

26. We are primarily not laying out categorical inventories here; the disintegration of such antagonistic levels of reality (dimensions), of which we know that they initially constitute the most diverse constellations and movements (aggregates), presented us with considerable difficulties. For more on this, see chapter 8 in the original German edition, pp. 652–75.

27. Hegel, *Elements of the Philosophy* of Right, p. 56.

28. *Ibid.*, pp. 56–57.

29. From a crude physical perspective, the glass on the table consists of a mixture of elements that appear solid. From a microphysical perspective, it contains massive amounts of material emptiness in which electrons and protons—removed from one another like distant stars—scurry around one another. As a relation of relationships, that I know I am supposed to drink out of such an object is a part

of acquired childhood habits. As a commodity, it is the exchange value, in other words, the objects that I can trade for the value of this glass. As a product of history, it is, for example, Bohemian, Venetian, or ordinary German glassware with which I associate social value. If the glass in question is German, the history of glassblowing would reveal the movements of German history. Lenin explained the materialist method using a similar example. In this respect, however, only an esoteric critique of knowledge emerges from the textbook example, because the stockpiling of analytic faculties is disproportionate. I can easily know much less by way of the glass sitting on the table. The procedure belongs to the expressive poverty of the philosophical method. A kind of permanent Hamlet emerges (a Hamlet machine).

30. In the industrial process, the tendency arises to limit the disposition of labor capacity. Many examples that interest us would need to be abbreviated. Entirely deployable situations always occur where labor power battles against the elimination of its freedom of disposition.

31. On the element of qualification for responsibility in business operations, see Horst Kern and Michael Schumann, *Industriearbeit und Arbeiterbewusstsein: Eine empirische Untersuchung über den Einfluss der aktuellen technischen Entwicklung auf die industrielle Arbeit und das Arbeitsbewusstsein* (Frankfurt am Main: Europäische Verlagsanstalt, 1970), p. 91.

32. The technical officer's statement before Congress sparked off a political storm that contributed to Nixon's downfall.

33. [*Translator's citation*: Marx, *Capital, Volume 1*, in *MECW*, vol. 35, p. 85. English Marx translation slightly modified.]

34. [*Translator's citation*: *Ibid.*, p. 83. English Marx translation slightly modified.]

35. [*Translator's note and citation*: Because the translation in Marx, *Capital, Volume 1*, in *MECW*, vol. 35, pp. 82–83 diverges sharply from the German original, the following translation is used: Karl Marx. *Capital, Volume One*, trans. Ben Fowkes (London: Penguin Books, 1982), pp. 164–65.]

36. Marx, *Capital, Volume 1*, in *MECW*, vol. 35, p. 84.

37. [*Translator's note and citation*: Schopenhauer's concept of the *Quietiv* is translated here as "tranquillizer," as found in Arthur Schopenhauer, *The World as Will and Representation*, vol. 1, trans. and ed. Judith Norman, Alistair Welchman, and Chistopher Janaway (Cambridge: Cambridge University Press, 2010), p. lii. Negt is referring here to Marx's "Critique of Hegel's Philosophy of Right," in *MECW*, vol. 3, pp. 3–210.]

38. Marx, "A Contribution to the Critique of Hegel's *Philosophy of Right*," in *MECW*, vol. 3, p. 175. [*Translator's note*: italics in the original Marx translation.]

39. Marx, *Capital Volume 1*, in *MECW*, vol. 35, p. 26.

40. In order to characterize the rigidity of this ban on experience, no other example crosses our mind than that of the prison. It is here where we find the institution of the visitor area. This is the sole point of contact between the realm of experience of those inside and that of those outside, assuming that every prisoner belongs to both realms. In the world of manufacturing, however, this inversion of the visitor's cell intended for the exchange of what a worker, as a living being, inseparable both inside and outside, requires by way of an entire plane of contact, does not exist at all. The two zones of experience in which the potential for living labor really exists are separated into two worlds by fences and internal organizations. The differentiation between secular reality and sacred reality in religion repeats itself in the encirclement of multiple realities into which one and the same real person is separated in terms of consciousness production. Strictly speaking, such a person produces roots of consciousness separately on the basis of every one of these encirclements.

41. We are following here the dark passages in Hegel. For more, see Theodor W. Adorno, "Skoteinos, or How to Read Hegel," in *Hegel: Three Studies*, trans. Shierry Weber Nicholsen (Cambridge: MIT Press, 1993), pp. 89–148. The essay begins with the epigraph "I have nothing but murmuring. (Rudolf Borchardt)." [*Translator's note*: on the dialectic as reality, see Chapter 1, note 13; "The Principle of 'Cowardice in Thought,'" in Chapter 4; "The Idiosyncrasy of Everyday Movements," in the present chapter; and the Glossary.]

42. [*Translator's citation*: Rosa Luxemburg, "Order Reigns in Berlin," in *Selected Political Writings of Rosa Luxemburg*, ed. Dick Howard (New York: Monthly Review Press, 1971), p. 415.]

43. At the beginning of *Being and Time*, Heidegger asks quite precisely why the third person singular present and not, for example, "we are" or "you are"—in other words the collective infections—have become the object of philosophy. [*Translator's citations and note*: Martin Heidegger, *Being and Time*, trans. Joan Stambaugh (Albany: State University of New York Press, 1996), pp. 1–3. A precise formulation of Heidegger's observation can be found in Günther Anders, *Über Heidegger*, ed. Gerhard Oberschlick (Munich: Beck, 2001), p. 232.]

44. Norbert Elias, *The Civilizing Process: Sociogenetic and Psychogenetic Investigations*, ed. Eric Dunning, Johan Goudsblom, and Stephen Mennell, trans. Edmund Jephcott (Oxford: Blackwell, 2000), p. 475.

45. Thought is analogous to the building of Noah's Ark. The opposite of this would be to jump back into the deluge and learn to swim. The image of "swimming like a fish in the waters of the people" derives from the combat situation of partisans. However, it is not a praxis of perception in highly industrialized

societies. Even if it were certain that every conceivable ark of Noah's would sink, the mass of the powers of perception would initially attend to the hopeless task of plugging the leaks.

46. They can push themselves away. They can imitate. But without any primary objects, no human labor power arises. A child would be hospitalized or die. It is said that Friedrich II of Hohenstaufen tried to lock children in a tower in order to research what kind of creatures result without any parental influence. They all died. He wanted to know which language children speak if they do not learn it from their parents: Could it be determined whether the original language of human beings is Hebrew, Greek, Babylonian, or German? He consequently had children locked in a tower full of mothers whose tongues were ripped out.

47. [*Translator's citation*: See Oskar Negt and Alexander Kluge, *Public Sphere and Experience: Toward an Analysis of the Bourgeois and Proletarian Public Sphere*, trans. Peter Labanyi, Jamie Owen Daniel, and Assenka Oksiloff (Minneapolis: University of Minnesota Press, 1993), pp. 32–38.]

48. [*Translator's note*: Roland Freisler (1893–1945) served under Hitler as state secretary of the Reich Ministry of Justice and was the president of the People's Court (*Volksgerichtshof*) from 1942 to 1945. He was killed on February 3, 1945, in an aerial bombing while his Berlin courtroom was in session.]

49. [*Translator's note*: The phrase appears originally in English.]

50. The expert witness was Chief Physician Hans Albert Müller of Hamburg-Ochsenzoll's psychiatric clinic. He formulated the following: "Whoever is unable to hear from birth onward cannot hear the soothing words of a mother, the chirping of birds, the roar of the sea, or the pillow talk of a first romance; music does not get through to him, and he hears no screams when he inflicts pain onto someone." The murder in the home for the hearing impaired played itself out for both perpetrator and victim **in total silence**.

51. [*Translator's note and citation*: For more on Adorno's plans, see the film and stories contained in Alexander Kluge, *Wer sich traut, reißt die Kälte vom Pferd: Landschaften mit Eis und Schnee* (Frankfurt am Main: Suhrkamp, 2010).]

52. Horkheimer and Adorno, *Dialectic of Enlightenment*, p. 35. See also chapter 12, "Dealing with Horizontal Displacement: The Need for Orientation," in the original German edition of *Geschichte und Eigennsinn*, pp. 1001–1089.

53. *Ibid.*, p. 38. "The faculty by which the self survives adventures, throwing itself away in order to preserve itself, is cunning" (p. 39).

54. Homer, *The Odyssey*, book 20, verses 13–24, trans. Edward McCrorie (Baltimore: Johns Hopkins University Press, 2004), p, 292. See also Horkheimer and Adorno, *Dialectic of Enlightenment*, p. 38 n.5 and pp. 258–59.

55. Adorno, *Hegel*, p. 40.

56. Friedrich Hölderlin, "The Nearest the Best," *Hymns and Fragments*, trans. Richard Sieburth (Princeton: Princeton University Press, 1984), pp. 175–76. The wind makes the *eyes* "quickened" [*scharfwehend*].

57. Such myths are told not once, but many times. They actually form the basis of all experiences with a mutual temporal core. André Gide tells in "Thésée" (1946) not the story of Odysseus, but rather of the departure and homecoming of the tricky Theseus, his experience in the Labyrinth, and his deceitfulness toward Ariadne, whom he leaves in the lurch in Naxos.

58. "It is well known that Greek mythology is not only the arsenal of Greek art but also its foundation. Is the view of nature and of social relations on which the Greek imagination and hence Greek [mythology] is based possible with self-acting mule spindles and railways and locomotives and electrical telegraphs? What chance has Vulcan against Roberts and Co., Jupiter against the lightning-rod and Hermes against the Credit Mobilier?... There are unruly children and precocious children. Many of the old peoples belong in this category. The Greeks were normal children. The charm of their art for us is not in contradiction to the undeveloped stage of society on which it grew. [It] is its result, rather, and is inextricably bound up, rather, with the fact that the unripe social conditions under which it arose, and could alone arise, can never return." Karl Marx, "Introduction to Outlines of the Critique of Political Economy," in *MECW*, vol. 28, *Karl Marx: Economic Works, 1857–61*, pp. 47–48.

59. See Hermann Fränkel, *Noten zu den Argonautika des Apollonios* (Munch: C. H. Beck, 1968).

60. Chosen by his peers with acclamation, the leader of this band of Argonauts is Jason. The Greek name means "savior." Theseus, Odysseus, and Jason are able to disguise themselves (that is, to act, to be deceitful, to make and break contracts); they are all equal masters in the art of the precision grip. Their leadership is based on the fact that theirs is the most general of specialties, that they possess no one particular ability that is specialized, other than to involve themselves in all the necessary abilities during the course of the voyage.

61. The strait between Greece and Asia Minor was called the Hellespont because Helle drowned there: "Helle's sea." The strait is also called the Bosporus, meaning "cow crossing," after Io, who was seduced by Zeus and discovered and pursued by the guardian of marriage, Hera, and who saves herself. Hera sends a horsefly to torment this lover transformed into an animal; on the run from the stinging insect, the animal swims swiftly across the inlet toward Egypt, where she then settles.

62. Fränkel, *Noten zu den Argonautika des Apollonios*, pp. 59 and 58–60. [*Translator's note and citation*: See Apollonios Rhodios, *The Argonautika*, trans. Peter

Green (Berkeley: University of California Press, 2007), book 1, verses 256–59, pp. 49–50. Negt and Kluge are quoting from both an unidentified German edition of *The Library*, once attributed to Apollodorus, and Manfred Hausmann, *Sternsagen* (Gütersloh: S. Mohn, 1965), pp. 24, 26, respectively.]

63. [*Translator's citation*: Fränkel, *Noten zu den Argonautika des Apollonios*, p. 313.]

64. [*Translation's citations*: Ibid., p. 313 n.420. See Apollonius, *Argonautika*, book 2 verses 1141–49, p. 108.]

65. [*Translator's citation*: Apollonios, *Argonautika*, book 3, verse 857, p. 135.]

66. Fränkel, *Noten zu den Argonautika des Apollonios*, p. 396.

67. [*Translator's citation*: Apollonius, *Argonautika*, book 4, verses 552–55, p. 165.]

68. Fränkel, *Noten zu den Argonautika des Apollonios*, p. 22.

69. See also Apollonius, *Argonautika*, book 4, verses 72–80, p. 153. On "brisk pace": "The poet's representation is here equally meager as it races the participants to finish the situation. When for the third time the call goes back and forth, the companions were already at the 'quick' oars and under way...and Jason already had set his 'nimble feet' on the other shore before the landing lines were thrown overboard (the pace will possibly become brisker as soon as the Argonauts have heard what Medea says in verses 83–86; hence verse 103)." And they act without delay thereafter; not a moment may be lost Fränkel, *Noten zu den Argonautika des Apollonios*, p. 461. [*Translator's note and citation*: the above quotation in this paragraph is taken from Pindar, "Pythian 4: Jason and the Argonauts," in *Odes for Victorious Athletes*, trans. Anne Pippin Burnett (Baltimore: Johns Hopkins University Press, 2010), verses 128–30, p. 83.]

70. [*Translator's citation*: Fränkel, *Noten zu den Argonautika des Apollonios*, p. 318.]

71. [*Translator's citation*: Ibid., p. 319.]

72. [*Translator's citation*: Apollonius, *Argonautika*, book 2, verse 1255, p. 111.]

73. [*Translator's citation*: Ibid., book 2, verses 1251–52, p. 111. See Fränkel, *Noten zu den Argonautika des Apollonios*, p. 319.]

74. Fränkel, *Noten zu den Argonautika des Apollonios*, p. 319 n.433.

75. Ibid., p. 337. See also Apollonius, *Argonautika*, book 3, verses 171–75, p. 117. Our choice of words follows here the category of hospitality as it is developed by Immanuel Kant in "Perpetual Peace: A Philosophical Sketch," in *Political Writings*, ed. Hans Reiss, trans. H. B. Nisbet (Cambridge: Cambridge University Press, 1991), pp. 105–108. See also commentary 12 in the original German edition of *History and Obstinacy* [*Translator's citation*: Negt and Kluge, *Geschichte und Eigensinn*, pp. 1193–97].

76. [*Translator's citation*: Fränkel, *Noten zu den Argonautika des Apollonios*, p. 338.]

77. [*Translator's note and citation*: In epic diction, *xeinoi* refers to a bond between strangers, usually translated as "guest friendship." The term *xenios* refers to "friend and host." See David Konstan, *Friendship in the Classical World* (Cambridge: Cambridge University Press, 1997), pp. 33–34.]

78. [*Translator's citation*: Fränkel, *Noten zu den Argonautika des Apollonios*, p. 489.]

79. [*Translator's citation*: Apollonius, *Argonautika*, book 4, verses 135–38, p. 154.]

80. [*Translator's citation* Fränkel, *Noten zu den Argonautika des Apollonios*, p. 465.]

81. [*Translator's citation and note:* Negt and Kluge are quoting here a paraphrase in Fränkel. See *Ibid.*, p. 316. Fränkel is referring here to Medea's lament in book 4, verses 355–90.]

82. *Ibid.*, 488.

83. Claude Lévi-Strauss, "The Structural Study of Myth," in *Structural Anthropology*, trans. Claire Jacobson and Brooke Grundfest Schoepf (New York: Basic Books, 1963), pp. 213, 212. "From this springs a new hypothesis...The true constituent units of a myth are not the isolated relations but *bundles of such relations*, and it is only as bundles that these relations can be put to use and combined so as to produce a meaning" (p. 211). We also read, for example, the following: "Cadmos kills the dragon/Oedipus kills the Sphinx" but at the same time: Theseus kills the alleged robber/he kills the Minotaur/he sacrifices Ariadne/he kills his father/he kills his son, etc. Next to this Labdacus's group (father of Laius), "*lame* (?)/Laius (Oedipus's father) = *left-sided* (?)/Oedipus = *swollen foot* (?)" Or: Oedipus marries his mother Jocasta/Antigone buries her brother Polynices, violates the prohibition (p. 214). "All the relations belonging to the same column exhibit one common feature which it is our task to discover" (p. 215). In other words, incidents among relatives, whose close familial relations are overexcited; the difficulty to walk upright that reveals itself as "*left-sided*" or "*swollen foot*," and so on.

84. We follow Lévi-Strauss's careful method here, which indeed goes much further: myth "explains the present and the past as well as the future. This can be made clear through a comparison between myth and what appears to have largely replaced it in modern societies, namely, politics." He treats everything as myth, as having "that double structure, altogether historical and ahistorical." In this regard, he refers to Michelet when Michelet invokes the French Revolution: "That day...everything was possible.... Future became present...that is, no more time, a glimpse of eternity." Lévi-Strauss, "The Structural Study of Myth," pp. 209–210.

Accordingly, portions of reality—e.g., the *Sosein* of industrial landscapes or the narrative conventions in contemporary reality novels (they do not invent fairy tales or myths according to the old forms, but rather build collective myths as worlds of things)—are to be analyzed as well using the manner of speech of myths. Myth could be rewritten as every kind of speech, "where the formula *traduttore, traditore* reaches its lowest truth value. From that point of view it should be placed in the gamut of linguistic expressions at the end opposite to that of poetry..." (210). In opposition to poetry, which can be translated into another language with only the greatest of difficulties, "the mythical value of the myth is preserved even through the worst translation" (210); in other words, also without every speech, as enclosed space, cement, machinery, reciprocal relations of bondage between above and below, working contradiction, etc.

85. Marx, *Economic and Philosophic Manuscripts of 1844*, in *MECW*, vol. 3, p. 302.

86. Many children who hear the fairy tale of "Little Red Riding Hood" over and over reply to the question "And who came out?" posed at the point where the hunter cuts open the wolf's belly with the answer "the seven little kids." Jacob W. Grimm and Wilhelm K. Grimm, "The Wolf and the Seven Young Kids," *Complete Fairy Tales of the Brothers Grimm*, ed. and trans. Jack Zipes (Westminster: Bantam Books, 1992), pp. 18–20. [*Translator's note*: See also "Little Red Cap," in *ibid.*, pp. 93–96.]

87. [*Translator's note and citation*: Negt and Kluge are deploying here Hegel's concept of *Dasein* in order to convey that sense of determinate, mediated being in contrast to the more essential meaning Hegel associates with *Existenz*. See: Georg Wilhelm Friedrich Hegel, *The Science of Logic*, ed. and trans. George di Giovanni (New York: Cambridge University Press, 2010), p. 69.]

88. Gilles Deleuze and Félix Guattari, *A Thousand Plateaus: Capitalism and Schizophrenia*, trans. Brian Massumi (Minneapolis: University of Minnesota Press, 1987), p. 6.

89. *Ibid.*, p. 2.

90. [*Translator's citation*: Jacob W. Grimm and Wilhelm K. Grimm, "The Frog King, or Iron Heinrich," in *Complete Fairy Tales*, p. 2.]

91. [*Translator's citation*: Jacob W. Grimm and Wilhelm K. Grimm, "The Twelve Lazy Servants," *Complete Fairy Tales*, pp. 466–67.]

92. [*Translator's citation*: Jacob W. Grimm and Wilhelm K. Grimm, "Freddy and Katy," in *Complete Fairy Tales*, p. 207.]

93. [*Translator's note and citation*: This and all subsequent quotations from Grimm and Grimm, "The Wolf and the Seven Young Kids," pp. 18–20.]

94. [*Translator's note*: The original German fairy tale is entitled "Der Wolf und die sieben jungen Geißlein"; the young kids in question are little goats, hence the child's insistence here that it is an animal, as well.]

95. [*Translator's note and citation*: All subsequent quotations from Jacob W. Grimm and Wilhelm K. Grimm, "The Animals of the Lord and the Devil," in *Complete Fairy Tales*, p. 463.]

96. [*Translator's note*: Italics in the Negt and Kluge original.]

97. [*Translator's citation*: Grimm and Grimm, "The Animals of the Lord and the Devil," p. 463; "The Wolf and the Seven Young Kids," p. 18.]

98. [*Translator's citation*: Grimm and Grimm, "The Wolf and the Seven Young Kids," p. 20.]

99. Felix Genzmer, introduction, *Die Edda*, trans. Felix Genzmer, vol. 1 (Düsseldorf: E. Diederichs, 1963), pp. 17–26.

100. [*Translator's citation*: *The Poetic Edda*, trans. and ed. Carolyne Larrington (Oxford: Oxford University Press, 1996), p. 106.]

101. Jacob W. Grimm and Wilhelm K. Grimm, "The Rejuvenated Little Old Man," in *Complete Fairy Tales*, pp. 462–63.

102. Jacob W. Grimm and Wilhelm K. Grimm, "The Domestic Servants," in *Complete Fairy Tales*, pp. 451–52.

103. Jacob W. Grimm and Wilhelm K. Grimm, "Lean Lisa," in *Complete Fairy Tales*, p. 499.

104. Jacob W. Grimm and Wilhelm K. Grimm, "The Stubborn Child," in *Complete Fairy Tales*, p. 422. No other collection of fairy tales contains such a thematic core. Obstinacy is what stubbornly continues to have an effect well beyond the grave. It cannot be killed, nor does it die. It merely *withdraws itself* inward. [*Translator's note*: In keeping with the English-language title of *History and Obstinacy*, the title of Grimms' fairy tale, "Das Eigensinnige Kind," is rendered here as "obstinate" and not "stubborn" as is used in the Zipes' translation of the story. Other editions have translated the tale as "The Willful Child."]

105. [*Translator's citation*: Gottfried Keller, *Green Henry*, trans. A. M. Holt (New York: Grove Press, 1960), p. 28.]

106. [*Translator's citation*: Ibid., p. 29.]

107. [*Translator's citation*: Ibid.]

108. [*Translator's citation*: Ibid., p. 36.]

109. Various female figures are to be found in the Oedipus context: Europa (sister of Cadmus), Sphinx, Jocasta, Ismene, and Antigone.

Freud's analysis of the female dynamic avoids mythical references altogether: "I do not see any advance or gain in the introduction of the term 'Electra complex,' and do not advocate its use." Sigmund Freud, "The Psychogenesis of a Case of Homosexuality in a Woman," in *The Standard Edition of the Complete Psychological Works of Sigmund Freud*, vol. 18, ed. and trans. James Strachey (London: Hogarth Press, 1955), p. 155 n.1. "What we have said about the Oedipus complex applies with complete strictness to the male child only and that we are right in rejecting the term 'Electra complex' which seeks to emphasize the analogy between the attitude of the two sexes." Freud, "Female Sexuality," in *The Standard Edition of the Complete Psychological Works of Sigmund Freud*, vol. 21, ed. and trans. James Strachey (London: Hogarth Press, 1953), pp. 228–29. "It does little harm to a woman if she remains in her feminine Oedipus attitude. (The term 'Electra complex' has been proposed for it)," Freud, "An Outline of Psycho-Analysis," in *The Standard Edition of the Complete Psychological Works of Sigmund Freud*, vol. 23, ed. and trans. James Strachey (London: Hogarth Press, 1953), p. 194.

Bion Steinborn undertook probably one of the first attempts at interpreting the "Electra complex" in terms of its derivation from the context of incest in his chapter "Offene Fragen zur Sexualität: Der Antigonekomplex der weiblichen Sexualität" in his unpublished manuscript "Zur Psychologie der Frau im Film" (Frankfurt am Main, 1971).

110. Georg Wilhelm Friedrich Hegel, *Lectures on Philosophy of Religion*, vol. 3: *The Consummate Religion*, ed. Peter C. Hodgson, trans. R. F. Brown (Oxford: Oxford University Press, 2007), p. 134. [*Translator's note*: Slightly modified translation.]

CHAPTER SIX: WAR AS LABOR

1. Ludwig Renn and Helmut Schnitter, *Krieger, Landsknecht und Soldat* (Berlin: Kinderbuchverlag, 1973). p. 78.

2. Initially, it was possible only to stab. After the introduction of the halberd, it was possible to swipe with the blade and stab with the spike. At the battle of Morgarten, Herzog Leopold of Austria—his army of knights was held up by a roadblock—was ambushed by a pike-square formation storming down a slope from the mountainside above. Prior to this, the Swiss had showered the knights with stones. This tactic brought the pike square into confusion, however, and counts as atypical. The pike square nevertheless triumphed because it had greater strength in numbers, the advantage of surprise, and because the army of knights was still, in part, advancing.

3. [*Translator's note*: The "maniple" was a organizational unit used to define an intermediate-sized group of infantry (120 men) within an ancient Roman legion. Approximately three maniples formed a cohort and ten cohorts made a legion, the basic military unit.]

4. Already at the battle of Breitenfeld (1631), the ponderous pike squares of the imperial commander Tilly faced the more loosely ordered Swedish lines, which could be ranked in companies and regiments.

5. Renn and Schnitter, *Krieger, Landsknecht und Soldat*, p. 105.

6. According to legend, the Swiss Winkelried is said to have thrown himself onto the spears of the Austrians, thereby opening up a gap. Historically, a mercenary named Winkelried lived about one hundred years later; the deed cannot have happened during the battle of Sempach, since the enemy consisted of a cavalry force four thousand strong that could not have formed a wall of spears. The compelling motives of townspeople and farmers, who were not mercenaries (as was the case in later years), but rather were people fighting for their own land, played a part in these battles.

7. Carl von Clausewitz, *On War*, ed. and trans. Michael Howard and Peter Paret (Princeton: Princeton University Press, 1984.) p. 358. [*Translator's note*: italics in the Causewitz translation.]

8. The czar was just as amazed by this as Bonaparte.

9. "With the exception of the extractive industries, in which the material for labor is provided immediately by Nature, such as mining, hunting, fishing and agriculture (so far as the latter is confined to breaking up virgin soil), all branches of industry manipulate raw material, objects already filtered through labor, already products of labor. Such is seed in agriculture. Animals and plants, which we are accustomed to consider as products of Nature, are in their present form, not only products of, say last year's labor, but the result of a gradual transformation, continued through many generations, under man's superintendence." Karl Marx, *Capital, Volume 1*, in *Collected Works*, vol. 35 (London: Lawrence and Wishart, 1996), p. 191. [*Translator's note*: The *Collected Works* are hereafter cited as *MECW*.]

10. The objective result is little more than zero. The American military headquarters was particularly stuck on the idea that a short distance away, behind what for them was the mysterious border with Cambodia, there had to be an underground North Vietnamese Pentagon; this is what they wanted to shell. They assumed that the enemy was doing exactly what they themselves would try and imagined that somehow around five thousand specialists must have set up a bunker to direct the battles in South Vietnam. This idée fixe was maintained for a long time, finally to be abandoned only a few weeks before the armistice.

11. The quotes in the subhead are from Leo Tolstoy, *War and Peace*, trans. Richard Pevear and Larissa Volokhonsky (New York: Alfred A. Knopf, 2007), p. 217.

12. A representative from the warring party who travels for a few days in neutral foreign territory (for example, Schellenberg in April 1945 in Sweden) may be able to grasp such a neutral viewpoint; it is always unexpected. [*Translator's note*: Walter Schellenberg (1910–1952) was a high-ranking SS officer who tried to arrange a separate peace with the Western allies.]

13. Clausewitz, *On War*, p. 90. "Force—that is, physical force, for moral force has no existence save as expressed in the state and the law—is thus the *means* of war, to impose our will on the enemy is its object" (p. 75). Disarming the enemy "takes the place of" this aim in the individual actions of war, "discarding it as something not actually part of war itself" (p. 75). The relation between war and **breaking** an opposing **will** is thus veiled in practice.

14. *Ibid.*, p. 69. The entry is listed under the heading "Notes." The author wanted to revise his book on war around the core of this distinction. [*Translator's note*: italics in the Clausewitz translation cited.]

15. *Ibid.*, p. 69. "The continuation of policy with other means" is only the *title of the subhead* (p. 87); in the text itself, it is more precisely "state policy" [*Staatspolitik*], on the one hand, and the "continuation of political activity," on the other. This is not the political in the conventional sense, such as, for example, the struggle over political opinion, but rather organized political production, such as the constitution of consciousness (the form of consciousness, the form of intercourse; in other words, it is also economic determination), the political constitution and the state. [*Translator's note*: italics in the Clausewitz translation cited.]

16. *Ibid.*, p. 75.

17. See *ibid.*, pp. 77–78.

18. *Ibid.*, pp. 80, 83, 84, 86. "From the very start there is an interplay of possibilities, probabilities, good luck and bad.... In the whole range of human activities, war most closely resembles a game of cards" (p. 86).

19. *Ibid.*, p. 89.

20. Clausewitz ascertains that the first of these aspects mainly concerns the people, the second the "commander and his army," the third "the government." War is a "true chameleon that slightly adapts its characteristics to the given case" (*ibid.*, p. 89). The relations between its three contradictory and fundamental characteristics thus also change. In the Vietnam War, for example, the factor of the *creative spirit*, the subjective work of motivation, is almost completely absent from the professionalized battles carried out by American forces and determines instead the power of the *anti-Vietnam movement* in the United States, while the government, "the commander," and the specialists make their calculations, and the element of blind natural force becomes independent of both calculation and emotion.

21. [*Translator's citation*: See. Carl Schmitt, *The Concept of the Political*, trans. George Schwab (Chicago: The University of Chicago Press, 2007), p. 52.]

22. [*Translator's citation*: Marx, *Capital, Volume 1*, in *MECW*, vol. 35, p. 331.]

23. [*Translator's note*: Kluge and Negt originally use "unconditional surrender" in English.]

24. [*Translator's citation*: Max Weber, "The Profession and Vocation of Politics," *Political Writings*, ed. Peter Lassman, trans. Ronald Speirs (Cambridge: Cambridge University Press, 1994), p. 369.]

25. [*Translator's note and citations*: Of the stories that follow in Commentary, 13, the first, second, fourth, fifth, and sixth originally appeared in German in Alexander Kluge, *Tür an Tür mit einem anderen Leben* (Frankfurt am Main: Suhrkamp, 2006), pp. 61, 76, 67–68, 328–29, and 256, respectively; the third originally appeared in Alexander Kluge, *Chronik der Gefühle*, vol. 1, *Basisgeschichten* (Frankfurt am Main: Suhrkamp, 2000), p. 750.]

26. The book *Europe's Last Summer: Who Started the Great War in 1914?*, by David Fromkin (New York: Vintage, 2005) had just appeared.

CHAPTER SEVEN: LOVE POLITICS

1. [*Translator's note and citation*: Untranslated into English in its entirety, the volume's most relevant contribution for Kluge and Negt can be found in Max Horkheimer, "Authority and the Family," in *Critical Theory: Selected Essays*, trans. Matthew J. O'Connell (New York: Continuum, 1982), pp. 47–128.]

2. [*Translator's note and citation*: this passage originally appeared in Alexander Kluge, *Das Bohren harter Bretter: 133 politische Geschichten* (Frankfurt am Main: Suhrkamp Verlag, 2011), p. 308.]

3. [*Translator's citation*: Karl Kraus, *Die Fackel*, September 19, 1913, nos. 381–83,p. 73.]

4. [*Translator's citation*: Horkheimer, "Authority and the Family," p. 52. This and all subsequent Horkheimer translations slightly revised.]

5. [*Translator's citation*: Ibid., p. 54.]

6. [*Translator's citation*: Ibid., p. 128.]

7. [*Translator's citation*: Ibid., pp. 109–10.]

8. [*Translator's citation*: Ibid., p. 98.]

9. [*Translator's citation*: Ibid., pp. 114–15.]

10. Georg Wilhelm Friedrich Hegel, *Phenomenology of Spirit*, trans. A. V. Miller (Oxford: Oxford University Press), 1977, pp. 267–78; Horkheimer, "Authority and the Family," p. 117: "He regarded the relations between brother and sister as the most unalloyed on in the family. Had he discovered that this human relationship, in which 'the moment of individual selfhood, recognizing and being recognized, can...assert its right,' need not simply accept the present in the form of mourning for the dead but can take a more active form in the future, his dialectic with its closed, idealistic form would have broken through its socially conditioned limitations."

11. [*Translator's citation*: Horkheimer, "Authority and the Family," p. 118.]

12. A woman falls in love with her husband's best friend. A man falls in love with his wife's best friend. It could be said that this is the attempt to preserve the closeness of a relationship. Presumably, closeness in a relationship even produces the original necessary "disreputability." Right next to my wife or right next to my husband, my love can once again come alive.

13. For this reason, in Kierkegaard's *Either/Or*, this is said as follows: "Whether you marry or you do not marry, you will regret both." Søren Kierkegaard, *Either/Or: A Fragment of Life*, trans. Alastair Hannay (London: Penguin, 1992, p. 54.)

14. [*Translator's citation*: Sigmund Freud, "Thoughts for the Times on War and Death," in *The Standard Edition of the Complete Psychological Works of Sigmund Freud*, trans. James Strachey, vol. 14. (London: Hogarth Press, 1955), p. 218.]

15. There is also the countermovement that sexuality has the character of the sum of all quests for desire as well as protest. In this case, those organs that appear specialized for sexuality assume a greater amount of disappointment than cathexis. In this respect, sexual interest can fortify itself to a certain extent from within, much like a fortress. In other words, organs vitally essential for immediate sexual contact, such as the respiratory system or the heart, acquire a high interest in sex and a negligible potential for protest and therefore become organs of refuge: the beating of a heart, the solar system, for example, are eroticized more unequivocally than the laboring hand or the so-called erogenous zones, which praxis can disturb completely. This would not be a diagnosis of illness, but a pure consequence.

16. [*Translator's citation*: Michael Balint, *Primary Love, and Psycho-Analytic Technique* (London: Hogarth Press, 1952), p. 42.]

17. [*Translator's citation*: Georg Wilhelm Friedrich Hegel, *Elements of the Philosophy of Right*, ed. Allen W. Wood, trans. H. B. Nisbet (Cambridge: Cambridge University Press, 1991), p. 202. Italics in the Nisbet translation.]

18. [*Translator's citation*: Ibid., p. 199.]

19. [*Translator's citation*: Ibid.]

20. [*Translator's citation*: Hegel, *Ibid.*]

21. [*Translator's citation*: Barbey D'Aurevilly, *Les diaboliques* = *The She-Devils (Empire of the Senses)*, trans. Ernest Boyd (Sawtry, UK: Dedalus, 1996), p. 216. Translation slightly modified.]

22. [*Translator's citation*: Edgar Reitz, Alexander Kluge, and Wilfried Reinke, "Word and Film," trans. Miriam Hansen, *October* 46 (Autumn, 1988), pp. 85–86. Translation slightly modified.]

23. Children who observe their parents fighting see with their own eyes as well as with the representational authority of their parents' eyes and sometimes even with that of their grandparents. These authorities are something different from the actual parents and grandparents, because the children created them.

24. [*Translator's note*: Negt and Kluge invoke "Celtic communities" here to signify in general terms premodern cosmologies and their attendant temporalities characteristic of European societies dating back to the Iron Age.]

25. The more unconsciously the subtle maneuvering is carried out, the more likely it is to succeed. If it is attempted ingeniously, the historical form of spirit initially will suppress the mimetic ability uniquely suited for propelling self-regulation far enough forward so that proportions and weights are replaced. For everything to go well, something other than so-called goodwill must be relied upon, because ruling consciousness resides in a portion of goodwill that destroys subtle maneuvering.

26. "Forms pregnant with potential development are…always unspecialized and small." Bernhard Krebs, "Die Archosauier," *Naturwissenschaften* 61 (1974), pp. 17–24.

27. Accordingly, the selection and variety benefited those dinosaurs whose amniotic eggs already had a tanklike structure. The firm shell of the egg could always be pierced, but the flexible armor of its occupant could not. At birth, carrying such armor was unbearable for such beings. In life, carrying this armor around was superfluous. Their covering made them inefficient. Paleontologists have always disputed whether so many different kinds of dinosaurs could have died out due to mere climate change or fights between aggressive and armored dinosaurs. A more plausible interpretation of the demise of these gigantic reptiles suggests that the protection of the spawn entails a selection that favors armor unsuitable for the praxis of life.

28. See Immanuel Kant, "An Answer to the Question: 'What is Enlightenment?,'" in *Kant's Political Writings*, ed. Hans Riess, trans. H. B. Nisbet (Cambridge: Cambridge University Press, 1991), pp. 54–60. (Originally published in *Berlinische Monatsschrift* 2, December 5, 1783, pp. 481–94). The cross-reference in the title as it appeared in the *Berlinischen Monatsschrift* alludes to the essay by minister Johann Friedrich Zöllner: "Ist es rathsam, das Ehebündnis ferner durch die Religion zu sanciren?" (Is it advisable to sanction matrimony further through religion?). "*What is enlightenment?* This question, which is almost as important as the question *What is truth?*, should indeed be answered *before* one begins to enlighten! And still I have never found it answered!" [*Translator's citation and note*: The quotes are from *ibid.*, pp. 54, 54, 55, 58, 59–60. Italics in the Kant translation; boldface in the Negt and Kluge text.]

29. [*Translator's note*: The commonly accepted English translation of the German *Ausgang* (literally "way out") in Kant's famous formulation "Aufklärung ist der Ausgang…aus…Unmündigkeit" ("Enlightenment is man's emergence from… immaturity") does not lend itself to all the permutations that Negt and Kluge

subject it to in this final section of Chapter 7. In order to call attention to the many plays on Kant's idea of emergence, deviations in the standard translation are called out using brackets.]

30. [*Translator's citation*: Friedrich Wilhelm Nietzsche, *The Will to Power*, ed. Walter Kaufmann, trans. Walter Kaufmann and R. J. Hollingdale (New York: Random House, 1967), p. 327.]

31. An abbreviation must therefore be cultivated stating "Man is mature if he can take leave [*wenn er Ausgang hat*]," just as when spare time is called "taking leave." [*Translator's citation*: Immanuel Kant, "An Answer to the Question: 'What is Enlightenment?,'" p. 55. Italics in the Kant translation.]

32. [*Translator's citation*: ibid., p. 59.]

33. It should come as no surprise that some scholarly schools indebted to Kant merely focus on methodology. In so doing, they create a sense of tidiness in their ranks and a purification of their methodological instruments. This ensures that they are not exposed to any friction with the subject matter, which would either damage or deform their instruments. We are not referring here to the Neo-Kantianism of Southern Germany or the critical epistemology of the Marburg School.

34. It must be insisted that Kant speaks of reason as if he were speaking of an unborn child.

35. [*Translator's citation*: Kant, "An Answer to the Question: 'What is Enlightenment?,'" p. 54.]

36. Friedrich Nietzsche uses the category of dancing emphatically, but so does Marx when he speaks of the particular melody of German relations. In this instance, we initially define dancing literally, in contrast to dance lessons, in which the tools of learning still fumble.

37. "He trampled on her toes obstinately. She no longer wanted to dance." This obstinacy (clumsiness) has to fall away. Obstinacy reveals itself in yet another way. Public dances were forbidden during wartime. However, the prohibition did not function in practical terms because those who had a pass [*Ausgang haben*] did not heed the authorities' ban on dancing. While Adolf Hitler put an end to his life in a bunker in Berlin, a lively dance took place in the bunker.

38. Courage or bravery cannot be used as simple inversions. According to the Socratic method, bravery is knowing "what to fear and what to love" (Plato, *Republic* 4.430b). Being courageous in a context lacking solidarity will only plunge me into misfortune. The material core of bravery is therefore trust, as is also the case with knowledge.

39. [*Translator's citation*: Kant, "An Answer to the Question: 'What is Enlightenment?,'" p. 54. Italics in the Kant translation.]

40. [*Translator's note and citation*: Negt and Kluge refer here to the title of Kluge's 2009 compilation of new and old love stories, *Das Labyrinth der zärtlichen Kraft* (Frankfurt am Main: Suhrkamp, 2009), in which a revised version of the original chapter 11 from *Geschichte und Eigennsinn* originally appeared ("Love Politics: Der Eigensinn der Intimität," pp. 519–68). See Oskar Negt and Alexander Kluge, "Beziehungsarbeit in Privatverhältnisse," in *Geschichte und Eigensinn*, vol. 2, *Der unterschätzte Mensch: Gemeinsame Philosophie in zwei Bänden* (Frankfurt am Main: Zweitausendeins, 2001), pp. 863–1000.]

41. [*Translator's note and citation*: Kant, "An Answer to the Question: 'What is Enlightenment?,'" p. 54. Of the following stories, the first and fifth originally appeared in German in Kluge, *Das Bohren harter Bretter*, pp. 303 and 308; the second, third, and fourth originally appeared in Alexander Kluge, *Das fünfte Buch* (Frankfurt am Main: Suhrkamp, 2012), pp. 527, 303–304, 167–68.]

42. [*Translator's citation*: Steve Jones, *Darwin's Ghosts: The Origin of the Species Updated* (New York: Random House, 1999), p. 215.]

43. [*Translator's citation*: See Jacques Derrida, "*Geschlecht I*: Sexual Difference, Ontological Difference," trans. Ruben Bevezdivin, and "Heidegger's Hand (*Geschlecht II*)," trans. John P. Leavey, Jr. and Elizabeth Rottenberg, in *Psyche: Inventions of the Other*, vol. 2, ed. Peggy Kamuf and Elizabeth Rottenberg (Stanford: Stanford University Press, 2008) pp. 7–26, and 27–62.]

44. [*Translator's citation*: Hans-Dieter Gondek, in Jacques Derrida, *Geschlecht (Heidegger): Sexuelle Differenz, ontologische Differenz*, ed. Peter Engelmann, trans. Hans-Dieter Gondek (Vienna: Passagen-Verlag, 1988), p. 111 n.45.]

APPENDIX: AN ATLAS OF CONCEPTS

1. [*Translator's note*: On the semantic field deployed for the permutations of *Steuerung* here, see footnote 4 in Chapter 1. See also "Navigational Labor" in Chapter 3.]

2. [*Translator's note and citation*: English equivalents for Hegel's triad are taken from Michael Inwood, *A Hegel Dictionary* (Oxford: Blackwell, 1992), p. 302.]

3. [*Translator's citation*: Wolf Singer, "The Brain: An Orchestra without a Conductor," *MaxPlanckResearch* 3 (2005), pp. 14–18.]

4. [*Translator's note*: On the title of this sidebar, see Friedrich Nietzsche, *The Gay Science: With a Prelude in German Rhymes and an Appendix of Songs*, ed. Bernard Williams, trans. Josefine Nauckhoff (Cambridge: Cambridge University Press, 2001), p. 221. The epigraph is from Oswald Spengler, *The Decline of the West*, vol. 1, *Form and Actuality*, trans. Charles Francis Atkinson (New York: Knopf, 1926) p. 59.]

5. [*Translator's note and citation*: See Jacob W. Grimm, and Wilhelm K. Grimm, "Brier Rose," in *Complete Fairy Tales of the Brothers Grimm*, ed. and trans. Jack Zipes (Westminster: Bantam Books, 1992), pp. 171–74.]

6. [*Translator's citation*: See "Mega-City Shanghai: Auf dem Wege zu einer neuen Wirklichkeit," *News & Stories*, dirrected by Alexander Kluge, SAT 1, October 16, 2005.]

7. [*Translator's citation*: Plato, *Laches* 199b.]

8. [*Translator's note*: On the origins of this quotation, see Chapter 2, note 6.]

9. [*Translator's citation*: Immanuel Kant, "An Answer to the Question: 'What is Enlightenment?,'" in *Kant's Political Writings*, trans. H. B. Nisbet (Cambridge: Cambridge University Press, 1991), p. 54.]

10. [*Translator's citation*: Karl Marx and Frederick Engels, *Collected Works*, vol. 28, *Karl Marx: Economic Works, 1857–61* (London: Lawrence and Wishart, 1986), p. 48.]

11. Monem Abdel-Gawad, "Wrench Movements in the Baluchistan Arc and Relation to Himalayan-Indian Ocean Tectonics," *Geological Society of America Bulletin* 82.5 (1971), pp. 1235–250. An assistant wrote Holbrooke a memo about the tectonics in northern Afghanistan so the ambassador would be on solid ground any moment the conversation turned to the country's substratum.

12. [*Translator's citation*: "Die Riesin liegt in den Wochen/Drei Wölfe sind ausgekrochen./Sie liegt zwischen Eis und Nebel und Schnee." Johann Wolfgang von Goethe, Letter to Friedrich Gottlob Konstantin von Stein, February 16, 1788, in *Goethe: Begegnungen und Gespräche*, ed. Renate Grumach, vol. 3, 1786–1792 (Berlin: Walter de Gruyter, 1977), p. 194.]

13. Theodor W. Adorno, "Marginalia to Theory and Praxis," in *Critical Models: Interventions and Catchwords*, trans. Henry W. Pickford (New York: Columbia University Press, 1998), p. 265.

Index

495 n.13; knowledge and, 409; solidarity
and, 382, 518 n.38.

Couthon, Georges, 431.

Craftsmanship, 188.

Critical Theory, 33, 76, 92, 198, 199; on
authority and the family, 348; historical
subject of emancipation and, 220; love
politics and, 341; objective possibility and,
397; proletariat as revolutionary subject
and, 419. *See also* Frankfurt School

Cross-mapping, 76, 93, 332.

Cultural Revolution, Chinese, 257, 421, 433.

Culture industry, 42.

Cybernetics, 47.

DANCING, 382, *388*, 518 nn.36–37.

Darwin, Charles, 94.

Dasein concept, 244, 280, 510 n.87.

David, Gérard, 119.

David, Jacques-Louis, 367.

Davidson-Miller, E. S., 204, 205.

Dead, resurrection of the, 49–50.

Dead labor, 48, 123, 128–30, 156, 390, 492
n.41; alienation and, 434; contained in
war technologies, 264; ethics and, 358;
intelligence labor and, 183, 189, 494 n.13.

Deafness, 267, 506 n.50.

Death, 113, 158, 294, 325.

Death drive, 43.

Debt, 427, 429–30.

De Gaulle, Gen. Charles, 329.

Deleuze, Gilles, 23, 39, 92, 200, 281–82,
449 n.31.

De Man, Paul, 468 n.179.

Democracy, 44, 329, 347, 430–31, 452 n.49.

Deng Xiaoping, 432–33.

Denmark, 333–34.

Deobjectification, 226.

Dependent annex, 423.

Derailment, 327–29, 401.

Derrida, Jacques, 31, 92, 385–86.

Descartes, René, 209, 245.

Determinacy, 158, 229.

Determination, 259.

Deterrence, theory of, 319.

Diaboliques, Les (Barbey d'Aurevilly), 359.

Dialectic, 63, 156, 480 n.13; damaged, 431; of
enlightenment, 239; of master and slave,
262–63; Nietzsche's critique of, 199–200;

of power grips and precision grips, 89;
sensuousness and, 257–59; of temporal
movement, 266–67; ungrammatical
nature of, 256–57. *See also* Contradictions

Dialectic of Enlightenment (Horkheimer and
Adorno), 21.

Dialectics of Nature (Engels), 23, 47,
466 n.160.

Diaphragm, intelligence of the, 202.

Dilthey, Wilhelm, 486 n.14.

Dinosaurs, 372, *374*, 517 n.27.

Disobedience, 105–06.

Displacement, 142.

Dispositifs, 356.

Disruption, 107–08, 114, 125.

Distribution, 126, 260, 267, 362; of commodities, 274; economic clocks and, 265, 266;
intelligence labor and, 186; redistribution,
102, 354, 447 n.23; social war over, 129.

"Domestic Servants, The" (fairy tale), 290.

Domination, 170, 188, 245, 348, 406.

Dostoevsky, Fyodor, 488–89 n.27.

Drives, 26, 436, 452 n.46, 491 n.35;
cognitive, 173; economy of, 337, 484 n.5;
labor and, 173; libidinal, 172, 489 n.31,
493 n.5; primary, 149; self-regulating
economy of, 114, 124–25, 483 n.18;
stubborn demands of, 36.

ECONOMIC AND PHILOSOPHICAL MANUSCRIPTS
["The Paris Manuscripts"] (Marx), 201,
434, 485 n.17.

Economies, 85, 86; black market, 35; Black-
Scholes model, 397, 401; computers and,
398–400, 403; loyalty tax and, 494 n.10;
property forms and, 413; psychic, 47;
socialist, 213. *See also* Balance economy

Economists, classical, 218.

Education, 115, 193–94, 408, 500 n.13.

Ego, 148, 158, 356; in ancient world, *160*;
private property and, 370; stone statue of
Kurlil, *161*.

Ego psychology, 40, 44.

Egypt, ancient, 62, 393–94, 435.

Einstein, Albert, 165, 176, *177*, 247, 299.

Eisenstein, Sergei, 428–29.

Either/Or (Kierkegaard), 516 n.13.

Electra complex, 511–12 n.109.

Elements of the Philosophy of Right (Hegel), 243,

Königgrätz, Battle of (1866), 317.
Konrad, Kai A., 427.
Korean War, 318.
Korsch, Karl, 330, 331, 336–37.
Kosovo conflict (1991), 62.
Kraus, Karl, 348.
Kriege dem Kriege (Friedrich), *310*.
Krieg und Frieden (Kluge), *241*.
KuhleWampe (Brecht film), 466 n.153.
Kyrgyzstan, 210, 218.

LABOR, 15, 19, 95–96, 144–45, 390–91,
402; alienated, 237; antagonistic reality
of, 145–47; anthropology of labor power,
22; balance labor, 24, 414, 450 n.36;
as category of reality, 457 n.91; as
category of social transformation,
143; disappearance of work, 391–92;
disposition to work, 123; evolution
and, 94; haptics of, 42; individual
labor and total labor of society, 130–31;
internalization of labor characteristics,
92–93; lived time exchanged for cash,
400–01; migration of, 391; navigational,
136–37, 395–96, 402; political economy
of, 37, 458 n.98; precision grips, 24;
primitive accumulation and emergence
of, 81; as process of metamorphosis, 48;
productive and unproductive, 347–48;
relationality of living labor, 113; simple
labor, 420; supplemental, 98, 124, 186;
theory labor, 172, 201, 439–40; unreality
of abstract labor, 133–34, 486–87
nn.18–19; violence as characteristic of,
88–89. *See also* Dead labor; Intelligence
labor; Living labor
Labor, division of, 127, 181, 189, 254;
in primary production, 406; in war,
300–05, *303*.
Labor capacities, 83, 88, 120, 127, 145;
balance economy of, 135–36; "collective
worker" and, 409; defined, 395; fulcra of,
143; historical, 92; incongruence between
process and result, 132; intelligence and,
202; materiality of, 147; responsibility
and, 247, 249; separation from object of
labor, 125; separation processes and, 225;
social factory and, 216, 218, 219; trust
and realism, 139–40; unification of forces

and, 137–38; war economy and, 328.
Labor power, 117, 217, 224, 503 n.25; as
commodity, 225; consciousness and,
126; exclusionary mechanisms and, 402;
genealogies and, 260; materialized in
bombs, 264; primitive accumulation
and, 274; as result and process, 131–34;
self-regulation and, 108; self-will of, 127;
valuations of political labor power, 347.
Labor power, political economy of, 23, 73,
120–23, 133, 493 n.5; first contradiction
in, 124–28; intelligence and, 170–72;
metaphoric concept and, 398; primitive
accumulation and, 413; real subsumption
and, 424; relation of flow and disruption
in, 134–35; separation and, 435.
Labyrinth der zärtlichen Kraft, Das (Kluge), *157*,
519 n.40.
Labyrinths, 315.
Lacan, Jacques, 453 n.51.
La Fontaine, Jean de, 2.
Language, 30, 94, 157, 256–66.
Lansing, Robert, *167*.
Laokoon (Lessing), 31.
Lask, Emil, 198.
Latour, Bruno, 476 n.253.
Laupen, Battle of (1339), 300.
Law, Bonar, *167*.
"Lay of Hildebrand," 280.
Leapfrogging action, in politics
(*Übersprungshandlung in der Politik*), 323,
425.
Learning Processes with a Deadly Outcome (Kluge),
17.
Le Corbusier, 501 n.18.
Lee, Gen. Robert E., 316–17.
Left, the: distant historical epochs and, 17,
18; dramas of historical rupture and, 23;
failures of, 15; political messianism
and, 61; spontaneist "infantile disorders"
of, 33–34; utopian ideals of, 65.
Legitimation, market versus popular, 430–31.
Lehman Brothers, crash of, 401.
Leibniz, GottfriedWilhelm, 66, 206–08.
Leimar, Olof, 192.
Lenin, Vladimir, 37, 64, 429, 479 n.13,
504 n.29.
Leonardo daVinci, 480 n.17.
Leopold of Austria, Herzog, 512 n.2.

Netherlands, 217, 326.

New German Cinema, 18.

News from Ideological Antiquity [Nachrichten aus der ideologischen Antike] (Kluge), 18, 445 n.14.

Newspapers, 196, 197.

Newton, Isaac, 156, 259.

Niagara (film), *360.*

Nietzsche, Friedrich, 27, 60, 199, 210, 351; on dancing, 518 n.36; on reality and illusion, 412.

Night at the Opera, A (film, 1935), *344.*

9/11 (September 11, 2001) attacks, 30, 320, 322–23, 425.

Nixon, Richard, 504 n.32.

Noah's Ark, 251, 505–06 n.45.

Nostalgia, 378.

Nunn, Sam, 319.

OBAMA, BARACK, 391.

Objectification, 140.

Objectivity, 245, 251, 353.

Objects, 116, 155, 181, 245, 254, 351, 478 n.4; appropriation of, 117; consciousness and, 252, 269; exchange value and, 504 n.29; existence and, 244; experience and, 262–63; friction of, 140; graspable, 91; *Homo clausus* and, 257, 258; inner power relations of, 89; intelligence labor and, 184; knowledge and, 242, 243; myth in ancient world and, 269, 273; primary, 223–24, 231, 253, 260, 345, 357, 380, 382, 488 n.25, 506 n.46; primitive accumulation and, 407 n.91; produced by labor, 247, 407, 492 n.41, 513 n.9; separation and, 125, 126, 232; signs and, 30; subjective-objective relation and, 236; transformed by labor, 143; value and, 110.

Obstinacy (*Eigensinn*), 66, 73, 93, 145, 390; of children, 224; female, 464–65 n.148; obstinate traits, 34–41; as "one's own self," 292; self-regulation and, 98; subnational regions of, 326.

"Obstinate Child, The" (fairy tale), 37, 292–95, 511 n.104.

Odysseus (mythological), 21, 165, 185, 186, 435, 507 n.60; as metaphor for the Enlightenment, 268–69; oral tradition and, 194.

Odyssey, The (Homeric epic), 268–69, 287.

Oedipus story/complex, 294, 354, 511–12 n.109.

Offenbach, Jacques, 490 n.33.

O'Hara, Scarlett (fictional character), 132, 317.

"On Rights to Persons Akin to Rights to Things" (Kant), 230.

On the Origin of Language (Herder), 27.

Opera, 42, 463 n.135, 476 n.255.

Oppenheimer, Robert, *177.*

Oral tradition, 194.

Orientation, 440.

Otto engine, 89.

Ottoman Empire, 333, 338–40, 430.

Ovid, 47, 48, *270.*

Owen, Robert, 484 n.2.

PAIN, 109, 149, 482 n.11.

Pakistan, 319, 437.

Papen, Franz von, *166.*

Parenting, 345, 356, 357, 359. *See also* Child rearing

Paris Commune (1871), 185, 205, 257.

Parsons, Talcott, 92, 216, 341, 420.

Pasha, Gen. Nazim, 338.

Passion (Godard film), 42, 463 n.134.

Patriot, The (Kluge film), 49, 50, 464 n.148.

Patton, Gen. George, 329.

Peasants, 66, 212, 486 n.13; enclosures of the commons and, 34, 404; German peasants' war, 222, 306, 330, 337; primary production of, 406; primitive accumulation and, 86–87; uprisings in China, 221.

Perle, Richard, 319.

"Perpetual Peace" (Kant), 58.

Perry, William, 319.

phenomenology, 22.

Phenomenology of Spirit, The (Hegel), 439.

Philosophy, 27, 48, 192, 472–73 n.220; experience and, 251; lived experience as object of, 59; Marx and classical philosophy, 201; neo-Kantianism, 198; positivist, 31; Stanford Encyclopedia of Philosophy, 191, 196

Phylogeny, 89, 159, 172, 382; dead labor and, 129; development of hand and, 357; epiphylogenesis, 26, 30; knowledge

Zone Books series design by Bruce Mau
Typesetting, page layout, and production by Julie Fry
Printed and bound by Maple Press